Christoph Ernst Luthardt, Caspar René Gregory

St. John's Gospel:

Described and explained according to its peculiar character

Christoph Ernst Luthardt, Caspar René Gregory

St. John's Gospel:
Described and explained according to its peculiar character

ISBN/EAN: 9783337714253

Printed in Europe, USA, Canada, Australia, Japan

Cover: Foto ©ninafisch / pixelio.de

More available books at **www.hansebooks.com**

CLARK'S

FOREIGN

THEOLOGICAL LIBRARY.

NEW SERIES.
VOL. LV.

Luthardt on the Gospel of St. John.
VOL. II.

EDINBURGH:
T. & T. CLARK, 38 GEORGE STREET.
1877.

PRINTED BY MURRAY AND GIBB,

FOR

T. & T. CLARK, EDINBURGH.

LONDON,	HAMILTON, ADAMS, AND CO.
DUBLIN,	ROBERTSON AND CO.
NEW YORK,	SCRIBNER, WELFORD, AND ARMSTRONG.

ST. JOHN'S GOSPEL

DESCRIBED AND EXPLAINED ACCORDING
TO ITS PECULIAR CHARACTER.

BY

CHRISTOPH ERNST LUTHARDT,
PROFESSOR OF THEOLOGY AT LEIPZIG.

TRANSLATED BY

CASPAR RENÉ GREGORY,
DOCTOR OF PHILOSOPHY, LEIPZIG.

VOL. II.

EDINBURGH:
T. & T. CLARK, 38 GEORGE STREET.
1877.

PREFACE.

WHEN I revised the first volume for this new edition, I had just completed the treatment of the critical question, which I presented in my book on St. John's authorship of the fourth gospel. It will be easy to understand that, after busying myself for some time with the assertions of the critics, I was eager to sink into the very words of the Scriptures, and to let them speak to me as well as to the readers. For this reason, the attention paid in that volume to the later works of the so-called critical party was perhaps scarcely so great as it should have been. That, however, is hardly to be charged upon the second volume. It is true that, with the most hearty desire to learn even from them, I cannot say that I owe them much help in understanding our gospel. In my opinion, these scholars would further the understanding of the Scriptures in general much more if, instead of making them so exclusively the object of merely historical-critical inquiries and observations, they would occupy themselves more with the exposition of them. Wieseler complained lately, and with justice, of the cessation of the true exegetical activity. Were exegesis more practised, there would be more loving devotion to the Scriptures. This would prevent many strange and incomprehensible fancies, which now throw various stones in the way, stones that must always be disposed of before we can move forward in the path of the real understanding of the Scriptures.

If this new edition of my work upon St. John's gospel

be compared with the first edition, it will easily be seen that, although the fundamental view and the essential understanding of it remain the same, yet it has undergone a thorough revision and working over in details. The very increase in size, which I did not know how to avoid, shows that. And every page can testify to it, for probably no single one stands unchanged. The proof-reading and the verification of the numerous citations were attended to by Dr. Gregory. I have also to thank him for an English translation of my book on the origin of the fourth gospel, which he has enlarged greatly in the literature: *St. John the Author of the Fourth Gospel.* Revised, translated, and the literature much enlarged. Edinburgh, T. & T. Clark, 1875.

May my book, then, be to many a welcome expositor.

Dr. LUTHARDT.

Leipzig, 14 June 1876.

NOTE.

The list of books in volume first, pages ix.–xiii., which the translator neither prepared nor saw, having been inadvertently inserted by the publishers, will be replaced by another list in volume third.

Caspar René Gregory.

Leipzig, 15 October 1877.

CONTENTS.

EXPOSITION.

I.

JESUS THE SON OF GOD.

CHAPTERS I.–IV. (*continued*).

	PAGE
3. *Jesus' first public Testimony to Himself as the Son of God; Unbelief, Half-Belief, Belief*, ii. 12–iv. 54,	3
A. Jesus in Jerusalem and Judea, ii. 12–iii. 36,	4
(1.) Jesus and the Judaism of that day, ii. 12–22,	5
Ver. 15, purging the temple,	7
Ver. 19, 'Destroy this temple,'	10
Ver. 20, 'Forty and six years,'	11
(2.) Jesus and the half-belief of the Jews, ii. 23–iii. 21,	13
Jesus and the half-belief of Nicodemus, iii. 1–21,	15
✓ Ver. 2, Nicodemus,	17
Ver. 3, 'The kingdom of God,'	18
Γεννηθῆναι ἄνωθεν ('to be born again'),	20
✓ Ver. 4, Nicodemus does not understand,	22
Ver. 5, 'Water' and 'Spirit,'	23
Ver. 13, 'No man hath ascended,'	30
Ver. 16, 'God so loved the world,'	33
Ver. 21, 'He that doeth the truth,'	39
(3.) Jesus in Judea, and the Baptist's testimony, iii. 22–36,	41
Ver. 23, 'Aenon, near to Salem,'	44
Ver. 25, John's disciples and the Jew,	45
Vers. 27–30, Christ and the Baptist,	46
Vers. 31–36, relation of Christ to world,	48
Ver. 36, 'He that believeth on the Son,'	51
B. The Belief of Samaria and Galilee, iv. 1–54,	52
✓(1.) Jesus and the Samaritan woman, iv. 1–26,	55
Ver. 5, Sychar,	56
Ver. 10, Living water,	59
(2.) Jesus and the Samaritans, iv. 27–42,	73
Ver. 35, 'White already to harvest,'	74
(3.) Jesus and the Galileans, iv. 43–54,	80
Conclusion of First Part,	85

II.

JESUS AND THE JEWS.

CHAPTERS V.-XII.

	PAGE
1. *Jesus the Life.—Beginning of the Contest,* chap. v., vi.,	89
A. The God-like activity of Jesus the Son of God, and the Beginning of the Opposition, v. 1–47,	91
(1.) The occasion, v. 1–9,	91
Ver. 1, 'a feast,'	92
Ver. 2, Bethesda,	93
(2.) The antagonism, v. 10–18,	98
Ver. 17, 'My Father worketh hitherto,'	100
(3.) Jesus' self-witness, v. 19–47,	104
Vers. 21–23, Jesus' future work,	107
Ver. 24, belief and life,	112
Vers. 27–30, judgment entrusted to the Son of man,	116
Vers. 31–47, the testimony to Jesus,	123
Vers. 33–35, the Baptist and salvation,	124
Vers. 36–39, Jesus' own testimony,	126
Ver. 39, 'Ye search the Scriptures,'	130
Vers. 40–43, they will not believe,	132
Vers. 45–47, judgment on unbelief,	137
Summary,	139
B. Jesus the Life in the Flesh. The Progress of Belief and of Unbelief, vi. 1–71,	140
(1.) Feeding five thousand. Walking on sea, vi. 1–21,	142
Ver. 7, 'two hundred pennyworth,'	146
Ver. 13, fragments that remained,	148
Vers. 16, 17, disciples on sea,	152
Ver. 21, 'the ship was at the land,'	154
(2.) A discourse, vers. 22–59,	157
(*a.*) Jesus gives to belief the true bread, vers. 22–40,	157
(*b.*) Jesus the bread of life, vers. 41–51,	169
Ver. 51, 'I am the living bread,'	174
Does this refer to the Lord's Supper?	177
(*c.*) Jesus repeats the lesson, vers. 52–59,	179
Summary of this discourse,	185
(3.) The crisis, vers. 60–71,	185
Ver. 60, disciples offended,	185
Ver. 62, the ascension,	187
Ver. 63, the Spirit and the flesh,	189
Ver. 69, 'we have believed and known,'	193
2. *Jesus the Light.—The Struggle at its Height,* chap. vii.–x.,	197
A. Jesus' Meeting with the Unbelief of the Jews at Jerusalem, vii. 1–52,	199
(1.) The situation, vers. 1–13,	199
Ver. 8, 'I go not up,'	207
(2.) Jesus speaks at the feast, vers. 14–39,	211
Ver. 28, 'Ye both know me, and ye know whence I am,'	224

CONTENTS. ix

	PAGE
Ver. 37, 'If any man thirst,'	229
Ver. 39, 'But this he spake of the Spirit,'	233
(3.) The success of Jesus' words, vers. 40-52,	235
Ver. 46, 'Never spake man,'	237
Ver. 50 f., Nicodemus,	239 ✓
[The adulterous woman, vii. 53-viii. 11],	242 ✓
This paragraph not genuine,	242
B. The Antagonism between Jesus and the Jews in its Greatest Sharpness, viii. 12-59,	250
(1.) Jesus' testimony to himself, vers. 12-20,	254
Ver. 12, 'I am the light of the world,'	254
Vers. 17-19, Jesus' testimony twofold,	261
(2.) Whence Jesus came, vers. 21-29,	264
Ver. 23, 'beneath' and 'above,'	266
Ver. 25, τὴν ἀρχήν,	270
Ver. 28, 'When ye shall lift up the Son of man,'	275
(3.) The severest antagonism, vers. 30-59,	277
Ver. 33, 'we were never in bondage,'	280
Vers. 37-47,	284
(a.) Vers. 37, 38, Abraham's seed only historically,	284
(b.) Vers. 39-41a, actions test origin,	288
(c.) Vers. 41b-47, their relation to God,	289
Ver. 44, children of devil,	291
Vers. 48-59, their future,	298
Ver. 56, Abraham saw Jesus' day,	303
Ver. 59, Jews would stone him,	307
C. Jesus the salvation-bringing Light of the World; to the Jews unto judgment, chap. ix., x.,	310
(1.) The blind man healed, ix. 1-41,	312
(a.) The healing, vers. 1-12,	312
Ver. 2, 'Who did sin,'	314
Ver. 7, the pool of Siloam,	321 ✓
(b.) Healing doubted, vers. 13-34,	325
Vers. 13-16, man led to Pharisees,	325
(c.) The blind man believes,	334
Vers. 39-41, Jesus come for judgment,	339
(2.) Jesus the Shepherd, x. 1-21,	342
(a.) The picture, vers. 1-5,	344
Ver. 3, 'sheep hear his voice,'	346
(b.) Jesus the mediator, vers. 6-10,	349
Ver. 7, Jesus the door,	350
Ver. 8, 'All that came before me,'	351
(c.) Shepherd giveth his life, vers. 11-18,	355
Ver. 11, 'I am the good shepherd,'	357
Vers. 14-16, Jesus applies parable to himself,	359
Ver. 16, 'other sheep,'	362
Ver. 18, 'I lay it down of myself,'	367
(3.) Hostility renewed, x. 22-42,	370
Ver. 23, 'Solomon's porch,'	373
Vers. 27, 28, 'My sheep hear my voice,'	377

Predestination,	378
Ver. 30, 'are one,'	379
Ver. 32, 'good works,'	382
Ver. 34, 'your law,'	384
D. Jesus, given up unto death, is the Life and the Judgment, chap. xi., xii.,	393
The raising of Lazarus, xi. 1–57,	399
(1.) The preparation, vers. 1–16,	399
Ver. 2, Bethany,	400
Ver. 11, death a sleep,	407
(2.) The event, vers. 17–44,	412
Vers. 25, 26, 'I am the resurrection and the life,'	417
✓ Ver. 27, Martha's confession,	420
Ver. 33, ἐμβριμᾶσθαι,	424
Ver. 35, 'Jesus wept,'	428
Ver. 44. the dead comes forth,	437
(3.) The effect, vers. 45–47,	439
Ver. 47, Sanhedrim meets,	440
✓ Ver. 49, Caiaphas' words,	443
Ver. 51, high priest of year,	445
Vers. 54–57, conclusion,	449
Ver. 54, Ephraim,	450

EXPOSITION.

I.

JESUS THE SON OF GOD.

Chapters I.–IV.

(Continued.)

I.

JESUS THE SON OF GOD.

CHAPTERS I.–IV.—*(continued)*.

II. 12–IV. 54. JESUS' FIRST PUBLIC TESTIMONY TO HIMSELF AS THE SON OF GOD: UNBELIEF, HALF-BELIEF, BELIEF.

WE have already seen that the fourth chapter closes a section. The fifth chapter begins the opposition, which in this part only shows itself from a distance, though an expectation of it is excited at the first appearance of Jesus. Yet the section now before us is made up of two parts. Jerusalem and Judea on the one side, and Samaria and Galilee on the other side, are contrasted with each other. It is true that Jesus began to reveal his glory by miraculous signs in Galilee, as we understand from ii. 11. Still this was but a single miracle which took place in a limited circle. In Jerusalem, on the contrary, he works many miracles, ii. 23, iv. 45, and that openly, before all the people, at the feast, and with clear testimony to himself as the Son of God. When he returns to Galilee he works one miracle only, upon an urgent prayer, when he is again in Cana itself. This is in all the second Galilean miracle; till now he has done so little in this land, iv. 54. Still less can his activity in Samaria be compared with that in Judea. And yet here he found belief; there, unbelief, or at most half-belief. This section moves in the most manifold contrasts, and hence is unmistakably double. Internal and external history, thought, and geography meet in it.

II. 12–III. 36. *Jesus in Jerusalem and Judea.*

We have here the first public self-revelation of Jesus as the Son of God. It is, however, kept more general than the later self-witness, from chap. v. onwards. Here all has the stamp of opening, of beginning, of foundation-laying. His appearance in the temple announces him only as the one that he is, rather than testifies to him as such in a detailed and instructive way. So likewise the talk with Nicodemus is of an introductory character. Hence it has often been compared to the sermon on the mount. The circumstance that Jesus is brought forward as baptizing in Judea, shows him more in a foundation-laying than in a completing activity. At the same time, as we shall see, all has a universal comprehensive meaning. All announces the new time which begins with Christ. This gives a peculiar mark to the whole of this section. The single paragraphs of this section correspond to the preceding ones in a reverse order. The contrasted analogy between the cleansing of the temple and the miracle at the marriage has already been noticed. In what succeeds, it is said that Jesus knew what was in man, ii. 25, and the talk with Nicodemus follows that directly. This recalls the displays of such knowledge reported at his first meeting with his disciples, i. 43, 48, and the words which he exchanged with them. In these words, just as to Nicodemus, though in a different way, he announces the new time of the Spirit, which he brings. The testimony of the Baptist closes this section, as it began the preceding, only that in comparison with that it is enlarged by what has happened in the meantime. Thus this circle closes and completes itself.

What has been said contains at the same time the justification of the triple division [1] of the first half of this section into (1.) ii. 12-22 ;—(2.) ii. 23–iii. 21 ;—(3.) iii. 22-36.

[1] See vol. i. p. 203.

(1.) II. 12-22. *Jesus and the Judaism of that day.*

Jesus and the Judaism of that day, the Son of God and the Jewish authorities, the new temple of the New Testament and the polluted temple of the Old Testament church, are here set over against each other.

VERSE 12.

This leads over to what follows, and is to be understood as a comprehensive account. Jesus must have gone to Nazareth before he went down ($κατέβη$, because to the sea) to Capernaum with his mother, his brethren, and his disciples. The question as to the brothers of Jesus has been much discussed.[1] Four brethren are called by name, James, Joses, Simon, and Judas, Matt. xiii. 55; Mark vi. 3. Two of these names, James and Jude, occur also among the apostles. Are these identical, so that James the brother of the Lord and James the son of Alphaeus, the apostle, were one and the same person? Then the brethren of Jesus would be his cousins. The two are clearly distinguished in John's gospel. According to vii. 5, the brethren, who at that time did not yet believe, cannot have belonged to the apostles. But the union with the mother of the Lord in which they here occur, makes their sonship of Mary and their bodily brotherhood of Jesus appear the most natural thing, and this is confirmed by the other statements of the Scriptures and by the oldest tradition. The family of Jesus is named here, to which the disciples of Jesus now also belonged. Mary's husband is not named. Probably he was no longer among the living. The visit in Capernaum was a passing visit, $οὐ πολλὰσ ἡμέρασ$ ('not many days'), in distinction from the later abiding residence of Jesus at Capernaum; this is a conscious reference of the evangelist to the synoptic account, Matt. iv. 13. It was a friend's house in which they stopped on the way before wandering towards Jerusalem to the passover-feast.

---

[1] See Winer, *Biblisches Realwörterbuch*, 3d ed., Leipzig 1847, vol. i. p. 525 ff., where the remaining literature is noted; and Lichtenstein, *Lebensgeschichte des Herrn Jesu Christi in chronologischer Uebersicht*, Erlangen 1856, pp. 100-124.

Verse 13.

Jesus is to appear publicly and announce himself as the one who he is. Where can he do this better than in Jerusalem? When, better than at the time of the passover? At the beginning of the history we lighted upon deputies of the authorities in Jerusalem, who advanced to meet the Baptist. This, as we saw, was already a hint as to, and a reference to, the future. Doubtless we are to think of like persons in the Jews, vers. 16 and 20. They are called Jews here, as they were there, because they represent this nation, which has become hostile to Christ. There is no need of recalling further how this first meeting of Jesus with the Jews is an index to the future development of their mutual relation. He begins his public career at a passover in Jerusalem. He is to close it at a passover in the same place. Thus the end contrasts itself with the beginning. The words of Jesus and of the evangelist, vers. 17, 19, and 22, point clearly to the end, as we shall see. To try to make out from this that the evangelist has put the end at the beginning, is only one of Baur's[1] many hasty conclusions. It has already been remarked [2] that, according to the synoptists also, Jesus must have often been in Jerusalem before his end. And if he wished to appear as a prophet in Israel, where else should he appear first, than in the religious centre of Israel, and at the time of the chief feast? All internal probability speaks for this. If, however, he wished nothing further than the elevation of Judaism or the like, he must begin with a judgment upon the existing condition of religious life. They would then have wished to say that the existing Judaism corresponded to its Old Testament ideal. What was fitter for him in such a case than to speak out his condemnatory judgment in an act of the kind here reported?

---

[1] Baur, *Kritische Untersuchungen über die kanonischen Evangelien*, Tübingen 1847, p. 126 ff.

[2] See Luthardt, *Der johanneische Ursprung des vierten Evangeliums*, Leipzig 1874, p. 163 f.; English edition, *St. John the Author of the Fourth Gospel*, T. & T. Clark, Edinburgh 1875, p. 206 f.

VERSE 14.

Wherein lay the fault on account of which Jesus carried out this act of judgment? He *found in the temple*, namely, in the outer court, the so-called court of the Gentiles, *those that sold oxen and sheep and doves, and the changers of money sitting*. That selling served the convenience of the sacrifices. This exchange business was to make easier the change of the double-drachma, which must be paid as temple tax.

VERSE 15.

And when he had made a scourge of small cords, he drove them all out of the temple, etc. Why? Some like to lay stress on the hindrance which this traffic must have been to devotion (Lücke, Baumgarten-Crusius). This is hardly given to us by the text. Jesus contrasts Father's house and house of merchandise. This is a contrast which goes beyond that of the common and the sublime (Baumgarten-Crusius and others). It rather agrees with that other saying kept for us by the synoptists: a man cannot serve God and mammon. This idolatry which is carried on in the house of God must be condemned. Whether his cleansing did not disturb the devotion more than the traffic, and whether the same thing did not soon find its way back, these and like matters did not come into consideration, and did not trouble Jesus. He had simply to do with a testimony against the idolatrous perversion of the holy place. He was only bent on giving this testimony. Without giving it, he thought that he could not enter his public office, and we may well add, could not close it. The judicial zeal is the same against all parts of this idolatry. Some, indeed, have found a greater mildness in the treatment of the doves, according to De Wette and Lücke because they belonged to the poor, according to Baumgarten-Crusius because perhaps they did not cause such a disturbance. Could not a piece of gold be changed as quietly as a dove could be bought? He treated all alike. He throws the money-table over, and throws the money on the ground; he drives the oxen out; and he bids them take the doves away.

Ought he to have made them fly in the temple, so that at the end the seriousness should have been turned into a jest? It is not necessary to repeat that it was not the whip which did it, but that it was the impression of the personality before which sin involuntarily bowed. Thus this fact is a proof of the uncommon personality. First of all, it is the power of the holy personality. But there is still something different which forces even external obedience. It is a deed of the Son of God.

Verse 16.

To this he himself appeals: *Make not my Father's house a house of merchandise.* 'My Father's.' 'Wonderful authority,' says Bengel.[1] He brings to bear the right of a son in his father's house.

A right of zealots has often been spoken of, because of the ζῆλοσ ('zeal') in ver. 17. This is wrong. There was a right of reformation in Israel, but that was no other than that of the prophets and of the Spirit of God which moved them. Baumgarten-Crusius speaks of 'a mere act of Old-Israelitic zeal.'[2] But aside from that prophetic right, the right of such a zeal never existed. Hence Jesus could as a prophet act as he did act. Here, however, he does not appear as a prophet. It is true that in the synoptists, who paint him in general as the prophet of Galilee, it is the prophet who carries out that act, and carries it out on the ground of a prophetic right. There, he protects the place of prayer in its rights (Matt. xxi. 13, οἶκοσ προσευχῆσ). Here, as the son of the father to whom the house belongs, he exercises the right of the house against the disorder. That is the reason he speaks purposely of his father's house. Hence the two facts differ essentially, much alike as they may seem externally. Least of all has anybody a right to talk of the identity of the act, and from that to charge with error either the fourth evangelist (thus Strauss, Baur, Hilgenfeld) or the first three evangelists (thus

---

[1] Bengel, 'Admiranda auctoritas,' *Gnomon*, 3d ed., Tübingen 1773.
[2] Baumgarten-Crusius, *Theologische Auslegung der Johanneischen Schriften*, Jena 1843, vol. i. p. 88.

De Wette, Lücke, Neander, Bleek). On the contrary, this testimony is alike suitable and convenient at the beginning and at the end of his activity.

In that Jesus thus appears as the Son of God in the house of his Father, the old promise has begun to be fulfilled, that Jehovah would come to his house. But, of course, if the time for the salvation of Israel was therewith to dawn, there was need of belief, so that it should not stumble at the humbleness of the Son of God, in whom Jehovah visited his people. This belief, however, presupposed that Israel, ready for repentance, bowed itself to the judicial testimony which Jesus here gave against the distortion of Old Testament truth. Israel could well know from the prophetic words of the Old Testament that this was necessarily presupposed.

But it was only too clear that those punished, though they yielded indeed to the power of Jesus' personality, because they could not withstand it, yet did not, as their very yielding showed, inwardly own and bow before it. The chief of the people, the people in its representatives, desired a miraculous sign in justification of his deed, so as to be satisfied with the deed on that account and to acknowledge him. This showed that they wished to believe without repenting, and wished to believe, not for his sake, but for the sake of sensible miracles, and so really did not wish to believe at all. Therefore, as neither the former nor the latter showed either repentance or belief, it was clear that the hour of visitation would be in vain for Israel as a whole. The feeling pressed itself involuntarily on the disciples, that Jesus would waste himself in useless work.

Verse 17.

Hence the remark: *His disciples remembered*[1] *that it was written, The zeal of thine house will eat me up*, Ps. lxix. 10. Whether the psalm be Davidic, as the heading says, or Jeremianic, as Hitzig thinks, it portrays a suffering in the service of Jehovah, and so points out beyond itself to the fulfilling of all suffering in the final servant of Jehovah.

[1] Namely, then, and not after the resurrection of Jesus; Olshausen.

Hence no psalm, except the twenty-second, is so often referred to in the New Testament as the sixty-ninth.[1] Καταφάγεταί με ('will eat me up,' Hellenistic future from ἐσθίω) is not to be understood of the future death, as I explained it formerly.[2] The disciples could not have thought of that then, and that would not fit the psalm. The thing that struck them in Jesus, was the impression of Jesus' devouring zeal for the house of God. This will consume him before the time (thus also Lücke, Meyer). The scene Mark iii. 21 may be compared with this.

VERSE 18.

The gaze of Jesus went farther. To him the picture of Israel's future, as well as of his own, came to him from the situation of the present. The question and demand to prove his authority for such a deed by a miraculous sign, disclosed to him the whole abyss of the opposing will. This opposition of unreadiness to repent and of unbelief, which he found, showed him that the judgment of God must first pass over Israel as God's house before it would reach the goal of its history.

VERSE 19.

Hence he speaks those words as to the breaking and building of the temple. The evangelist has often been accused (as by Lücke and De Wette) of not understanding these words, because of the way in which he interprets them. The accusation is unfounded. Jesus speaks of 'this temple.' It is unquestionable (so Bengel) that τοῦτον ('this') could not refer to his body. And yet the evangelist refers it to his body. Jesus' words refer to the one while referring to the other. Λύσατε ('destroy'), not hypothetically. (Lücke, Baumgarten-Crusius, De Wette), but imperatively: go on and break. That implies that they will surely do it. 'This temple'—that is, not the Old

---

[1] See Delitzsch, *Biblischer Commentar über die Psalmen*, 3d ed., Leipzig 1873, vol. i. p. 486.

[2] With Bengel, Olshausen, and Hofmann, *Weissagung und Erfüllung im alten und im neuen Testamente*, Nördlingen 1844, vol. ii. p. 111.

Testament religion in general, in whose place Christ will put a new religion (thus say many), but the temple which they see. Yet that is meant not simply as a stone building, but as the dwelling of God. As such, however, the temple is a type of Christ, in whom the glory of God has, and was intended to have, its dwelling bodily. This contrasted figurative relation is at once allowed by Jesus, in his enigmatical words, to enter in thought upon the place of the external temple. It was clear to him from the first opposition which he found, that the authorities of Israel would go to the most extreme refusal of belief, and so to the rejection of his person. But when they bring him to death, they thereby break the temple. It ceases therewith to be the dwelling of God. It is thereby broken in its essential importance. But Jesus will raise the temple up again: after three days, in his resurrection. His glorified body is the right place of the presence of God. From that, then, shall the temple of the New Testament church build itself, Zech. vi. 12. As the real meaning of Jesus' words aimed at this, the evangelist lays stress on this sense as the substance of those words.

Verse 20.

It was natural that the Jews should not understand this mysterious saying. They were not intended to understand it. *Forty and six years was this temple in building* (till now: and it was not nearly done then). Herod had begun the rebuilding in the eighteenth year of his reign, and it was only finished under Herod Agrippa II. in the year 64 after Christ. It is not entirely certain how the forty-six years are to be counted. Herod's eighteenth year runs from the 1st of Nisan 734 to the 1st of Nisan 735. If this be the first year of the building, the forty-six will end with Nisan 780. Hence the passover of the cleansing of the temple falls in the year 780, and not 782, as Meyer assumes, referring to Luke iii. 1, or 781, as Godet and others assume.

Verse 22.

Nor do the disciples understand the words of Jesus. But they keep them in heart, and they become clear to them after the resurrection of Jesus. *They believed the Scripture;* not as to the resurrection of Jesus, say Ps. xvi. 10 (Meyer). That was not the point. It was as to the raising up of the new temple, Zech. vi. 12.

Thus this first appearance of Jesus is comprehensive and decisive as no other fact is. The whole history of Israel is in question. It is decided that the spiritual house of God must be built upon the ruins of the condemned people of God. This is decided because it is decided that Jesus will first be brought to death by his people before he will be glorified, and before his glorified body can be changed into the temple of God. The fact of the glorification of Jesus' body made the disciples understand the words of Jesus and the promise of the Old Covenant. And the disciples believe the former for the sake of the agreeing testimony of both sayings and of the fulfilling history. That word, however, which the disciples believe, is the word of him who had here owned and testified to himself as the Son of God in his Father's house. And he, in his resurrection and glorification, and in the thereon conditioned founding of his church, is proved, because Lord of the house, also to be the Son of God. Hence everything here treats of the Son of God, and of belief on him. His self-witness in the word is the first object and ground of this belief, and the conclusive facts of his life are the confirmation and reward of this belief. In the case of the Jews, as we see, Jesus' words of self-witness produce only the opposition of unbelief, which has as its consequence, judgment.

But Jesus witnesses to himself also by signs of a miraculous character. These cannot remain entirely without impression. They call forth a certain kind of belief. Yet this is not the right kind. The great point is, whether or not this half-belief permits itself to be raised to the right belief by Jesus' self-witness in his word. This forms the contents of the next section.

(2.) II. 23–III. 21. *Jesus and the Half-Belief of the Jews.*

The half-belief of the Jews, as it is called out by the miraculous signs of Jesus, is here brought before us.

VERSE 23.

As it appears, Jesus wrought not a few signs at the passover in Jerusalem. Ἐν τῇ ἑορτῇ is, for closer definition, *in the feast*. Meyer's explanation, 'in the act of celebrating the feast,' would be better expressed by the participle or the like; it would also bring a useless point into the connection. For the result also, outwardly considered, is no small one : πολλοὶ ἐπίστευσαν εἰσ τὸ ὄνομα αὐτοῦ ('many believed in his name'); it reads : So there are many that believe, and they believe in his name—namely, that he is the one whom he testifies that he is. It all gives the impression of a comprehensive attempt on the part of Jesus. He had indeed seen that Israel met him only with an unbelief which was not ready to repent. But still, to fulfil all righteousness, another attempt must be made. He might, perhaps, be able to separate the people from the authorities. His miraculous appearance in Jerusalem turns itself to the nation as a whole. The only thing, however, that makes any impression, is the miraculous part of his signs. The belief born of this is no moral act, and in so far is at heart not belief. It is unbelief in the form of belief, as Baur likes to say of the belief of the Jews. Only we must not forget that this half-belief is only unbelief in so far as it fixes itself on its standpoint of mere amazement, which has no moral value. It is, however, not unbelief, but the beginning of belief, as soon as it fails to find its rest in itself and strives to go beyond itself. The first was the case with the many spoken of in ver. 23, the latter was the case with Nicodemus.

VERSE 24.

Because the former did not reach a moral bearing towards Jesus, He also could enter on no moral relation to them. This is meant by the οὐκ ἐπίστευεν ἑαυτὸν αὐτοῖσ ('did not commit himself unto them'), which is based on a πιστεύειν ('believing') that Jesus recognised as a not believing. These words are as a rule translated: he did not entrust himself to them, and are understood either of his doctrine (Bengel) or of his person (Lücke, Baumgarten-Crusius). If they explain this, they explain it away, perhaps, with Lampe, by saying that he did not walk so freely among them as he otherwise would have done. But they can find in the text, and in the directly following account, as little of a reserve of the first kind as of the second. The understanding of it must be won from the contrast. The repetition of πιστεύειν is neither a play on the word (De Wette, Lücke) nor a mere coincidence in sound (Baumgarten-Crusius). It is a real analogy. It is not hard to see what is meant when it is said that in the case of such as did not enter into the moral relation and bearing of belief towards him, he on his part did not enter into the corresponding moral relation. The relation of communion is meant, into which relation he ought to have entered with Israel as his people, but could not enter. We may recall such passages as Hos. ii. 20: μνηστεύσομαί σε ἐμαυτῷ ἐν πίστει καὶ ἐπιγνώσῃ τὸν κύριον ('I will even betroth thee unto me in faithfulness; and thou shalt know the Lord'). The relation here, however, is taken from the other side, and is designated the less with a sensible expression. There is not a word here of prudence, or of public conversation, or of plain-dealing, and the like. It is the moral devotion, as it existed, for example, between Jesus and the disciples, as it existed between him and Nathanael at the very first meeting. The reason is the same here as there, namely, that Jesus possessed a knowledge of the internal position of the hearts of men who came into contact with him. No absolute knowledge on the part of Jesus is here meant, as our old dogmatists understood this word. All of the knowledge and power of Jesus is determined in accordance with his calling. The calling of the Baptist involved his recognising in those who came to his baptism, whether they came with a disposition ready or not ready for repentance. And thus Jesus' calling involved his recognising the internal position of the hearts of all in reference to the kingdom of God. *He himself*, that is, without needing to to be taught by another.

VERSE 25.

This negative point brings in the next: He *needed not that* (ἵνα in the weakened sense of later Greek, against Meyer's forced holding of the strict telic sense), etc. *For he himself*, without foreign help, *recognised what was in man;* the internal posture of the heart towards the kingdom of God or towards his person. In this sense, however, this knowledge was a testimony to his divine Sonship, for the point is the posture towards him, and it affects all men. Therefore it is a witness to his absolute importance. The supernatural direct knowledge of Christ is often made prominent in the gospel of John: i. 49; iv. 17; vi. 64; xi. 4, 14; xiii. 11; xxi. 17 (Meyer). Look also at the Revelation, ii. 2, 9, 13, 18, 19, 23, etc.

III. 1–21. *Jesus and the Half-Belief of Nicodemus.*

When the apostle reports the conversation with Nicodemus in chapter third, he certainly does not do it merely to lay stress on a particularly weighty story from that first time of residence at Jerusalem (Meyer). He did not compose his gospel so externally as that. The connection is more internal. Nor is the conversation with Nicodemus meant as a single example of that complete knowledge, or 'of the complete wisdom' (Lücke). To say this, ruins beforehand the right understanding of what follows. De Wette, and likewise Hengstenberg, are more correct in wishing to explain the conversation by reference to the belief in miracles, of which Nicodemus was an example. Baur has tried still more decidedly to develop the understanding of it from this thought. Nicodemus, says Baur, represents the believing Judaism, whose belief is but the cloak and form of unbelief. Hence this talk forms the first point in the process of belief and of unbelief which develops itself thence onward. In presenting this, the evangelist intends to reveal the fact, that the unbelief,

which comes out more and more openly, is and has been
from the beginning the contents of the external belief of
the Jews.¹ But this conception is opposed by the fact
that, in the course of the gospel, Nicodemus appears as a
believer, and indeed as believing not without the effect of
this talk.² Hence the evangelist cannot well have used him
here as a type of the absolutely unbelieving and 'unsusceptible' Judaism. Besides, he seeks the words of Jesus,
and though he reaches the understanding of them only with
difficulty, yet he does not gainsay them. At the close of
the talk, the matter stays in suspense, and so in the real
possibility and in the easy beginning of belief. It certainly,
however, is an example of belief, which is not yet belief,
but which is a possibility of the right belief if it tries to
pass beyond itself. Accordingly, we have here a sketch of
the other side of the Jewish belief in miracles. At the
same time, as the question at the end remains in suspense,
it also shows how hard it is to come to the right belief in
Judea. At this conversation, we still remain within the
realm of not yet believing. This, as well as the really
unbelieving belief in miracles, is touched by the words of
the Baptist, iii. 32: καὶ τὴν μαρτυρίαν αὐτοῦ οὐδεὶσ λαμβάνει ('and no man receiveth his testimony').

VERSE 1.

Stier³ was right in calling attention to the fact that
iii. 1 is connected with ii. 25 by the repetition of ἄνθρωποσ
('man'). By the repetition of the word, Nicodemus is held
up as a single one, from the collective whole, of whom it
was also true that Jesus knew what was in man. That
shows us one side in the progress of the history. The
people as a whole will remain unsusceptible. But single
ones will turn to Jesus, joining him and freeing themselves
from the mass. The evangelist here brings in this cutting
loose of single persons which is just beginning.

---

[1] Baur, *Kritische Untersuchungen über die kanonischen Evangelien*,
Tübingen 1847, pp. 143, 145.
[2] See vol. i. p. 104 f., and see vii. 50.
[3] Stier, *Reden Jesu*, 3d ed., Barmen and Elberfeld 1870, vol. iv. p. 22, note.

Verse 2.

In the Talmud, a Nakdimon, also called Bunai, is mentioned. He was very rich, and survived the destruction of Jerusalem. And this name is at another place given to a disciple of Jesus.[1] But nothing is said of his being a master in Israel. Nicodemus belonged to the strict legal and national party of the Pharisees, and was ἄρχων τῶν Ἰουδαίων ('a ruler of the Jews'), that is, a member of the high council, see vii. 50. *This one came to Jesus by night.* We are hardly to look for a special emphasis in the οὗτοσ ('this one,' Stier says, 'this one, a Pharisee and a ruler!'). It is a simple repetition, in hastening to what follows, on which the whole gaze of the evangelist is directed.[2] Νυκτόσ ('by night') is not a symbol of his benighted disposition (Hengstenberg); it served to characterize him. He chooses the night, not to be able to talk with Jesus without interruption, but from fear of his colleagues, and seeks Jesus in the circle of his disciples, for we must think of him as in that circle. Still he, the learned, comes and salutes Jesus the unlearned as a teacher sent from God. Indeed, he also joins himself here with others: οἴδαμεν ('we know'). That fits his whole nature. The most natural thing here is to think of colleagues of like mind; see xii. 42. Hence Jesus' appearance has not failed of a certain impression in the highest circles. But while the most were wanting in that moral earnestness which let itself be led farther, and while they thus lost the blessing, Nicodemus was forced to reach full certainty. He therefore frees himself internally from his colleagues. Of course, he still stands on quite the same ground as they. His recognition of Jesus rests only on the σημεῖα ('signs') which Jesus does. Because he works uncommon things, he is also a teacher in the uncommon sense. Indeed, he is a teacher with a divine commission, for his uncommon deeds can only be traced to

---

[1] See Delitzsch, *Talmudische Studien*, III., *Zeitschrift für die gesammte lutherische Theologie und Kirche*, 1854, pp. 643-647.

[2] As to Nicodemus in general, and as to his coming at night especially, see vol. i. p. 104 f.

uncommon help from God. The belief which he here confesses, is belief as it is described in ii. 23 ff., but it has the tendency to a progressive development. Thus he is the representative of half-belief, which forms the transition from unbelief to belief.

Verse 3.

Jesus' return to this address is called an answer (ἀπεκρίθη). A question lies in the address. Jesus does not let him go on far enough to express it. We do not need to presuppose gaps in the account. Nor have we a right to fill out the question as we like; as, for example, when Meyer says: What must we do to come into the kingdom of the Messiah? or when Bäumlein says: Does the baptism of John suffice for membership in the Messianic kingdom? As a matter of course, Nicodemus has the Messianic kingdom in mind. Jewish thoughts were directed to that above all. Jesus' answer confirms this. Nicodemus emphasizes the teacher and his divine miracles. That contains the question, whether this be the opening and the founding of the Messianic kingdom. In that case, it would be enough for membership therein to acknowledge the miracles of Jesus and his calling as a teacher. To this Jesus answers with the demand for the new birth. That is as much as to say: It does not come so externally in the external miracles, but internally; and it is not mediated to separate persons by that external recognition, but by this internal experience. Hence it is certainly right (against Meyer), though it is not everything, when De Wette, Brückner, and Ebrard, following Augustine, assume that Jesus wished to lead Nicodemus from the belief in miracles to the belief which brings a moral change; or when Godet says that Jesus contrasts the new birth with works.

Jesus speaks of the kingdom of God.[1] It has often

---

[1] Τῶν οὐρανῶν is not sufficiently attested. Justin cites thus in the well-known passage, *Apologia*, i. 61 (*Opera*, ed. Otto, Jena 1842, vol. i. p. 258); but that is clearly according to the common use of speech : on this point, see vol. i. p. 219 f., and Luthardt, *St. John the Author of the Fourth Gospel* (Edinburgh, T. and T. Clark, 1875), p. 61 ff.

been remarked that this expression is found nowhere else in the gospel of John (xviii. 36 is specially occasioned), and that it is therefore a testimony to the historical character of the account. 'Kingdom of God' is the popular expression for the Messianic state of salvation. The gospel of John likes in its own way to characterize this more really as life and the like. 'Kingdom of God' rests on the Old Testament prefiguring and prophecy. Jehovah was the real king of Israel, and his will was the law of the nation. To this was added the prophecy of the final position of things, when, after the time of the worldly kingdoms, Jehovah and his will should come to full dominion.[1] Nicodemus thought of this kingdom of God. All the hopes of Israel aimed at it. When will the dominion of the earthly kingdoms come to an end and Jehovah set up his dominion in Israel, and the καιροὶ ἀναψύξεωσ ἀπὸ προσώπου τοῦ κυρίου ('times of refreshing from the presence of the Lord,' Acts iii. 19) begin? That was the constant question of Israel. Israel thought of an external change of things by means of a revelation of power. But Jesus pointed from the outside to the inside. That is the sense and the progress of his discourse. It is true that he speaks also of a seeing (ἰδεῖν, and afterwards in ver. 5 εἰσελθεῖν, 'a coming in'), but it is not with a wish to confirm the thoughts of the externality of the kingdom of God; see Luke xvii. 20 f. Nicodemus thought that he had already beheld in the miracles the dawn of the kingdom of God. Hence Jesus chooses this word, which is an expression for an experience which a man goes through with. It is, however, a correct principle of the ancient philosophy, that like can only be recognised by like. How could the eye behold the sun, were the eye not fitted for the sun? A man must bear in himself the manner of the kingdom of God if he wishes to see it—that is, to experience it.

[1] On the Old Testament doctrine concerning the kingdom of God, see Oehler, *Theologie des Alten Testaments*, Tübingen 1874, vol. ii. p. 215 ff. On the New Testament, see Schmid, *Biblische Theologie des Neuen Testaments*, Stuttgart 1853, part i. p. 324 ff.; and Weiss, *Lehrbuch der biblischen Theologie des Neuen Testaments*, Berlin 1868, p 49 ff.

Γεννηθῆναι ἄνωθεν.

This influence, which must come to us to make us fit for the kingdom of God, is called by Jesus γεννηθῆναι ἄνωθεν ('to be born again, or from above').

As is well known, it is an old question whether ἄνωθεν is to be understood of time or of place; whether it means 'anew' (really 'from the beginning on'), or 'from above.' It is taken in the first way by the Syriac version, Augustine, the Vulgate, Luther, and Calvin; and among later scholars, by Tholuck, Olshausen, Neander, Stier, Hengstenberg, Godet, Hofmann,[1] and Weiss.[2] But by far the larger number of later exegetes follow Origen, Cyril, Theophylact, Erasmus, and Bengel, in holding to the other sense; thus Lücke, Baumgarten-Crusius, De Wette, Bäumlein, Meyer, Lange, Baur, and Hilgenfeld. In the three other passages in this gospel, which they quote here, iii. 31, xix. 11, 23, ἄνωθεν only occurs in this meaning. Besides, γεννᾶσθαι ἐκ θεοῦ ('to be born of God') is a more familiar idea and expression for John. Should they, however, at once assert that John only knows this idea and does not know that of the new birth (De Wette, and Weiss too, though it is true with a distinction between new birth and second birth), they are at fault; because in this place the thing in point as to matter no less than as to expression (δεύτερον γεννηθῆναι, ver. 4, see ver. 6) is a new birth which takes place from the Spirit. It seems to me (Stier, Hofmann, and others think so too) to be decisive against that view that Nicodemus must then have failed to hear this sentence (thus Bengel), which nevertheless stands at the emphatic part of the sentence, and expresses the chief point of the thought. Had he heard it, he could not well have put the question which he then puts. The ἐκ θεοῦ ('from God') must otherwise have solved the riddle for him, or at least have made him put that question in this direction.

Thus we see him moving entirely in the circle of thought of a second birth. In this case, Jesus would only emphasize

---

[1] Hofmann, *Der Schriftbeweis*, 2d ed., Nördlingen 1859, vol. ii. part i. p. 11.
[2] Weiss, *Der Johanneische Lehrbegriff*, Berlin 1862, p. 94.

the essential difference between this second and the first birth, in what follows. If it be objected that ἄνωθεν never means 'again,' but only 'from the beginning' (see Luke (i. 3; Acts xxvi. 5; and Gal. iv. 9, πάλιν ἄνωθεν), the objection has no force; since 'from the beginning' is exactly what it is said to mean here, and just for that reason δεύτερον ('second time') or the like was not chosen. As to the usage of the language, look at Josephus:[1] φιλίαν ἄνωθεν ποιεῖται: he binds himself from the beginning, that is, anew, in friendship with him. See especially the passage quoted by Tholuck, following Wetstein, from Artemidorus.[2] 'When a man's wife is with child, and he dreams that he is born of a woman, it means: παῖδα αὐτῷ γενήσεσθαι ὅμοιον κατὰ πάντα· οὕτω γὰρ ἄνωθεν αὐτὸσ δόξειε γεννᾶσθαι' ('that the child will be like him in all respects; for thus he himself will seem to be born again'). Meyer has no reason for his assertion that ἄνωθεν here also means ἐκ θεοῦ ('of God'). The point is not, as he says, that the dream comes from God, but that he himself is born anew, and thus begins to live in his son so like to him. Thus also here. The παλιγγενεσία ('regeneration') of Tit. iii. 5, and the ἀναγεννᾶσθαι ('to be born again') of 1 Pet. i. 3, 23, mean something else. In them the new birth is the changing about of the preceding life; in our passage it is a new beginning of life which puts itself in the place of the first one. Jesus intends to lay stress on this point of making a beginning; the whole life must start over—that is to say, the time now dawning is not merely a higher degree of the preceding, but a new time, which in the single person must put itself as a new beginning of life. He wishes to impress this on Nicodemus before he proceeds to explain that this new beginning of life is a working of the Spirit of God. By the idea and the mention of a birth from above, Jesus would have purposely made the whole matter from the first unintelligible

---

[1] Josephus, *Antiquitates*, I. xviii. 3; *Opera*, ed. Bekker, Leipzig 1855, vol. i. p. 49, line 26.

[2] Artemidorus, *Onirocriticon*, lib. i. cap. 13, lines 14-25, ed. Hercher, Leipzig 1864. [Hercher reads ἄν instead of ἄνωθιν; but the latter is supported by two good MSS.—C. R. G.]

to Nicodemus. On the other hand, the new beginning of life could not be so entirely strange to him, when he thought of the promise of the new heart and of the new spirit, Ezek. xi. 19 f., xxxvi. 26, 27, of Ps. li. 12 (English version 10), and the like.

Verse 4.

In spite of the accord with the Old Testament, Nicodemus does not understand Jesus. The reason probably is, that he was before this accustomed to understand the word as to a new birth, only figuratively of a changing about or of a transposition, while he thought that Jesus decidedly seemed to take the matter exactly 'from the beginning on.' Hence his answer refers to this point ($\epsilon\iota\sigma$ $\tau\dot{\eta}\nu$ $\kappa o\iota\lambda\acute{\iota}\alpha\nu$ $\kappa.\tau.\lambda.$, 'into the womb'), and Jesus gives him information about it.

A multitude of hypotheses arise from this reply of the 'Israelitic scholar:' they frame from them an accusation against the evangelist (Bruno Bauer); they put it at least to the charge of the narrative (De Wette); they determine the possibility that 'John emphasizes somewhat too strongly' Nicodemus' want of understanding (Lücke); they assume real want of understanding (Reuss);[1] they explain the preposterous character of his question from the natural mental narrowness of the man, as well as from the confusion of the moment (Meyer); they explain the question by the excitement of his disposition at the moment, owing to the strange answer of Jesus (Bengel, Stier); they explain it in the sense of irony (Godet), which does not suit his character; or they interpret (Baumgarten-Crusius and Schleiermacher) Nicodemus' words more ingeniously than they sound (the words about the womb are only a figure to denote the change in age), so as to free him from the charge of narrowness. If we hold fast to the real meaning of the words, Nicodemus is not charged with asking about the possibility of a second bodily birth. Nor does he merely say what Lücke makes him say: If the repetition of bodily

---

[1] Reuss: 'All attempts to save the sound understanding of Nicodemus have been wrecked on the palpable absurdity of his objection.' *Histoire de la théologie chrétienne*, 2d ed., Strassburg and Paris 1860, vol. ii. p. 413, note.

birth is such an absolutely impossible thing, how am I to understand the ἄνωθεν γεννηθῆναι ('to be born again')? He asks how this ἄνωθεν γεννηθῆναι can take place without a second bodily birth. He takes the ἄνωθεν γεννηθῆναι rightly of a new beginning of personal life. But the inward life seems to him so closely chained to and dependent on the natural life, that he cannot think of a new and real (not figurative) beginning of the former without a new and real beginning of the latter. He does not say, as some have imputed to him, that the second coming out of the womb is one and the same with the ἄνωθεν γεννηθῆναι of Jesus, but that it is the necessary natural presupposition, in and with which alone he is in a position to think of the new beginning of personal life.

This is verily a novelty in the whole arrangement of things, that there shall hence be a new beginning of personal life, which does not presuppose, but is followed by, the new beginning of the natural life. This finds its actual and conceivable possibility only in the typical and causal fact and knowledge of the birth of Christ the Son of God, the beginning of whose personal life is also independent of the beginning of his earthly natural life. The Old Testament did not know of such a Son of God, but of such as were in a certain sense raised to be sons of God by their position in their earthly life. To that degree, also, it does not know of the new birth, in the New Testament sense, which was first given by Christ. It knows only of a conversion, and that only as a not understood fact of the future. Hence, therefore, Nicodemus cannot understand the saying as to the new birth. He sees in Jesus only a human teacher, who, though divinely gifted-and endowed, is not thereby removed from the common order of things. He cannot understand this saying, because he takes it seriously and exactly, and because the person of Jesus, not being understood by him, does not give him the key to it.

Verse 5.

Jesus assures him that the point is a new birth in the real sense. It is as real as the first birth. As in the one the man comes from the earthly element and from the divine creative Spirit of the natural life, so in the other he comes from the earthly element and from the divine creative Spirit of the new time and new order of things. Πνεῦμα ('spirit') is contrasted with σάρξ ('flesh'), and not with πνεῦμα τῆσ σαρκόσ ('spirit of the flesh'). This birth must be produced by the πνεῦμα in the real sense, because it is produced for the time of the πνεῦμα, which time has dawned in Jesus the Son of God. Jesus here joins what the Baptist had contrasted: water and Spirit; see i. 26, 31, 32, 33. He adds the Spirit to the water, for He bears the Spirit without measure in himself, because He is the incarnate Word and the Son of God. We are not to take ὕδωρ ('water') as the figurative designation of the cleansing of the heart, and πνεῦμα ('spirit') as an unfigurative expression (Lücke[1]), or ὕδωρ as a figurative expression for the Spirit (Calvin), or for the human soul (Olshausen). Both words are alike exactly meant, and both are to be so joined in thought, that the baptism with the Spirit by Jesus is to be added to the baptism with water, which Nicodemus knew from John.[2]

Both points, the water of the Baptist and the Spirit of Christ, are well known to him; the first, from the immediate history, and the second, from the promise. When Christ combines them to the united divine act of the new birth and human act of believing obedience, the account remains strictly within the bounds of historical possibility and probability. On the other hand, to understand the words in the mouth of Jesus as a direct designation of Christian baptism, as Meyer does, neglects too much the historical connection in which they are spoken. They were not meant to make what had already been said to Nicodemus still more unintelligible by a fact of the future that was necessarily unknown to him, but to make it more intelligible. We may, however, well infer from the words of Jesus, that when the Baptist is no longer living, and yet the entrance into the kingdom of God is to be continually

---

[1] Lücke, *Commentar über das Evangelium des Johannes*, 3d ed., Bonn 1840, vol. i. p. 521 f.

[2] Hofmann, *Der Schriftbeweis*, 2d ed., Nördlingen 1860, vol. ii. part ii. p. 12.

mediated by the new birth produced through the two elements of the water and the Spirit, that these two points shall be combined into one act. Therefore, for us this saying speaks in the second place of a water baptism, which at the same time is a Spirit baptism. It is true that Nicodemus could not understand this, but he was not meant to understand it. He was merely to combine that which in time lay separated, that which is united for us by the fact of the Christian baptism into λουτρὸν παλιγγενεσίασ ('washing of regeneration,' Tit. iii. 5). In this, however, the Christian baptism is nothing else in reality than that which Jesus here intends by the πνεῦμα, only it is in a form different from that in which Nicodemus had occasion to think of it.

Verse 6.

But man needed such new birth because he is σάρξ ('flesh'), while the βασιλεία τοῦ θεοῦ ('the kingdom of God') is spiritual, and so man must become of the same kind as this in order to enter into it. As a matter of course, this does not refer merely to a part of men, as Hilgenfeld asserts from his presupposition of Gnostic dualism in the gospel of John,[1] but to men in general. All men are σάρξ. Weiss[2] thinks that i. 13 is decisive for the meaning of this word in this passage, in the sense that we are to understand it merely of the bodily sensuous side of human nature, and to reject all reference to the sinful character thereof as a Pauline addition. That is not right. The Old Testament circle of ideas which Nicodemus brought with him, and the whole connection in which the word here stands, must also speak. In the Old Testament, the statement that man is flesh does not designate merely the sensible existence of man, aside from all moral reference. According to the whole Old Testament conception, this is closely linked to the fact that man also morally is not what God would have him be.[3] In the context of the passage before us, the

---

[1] Compare against him, Weiss, *Der Johanneische Lehrbegriff*, Berlin 1862, p. 128 ff.   [2] *Ibid.* p. 130.
[3] See Hofmann, *Der Schriftbeweis*, 2d ed., Nördlingen 1857, vol. i. p. 503 ff.; and Oehler, *Theologie des Alten Testaments*, Tübingen 1873, vol. i. p. 253 ff.

necessity of the new birth is based upon the σάρξ of man. Clearly that cannot be intended to express merely the corporeality. It must mean the moral character of his human nature, which excludes from the kingdom of God. Indeed, this alone can make that divine influence upon him necessary.[1] The question is not merely about a difference between a lower and a higher stage,[2] but about an opposition.[3] The first birth of the flesh to the flesh has happened to the man, and thus too the second birth of the Spirit to the Spirit is something which happens to the man. Hence it is not identical with the μετάνοια ('repentance') (against Meyer), which the man has to perform himself (μετανοεῖτε), but is an influence ἐκ τοῦ πνεύματοσ, namely, from God's Spirit. The effect corresponds to the cause. There the man is flesh, namely, in kind; here, he is Spirit in kind. The substantives are more emphatic than the adjectives σαρκικόσ, πνευματικόσ ('fleshly,' 'spiritual') would have been.

VERSE 7.

This circumstance, that it is an act of the πνεῦμα ('Spirit') which is to happen to him, is to help Nicodemus understand, as far as he needs to, the demand for a new birth, which seems strange to him. This is to show him how a new beginning of life in the Spirit can be spoken of without a new beginning of the natural life. In order to understand the spirit of the ethical life, he is referred to its analogue in the natural life.

VERSE 8.

It is as free as the wind in its motion, and as undiscoverable in its origin, although perceptible and recognisable in its effects. Οὕτωσ ἐστίν ('so is'): this is the case with every one, etc. That is to calm Nicodemus. This working of the Spirit (πᾶσ ὁ γεγεννημένοσ ἐκ τοῦ πνεύματοσ,

---

[1] See Luthardt, *Lehre vom freien Willen*, Leipzig 1863, p. 393.

[2] Thus Julius Müller, *Lehre vom der Sünde*, Breslau 1844, vol. ii. p. 367.

[3] See Hofmann, *Der Schriftbeweis*, 2d ed., Nördlingen 1857, vol. i. p. 512 f.; and also Meyer.

'every one that is born of the Spirit') is a fact of experience which he likewise can and is to experience in himself.

That closes the first circle, vers. 3–8, of the instruction of Jesus. Its thought is: The wonderful fact of the new birth must happen to every one who wishes to belong to the kingdom of God, whose time had dawned in Jesus the Christ. The second circle, vers. 9–15, follows with: The said fact happens to him who believes on Jesus the Son of God, whose person and testimony are to be accepted in belief. And the third circle, vers. 16–21, continues: For whosoever believes on this one has therewith eternal life, while he who does not believe remains subject to judgment. The discourse falls into these three parts of like extent, the development of three sentences joining closely together logically. These sentences, the contents of the discourse, show nothing different from that which is the contents of the whole gospel.

VERSES 9–15.

The point here is belief on the Son of God. The matter in general, and Nicodemus' question, lead Jesus to speak of this. Nicodemus does not ask so as to comprehend the necessity and possibility of this (Lücke). He wishes to know the manner and the way in which this fact of the new birth can complete itself. Jesus then takes occasion to refer him to the belief on His person.

VERSE 9.

As a rule, the questioner has been wrongly treated; because commentators have only found here a repetition of the first failure to understand, and of the first want of understanding. On the contrary, he lets the fact of the new birth stand in some measure as believed, although not comprehended: he only wishes instructions as to the way it is to be completed. He still fails here, in that he stands objectively towards it, instead of asking how he himself can come to experience it, and what he has to do on behalf of it.

Verse 10.

Jesus reproaches him with a wondering question for not knowing this. 'Art thou the master?' This means, the well-known, recognised (thus commonly), not the ideal person of the teacher, which had become concrete (Hengstenberg), or the representative of the Israelitic teaching office (Godet): these would make too much out of Nicodemus. And then, in nice contrast to 'the teacher,' stands: καὶ ταῦτα οὐ γινώσκεισ ('and knowest not these things?'). As a teacher of Israel, he ought to know these things. As such it must be known to him from the Old Testament and from the history of salvation, that the only way to the communion of salvation from the very outset has been that of a believing obedience towards God's word and messenger. Thus also this New Testament saving fact of the new birth can only be experienced by believing obedience towards him who has the Spirit of the new birth and the divine testimony of this New Testament salvation. Jesus reproaches him for not coming to Him in such right believing obedience, and for not bearing himself thus towards Him even now in this conversation.

Verse 11.

He can do that the better, the more He has a right to demand belief in His testimony. If Nicodemus deserves to be called ὁ διδάσκαλοσ τοῦ 'Ισραήλ ('the master of Israel'), Jesus was the same in an entirely different way. In ver. 11, Jesus contrasts himself with that teacher. The contrast here is like the one in vii. 15, where the Jews ask in wonder: πῶσ οὗτοσ γράμματα οἶδεν μὴ μεμαθηκώσ ('How knoweth this man letters, having never learned?'). Nicodemus and his friends whom he represents ('ye') have a knowledge as far as study goes. Jesus has a knowledge based on direct acquaintance with that of which he gives witness. *We speak that we do know, and testify that we have seen.* Who are the 'We'? De Wette, Lücke, Meyer, and Stier make it a rhetorical plural. This, however, does not occur elsewhere in the words of Jesus or of John, not even in iv. 38, to which Meyer appeals. Some call it the plural of category: 'such teachers as I' (Meyer). But there were no other ' such teachers.' There is no need of proving that we are not to think of God (Chrysostom and others), or of the Holy Ghost (Bengel). The Old Testament prophets (Tholuck) are too distant. The disciples (Hengstenberg and Godet) do not 'speak' and 'testify' yet. Only the Baptist is left (Knapp, Hofmann, Weiss[1]). He also testified of the Spirit of the new time on the basis of direct divine revelation. Jesus had just recalled the Baptist by the water. Nicodemus knew that the Baptist had announced the Messianic baptism with the Spirit. So it must have been easy for him to think of the Baptist in this 'We.'

The first thing we are to think of here is the Spirit of the new time, which came upon Jesus at the baptism, so that he should impart it. That explains the 'we know' and 'we have seen;' the second is presupposed in the first. Jesus does not speak of his premundane perception, but of the revelation of God which he had received in the midst of men. If Jesus speak with such direct certainty and perception, they ought to believe him. *And ye receive not our witness.* The Pharisees believed neither in the Baptist nor in Jesus. In this Nicodemus is like the 'Ιουδαίοισ (' Jews'), ' ye' οὐ λαμβάνετε (' do not receive'), he is wanting in right belief. As long as Nicodemus has not right belief in the person of Jesus, he belongs to those Jews, although he may already have taken steps towards belief. He still ever has this in common with them, that he does not answer the real demand of Jesus. Hence Jesus in this paragraph presses throughout upon belief, and to this-end testifies to himself as the Son of God.

Verse 12.

But the testimony which is to be received in belief has hitherto had τὰ ἐπίγεια ('earthly things') for its contents. There is another contents that he must also proclaim, that is, τὰ ἐπουράνια ('heavenly things'). He names his testi-

---
[1] Weiss, *Der Johanneische Lehrbegriff,* Berlin 1862, p. 111.

mony as to the heavenly things not as a possibility, which remains only in thought, and perhaps will not be fulfilled, but as something which will be realized. Otherwise the hypothetical form with ἐάν would not be used. These two contrasted things, the earthly and the heavenly, have been explained in the most different ways, but the reference to the connection has been neglected, especially in the case of the last. The article in ἐπίγεια κ.τ.λ. ('earthly things') shows that we are here to think of something distinct, namely, of the testimony as to the kingdom of God. 'Earthly things' designates, not the whole category of the things to be found on earth, to which 'also' the birth from above belongs' (Meyer), but the shape and realization of the kingdom of God as it belongs to earth, which completes itself in this very new birth. Jesus had spoken of that until now (εἰ ... εἶπον, 'if I have told'). Hence τὰ ἐπουράνια ('heavenly things') does not betoken merely divine decrees for redemption (Meyer, Godet, and others). Still less is it to be generalized to the higher ideas of the gospel as a whole (Lücke, Reuss). Nor is it to be limited to the divinity of Jesus (Hengstenberg), or to the Trinity (thus often the popular interpretation of the gospel for Trinity Sunday). Nor is it to be extended to 'very many and manifold things' (Stier[1]). It is the heavenly reality which the kingdom of God has in its relation to the Father. That is to say, it is the Christological contents of his preaching, in distinction from the anthropological or moral, before treated of.

Verse 13.

And yet (καί) they must believe on him, for He alone can give testimony thereto. *No man hath ascended up to heaven, but he that came down from heaven, the Son of man.* 'No man hath ascended up to heaven,' so that he could speak from his own perception of those heavenly things (τὰ ἐπουράνια). It is true only of the Son of man that he was in heaven, and can speak from his own perception of these heavenly things. It does not mean: will ascend to

---

[1] Stier, *Reden Jesu*, 3d ed., Barmen and Elberfeld 1870, vol. iv. p. 22, note.

heaven (Bengel), the tense is against that; or: has raised himself in spirit to God (thus commonly; Lücke, Olshausen, Baumgarten-Crusius, De Wette, and even Beyschlag and Weiss[1]), for this tropical way of taking it is excluded by the verb and the contrast to καταβάσ ('came down'), and would not hold exclusively of Christ (see Hengstenberg and Meyer); or: he was by 'raptus in cœlum' ('a being caught up into heaven') taken away to God, as the Socinians fantastically explained. He 'ascended up,' which would be necessary for the men living on earth, is intended only as the necessary presupposition for the direct perception and the testimony made possible by it.

At the transition to Jesus (εἰ μή, ' but'), therefore, this point (direct perception as a basis of eye-witness) is to be emphasized. This holds good only of him, for he alone has come down from heaven—that is, has come out from a being with God. At καταβάσ ('came down') we think naturally of the incarnation. He became thereby the goal of the history of humanity: the Son of man. The phrase ὁ ὢν ἐν τῷ οὐρανῷ ('which is in heaven') is not to be taken as a present, so as to mean his then being present, and to be referred to his internal relation of communion with God (thus most later commentators). That would not suit the exact way of taking καταβάσ, or the whole thought. On the contrary, it would confuse the thought. It must be understood as an imperfect, and resolved into ὃσ ἦν (Bengel, Hofmann, Weiss[2]). This ὃσ ἦν ἐν τῷ οὐρανῷ ('who was in heaven') would not be 'unbearably useless' (Lücke). Jesus would emphasize his being ἐπουράνιοσ ('heavenly'), so as to confirm his knowledge and hint at his future. Since, however, these words are lacking in B L as well as in the Sinaitic manuscript, the right thing certainly is to leave them out, especially as the addition of them would be very easily explained, and the leaving them out would be much harder to explain. At the same time, the dogmatic use made of them falls away. The old doctors used this passage as a proof of their doctrine of the participation of the human

---

[1] Weiss, *Der Johanneische Lehrbegriff*, Berlin 1862, p. 213 f.
[2] *Ibid.* p. 214.

nature of Christ, in the omnipresence of the divine Logos, in the state of humiliation, on the basis of 'genus majestaticum communicationis idiomatum'[1] ('the majestic genus of the communion of attributes').

VERSE 14.

As now that fact, that He has come down from heaven, must be believed, so also is his exaltation an object of belief: for only he who believes on Him has eternal life. The connection with what precedes has been taken in very different ways: before, it spoke of the necessity; here, it speaks of the blessedness of belief (Meyer); but the wording of ver. 14 is against that; Jesus now goes to the ἐπουράνια ('heavenly things') (Tholuck and others); he passes from the possibility of the revelation through him to the necessity thereof (Lücke); or he passes from his divine person to his work of atonement (Hengstenberg). All this is arbitrary, because the progress of the discourse is evidently completed by the ὑψωθῆναι ('be lifted up'), in contrast to the preceding (see also Godet); yet not to designate the cross of Christ as the means of redemption (Godet), but to own the exaltation as an object of belief. If ὑψοῦν ('lifted up') stands also in that contrast, it is first of all the exaltation on the cross as the step to the exaltation on the throne. If Jesus, as is likely, used the Aramaic זְקַף, this served for the hanging of ill-doers on the stake. That suits also the comparison with the lifting up of the serpent in the wilderness, Num. xxi. 8, to be the means of salvation for those who directed their gaze unto it in belief.

The 'tertium comparationis' ('middle term of the comparison') lies in this. Jesus does not compare the subjects, himself and the snake, so that we should have a right to seek out all possible points of comparison between the two.[2]

---

[1] See Luthardt, *Compendium der Dogmatik*, § 49, 4th ed., Leipzig 1873, p. 160. [According to the old dogmatists, the 'communicatio idiomatum' was divided into three classes: 'genus idiomaticum,' 'genus majestaticum,' and 'genus apotelesmaticum.'—C. R. G.]

[2] Bengel, *Gnomon, in loco*, 3d ed., Tübingen 1773, 'ut serpens ille fuit serpens sine veneno contra serpentes venenatos; sic Christus homo sine peccato contra serpentem antiquum' ('as that serpent was a serpent without venom

That leads to a play of wit that has no right to a place in exegesis at least. The lifting up is what Jesus compares; in both cases a paradoxical means unto belief for salvation. He will indeed be lifted up, but so that his lifting up also demands belief. He will be lifted up on the cross; if he then be lifted up to God, it will be invisibly. Jesus leaves that continuation of the thought unspoken. This is a divine necessity: δεῖ ('must be') by divine decree, Matt. xvi. 21; Luke xxiv. 26.

VERSE 15.

This is the aim: *That whosoever believeth in him.* That is, reading εἰσ αὐτόν with the received text and the Sinaitic, which is the simplest and the best suited to John's use of the words. 'Επ' αὐτῷ (Γ) and ἐν αὐτῷ (B) have this usage against them, whence Meyer would join ἐν αὐτῷ with ἔχῃ κ.τ.λ., which does not fit the order of the words so well. The following words: μὴ ἀπόληται, ἀλλά ('should not perish, but'), which are lacking in ℵ B L, could certainly be taken up from ver. 16 (Meyer). The gift of eternal life (see on i. 4), the gift of the essential life of divine communion, is designated by ἔχῃ (present 'has') as one given at once with belief. It is given in Him because he is the Son of God, and so includes in himself the fulness of the divine life. Thus the close of ver. 15 leads us over from the necessity to the saving character of belief, that is, to the third paragraph of the whole discourse.

VERSES 16–21.

Thus far the discourse has turned on the necessity of belief, and on the right of Jesus to demand it; now it turns on the saving character of belief, according to the will of God, for salvation.

VERSE 16.

God aims at ζωὴ αἰώνιοσ ('eternal life') for the world, which life begins with the new birth, and is granted to faith. *For God so loved the world.* This will of God unto

against venomous serpents, thus Christ was a man without sin against the old serpent'); see also Menken, Olshausen, Jacobi, Stier, Lange.

salvation is designated as a will of love, because it realized itself by devotion (ἠγάπησεν). We are not to supply εἰσ θάνατον ('unto death') (Olshausen) to ἔδωκεν ('gave'), but τῷ κόσμῳ ('to the world'). The man Jesus is this gift: all else is but the historical consequence. In order, however, to enhance the greatness of the divine love, he is called the only-begotten Son; see on i. 14. The man Jesus is the Son of God by reason of his origin from God and of his communion with God, standing as 'the only-begotten' in a relation to God which no one else holds. God gave this one to the world. The emphasis lies, not on the greatness of the offering (in the death), but of the gift (in the incarnation). The design of God is to save the world from the destruction to which it would otherwise irremediably fall a prey, and to give it eternal life in Jesus as the Son who bears the fulness of life in himself. The destruction is the future, eternal ἀπώλεια (ἵνα μὴ ἀπόληται, 'that ... should not perish': the subjunctive instead of the optative demanded by the preceding praeterite, because this latter mood in general was less familiar to the speech of common life, and so also to the Hellenistic speech). With this design He was given to the whole world. We are not to make the 'universitas electorum' ('body of the elect') out of that, as Lampe does.[1] The whole κόσμοσ ('world') is the object of God's loving will. Jesus, however, is such salvation to the world under the condition of belief, or in belief. By the union of Son of God, eternal life, and belief, we easily perceive that the last is the essential appropriation of the person of Jesus, and therewith the possession of the true life which is in Him, and which he himself is.

If he who does not believe is thereby condemned, it is clear that the world is first of all under the ὀργὴ τοῦ θεοῦ ('wrath of God'), iii. 36. The decision is given in the person of Jesus, so that whosoever believes on Him is taken from destruction, and made a partaker of salvation; while whosoever does not believe, is thereby under judgment. We see that the essential relation between man and the

---

[1] Lampe, *Commentarius* . . . *Evangelii secundum Joannem*, Amsterdam 1724, vol. i. p. 615.

person of Jesus consists in belief. The evangelist names nothing else. Whatever things he mentions as forming communion or bringing salvation, are but as explanations or necessary consequences of the one πίστισ ('faith') in which all is given and decided. Again, we see that the whole decision as to the possession of salvation rests in the person of Jesus on the one side, in belief on the other side, and on nothing else. It is true that John likes to name salvation itself, life. As we remarked above, he gathers the whole of salvation in this word. Here, where he has spoken of the fact of the new birth, he chooses this expression of necessity. But we remember that he who believes unto eternal life is thereby taken from the wrath of God and put into loving communion with him, ver. 36. The life too is first of all communion in grace.

Verse 17.

When Jesus goes on, that he is not come to condemn but to save the world, we recall those passages in which he names the judgment as a thing kept for him until the future, as v. 22, 27 ff. He will do that when he comes the second time. It is true that we read in ix. 39, εἰσ κρίμα ἐγὼ εἰσ τὸν κόσμον τοῦτον ἦλθον ('For judgment I am come into this world'),[1] and κρίμα ('judgment') here refers, not to a future, but to a present thing. These words, however, do not mean to say that he is come to hold a judgment, but that a decision completes itself in him, namely, by the self-decision of men for or against him, in belief or in unbelief, to salvation or to judgment. The judgment itself, therefore, ever remains a future matter. That which now completes itself is that κρίσισ ('judgment') of which he speaks in vers. 18 and 19 as present; while his condemning judgment, as the external historical completion of that which now completes itself inwardly, always remains a thing of the future. This is the sense in which he denies the judgment as the aim of his mission. Lücke is wrong[2] when he says

---

[1] See Lücke, *Commentar über das Evangelium des Johannes*, 3d ed., Bonn 1840, vol. i. p. 547.
[2] Lücke, *ibid.* See also De Wette and Baumgarten-Crusius.

that he denies it in the sense 'in which the Jewish particularism asserted it, namely, with exclusion of the σωτηρία τοῦ κόσμου (" salvation of the world") ... as a condemning judgment in the Jewish sense over the not-Jewish world, before this has made its decision as to believing or not believing.' What would justify us in seeking the chief point in such nearer determinations and contrasts that were only thought out and added afterwards? Hence we cannot supply the words 'for this time' here. It is never said of the second coming unto judgment, that the Son will be *sent*.[1] We can easily see how he comes to speak of his being sent, not to judgment, but to salvation, if we remember that he is speaking to a teacher of Israel. The moment Jesus testifies to himself as the Son of God who has been sent, he must think of the Messianic prophecy of the Old Testament, according to which the day of Jehovah was to be joined with a great judgment upon the world. Nicodemus is to know that this judgment will remain a thing of the future. The presence of the Son is for the salvation of the world. Yet that future judgment is already decided internally by the relation which each man assumes towards the person of Jesus, and towards his self-revelation.

VERSE 18.

He that believeth on him is not condemned: but he that believeth not is condemned already, because he hath not believed in the name of the only-begotten Son of God. The world in itself is lost, and salvation is decreed alone in the person of Jesus, and is joined to his self-revelation (ὄνομα). Hence, therefore, belief is the only way of salvation, and the judgment is already decided (κέκριται) for unbelief.

VERSE 19.

This verse states, first, wherein the internal judgment consists, as to essence (αὕτη ἐστὶν ὅτι). It is, that a man shuts himself out from the light which has appeared in Jesus Christ. Instead of subordinating the first to the second grammatically, the evangelist put the contrasted phrases

[1] See Stier, *Reden Jesu*, 3d ed., Barmen and Elberfeld 1870, vol. iv. p. 113.

side by side, for the sake of emphasis: the light appeared, and man loved, etc.[1] The idea of light comes in here, instead of the idea of life, because Jesus wishes to pass to the moral sphere.[2] The point is a moral decision between the two great moral antagonists, between light and darkness. The light has appeared in Jesus Christ, in his incarnation, and in his entrance on his calling. Yet men loved the darkness more than the light. It might seem strange that Jesus should speak of the relation of men to him as of a completed fact: ἠγάπησαν οἱ ἄνθρωποι κ.τ.λ. ('men loved,' etc.). This is not meant as 'a general experience of history,' as Lücke has it,[3] but as the historical bearing towards Jesus, with which men answered God's deed of love.[4] He designates this just as the Baptist does afterwards in ver. 32, when he says: καὶ τὴν μαρτυρίαν αὐτοῦ οὐδεὶσ λαμβάνει ('and no man receiveth his testimony').

This is settled, although Jesus still is only at the beginning of his activity. The beginning decides as to the general bearing of Israel, and so of men, towards Him. In general he stands in contrast with unbelief, and there are but few believing exceptions. Thus the disciples are chosen, thus the church of Jesus is chosen out of the world, xv. 19. The world as a whole has closed itself to the light. This is essentially decided from the first. The relation of Jesus to the world became at once an opposition. The decision consists in the fact that men preferred (μᾶλλον) the darkness in which they lived to the light which came to them and wished to draw them to itself. It is true that μᾶλλον ('rather') is not an expression of opposition, but of comparison (Bengel, Stier); but here it does not point merely to a difference of degree in the ἀγαπᾶν ('love'); it does not belong to this verb, but to the substantive τὸ σκότοσ ('the darkness'). Their love (ἠγάπησαν put first for the sake of emphasis) was directed rather (μᾶλλον, 'potius,' not 'magis') to the

---

[1] See vol. i. pp. 36 f., 43.   [2] See the discussion of i. 5.
[3] Lücke, *Commentar über das Evangelium des Johannes*, 3d ed., Bonn 1840, vol. i. p. 550.
[4] On ἠγάπησιν, ver. 16, and ἠγάπησαν, ver. 19, see Stier, *Reden Jesu*, 3d ed., Barmen and Elberfeld 1870, vol. iv. p. 117.

darkness than to the light. 'Darkness' indicates the ungodly, sinful, worldly essence, to which they originally belonged. Hilgenfeld (so also Baur and Keim), with the notion of a metaphysical dualism, which he brought in so arbitrarily, thinks that this applies merely to a single class of men.[1] He is wrong. It is clear that the sentence is true of men in general. If they choose the darkness instead of the light, there must be a possibility of deciding for the light. They must have had historical experience of the light, not by the testimony of the conscience or the like, but, as what precedes shows us, in the appearance and words of Jesus Christ. The deeper reason for this unbelief is a moral one; the religious conduct has a moral root. The reason, namely, is given, that *their deeds*, that is, their whole action wherein their moral disposition and character proved itself in detail, *were evil*. The contrast, $\pi o \iota \epsilon \hat{\imath} \nu \ \tau \grave{\eta} \nu \ \dot{a} \lambda \acute{\eta} \theta \epsilon \iota a \nu$ ('to do the truth,' ver. 21), shows that $\tau \grave{a} \ \check{\epsilon} \rho \gamma a$ and $\phi a \hat{\upsilon} \lambda a$ betoken not single acts, but the whole moral bearing. The posture towards Christ is therefore conditioned by the original moral tendency.

VERSE 20.

It is necessarily so. *Every one that doeth evil* (not in one or another single case, but whose $\pi \rho \acute{a} \sigma \sigma \epsilon \iota \nu$, 'action,' in general is not moral; observe the present) *hateth the light, neither cometh to the light*.[2] This sentence, it is true, contains a general truth; but it is here to be taken only in relation to the revelation in Christ. 'The light' must be understood as before: the light as it has appeared in Christ. That moral species forms a contrast to the moral character of the revelation, and hence it denies this revelation. Such a one does not come to the light, that is, does not follow Jesus in belief, because this is a moral decision which stands in contradiction to his whole moral (or rather immoral) course of life, so that this relation of belief could only be completed by the denying of this course of life.

---

[1] See vol. i. p. 122.

[2] The καὶ οὐκ ἔρχεται πρὸς τὸ φῶς is probably left out by ℵ through mere accident.

Lest his deeds should be reproved. That does not mean external, but internal reproof and condemnation, since the processes in question are psychological.

Verse 21.

Unbelief has moral roots, and so has belief: *But he that doeth truth cometh to the light, that his deeds may be manifest that they are wrought in God.*[1] Truth is, first of all, the being which agrees with itself, which excludes all internal contradiction; then it is used of knowledge and of words, so far as they agree with the reality without contradiction, and so bear it in themselves. The former exists in its absolute sense in God, and God is revealed in Christ Jesus. Hence He is the truth, and the truth has appeared in Him, so that we recognise it and let it become the determining power of our thought, will, and life. In agreement with all the rest of John's use of language (especially in the first epistle), the doing of the truth must here be taken in this absolute sense.

The possibility of this action, therefore, presupposes the revelation in Jesus Christ. Hence it does not betoken a moral possibility or degree upon the pre-Christian sphere.[2] The expression would clearly be too strong for that. For that reason Hengstenberg reminds us that Jesus is talking to a member of the covenant people of the Old Testament. This, however, all steps into the background, and the discourse keeps itself wholly in the general human sphere (κόσμοσ, ἄνθρωποσ, πᾶσ, 'world, man, all'). It treats of the man, not of the Jew. But it treats of his posture towards Christ. To be able to do the truth he must know the truth, and the truth must have met him in Christ. He who does the truth (that is, not he who does it in this or that single case, but for whom it has become the determining power of his moral will and conduct) cometh to the

---

[1] On the biblical conception of truth, see Hoelemann, *Bibelstudien*, Leipzig 1859, vol. i. p. 1 ff.

[2] Against my article on ἔργα τοῦ θεοῦ and πίστισ in their mutual relations, according to the representation of John's gospel. *Studien und Kritiken*, 1852, pp. 333-374.

light, that is, follows Christ in belief. Thus the religious posture of belief in Christ has as its presupposition and as its base a moral self-decision with regard to Christ, which has been made possible by Christ.

Hence the question at each place, at the $\phi a\hat{v}\lambda a\ \pi\rho\acute{a}\sigma\sigma\epsilon\iota\nu$ ('doing evil') as well as at the $\pi o\iota\epsilon\hat{\iota}\nu\ \tau\grave{\eta}\nu\ \grave{a}\lambda\acute{\eta}\theta\epsilon\iota a\nu$ ('doing the truth'), is not with reference to degrees of natural morality in the pre-Christian sphere, but with reference to moral self-decisions as they are called forth by the revelation of and by the words of Christ; upon these decisions the religious conduct depends. To love the darkness is to do evil; to love the light is to do the truth. In the former, the man shuts himself up selfishly in himself against the light; in the latter, he opens himself to Christ, devoting himself to Him. 'That his deeds may be manifest that they are wrought in God.' The internal decision will come out. The moral posture being towards God, and therefore belonging to God and agreeable to his will, presses on to the union, by belief, with the revelation of God in Christ. Belief has as its base the moral self-decision for God in Christ; and moral self-decision for God in Christ has belief as its necessary effect and phenomenon. Such is the thought of this passage, which sounds difficult, which has been often treated, and which has commonly, though as we have seen probably incorrectly, been understood of a preparatory stage of belief or of conversion.[1]

The conversation closes fitly with the reference made by Jesus to the innermost moral root of belief. It goes from the objective to the subjective, from without, within. Jesus had passed from the new birth as the presupposition for participation in the kingdom of God, to belief as the presupposition for the new birth. This he did in order to show the necessity and the blessing of belief, and finally to reveal the moral presupposition of belief and of unbelief, thus leading Nicodemus to the subjective sphere of his life within—to his conscience. The objective side of the discourse corresponds to that subjective side: it is the testimony to the divine Sonship of Christ. Both are meant to

---

[1] See Luthardt, *Lehre vom freien Willen*, Leipzig 1863, p. 418 f.

knit a personal relation that shall take the place of the mere external amazement at his miracles. This comprehensive and peculiar character of the discourse gives it a fundamental value for John's gospel and its testimony. Hence the evangelist picked out this very discourse, put it at the head of his account of the public activity of Jesus, and so reproduced it as to make it exactly fit to serve this purpose. We therefore need not assume that the evangelist, in the progress of the discourse from ver. 16 on, has passed from the report to his own reflections and explanatory considerations (for example, Neander, Tholuck, Olshausen), or at least has joined these to the account more strongly than before (Lücke, De Wette, Brückner, whom Meyer rightly opposes). We have only to acknowledge the subjective character in the form of the reproduction, as we have to admit it in the discourses of John's gospel in general.[1]

(3.) III. 22–36. *Jesus in Judea, and the Baptist's Testimony.*

Jesus widens the circle. He turns from Jerusalem to the whole land of Judah, from the few to the many. He begins the foundation of the kingdom of God, in the form which the Baptist used. It is true that his baptism is not essentially different from John's, and is not yet the real Christian baptism in the name of Jesus, for he is not yet glorified. Yet it is more than if he were merely active at the side of the Baptist, and in just the same way. We can already recognise the progress of the realization of salvation in the fact that, while those ready to repent must go out to John to show their readiness, Jesus on the contrary comes to them to bring salvation near to them. In consequence, John pointed to the Son of God who was to come; Jesus points to himself as being the Son of God. Thus he begins to gather about the present Redeemer, from separate

---

[1] See vol. i. p. 144 ff., and my *Der johanneische Ursprung des vierten Evangeliums*, Leipzig 1874, p. 196 ff. English edition, *St. John the Author of the Fourth Gospel*, Edinburgh 1875, p. 246 ff.

persons of Judea, the church of the kingdom of God, which kingdom was now revealing itself. It is the third attempt Jesus makes to win Israel to repenting belief in his person, so that he could go on with the revelation of the kingdom of God. Yet, though they came to him in greater numbers than to the Baptist, the latter could not but say: καὶ τὴν μαρτυρίαν αὐτοῦ οὐδεὶσ λαμβάνει ('and no man receiveth his testimony').

The matter is commonly put as if the Baptist's testimony were the only thing really meant to be reported here, and the rest were brought in only to make it possible to give the former. This can hardly be right. The evangelist is here busied with the historical progress, and this testimony forms a part of the history which he is reporting. Every particle of it is historical. Instead of saying himself that Jesus, with such an extended and heightened activity, has gradually taken the place of the Baptist, that the Baptist's time had begun to yield to Jesus' time, and that the former had not yet reached the right belief in Jesus' person and word, he gives us a testimony of the Baptist's which contains all this. He relates the history in the Baptist's words, because they at once help us to understand the historical position. If the relation of ver. 22 ff. to ver. 27 ff., and the meaning of the last, were not such as is here alleged, how could the evangelist, iv. 1, go on with the history, with οὖν ('therefore'), drawing a conclusion from what precedes?

If this be the case, then we shall have to explain ver. 22 f. from the words of the Baptist. He designates Jesus as a bridegroom, who is already on the way to take His bride home; he already hears His voice as He calls the bride, ver. 29. Hence his great joy, and hence he knows that his own time is almost at an end. According to this, the design of Jesus' deeds here will need to be taken as more comprehensive and more far-reaching than is commonly assumed. It is no longer mere preaching and preparation, but the beginning of founding and gathering.

But why does not Jesus appear to baptize after this?

It was not on account of the lack of faith,[1] nor because it was enough to have put his baptism once by the side of John's.[2] The real reason is that he took up another plan, and gave up the thought of gathering his church about himself in such a definite way during the days of his flesh. That is the very cause for the Baptist's mistake. He now saw the gathering of the church already beginning. But later he could see nothing more of such a beginning, and, on the contrary, found again mere preaching and preparation, like a simple continuation of his own activity. But, it may be objected, the Baptist knew by this time that the right belief was not afforded. Of course he understood the present, but not the future; and afterwards, when in prison, he did not understand even the later present, because the time of his calling was over. He might easily think that Jesus would reveal His kingdom in spite of the lack of belief. In fact, he saw Him busy therewith in the beginning of His activity.

This gives us the clue both to the account of Jesus' activity, and to the dispute between the Baptist's disciples and the Jew named in ver. 25.

Verse 22.

Μετὰ ταῦτα ('after these things'), a familiar way of continuing in John's gospel,[3] joins what follows to what precedes, only as a general matter of time. Jesus went from Jerusalem (that he was in Galilee in the meantime is not absolutely impossible from the account, but is improbable) into the land of Judea. Ἰουδαία γῆ is to be understood thus of the country in contrast with the capital. The imperfects διέτριβεν and ἐβάπτιζεν ('tarried' and 'baptized') express longer continuance. We see by iv. 2 that the disciples, and not Jesus himself, performed the baptism.

---

[1] Lücke, *Commentar über das Evangelium des Johannes*, 3d ed., Bonn 1840, vol. i. p. 559.

[2] Hofmann, *Weissagung und Erfüllung im alten und im neuen Testamente*, Nördlingen 1844, vol. ii. p. 90.

[3] See vol. i. p. 26.

VERSE 23.

John was active at the same time. *Ἦν βαπτίζων, he was busy baptizing;* more than a mere paraphrase for the finite verb: *in Ænon, near to Salem.* Whether we explain Ænon as עַיִן יוֹן, Dove-Fountain (Meyer), or as the intensive or adjective form of עַיִן, fountain, the name cannot but suggest a region that was rich in fountains, and therefore in water. Eusebius and Jerome put Σαλείμ ('Salem') eight Roman miles (about 8 English miles) south of Scythopolis, at a place where the Jordan was quite broad, towards the borders of Galilee. But according to the account here it must have been in Judea. Probably we should refer to Josh. xv. 32, שלחים ועין, in the south of Judea.[1] Shilchim (LXX. Salem) means those sent, hence brooks; and Ain means fountain, hence a region rich in water. Hence John went southward, perhaps towards his home. They must come to him at that point to be baptized. The fact that he did not give up his activity, although Jesus had come forth and was at work, is not to be considered improbable (Baur), because it would have been a split in the Messianic movement (Keim); nor does it stand in contradiction with the divine certainty the Baptist had as to Jesus' Messiahship (Weizsäcker); nor is it to be accounted for by the circumstance that Jesus had not really appeared yet as the Messiah (Meyer). The simple state of the case is, that as God had put him in his calling, he had no right to give it up of himself, but had to wait for the direction of God.

VERSE 24.

The evangelist remarks, by way of explanation, that John was then not yet cast into prison. In this he does not 'correct' the synoptic account (Meyer); that was unnecessary, as the synoptic account does not say a word about this time, and only begins at the imprisoning of the Baptist. He merely brings his account into connection with the synoptic account, which tells us that Jesus came

---

[1] So says Wieseler, *Chronologische Synopse der vier Evangelien*, Hamburg 1843, p. 247 f.; Ewald, and others.

forth as the prophet of Galilee in the stead of the imprisoned Baptist.

VERSE 25.

The position of affairs as just stated will help us to understand the dispute, ver. 25 f., which has given exegetes much trouble. The inferential relation of iv. 1 to what precedes, and John's use of 'Ιουδαῖοσ (' Jew'), allow us to conclude that the 'Ιουδαῖοσ here spoken of is a hostilely disposed Pharisee. We must learn what the dispute between the Baptist's disciples [1] and the Jew was about, from the statement they make to their master. The Jew had told them what they now tell John, and the Jew had drawn inferences therefrom about καθαρισμόσ (' cleansing'). The major premise for this conclusion was, that Jesus was the one testified to by the Baptist; the minor premise, that he is baptizing. What must the conclusion have been? It was not that Jesus' baptism was better, so that John's disciples became jealous (De Wette, Lücke, Meyer). The text says nothing about that, and that would not explain why it says περὶ καθαρισμοῦ (' about purifying'), and not περὶ τοῦ βαπτίσματοσ, sc. τοῦ 'Ιωάννου (' about baptism,' namely John's). The question referred to the necessity of a cleansing before the opening of the kingdom of heaven, resting on Ezek. xxxvi. 25; Zech. xiii. 1.[2] Perhaps the disciples of John had asked him to let himself be baptized, and thus had given him occasion to tell about the activity of Jesus, and to argue from it against John's baptism.

VERSE 26.

The tone in which the disciples speak to their master is excited and complaining. The reference to the Baptist's testimony, ᾧ σὺ μεμαρτύρηκασ (' to whom thou bearest witness'), does not emphasize the contents but the fact of that testimony: He who owes his authority to you, now rivals you so as to put you in the shade. *All come to him:*

---

[1] See vol. i. p. 115 ff.; ἐκ τῶν μαθητῶν, and therefore begun by the disciples, but, as is seen by what follows, occasioned by the Jew.

[2] See Hofmann, *Weissagung und Erfüllung*, Nördlingen 1844, vol. ii. p. 87.

passion speaks with exaggeration. Still it shows at any rate that Jesus had a great throng.

VERSES 27–36. *The Baptist's Answer.*

The Baptist's answer is in two parts, corresponding to the two points in the disciples' complaint. The first, vers. 27–30, discusses the relation between Jesus and him; the second, vers. 31–36, the relation between Jesus and the world.[1]

He answers with an 'Indeed . . . but.' 'The time of the kingdom has come, and Jesus the Christ already calls the church of the kingdom of heaven: my time, on the other hand, is almost at an end: as the friend of the bridegroom, standing at his side, it is my duty to rejoice in his increase. Still, great as is the applause found by Jesus, they do not give him real belief. And therefore I, his herald, must continue to bear witness to him, and to point to him as an object of belief, so that they may learn to escape the wrath over Israel.' The conclusion in reference to his own action is not drawn in definite words by the Baptist, only because it is to be seen clearly enough in his command to his disciples.

VERSES 27–30. *Christ and the Baptist.*

VERSE 27.

The explanation given shows of itself how we are to understand the general sentence with which the Baptist begins this verse. It is not to be referrred to the Baptist alone (Wetstein, 'non possum mihi arrogare et rapere quod deus non dedit,' 'I cannot arrogate to myself and seize what God has not given me;' Bengel, Lücke, Hengstenberg, Godet); that would not fit the complaints of the disciples about Jesus. Nor is it to be referred only to Jesus (Olshausen, De Wette, Baumgarten-Crusius, Meyer). It must be understood of both,—of the Baptist as well as of Jesus,—for the disciples need information as to both (Tholuck, Brückner). He must explain and justify not

---
[1] See Hofmann, *Der Schriftbeweis*, Nördlingen 1859, vol. ii. part i. p. 13.

only his own conduct, but also Jesus' action and success. Thus we have here in brief the relation between him and Jesus, which he then proceeds to give in detail with humility and with joy.

Verse 28.

First of all he reminds his disciples of his earlier testimony to Jesus. His disciples had laid stress on the fact of that testimony, he lays stress on the contents of it. He is only the forerunner ἐκείνου ('of him'), not of the Χριστόσ ('Christ'), but of Jesus (Bengel, De Wette, Baumgarten-Crusius, and Meyer). That is the way the thing stands.

Verse 29.

Both have a calling with regard to the church, Christ as its master, John as His servant and friend. The comparison of the church with a bride rests on the Old Testament view of the relation of Jehovah to the Old Testament church as a marriage, Isa. liv. 5; Hos. ii. 19 ff. This view passed over to the New Testament, Eph. v. 32, and is especially familiar in the Revelation, see Rev. xix. 7, xxi. 2, 9. The reference to the Song of Solomon (especially v. 1, Bengel, Hengstenberg) is problematical. The completion of communion with God, or the full institution of the kingdom, is represented as a marriage, Matt. ix. 25, xxv. 1 ff. Jesus has entered upon the position of Jehovah towards the church, as its Lord, and therefore as the bridegroom who has (ὁ ἔχων) the bride, and who is on the way to the wedding. The Baptist is his friend who stands by. That does not mean ἐπὶ τῇ θύρᾳ ('at the door;' Olshausen too), to hear the delight of the newly-married; aside from other reasons, things are not so far advanced. Nor is it 'tanquam apparitor' ('like an attendant') at the wedding (Bengel,[1] Meyer); it is too early for that. It is more general; he has announced Him and now waits for Him (Baumgarten-Crusius), and hears His voice as He approaches. Jesus is on the way to set up His kingdom, and John rejoices greatly because he hears His voice, simply hears His voice as He approaches, and

---

[1] Bengel, *Gnomon*, 3d ed., Tübingen 1773, vol. i. p. 390 b.

not the voice from the marriage-chamber (Paulus), or the voice of the marriage-joy (Meyer). Meyer's objection, that the παρανύμφιοσ ('friend of the bridegroom') had to accompany the bridegroom, does not apply, because the Baptist ἀπεσταλμένοσ ἐστὶν ἔμπροσθεν αὐτοῦ ('is sent before him,' ver. 28); this is enough to justify our (and Baumgarten-Crusius') way of taking it. The bridegroom calls ἔρχομαι ('I come'); the bride answers ἔρχου, κύριε 'Ιησοῦ ('Come, Lord Jesus,' Rev. xxii. 20). This was then in process. It is true that it has had a long delay, and that the Baptist's calling now continues itself in the church; see 2 Cor. xi. 2. Still he rejoices that it has gone so far. He contrasts his joy with the envy of his disciples.

Verse 30.

The conclusion follows of itself: Jesus' day is rising, his own is setting, and thus the Baptist has ended the explanation of his relation to Christ.

Verses 31–36. *The Relation of Christ to the World.*

He now turns to the relation between Christ and the world. He first emphasizes the absoluteness of Christ in comparison with all others, in order to put the conduct of the world in contrast with it.

Verse 31.

He that cometh from above, namely Jesus, *is above all,* and therefore has a claim upon the church as its Lord. 'Ερχόμενοσ ('cometh') is in the present; his coming is not yet finished. Hence we are to understand thereby not simply the incarnation, but also the whole historical activity of Jesus, with the setting up of his kingdom. Fitting this, then, the ἄνωθεν ἐρχόμενοσ ('cometh from above') is not to be understood of the pre-existence of the incarnate one, but of the divine origin of this historical fact in general. This phrase contains nothing that exceeded the Baptist's knowledge, though it later became for the evangelist also the expression of a more widely-developed knowledge.

By reason of this higher origin, Jesus is higher than all others: ἐπάνω πάντων ἐστίν ('is above all'); not merely above all interpreters of God (Meyer), that would be an unwarranted limitation; nor does the Baptist here speak of himself and the other messengers of God, for he has passed to the relation of Christ to the world, and emphasizes the contrast. The 'all' are those belonging to the earth, in contrast to the one coming from above. *He that is of the earth is earthly*, is not tautological. It means that character corresponds to origin, and hence that when such a one comes forth as a teacher, his words (λαλεῖ) correspond to his origin. It is not allowable to refer this to the Baptist (thus commonly, Meyer too). The Baptist does not speak from the earth, but from divine revelation. Had he referred, or even only partially referred, to himself in this, he would have contradicted his former testimony.[1] On the contrary, he avoids himself here altogether. The Sinaitic manuscript and D leave out the closing words: ἐπάνω πάντων ἐστίν, and also the following καί, thus joining ὁ ἐκ τοῦ οὐρ. ἐρχ. with ὃ ἑώρακεν κ.τ.λ. But the repetition of those closing words is exactly suited to John's style. The thought returns to its own beginning in order to pass to a new contrasted thought.[2]

Verse 32.

We probably ought to leave out the καί ('and') at the beginning of this verse, as ℵ B L D do. The asyndetic form of the progress of thought rules in this whole passage,[3] and the following καί is the καί of tragic contrast, peculiar to John's gospel.[4] The Baptist's tone, at first so joyful as he looks at Jesus and his own relation to Him, now becomes sad as he turns to the relation of the world to Jesus. *What he hath seen and heard;* i. 18 and iii. 11 speak only of seeing. Hearing betokens the internal intercourse of the Son with the Father; see what Jesus says of the ἐντολή ('commandment') which the Father gave him, x. 18.

[1] See Hofmann, *Der Schriftbeweis*, Nördlingen 1859, vol. ii. part i. p. 14.
[2] See vol. i. p. 48 f.   [3] See vol. i. p. 43.
[4] See vol. i. p. 43 f.

These words only reach their full truth in the knowledge of the pre-existence of Christ: in the Baptist's mouth they are the expression of the direct relation of Christ to the Father, and the direct knowledge which rests thereon. *Τοῦτο* ('that') refers back with emphasis, as John's gospel likes to do;[1] hence its omission in the Sinaitic manuscript is unjustified, indeed it is clear that all this part. in the Sinaitic is unfortunately corrected (thus also ὃν ἑώρ. κ.τ.λ. instead of ὅ). In contrast therewith: *and no man receiveth his testimony*, referring to the disciples' words: πάντεσ ἔρχονται πρὸσ αὐτόν ('all come to him'). The Baptist's grief makes him overlook the few who really believe, and only see the unbelief of the multitude; hence οὐδείσ ('no one').

VERSE 33.

In contrast with the preceding we have here the right behaviour, and this verse brings in the single exceptions as a fact, for the words are in the preterite. *He that hath received his testimony,* αὐτοῦ ('his') put first for emphasis, *hath,* namely thereby, *set to his seal,* that is, confirmed, *that God is true.* Belief is the seal which man on his side impresses on the testimony of God, owning it as true. Belief is the Yea and Amen to God's word. The testimony here meant is the preaching of Jesus Christ as the revelation of God.

VERSE 34.

God's word is the thing in question: *For he whom God hath sent speaketh the words of God.* This, according to the connection, relates clearly to Jesus, and so the question is not merely of divine words in general, but of God's words. He brings the absolute revelation of God. This gives a closer definiteness to the following words, which sound quite general: *for God giveth not the Spirit by measure.* It is true that there is no αὐτῷ ('to him') here, and that it is not put in the preterite: has given. Therefore the sentence is general: God does not give his Spirit to his

---

[1] See vol. i. p. 32.

ambassadors by measure,[1] so that we should have to distinguish between what is divine and what is not divine in their preaching, but he gives them the Spirit for all the preaching of their calling. Of course this is true in its way of all God's messengers, but especially of Him of whom the Baptist here speaks, who came from above before all others, and who has a comprehensive calling with reference to the church.

Verse 35.

This is not simply a 'further description of Christ's elevation' (Meyer), but a conclusion from what precedes. If that be true of Jesus and of his word in the absolute sense, then he and his word, and the posture towards him and it, are decisive. *The Father loveth the Son.* This does not refer to the eternal relation of love within the Trinity, but to the historical relation of love between God in heaven and the man Jesus on earth, though the latter relation is but the historical appearance and completion of the former. This love is the foundation of the absolute position which Christ assumes: He *hath given all things into his hand*, ἐν τῇ χειρί, so that they lie in his hand, that is, he is the absolute Lord; the absolute decision, life and death, for every one is joined to him, and is dependent on the relation to him.

Verse 36.

Hence: *He that believeth on the Son hath everlasting life: he that obeyeth not the Son* (rejects his word in unbelief) *shall not see life; but the wrath of God abideth on him.* This verse shows how we are to understand the πάντα-('all things') in the verse before. It does not refer to all things absolutely, but is defined more closely by the saving office of Christ. Belief is a personal relation of devotion and appropriation, and therefore of communion. Hence he who believes has; he has that which is determined in Christ, namely, the essential life which springs from God. Christ

---

[1] Winer, *Grammatik des N. T. Sprachidioms*, sec. 51, 7th ed., Leipzig 1867, p. 395.

demands such belief; therefore we read ἀπειθῶν ('disobeying'). 'The wrath of God abideth on him;' thus we are by origin under this wrath, and can only be taken from it and made partakers of life by belief. That is to say: salvation is absolutely united to Jesus Christ. This knowledge yielded itself to the Baptist of itself, from his knowledge of Christ. His discourse ends like an elegy. His last words in John's gospel are like a prophecy of judgment over Israel, which as a whole refused believing obedience.

This exposition shows that the discourse does not turn into the evangelist's own reflections (Bengel, Olshausen, Tholuck), but is the Baptist's to the very end. The two parts of it: his relation to Jesus, and Jesus' relation to the world, were both essential to the instruction of his disciples. But considering the likeness of the language of the Baptist to the language of the rest of the gospel, we should probably own that the evangelist makes the Baptist speak in his own language. Indeed, it is true of the discourses of the fourth gospel in general, that they are reported in the form which they have assumed in the course of time and in the process of internal reflection upon them in the mind of the evangelist. That, however, is no proof of a want of historical character. The evangelist is bent only on the thing itself, that is, on the inward historical character in the higher sense, and not on the outward historical character of the single words.[1]

IV. 1–54. *The Belief of Samaria and Galilee.*

This is the contents of the second half of the third section of the first part. The second half is contrasted with the first.

Jesus returns to Galilee, whence he had gone out. Thus the circle is closed. The first verse gives as a reason that Jesus perceived that the Pharisees had heard of his activity. How can that make him decide to give it up? He might easily have imagined from the first that his deeds would not

---

[1] See vol. i. pp. 144, 148 f.; also Luthardt, *Der johanneische Ursprung des vierten Evangeliums*, Leipzig 1874, p. 199 f. English edit., *St. John the Author of the Fourth Gospel*, Edinburgh 1875, p. 249 f.

long remain concealed from the Pharisees. The words must therefore mean more than they seem at first. There is no talk of persecutions and the like (De Wette, Lücke, Meyer), but we may unhesitatingly presuppose a hostile disposition. We have seen, in the case of the Jew spoken of above, how they used Jesus' action and success as a ground for argument against the Baptist's activity. Jesus wished to bring to nought such attempts to hinder the work of both of them. It is true he could only do this by giving up the effort he had made in Judea.[1] So he suspends his work. He withdraws into privacy, and only comes forth again later; then, however, as the prophet of Galilee. He begins to gather a church again, but only through his apostles, and in a higher way than before. He does what we so often see in the history of salvation. This history, namely, after having made important strides towards its goal, suddenly seems to stop, break off entirely, and soon fall farther and farther behind the point of development at which it already stood. As a matter of fact, however, it is moving towards the same goal on another road, the earlier road having become impossible by the unbelief of men. We could say at all the chief points of Israel's history, that in them salvation came very near to the goal of its realization, and would have reached it in the form of that time, had the people on their part offered the right believing obedience. It was the refusal of this latter which forced the history of salvation always to descend anew to the depths, so as to draw near to the heights again by new paths. In like manner we have here the same law of suspension and modification.

If we recall the position which the fourth chapter assumes towards its surroundings, we find the most manifold relations. In the first place, it joins itself most closely to what precedes, by the internal affinity of its contents. Jesus spoke before of the Spirit of the new birth to the new life, which Spirit adds itself to the water of purification, and here he makes the living water the figure of this

[1] See Hofmann, *Weissagung und Erfüllung*, Nördlingen 1844, vol. ii. p. 86; *Der Schriftbeweis*, Nördlingen 1859, vol. ii. part i. p. 163 f.

very Spirit of the new life. He had announced and tried to open the way for the new time which begins with him, and the Baptist had testified to it; here he finds occasion to proclaim himself in definite words, iv. 21 ff. Finally, Jesus as a teacher had endeavoured before to turn the belief produced by miracles away from them, and to make it rest on his word; and we behold him doing the same thing in Samaria and Galilee. This gives the progress of the fourth chapter in comparison with what precedes; the progress from unbelief and half belief to the right belief; he did not succeed in producing it in Judea, here he did.

This shows us of itself the contrast of the two parts. There, Jesus seeks fruit by public activity, and does not find it; here, he finds some fruit, though he did not seek it, but meant to remain hidden. There, he does many miracles, yet in vain; here, he does but a few, which are forced on him, and yet unto belief. He is busy in Jerusalem and Judea many months, from spring to late autumn, iv. 35; he only stays two days in Sychar, and that only at an urgent request. There, 'the greatest' of the Old Testament covenant is his herald, and the authorities and the people of Jerusalem and Judea do not receive him in belief; here, an unknown woman serves as his herald, and he finds belief accorded to her testimony. Those who have religious knowledge, and a certain righteousness of life, reject him; those who were neglected and despised by Israel's teachers, and who were lacking in that knowledge as well as in outward righteousness, unite with him in belief.

Again, the fourth chapter is related to what follows; it prepares for it. It leads us into the time of calm retirement which preceded the public appearance in chap. v., just as a like time of life in the family preceded the first public appearance in ii. 13. The display of miracles there served to instruct the disciples in belief, and here likewise they bear such reference; see iv. 35 ff. At the same time, the conduct of the Jews towards Jesus, as it is described from chap. v. on, forms a contrast to the conduct of the Samaritans and Galileans. Hence the fourth chapter has almost the character of a transition from the first to the second part of the gospel. This is also confirmed by the place it takes in the list of analogies, which reach as far as the sixth chapter. In the first part, in the first chapter, we have utterances as to Jesus' wonderful knowledge upon the way, and these are followed by the miraculous deed at Cana. The fourth chapter shows us the same thing. [The knowledge shown to the woman, and the miracle of healing at the close.] The miracles are followed, the former by Jesus' display of himself as Lord of the temple at Jerusalem; the latter, v. 17, 18, as Lord of the Sabbath. In the former case, this is followed by the talk with the teacher of Israel about the baptism of the Spirit, which he gives, unto the new life; in the latter case, by the talk with the Jews—doubtless Pharisees and scribes—about spiritual food, which he is, unto the true life. The discourse in the two places stands at least in some relation to baptism and the Lord's supper.

(1.) IV. 1–26. *Jesus and the Samaritan Woman.*

Verse 1.

When therefore Jesus knew that the Pharisees had heard, etc. Οὖν puts the next words as a conclusion from what precedes. Such occurrences as we read of in iii. 25, which could easily reach the ears of Jesus, showed him how the Pharisees misused his activity against the Baptist.

Verse 2.

Though Jesus himself baptized not, but his disciples:—because He himself had to bring the Messianic baptism of the Spirit, which was only a fact of the future—yet in their eyes this baptism was an act of Jesus'.

Verse 3.

Hence: *He left Judea and departed again into Galilee,* giving up his former activity, and therefore also the baptizing. Accordingly, he did not go to Galilee, there to carry on his ministry or to open a new one, but to lay it aside for the time.

Verse 4.

The way led him through Samaria. "Ἔδει ('must needs') shows that he did not mean to seek disciples in Samaria.[1] It was the common path for Galilean pilgrims. Hence it is unnecessary to assume that he wished to avoid Herod, who was in Perea (Baumgarten-Crusius); there was no occasion for that. At any rate, and that is the point here, he did not purposely seek out Samaria to work there.

Verse 5.

Hence also, when he comes to Sychar, he remains outside of the place, and lets his disciples go in alone to buy food. Εἰσ does not mean: into the city; but, as what comes after shows: unto the city of Sychar. Sychar is commonly, but arbitrarily, taken as identical with Sichem.[2] The meanings, drunkard's town, Isa. xxviii. 1, and lying-town (שֶׁקֶר, Hengstenberg), are unjustifiable in the simplicity of the account. Hug[3] upheld the distinction between Sychar and Sichem, and Delitzsch[4] has proved it. Nablus, half an hour distant from the well, is the ancient Sichem; and Ascar, עסכר, on the north side of the valley, which opens itself eastward from Nablous, is Sychar. This סוכר often occurs in the Talmud; the Talmudic עין סוכר, 'the well of Ascar,' is Jacob's well; בקעת עין סוכר, 'the plain of Ascar,' is Jacob's field. Consequently it was altogether unjustifiable, when many saw in this a want of knowledge of the place, and a sign of a distant, Gentile-Christian author; it is a direct proof of exact knowledge. The place was *near to the parcel of ground*, etc. Gen. xxxiii. 19 tells us that Jacob bought a

---

[1] Against Lücke, *Commentar über das Evangelium des Johannes*, 3d ed., Bonn 1840, vol. i. p. 576.

[2] See Wieseler, *Chronblogische Synopse der vier Evangelien*, Hamburg 1843, vol. i. p. 256 f.; and Winer, *Biblisches Realwörterbuch*, 3d ed., Leipzig 1848, vol. ii. p. 454 f.

[3] Hug, *Einleitung in die Schriften des Neuen Testaments*, 4th ed., Stuttgart and Tübingen 1847, part ii. p. 194; see also the discussion in Raumer, *Palaestina*, 3d ed., Leipzig 1850, p. 146 f., note.

[4] Delitzsch, *Talmudische Studien*, VIII. in *Zeitschrift für die gesammte lutherische Theologie und Kirche*, Leipzig 1856, p. 240 ff.; see also Ewald, *Jahrbücher der Biblischen wissenschaft*, vol. viii. 1856, p. 255 ff.

piece of land near Sichem (Godet appeals to Gen. xlviii. 22); later, Joseph's bones were buried here, Josh. xxiv. 32, and Joseph's sons received it as their possession.

VERSE 6.

There also was the well which tradition ascribed to Jacob, and which is still held in honour. Jesus sat down here οὕτωσ ('thus'), just as it happened, ἁπλῶσ ὡσ ἔτυχεν, that is, without further ado, on the ground (see Meyer), ἐπὶ τῇ πηγῇ, directly at the well. The disciples had gone to the town to buy food, for *it was about the sixth hour;*. that is, in Jewish reckoning, about noon. Nobody has a right to give up the common Jewish way of reckoning here. Ewald objects on account of the mid-day heat; but that is no hindrance, because, as we shall see, the journey fell in December. It is true that this hour was not the common time for drawing water, but it was simply an extraordinary case.

VERSE 7.

There cometh a woman of Samaria; that is, a Samaritan woman. It does not mean the city Samaria (Sebaste), which was two leagues off, but the country, with reference to what follows. Jesus asks for a drink, because he is thirsty—not with spiritual (Hengstenberg), but with bodily thirst.

VERSE 8.

His disciples had gone to the town to buy food, and had taken with them the ἄντλημα, the vessel for drawing water, which they used to have with them on journeys, and so he was thrown upon the woman's help. It is arbitrary to say that John was with Jesus (Hengstenberg, Godet). Probably the disciples learned of the conversation afterwards from the woman. However, Jesus perceives at once that this woman has been sent to him by the Father, and that he has a call here. His desire to withdraw for a time from his official activity, as his nearest need, now retires at once, yielding to the will of his Father. This will enters upon the place of that wish, and renders the satisfying of that need unnecessary, or makes him forget it. For the fulfilling the Father's will is to him an essential satisfaction, vers. 32–34. In the case of Nicodemus, he was ready at night to give him the time set for rest; here he does the same when tired and thirsty at noon. Perhaps the place, too, was a hint and a demand for Jesus. It is not mentioned merely as an important background (Baumgarten-Crusius), but as the place at which the age of the patriarchs awaited the promise, and which in a figure brought the word of the promise into connection with its fulfilment, Gen. xlix. 22; Deut. xxxiii. 28 f. Samaria was now to enter on possession of this promise, the inheritance of the patriarchs. The possession of Jacob's well was the token and pledge of this. With it, this land should also become the possession of Him who was prefigured in Joseph, the one whom his brethren despised, and yet who became their deliverer.

His preaching of salvation now contrasts with the gift which this nation holds from the patriarchs, the gift which He is able to bestow on it. He gives the truth of that which this water is in an inexact and incomplete way. He could not do this were He not himself also the truth, and the fulfilment of the time, from which the gift in which they rejoice comes. This is the fundamental thought in the first part of this conversation, vers. 10–15. It is essentially like what we have previously found; but it is kept more figurative and in a lighter tone, agreeably to the difference of the situation.[1]

VERSE 9.

The taunting word of the woman occasioned the conversation. She recognises the Jew in his speech. The evangelist's explanatory remark, that the Jews have no intercourse with the Samaritans, is omitted by ℵ, but given by B. In any case, it must be supplied in thought.

---

[1] See Hug, *Einleitung in die Schriften des Neuen Testaments*, 4th ed., Stuttgart and Tübingen 1847, part ii. p. 185.

Verse 10.

If thou knewest the gift of God, and who it is that saith to thee, Give me to drink, thou wouldst have asked of him, and he would have given thee living water. The gift of God is not the fact that Jesus has opened intercourse with her (Meyer), nor is it the person of Jesus (Hengstenberg, Godet); it is a gift which is the gift of God κατ' ἐξοχήν ('by way of eminence'), and which Jesus can bestow on her. It is the same as that which he afterwards calls living, namely, flowing water, of course figuratively. Compare Rev. vii. 17, ζωῆσ πηγαὶ ὑδάτων ('fountains of waters of life'); xxi. 6, ἡ πηγὴ τοῦ ὕδατοσ τῆσ ζωῆσ ('the fountain of the water of life'); xxii. 1, ποταμὸσ ὕδατοσ ζωῆσ ('river of water of life'). But he connects this gift with his person: *who it is*, etc. She is to put the gift into union with him, and is to receive an impression of the importance of his person. He designates the water that he gives as a gift of God, and yet he speaks throughout as if all depended upon him and upon the recognition of his person. Hence, in the course of the conversation, the former point disappears altogether in comparison with the latter. Thus the woman also is led on from the desire for this gift to the recognition of Jesus himself, ver. 15; compare ver. 19. And Jesus closes this conversation with the most decided self-witness, ver. 26. The course of the interview is intended to produce upon the woman the impression that that gift is given only in Jesus' person, and that, in fact, the only question is concerning the relation to this person.

Living Water.

What is it, however, that he denotes by the figure of the water, and announces as given in his person? His speech, it is true, treats at first of real life. He depicts it as a living water, ver. 10, and as a water unto everlasting life, ver. 14, and as bestowing a state of being, completely appeased and satisfied in itself, ver. 14. The αἰώνιοσ ζωή ('eternal life') is especially to be understood in this latter sense, as may be seen from the contrast between vers. 14

and 13. Yet even in this he distinguishes the ζωή (' life '), as an attribute and effect, from the ὕδωρ (' water ') itself, as a different thing. It seems unquestionable that he means by this the spirit of the new life which he proclaimed to Nicodemus; thus also Calvin, Baumgarten-Crusius, and Hofmann. Least of all could it be belief (thus Lücke); that would not suit the figure and its use at all, for the thing in question is an objective gift which we are to receive (by belief). It must, however, not be generalized to ' tota renovationis gratia ' (' the whole grace of renewing,' Meyer, after Calvin), since the water betokens something definite, which is then followed by the renewing.

The fact that he does not name the thing definitely, and that he speaks more largely as to its effect than as to it itself, is explained by the respect paid to the woman. If the master in Israel could not grasp the saying about the spirit of the new birth, how should this woman grasp it? Besides, she lacked the connection given by the Old Testament prophecy, seeing that the prophets did not exist for the Samaritan woman. Therefore, in speaking only of the effect, he connects himself with her share in the general human need. This life of need makes men desire and recognise as prophecy a life of the fullest satisfaction. This will serve as a measure of the gift which effects it. The unchanging foundation of the former life is the spirit of God the creator. The unchanging foundation of the latter life will therefore be the spirit of God the redeemer.

Verse 11.

The woman stumbles at Jesus' words. She has received a certain impression: κύριε (' Sir!'). What does he mean? *Thou hast nothing to draw with, and the well is deep; from whence then hast thou that living water?*

Verse 12.

Her curiosity passes over into a certain feeling of national sensitiveness: Is not the water of this well good enough for you? *Art thou greater than our father Jacob, which gave us the well?* Like a woman, her speech becomes diffuse: he *drank thereof himself, and his children, and his cattle.* But for that very reason this cannot be the true water.

Verse 13.

Jesus impresses this upon her in the 13th verse. *Whosoever drinketh of this water shall thirst again.* This water does not even satisfy the needs of the present life.

Verse 14.

But whosoever drinketh of the water that I shall give him shall never thirst, but the water that I shall give him shall be in him a well of flowing water unto everlasting life. Such a one shall have essential and lasting satisfaction; for this gift is not merely accompanied by a temporary effect, but becomes a source of life dwelling in the heart.

This gift, namely, the new spirit which he gives, Jesus designates as the abiding foundation of the new life by ἐν αὐτῷ ('in him'), and as the source of life by ἁλλομένου ('springing up'). The word 'spring, bubble up,' in the figure, is not intended to express essentially anything else than the ὕδωρ ζῶν ('living water') above mentioned. The living essence in its constant driving motion is so called.[1] But then it is a conception complete in itself, and does not need to be completed by εἰσ ζωὴν αἰώνιον ('unto eternal life') (against Meyer and others). What would be the idea of the phrase in that case? It has been explained as the thirst which is excited by the Holy Ghost (Starke, in his *Synopsis*), or by the fact that this stream flows back thither whence it proceeds (Besser); the former explanation is refuted by the fact that the matter in question here is ὕδωρ ('water'), and the latter is refuted by ἁλλομένου ('springing'). For my part, I cannot conceive what is meant, and what the representation is, when it is said that this fountain springs up into everlasting life.[2] If, in order to make sense of it, 'with the earthly life,' or the like, be added (Lücke), that is merely an

---

[1] See Hesychius: ἀεὶ ῥέοντοσ ἢ βλύζοντοσ ('ever running or flowing').

[2] Lücke, *Commentar über das Evangelium des Johannes*, 3d ed., Bonn 1840, vol. i. p. 585.

arbitrary interpolation. De Wette and Baumgarten-Crusius abandon all more detailed explanation, and call the whole passage a mere emphasizing or strengthening of ὕδωρ ζῶν ('living water'). It therefore is allowable to connect εἰσ ζ. αἰ. (' to eternal life'), not with ἀλλ. (' springing up '), but with πηγὴ ὕδ. ἀλλ. (' fountain of bubbling water'). In vi. 27 it is said of the ἄρτοσ ζῶν (' living bread ') that it is a lasting food, εἰσ ζ. αἰ.; and thus here it is said of this living water that it is a fountain of bubbling water unto eternal life— that is, sufficient for it, bestowing it.

The extent of the need of redemption is the measure of the extent of the new life, and therefore also of the effect of the spirit. It touches the whole man in soul and body. The woman, it is true, understands by the eternal life only a potentiating of the present life. Accordingly, the gift also appears to her to be a potentiating of that natural gift of God.

Verse 15.

In this sense she desires it of Jesus: *Sir, give me this water, that I thirst not, neither come hither to draw.*

Hence Jesus must, in the next part of the discourse, vers. 16–19, display to her the internal presupposition and the inward human beginning of that which she desires. This he does by leading her to recognise and to confess her sins.

Verse 16.

Jesus bids her call her husband. It does not mean that He now wishes to talk to her husband and direct the gift of salvation to him (Lücke). Jesus speaks of her husband only for her sake. The demand is not earnestly intended, but only serves Jesus' purpose concerning the woman; he wishes to touch her upon a sore spot (Meyer). Jesus knew the circumstances of the woman, as well as what he himself intended, he did not need to learn about her gradually in the course of the conversation.

Verse 17.

The woman is hit. She becomes sparing of her words: *I have no husband.* Jesus repeats these words to her, so as to let her feel their full force: *Thou hast well said, I have no husband.*

Verse 18.

For thou hast had five husbands; and he whom thou now hast is not thy husband (but thy lover): *in that saidst thou truly.* These five husbands have been interpreted symbolically of the idol-worship of the five nations of Samaria, upon which the reception of the worship of Jehovah followed,[1] in the interest of the mythical explanation (Strauss), and as mere poetry (Bruno Bauer), or as an unhistorical use of symbols by the evangelist (Keim), or as a typical conception of the evangelist's based on history (Weizsäcker), or as a divine ordering (Hengstenberg), or as a Jewish byword against the Samaritans which Jesus applied to the woman (Baumgarten-Crusius). Whatever turn be given to it, the allegory still remains, not merely indistinct, but also out of place.[2] On the one hand, the Samaritan heathenism would be represented as marriage, and the service of Jehovah as whoredom. And on the other hand, the heathen deities were worshipped simultaneously, while the woman had the five husbands one after the other.

The fact is, that Jesus, by calling this up, intends to bring the woman to a consciousness of her sins. Whether the dissolution of the marriage had been brought about by death, which is hardly probable for all five cases, or by other causes, this fivefold repetition of marriage was a token of sinful lust. And the context shows unmistakably that she is living with the sixth man in an illegal manner. Jesus bids the woman think of all this.

This knowledge on the part of Jesus has been declared to be different from his essential knowledge, and subordinate to it.[3] But it is arbitrary to try to make a distinction in

---

[1] See 2 Kings xvii. 24 ff.; compare also Josephus, *Antiquitates*, IX. xiv. 3, *Opera*, ed. Bekker, Leipzig 1855, vol. ii. p. 291: [five nations] ἕκαστοι κατὰ ἔθνος ἴδιον θεὸν εἰς τὴν Σαμάρειαν κομίσαντες ('each nation having brought its own god into Samaria').

[2] See Lücke, *Commentar über das Evangelium des Johannes*, 3d ed., Bonn 1840, vol. i. pp. 663 and 661.

[3] Lücke, *ut supra*, vol. i. p. 591.

the objects of knowledge, as to whether they be external or internal. In the case of Jesus, the knowledge, which stood related to his calling and to his necessary activity in his calling, was at every time essential, and therefore real, whether it touched upon the thoughts of the heart or upon the facts of the external life. It is, in fact, impossible to see why a knowledge in relation to the former should be more easily reconcilable with Jesus' human consciousness than a knowledge in relation to the latter (De Wette); unless, indeed, any one should think he might or could escape the impression of something miraculous more easily in the former than in the latter case. To assume that Jesus named a round number which fitted in a miraculous way (Ewald), or that Jesus at once observed in the woman the impressions (like the year-rings of a tree) of the various matrimonial relations (J. P. Lange), is all a mere additional fantastic indecision, which is of no avail. The knowledge is removed from mere chance and from magical immediateness by its connection with the saving activity which Jesus is exercising towards the woman. And that he really had the intention (against De Wette) of touching her conscience is shown by the result.

VERSE 19.

It is true that there are not many who are willing to find a confession in the woman's answer: *Sir, I perceive that thou art a prophet.* Even Ebrard thinks she wished to interrupt the conversation, or to avoid the point (thus Meyer and others), and De Wette calls it a 'piece of feminine artfulness.' Stier urges rightly the fact that these words, θεωρῶ ὅτι προφήτησ εἶ σύ ('I perceive that thou art a prophet'), contain the most decided and most earnest confession of sin.[1] She expresses it indirectly, in accordance with her manner and her position. Her succeeding question must be connected with this.

VERSE 20.

Our fathers worshipped in this mountain, and ye say that

[1] Stier, *Reden Jesu*, 3d ed., Barmen and Elberfeld 1870, vol. iv. p. 149.

in Jerusalem is the place where men ought to worship. That is to say, is Gerizim or is Jerusalem the proper place for worship? She points to Mount Gerizim, for the well is in the valley between Gerizim and Ebal. When the Jews returned from the exile they shut out the Samaritans from a share in the temple at Jerusalem, on the plea that they were of heathen origin, or, at least, because of certain constituent parts of their nation. Then the Samaritans built a temple for themselves upon Mount Gerizim, which they held to be holy by reason of the blessing spoken from it in preceding ages. See Deut. xi. 29, xxvii. 12, and xxvii. 4, where the Samaritan text has Gerizim instead of Ebal. Even after John Hyrcanus destroyed this temple, the place continued to be for them the holy place of worship. Who is right; our fathers,—namely, our Samaritan forefathers, not the fathers of Israel,—or you? For the woman this question has not only a national but also a personal interest. She intends to seek forgiveness of her sins by prayer at the holy place. But where is that place? Is it upon Gerizim or in Jerusalem? Jesus has shown her her sin, and now he must show her whence she is to obtain righteousness. Jesus answers this question in vers. 21-24, by pointing out to her the true internal character of the relation to God.

VERSE 21.

Woman, believe me, the hour cometh, when ye shall neither in this mountain, nor yet at Jerusalem, worship the Father. He begins by emphasizing his personal authority. He does not wish to free her from himself while he points her to the future. The future will bring freedom from all outward local obligation. In the Old Testament, Zion is the place of God's presence, הַר קָדְשׁ, 'holy mountain;' compare Ps. lxxiv. 2, 7, lxxvi. 3. They expected salvation from this point. The new era brings in a worshipping of the Father, which is independent of that place; τῷ πατρί ('the Father') in the New Testament sense, proleptically.

VERSE 22.

Israel, indeed, is right, however, and Samaria is not right, as to the *what* in the worship. *Ye worship what you do not know, we worship what we know.* That is to say, the God whom they worship is one whom they do not understand, and one who is better known to the Jews. Although it is not ὅν ('whom') (De Wette), still ὅ ('what') is the object of προσκυνεῖν ('to worship'),[1] since προσκυνεῖν is construed with the accusative as well as with the dative. God is here spoken of as neuter because it is not He, in and for himself, whom the Samaritans do not and the Jews do know, but the circumstance that he is a God of salvation, a God of redemption. Prophecy, which the Samaritans rejected, taught this of God. Such proper knowledge of God, therefore, is only found in Israel. That is the place of salvation. There dwells the future of salvation, and there it must be sought so long as it is not yet revealed. Yet it is now about to dawn, and that in his person. Therefore the importance of that place of worship ceases herewith, and Jesus takes its stead. The due relation to God from this time forth is to be mediated not locally, but personally; namely, through him, and through the communion with him in the Spirit. Jesus hints at this new relation to God by calling him the Father.

Some[2] have counted it strange that Jesus should here reckon himself as one with the Jews, whereas he elsewhere places himself in contrast with them. It is a matter of course that the ἡμεῖσ ('we') is to be understood of the Jews, and not of the Christians, as Hilgenfeld thinks. Were the Christians meant, the evangelist would have fallen too completely out of his *rôle*. The fact that the evangelist writes thus proves that the gospel is not so anti-Judaistic as it is commonly represented to be by Tübingen and other critics. The evangelist, of course, appropriates to himself this saying of Jesus. But Jesus speaks thus, not because He was born among the Jews, and lives among them, and belongs thus to their party (De Wette); nor

---

[1] Lücke, *Commentar über das Evangelium des Johannes*, 3d ed., Bonn 1840, vol. i. p. 594; and Baumgarten-Crusius.

[2] Baumgarten-Crusius, *Theologische Auslegung der Johanneischen Schriften*, Jena 1843, vol. i. p. 156; Lücke, *ut supra*, vol. i. p. 597.

because he wishes to refer to the corruption of Samaritan life (Baumgarten-Crusius), all of which is simply forced. He speaks thus because, after he has freed the woman from her sins, he must also free her from the untruth of her nationality, and bring her to acknowledge the essential truth of Israel, so that she may have a share in the historical salvation.

We possess the essence of salvation only in its historical character, and its historical character is settled for all time as Jewish.[1] Hence he adds with strong emphasis: *For salvation is of the Jews.* We must all agree to that, however hard it may be to own it. Salvation does not consist merely in ideas or general truths of reason. It was accomplished in a historical way, and had its historical growth upon Jewish ground. The woman must accept that. It was no little thing that the Lord asked of her. How many threads of national connection must she break to appropriate to herself these words of Jesus! These words, moreover, contain nothing else than Paul's instructions in the eleventh chapter of Romans, that the heathen must all be incorporated in the holy root-stem of Israel, only with the removal of national limitation.

Not until He has secured this truth does Jesus announce that with Him the time has come for the general human communion with God in the Spirit.

Verse 23.

It is true that the communion of salvation is to be free from Jewish limitations. That is the contrasted progress in the twenty-third verse: *But the hour cometh,* in the New Testament time, *and now is,* having begun with him, *when the true worshippers*—ἀληθινοί ('true'), in whom the idea of worship is realized—*shall worship the Father in spirit and in truth.* It is a question whether ἐν πνεύματι ('in spirit') is to be understood subjectively or objectively, whether it means the human or the divine spirit. It is contrasted with ἐν ὄρει κ.τ.λ. ('in this mountain,' etc.) not only in form

---

[1] See Stier, *Reden Jesu*, 3d ed., Barmen and Elberfeld 1870, vol. iv. p. 154 f.

(Baumgarten-Crusius), but also in substance. The former was a προσκυνεῖν ἐν σαρκί ('worshipping in the flesh') because it was still mediated cosmically. And although the Jews, as compared with the Samaritans, had the truth of God's worship, nevertheless, because this was bound to external things, and therefore mediated in a fleshly way, in accordance with the stage of preparation, it was not the essential truth.

Only now, when the worship shall stand and consist in the πνεῦμα ('spirit'), shall it be a worship of God in truth; no longer a type, and therefore unreal worship, but one which corresponds to the essence of worship. Hence ἐν πνεύματι ('in spirit') is contrasted with the fleshly externality of the worship, which is dependent upon place and the like. It is a designation of inwardness, and therefore of subjective inwardness, and not of the objective spirit of God (thus Stier, Brückner, Bäumlein, and I in my earlier edition). The place for worship is here, in the spiritual internality. Yet the inner man must, of course, previously become by the Spirit of God a place of worship, so that when the worshipper retires within himself, he thereby enters into communion with God, and stands in the Spirit of God. Augustine says: 'We had gone out of doors, we are sent within. . . . Go entirely within. And if perchance you seek some lofty place, some holy place, show yourself within a temple for God. For the temple of God is holy, which ye are. If you wish to pray in a temple, pray in yourself. But first be a temple of God, because he will hear the one who prays in His temple.'[1]

It is therefore not the spirit in its natural character, but in its renewal by the Spirit of Jesus Christ; not in its natural communion with God, but in a communion mediated and effected by the historical salvation. By this the worship

---

[1] Augustine, *In Johannis Evangelium*, cap. iv. tractatus xv., *Opera*, edit. Benedict., Antwerp 1700, vol. iii. part 2, p. 302 b, c: 'Foras ieramus, intro missi sumus. . . . Intus age totum. Et si forte quæris aliquem locum altum, aliquem locum sanctum, intus exhibe te templum Deo. Templum enim Deo sanctum est, quod estis vos. In templo vis orare, in te ora. Sed prius esto templum Dei, quia ille in templo suo exaudiet orantem.'

becomes a true worship, namely, removed from the σκιά ('shadow') and the τύποσ ('type') (Olshausen and Meyer), and raised to its truth, in that it corresponds to God himself. *For the Father seeketh also those who worship him in this way.*[1] Meyer refers καί ('also') to ὁ πατήρ ('the Father'): the Father also seeks, etc. But the progress of the thought cannot lie in ὁ πατήρ, because He was spoken of before. The progress must lie in what is new, that is, in ζητεῖ ('seeks') (against Meyer): for he seeks also, etc. The designation of God as the Father is to indicate the New Testament relation of God to the world, which has entered, by way of fulfilment, into the place of the preceding exclusive relation of God to Israel. If God previously chose a nation to himself for his son, now he seeks in all places such as shall and can enter upon a filial relation to him in spirit. The fact that God seeks such as are willing to enter upon a moral relation of that kind to him, teaches us that communion with God is no longer conditioned upon nationality. Τοὺσ προσκυν. ('those worshipping') is, as the article shows, the object, and τοιούτουσ ('such') is the predicate.

Verse 24.

Such a character in the worshippers corresponds to the will of the Father, for it corresponds to the essence of God: *God is a Spirit: and they that worship him must worship him in spirit and in truth.* Spirit is in contrast with corporality; therefore it is in the first place negatively meant. Isaiah xxxi. 3: Egypt is man and not God, and its horses are flesh and not spirit. With this, however, is given at the same time the positive point of inwardness. - That which corporally exists has the place of its existence in sensible externality. But God is Spirit in himself, '*in se ubique et totus*,' 'everywhere and entirely within himself.' Hence he is not bound to this or that space; but when we stand

---

[1] [The English version has: 'such to worship him.' Professor Luthardt translates: 'those who worship him, as such,' a sentence alike awkward in German and in English, but necessarily added here in explanation of a grammatical remark below.—C. R. G.]

in the spirit, we are near to him. According to the whole context, πνεῦμα ('spirit') is here meant in this sense of inwardness, of being in and with oneself. It does not betoken the perfection of God identical with itself,[1] nor, finally, does it express 'power, life, knowledge, will, action,' as Stier[2] arbitrarily heaps up the statement.

This knowledge of God, πνεῦμα ὁ θεόσ ('God is a Spirit'), was, however, nothing new, as De Wette has acknowledged by referring to the passages concerned in the Old Testament; for example, 1 Kings viii. 27. It lies at the base of the whole Old Testament by presupposition, as a matter of course, and a matter of necessity. Lücke is guilty of a gross misconception when he inclines to believe[3] that the Samaritan conception of God was more spiritual than that of the Old Testament. If that idea of God belongs to the Old Testament, it is clear that Köstlin[4] and Lutz[5] are quite wrong in finding in this the specific characteristic of Christianity according to John's representation, and in thinking that this saying was something utterly new in contrast with the Old Testament.[6] But the conclusion drawn from it is new. And this conclusion is only now drawn for the first time, because the time of the essential and adequate divine revelation, and therefore also of the essential and adequate divine communion in the Spirit of Jesus the Christ, is now for the first time present.

Verse 25.

The woman gives occasion for Jesus' testimony to him-

---

[1] Köstlin, *Der Lehrbegriff des Evangeliums und der Briefe Johannis*, Berlin 1843, p. 78.

[2] Stier, *Reden Jesu*, 3d ed., Barmen and Elberfeld 1870, vol. iv. p. 159.

[3] Lücke, *Commentar über das Evangelium des Johannes*, 3d ed., Bonn 1840, vol. i. p. 599. This Lücke bases on Gesenius, *De Samaritanorum Theologia*, Halle 1822, p. 12; and *De Pentateuchi Samaritani origine indole et auctoritate, commentatio philologico-critica*, Halle 1815, p. 58 ff.

[4] Köstlin, *Der Lehrbegriff des Evangeliums und der Briefe Johannis*, Berlin 1843, p. 77.

[5] Lutz, *Biblische Dogmatik*, Pforzheim 1847, p. 45.

[6] Compare against this view, Hofmann, *Der Schriftbeweis*, 2d ed., Nördlingen 1857, vol. i. p. 68 f.; and Weiss, *Der Johanneische Lehrbegriff*, Berlin 1862, p. 54 f.

self as the Christ by her words: *I know that Messias cometh, which is called Christ: when he is come, he will tell us all things.* This has been explained as an endeavour of the woman's to put Jesus off with a question (De Wette). Lücke[1] thinks that it was not agreeable to her that Jesus had not decided the debated question in her favour, and that, therefore, she wished to break off with the remark that all this will be taught one day when the Messias comes; there is always time for that yet. And did Jesus nevertheless see her to be so near a Messianic belief that he revealed himself to her as the Messiah?[2] Or is the woman so deeply impressed with Jesus' words, that she feels deeply the need of the Messianic appearance (Meyer)? But what brought her to the Messiah, if Jesus' person and the impression from it did not draw this thought near to her? Baumgarten-Crusius declares at least the possibility that this question was the utterance of a presentiment as to the higher personality of this Jew. Such is the case. This woman has already advanced to such a point that she is not only free from Gerizim, but also from the pre-Christian externality of divine worship in general. The divine communion that henceforward presents itself to her hopes will be, if anything, a matter of the Messianic time. Might not this Jew, then, himself be the Messiah, since he has given her this freedom of relation to God? Some think that this Samaritan reference to a Messiah is perhaps a new and essential step in advance, because the Samaritans rejected the Messiah as well as prophecy.[3] But even if there were no other proof, this story, in my opinion, is decisive as to a Messianic expectation in this nation—an expectation, it is true, only of a general character. The woman, indeed, uses a thoroughly Jewish form in expressing her belief, as was to be expected from her confessing the salvation which is from Israel. Yet, nevertheless, the

---

[1] Lücke, *Commentar über das Evangelium des Johannes*, 3d ed., Bonn 1840, vol. i. p. 600.

[2] *Ibid.*

[3] Bruno Bauer, *Kritik der evangelischen Geschichte des Johannes*, Bremen 1840, p. 415 ff., especially p. 433 f.

matter was her own before, otherwise she would have said πιστεύω ('I believe'), and not οἶδα ('I know').[1] Thus, again, in ver. 42, ὁ σωτὴρ τοῦ κόσμου ('the Saviour of the world') is spoken of as a known and looked-for person. This last phrase also shows us the shape of her expectation. The later Samaritan Messianic belief, as Gesenius has presented it, allows an inference back to its existence at this time as to substance, though not as to form,[2] since the latter before then would have been exposed to too many influences. Nor can I believe, with Hengstenberg,[3] that the Messianic hopes had come over from the Jews. Religious antagonism was too active for that, and the later prophetic element of the kingdom was wanting in its conception of the Messiah. The ruling view is that this is connected especially with Deut. xviii. 15, and that it saw in the Messiah the higher antitype of Moses the prophet. The Samaritan name הַשָּׁחֵב is taken either of the one bringing again (Ewald) or the one returning again (Hengstenberg), and in the last case is understood of the returning Moses (Meyer). The passage before us is too general to allow definite conclusions. If we might lay stress on 'the Saviour of the world,' in ver. 42, that would lead us to a somewhat different conception from that of the returning Moses. We should be forced rather to think of such utterances and thoughts as Lamech expresses at Noah's birth, Gen. v. 29. One who should free us from the neediness of life in general, and therefore a Saviour of the world, as Noah was typically; this would accordingly have been the hope of Samaria. This woman had let herself be led so far by Jesus' self-witness as to believe on this Saviour of the world, and that as the Christ prophesied by the prophets of Israel, in the person of this Jew:

[1] See Stier, *Reden Jesu*, 3d ed., Barmen and Elberfeld 1870, vol. iv. p. 165.

[2] See Baumgarten-Crusius, *Theologische Auslegung der Johanneischen Schriften*, Jena 1843, vol. i. p. 161 ff.

[3] Hengstenberg, *Beiträge zur Einleitung ins Alte Testament*, vol. ii., also entitled, *Die Authentie des Pentateuchs*, Berlin 1836, vol. i. p. 28 ff.

Verse 26.

Jesus could testify to himself as the Messiah before her, with a short decisiveness which he could not use towards the Jews: *I that speak unto thee am he.* This is the great ἐγώ εἰμι ('I am'), which recurs throughout John's gospel. What follows shows us that the woman accepted this self-witness of Jesus in belief.

(2.) IV. 27–42. *Jesus and the Samaritans.*

We take these verses together as one section, in spite of Stier's opinion.[1] Stier thinks that Jesus' conversation with the woman is followed by an explanatory supplement about his relation to his disciples, corresponding to the preceding about his relation to the Baptist, so that Jesus himself is put in between his forerunner and his deputies. But the conversation with the disciples has no independent value. It is only a part of the rest of the history, although Jesus gives the latter at the same time such a turn as makes it serve for the instruction of the disciples.

Verse 27.

The disciples had come back from Sychar, and were amazed to find their master talking to a woman. The rabbinical customs forbade such conversations in public places, especially about questions of law, and above all with a Samaritan woman. In their feeling of reverence, however, they did not dare to ask or to say anything.

Verse 28.

The woman, however, full of what she has heard and experienced, hurries to the city, leaving her water-pot so as to go faster.

Verse 29.

She calls on them to come and see the wonderful man who had revealed to her her sinful life.

---

[1] Stier, *Reden Jesu*, 3d ed., Barmen and Elberfeld 1870, vol. iv. p. 169.

Verse 30.

The people of the city, at the woman's call, start towards him.

Verses 31–34.

Meantime, the disciples' invitation to him to eat of what they had brought, gives Jesus occasion to utter weighty words about his calling, and the inward satisfaction which he finds in it,—a satisfaction which makes him superior to bodily needs. It does not mean that he in general had not the bodily need of eating; but this need retires into the background for him in comparison with the divine and rich-futured calling of his life, when that calling fills his whole soul.

Verse 35.

He adds to this a reference to the future of his work, which looks forth beyond his day unto the time of the apostles' activity. A wide range spreads itself before him here from this single point and this narrowly limited occasion.

Jesus had closed the conversation with Nicodemus by a reference to the inward religious life. Now he has passed beyond that, and can close with the most decided self-witness as the reward of a believing disposition. Nicodemus went forth silent and reflecting. This woman speeds forth in joyful certainty of belief, and with a burning heart, to be the herald of his name. In the former case, Jesus himself widens his sphere, and going out from Jerusalem passes through all Judea, teaching, baptizing, and exciting attention, and yet he does not find right belief. Here the multitudes come out to him and beg him to stay; and after two days they believe on him. In both cases the sphere is widened; in the former, from the centre of Israel within the bounds of Judea, in the latter from a chance point outside of the nation of promise. Thus we have two spheres. The kingdom of God is to be planted first in Israel, and then outside of Israel. These two sections of the gospel are a prophecy of these future events. In this sense Baur's [1] statement is true, namely, the present history presages the conversion of the Gentile world. Israel and not-Israel are to be called to the kingdom of God. Jesus is not merely the fulfilment of all the history of Israel, but is also ὁ σωτὴρ τοῦ κόσμου ('the Saviour of the world,' ver. 42). In the first case above, a few indeed believe, but on the whole, ἡ ὀργὴ τοῦ θεοῦ μένει ἐπ' [αὐτούσ], iii. 36. In the second case, the present case, on the contrary, Jesus sees a wide grain-field ripe for the harvest.

Say ye not, There are yet four months, and then cometh harvest? Behold, I say unto you, Lift up your eyes, and look on the fields; for they are white already to harvest. It was still (ἔτι) four months to harvest (τετράμενόσ ἐστιν, sc. ὁ χρόνοσ) when Jesus spoke these words. The harvest was in April, therefore these words and this event fall in December. Accordingly, it cannot have been a proverb (against Lücke, Tholuck, De Wette, Krafft [2]), since the sowing took place in November. Nor is there the slightest trace of such a proverb to be found. Hence Jesus journeyed back from Jerusalem to Galilee through Samaria in December. While the fields of the land, however, are but just beginning to show the new green, the fields of men's hearts are already ripe for the harvest. The multitudes who came to the Lord from Sychar reminded him of a waving harvest-field. But the Lord's words are not exhausted in the present (against Godet). The present is to him only the pledge of the future,—first of Samaria, and then of men in general (Meyer). Hence he can say ἤδη ('already') of the latter also. For ἤδη is most simply (Meyer) taken with verse 35 (against Tischendorf, Godet, and others). The statement that it never stands at the end in John (Godet) is refuted by 1 John iv. 3. Here it corresponds by contrast with ἔτι. Were it taken with what follows, it would put the harvest-work in the very present, notwithstanding that the further

---

[1] Baur, *Kritische Untersuchungen über die kanonischen Evangelien*, Tübingen 1847, p. 147, and note.

[2] Krafft, *Chronologie und Harmonie der vier Evangelien*, Erlangen 1848, p. 73.

declarations make it belong to the future, namely, to the time of apostolic work. The field, which the prophets, the Baptist, and Jesus himself worked, is the world, though they limited themselves in the first place to Israel's borders. Now this field is to be harvested. He alone knows that at first. It is a mystery to the disciples how he can talk to and teach those who are not Jews, and above all a woman who is not a Jew, and even testify to her of himself as the Christ. This is a mystery, because they do not yet know the general human mission of the gospel, and likewise they know nothing of that future of the kingdom of God. This future comes to Jesus' soul like a comfort, after the experience he had in Judea, and fills him with that joy and satisfaction which made bodily satisfaction unnecessary.

Verse 36.

He expresses his joy that the field stands already ripe before the eyes of his spirit: *He that reapeth receiveth wages, and gathereth fruit unto life eternal, that both he that soweth and he that reapeth may rejoice together.* The union by καί ('and,' the received text, against ℵ B etc.) would certainly suit John's style better, though it is not absolutely necessary. Was it perhaps left out on account of the false reference of ἤδη to what follows?

But a slight sadness mingles with this joyful outlook. He distinguishes between the sower and the reaper. He indeed has sowed, but others will reap. Had Israel showed at once a believing obedience, the harvest could have begun at once. But the gospel must go over from Israel to the Gentiles, and the time of the Gentiles is to begin thus. Jesus can only sow. Others will enter upon his work and gather the fruits. His very disciples, however, will begin this harvest, and his experience in the present case is a surety of that. That makes this experience of his a joyful one, and the tone of joy prevails in these utterances. He shows his disciples therewith what a blessed activity awaits them. It will consist in their gathering men into the church of Christ unto eternal life, and their reward will consist in their success. I say 'unto eternal life,' for

Baumgarten-Crusius is right in rejecting the local explanation of εἰσ (De Wette, Meyer), which would make it mean the same as 'into the barns' of eternal life. That figure can only be made possible by adding something to the account. Jesus rejoiced at the success of their activity, although he had to content himself with sowing. Ὁμοῦ is not to be taken temporally, but materially, as Baumgarten-Crusius has paraphrased it with 'as well . . . as also.'

VERSE 37.

For, to confirm the distinction between the sower and the reaper, *herein is that saying* (ὁ λόγοσ = τὸ λεγόμενον) *true*—that is, finds the reality which corresponds to its thought;—or, if we should read ὁ ἀληθινόσ, is that which corresponds to its thought; ἀληθινόσ, according to John's constant use of the word, is different from ἀληθήσ (against De Wette) : *one soweth and another reapeth.*

VERSE 38.

I sent you to reap that whereon ye bestowed no labour. He emphasizes the fact that he is the sender. The sending stands before his very eyes as a fact. Although it was implied in the choice to the apostolate (Meyer), yet in itself it was still a future fact, which Jesus handles here as at present complete. *Other men laboured, and ye are entered into their labours.*

Almost all the later commentators (not Olshausen) agree that Jesus thinks of himself in speaking of those who as sowers have prepared the harvest for the reapers. He also had had the 'toil and work,' and the disciples then began to bring in the ripe fruit at the day of Pentecost. Hence even Chrysostom put that fact as an explanation of these words. Nevertheless, I cannot agree that Jesus meant himself alone by the plural ἄλλοι ('others'), although most of the later writers explain it thus (Tholuck, Lücke, Baumgarten-Crusius, Meyer). Stier[1] asserts it with great zeal, and designates it as 'the most wretched thing,' and 'most thoroughly false,' and 'opposed to the whole of sacred

[1] Stier, *Reden Jesu*, 3d ed., Barmen and Elberfeld 1870, vol. iv. p. 177.

Scripture,' to think of Moses and the prophets as the sowers. Of course we do not hold that they are the only ones, but certainly they belong to the sowers. Christ is put with them only under a special point of view, namely, in so far as he did not himself in the days of his flesh, any more than they, gather the church of God, but merely prepared for it; at the same time, it is of course not thereby denied that he is the fulfilment of the Old Testament. Therefore as many of them as were busied with such preparatory work, which closed with the glorification of Christ and with the day of Pentecost, are meant in the ἄλλοι.

VERSE 39.

And many of the Samaritans of that city believed on him for the saying of that woman which testified, He told me all that ever I did. The preliminary fruit, which is a prophecy of the real fruit, is the coming of the Samaritans to Jesus. It is occasioned, indeed, by the words of a stranger, and that in an account of Jesus' wonderful knowledge.

VERSE 40.

So when the Samaritans were come unto him, they besought him that he would tarry with them. And he abode there two days. The belief shows itself to be a real longing, and does not stop at mere belief in authority.

VERSES 41 AND 42.

And many more believed because of his own word; and said unto the woman, Now we believe, not because of thy saying; for we have heard him ourselves, and know that this is indeed the Christ, the Saviour of the world. The belief perfects itself, and that in the hearts of many, by the reception of Jesus' self-witness, and by the experience they therewith make of him as the one he testified himself to be. And thus it rises to the true and right belief, namely, to belief on Jesus in his word, begotten by his word, and realized as an inward experiencing of Jesus.

The story here spoken of is prophetic of the future, and therefore Baur[1] holds it to be an invention; he thinks it was formed from the after fact of Samaria's conversion, and then transferred backwards.[2] But, as we have already seen, what is said about Jesus' success in Judea is prophetic, and the two sections correspond to each other, and therefore belong together. The same thing would in consequence have to be said of this previous statement, and yet Baur takes it to be only a transfer of the later activity of Jesus himself to an earlier time. Moreover, it is said that Luke ix. 52 does not agree with our account.[3] It is true that Jesus is there refused admittance to a Samaritan city, not merely because he is a Jew, and is travelling towards Jerusalem (thus commonly), for the usual course of pilgrims from Galilee was through Samaria; but also because he wished to be the Messiah, and as such owned his allegiance to the temple at Jerusalem. That, however, was in an altogether different part of Samaria. If they had heard there of the events in Sychar, the opposition would be more easily explained. Jesus, the Messiah from the Jews, had already found belief among other Samaritans, and antagonism had been excited by such apparent denial of the national Samaritan honour. That, too, explains more easily the success of Simon the sorcerer, which Baur uses likewise as an argument against our gospel, but which is rather an argument for it. If the Messianic hopes of the Samaritans had been once excited, and then had this Messiah of the Jews come to an end which did not seem directly to confirm him as Messiah, those hopes could the more readily fall upon one who flattered their national pride as a great miracle-worker and as a Samaritan Messiah. And just so much the better could they be won again for Jesus the Christ when it turned out that the miraculous power of that Simon was thrown quite in the shade by the deeds of Jesus' disciples, and that Jesus had been proved to be the Christ by the resurrection.

[1] Baur, *Kritische Untersuchungen über die kanonischen Evangelien,* Tübingen 1847, p. 147.
[2] *Ibid.* p. 147.   [3] *Ibid.* p. 143.

(3.) VERSES 43–54. *Jesus and the Galileans.*

Jesus had found work and fruit in Samaria, contrary to what was to be looked for. Still he knew that this ought to be to him only a prophecy of the future, and not a direction for the present. Hence he holds fast to his determination to withdraw into privacy. The evangelist intends to indicate this by the words found in the first two verses.

VERSES 43 AND 44.

Now after two days he departed thence and went into Galilee. For Jesus himself testified that a prophet hath no honour in his own country. Jesus went to Galilee after two days, because, as Jesus himself testified,—not at that time (Meyer), but on some other occasion, nor do we need in this case to take ἐμαρτύρησεν ('testified') as a pluperfect (Tholuck, Godet),—no honour is shown to a prophet in his own country. The first meaning of these words evidently is, that he went to Galilee exactly because there, in his own country, he could expect no honour. This thought, however, has been often regarded as an impossible one, and hence πατρίσ ('own country') has been understood of Judea, either as the country of the prophets (Origen, Baumgarten-Crusius, Baur), or as the land of Jesus' birth, the country containing Bethlehem (Lücke and Ebrard earlier).

But, in the first place, in spite of this, Judea is not his πατρίσ, since in the gospel history he is the Nazarene; compare i. 46. Again, this does not suit the connection. He is here leaving (ἐκεῖθεν, 'thence,' ver. 43; γάρ, 'for,' ver. 44), not Judea, but Samaria, in which he had found belief. As little are we to understand by πατρίσ Nazareth in contrast with Galilee, so that it would here be told why he went to Galilee, yet not to Nazareth, his old home (Calvin, Bengel, Olshausen, Hengstenberg). Indeed, this is utterly impossible, because the evangelist in no wise hints at such a distinction between Galilee and Nazareth. The appeal to the 'land of Judea,' iii. 22 (Hengstenberg), is not available; in that case the capital had been previously mentioned, and the 'land' is clearly distinguished from it.

Γάρ (' for ') has not lost its confirmatory force, and assumed instead the force of an explanatory introduction (Lücke), since this would correspond neither to the New Testament nor to Johannean diction. Nor is it intended to tell here the reason why he went to Galilee only at such a late date, namely, to obtain from foreign parts the honour he could not expect at home (Meyer). Nothing is said about his going there at a 'late' date, nor are Judea and his miracles there, mentioned directly before this; here we also oppose Godet's: only now, and not right after the baptism. Nor can the meaning be, that just because he could expect no honour he intended to try to obtain it (Brückner), for the succeeding context does not relate an activity in Galilee; he works but one miracle, and that only when compelled. The evangelist's counting, at the close in ver. 54, expressly calls attention to this.

Γάρ gives the reason for his going to Galilee, although he had found in Samaria such a hopeful field of activity; for that very reason, because he could not count upon honour there. Hence he could hope there not to be observed, but to be able to remain in rest and quiet.[1] He wished to withdraw a while from that scene of public activity. This would most probably be possible in Galilee. The difficulty, therefore, of this passage is not so utterly inconceivable.[2] The following sentence is connected with this one by οὖν (' then '), and not by δέ (' and '); not because the reception Jesus found is to be contrasted with his word (Tholuck, compare De Wette), although both as to substance are in contrast with each other, but because it is only to be added, by way of conclusion to what precedes, that he has accordingly now come to Galilee. Therefore οὖν refers not to ver. 44, but to ver. 43.

---

[1] See Hofmann, *Weissagung und Erfüllung im alten und im neuen Testamente*, Nördlingen 1844, vol. ii. pp. 86, 87 ; *Der Schriftbeweis*, 2d ed., Nördlingen 1859, vol. ii. part i. p. 171 f.

[2] Schwegler, *Theologische Jahrbücher*, Tübingen 1842, I. i. pp. 164–166 ; compare Baumgarten-Crusius, *Theologische Auslegung der Johanneischen Schriften*, Jena 1843, vol. i. p. 173.

Verse 45.

Then when he was come into Galilee, the Galileans received him, having seen all the things that he did at Jerusalem at the feast; for they also went unto the feast. We here find the same contrast between Jesus' design and the reality that appeared in the journey through Samaria. He had hoped to be able to remain unnoticed, but he met with a joyful welcome. Yet he had not worked his miracles among them, but in Jerusalem.

Verse 46.

So Jesus came again into Cana of Galilee, where he made the water wine. He had it in mind to withdraw for a while into stillness. Hence he went to Cana, to the retirement of that house the founding of which he had consecrated. This is probably what the evangelist means to say when he recalls the miracle of changing the water into wine. *And there was a certain nobleman whose son was sick at Capernaum.*

Verse 47.

When he heard that Jesus was come out of Judea into Galilee, he went unto him, and besought him that he would come down and heal his son; for he was at the point of death. Baur and others have made this nobleman a heathen, so as to be able to identify him with the centurion in Matt. viii. 5 ff., and then to refute or correct either John by Matthew (Strauss, Bruno Bauer, Baur, Hilgenfeld), or Matthew by John (Weizsäcker). But this is all arbitrary, since the two incidents are in every respect different. The unyielding belief of this βασιλικόσ ('nobleman,' namely, an officer in the service of Herod Antipas at Capernaum) compels Him to do a miracle, although He at first answered the request unfavourably, and with a reproof.

Verse 48.

Except ye see signs and wonders, ye will not believe. The belief of the Galileans and of this man of Capernaum was at first only a belief like the Judean belief in miracles, ii. 23. They received him joyfully, ver. 45, because of the signs which they had seen. And Jesus must utter the reproof to this man, that their belief is never willing to have any other foundation than miraculous signs. Yet they were inclined towards Him though He had hitherto done miracles, and wrought, not among them, but only in Jerusalem and Judea. And this man holds so confidently to his belief in Jesus' person, that His word is enough to make him sure of the thing he wished for.

VERSE 49.

Unmoved by Jesus' reproof, the father continues: *Sir, come down ere my child die.*

VERSE 50.

This urgency of the father's prayer, born of anxiety, decided Jesus to consent: *Go thy way; thy son liveth.* And he went his way. As a reward for this, even before he reaches his home he learns the certainty of the answered prayer.

VERSES 51–53.

On the way he receives the joyful news from his servants, *Thy son liveth,* and at the same time finds that the beginning of the recovery dates from Jesus' words: *Yesterday at the seventh hour the fever left him.* According to the Jewish reckoning, which we have no right to exchange with the Roman (Ewald: seven o'clock in the evening), that was one o'clock in the afternoon. Since Cana is about three geographical miles distant from Capernaum, we must either assume an unknown delay, or else put the meeting in the evening, which begins a new day for the Jews (Hengstenberg, Brückner).

Jesus had so arranged his miraculous help, that he freed the belief from the miraculous activity and referred it to His word.[1] It is said of the Samaritans in ver. 41: ἐπίστευσαν διὰ τὸν λόγον αὐτοῦ (they 'believed because of

---

[1] Compare Baur, *Kritische Untersuchungen über die kanonischen Evangelien,* Tübingen 1847, p. 152.

his word'), and here, in ver. 50, we read ἐπίστευσεν τῷ λόγῳ (he 'believed the word'); in both cases alike, the ground and object of belief is Jesus' word. This is the progress of belief, which the evangelist intends to depict by the two examples from Samaria and Galilee. He presents it as contrasted with the Judean belief in miracles, which concealed within itself real unbelief. The last words of Jesus quoted by the evangelist, which denote the true constitution of belief, apply entirely to the man before us, xx. 29: μακάριοι οἱ μὴ ἰδόντεσ καὶ πιστεύσαντεσ ('blessed are they that have not seen and have believed'). The whole gospel is so planned as to enable us to behold the development of belief towards this end.

VERSE 54.

The incident in Samaria, however, had an importance not simply as standing alone, and in reference to that day, but also as prophetic of the future. The case is the same here. Jesus does not yet open a course of Galilean activity. His action on this occasion is only an exception. The evangelist calls attention to that fact: *This is again the second miracle that Jesus did, when he was come out of Judea into Galilee.* Τοῦτο ('this') is the subject, δεύτερον σημεῖον ('second miracle') is the predicate, and πάλιν ('again') lays special emphasis on the point contained in δεύτερον ('second'). The first miracle was upon the occasion of the marriage, this second miracle is again in Cana. We therefore have not a miraculous activity, but only these two miracles, both of a private character. The whole scene, however, is a prelude to the future.

That man from Capernaum represents Galilee in general. Christ speaks to him, ver. 48, in the plural; and what is true of him is true of all. In Galilee, as in Judea, it is only by miraculous signs apparent to the senses that Jesus can hope to awaken belief. But the result in Galilee is a different one from that in Judea. Here he will succeed in finding a larger circle of disciples, who no longer need the sensible miracles for their belief, but who hold simply to his word. This presupposes, it is true, that the one who begged the favour from Jesus was not a heathen, as many have made him out to be. Jesus, in ver. 48, does not mean this man alone, nor the nation aside from this man (Baumgarten-Crusius), but both, and therefore the man is a Galilean, and is a Jew. Although he came with belief, yet it was a lack in his belief (against Baumgarten-Crusius) that he asked Jesus to come with him and heal his son. The centurion spoke very differently, Luke vii. 2 ff.: ver. 7, εἰπὲ λόγῳ καὶ ἰαθήτω ὁ παῖς μου ('But say in a word, and my servant shall be healed'). Hence Jesus could say in ver. 9: οὐδὲ ἐν τῷ Ἰσραὴλ τοσαύτην πίστιν εὗρον ('I have not found so great faith, no, not in Israel'). Yet, on account of this lack of belief, the nobleman does not deserve the accusations Stier[1] makes against him. For, in the first place, he clings to the LORD like the wrestling Jacob, as if he would not leave him till he blessed him. And, in the next place, he at once sustains the trial of belief—no small trial—which Jesus lays upon him by commanding him to believe without seeing, ver. 50. In the renewed life of his son, he and his household themselves find eternal life in belief, iii. 36. Thus Jesus rewards belief on his word, while the wrath of God remains upon the unbelievers of Judea.

Conclusion of First Part.

With this, the first part of the gospel closes. Jesus, the Son of God, the incarnate Word, the truth and the fulfilling of the Old Testament and of all Old Testament revelation, the essential satisfaction of human need, is introduced and introduces himself as such, is witnessed to and witnesses to himself. On the other hand, we have seen belief and unbelief, and half-belief, which contains unbelief in itself or which develops into true belief—a belief needing miracles no longer, but holding only to the word, and finding its reward in living communion with

[1] Stier, *Reden Jesu*, 3d ed., Barmen and Elberfeld 1870, vol. iv. p. 183 ff.

Jesus. The first swift beginning and comprehensive attempt of Jesus, his limiting himself to special persons, and his return into quietness,—all this is brought before us in a movement which is spirally progressive, and which displays the most various contrasts. One phrase, however, is the centre and union of the whole: Jesus, the Son of God, must be believed in; He is believed in by God's decree, and unto eternal life; and men are to believe in him for the sake of his self-witness.

In the last event, however, a self-revelation of Jesus is reported which is not so general and comprehensive as the preceding, but more special. In ver. 53 he speaks the words ὁ υἱός σου ζῇ ('thy son liveth'), and thereby revealed himself as the one who gives life. This forms the transition to the next section. Hence Stier[1] has connected this account with the fifth and sixth chapters as one section; but that is because he does not understand the peculiar construction of our gospel. After what was said above, we hardly need any further proof that vers. 46–54 necessarily belong to what precedes. We have, however, already seen that in this gospel the close of one section is usually at the same time the transition to the next section. We do not need, therefore, to be led astray in our division by the certainly apparent relation of these verses to the fifth and sixth chapters.

Jesus reveals himself as the life, then as the light; both in a rising climax, and both in contrast with and under the contradiction of the unbelief of Israel. The fifth chapter leads us directly into this contest.

[1] Stier, *Reden Jesu*, 3d ed., Barmen and Elberfeld 1870, vol. iv. p. 181.

EXPOSITION.

II.

JESUS AND THE JEWS.

Chapters V.–XII.

II.

JESUS AND THE JEWS.

Chapters V.–XII.

V., VI. Jesus the Life.—Beginning of the Contest.

THE evangelist leaves the thread of continuous historical narration. He has, indeed, led Jesus to Galilee. But he is silent as to His stay there, and likewise at the beginning of the next section, chap. vii., as to His activity there. He simply ranges one upon the other, single fragments, chiefly from Jerusalem, as a clear sign that the history serves him as a means of instructing, as a demonstration of the doctrine.

The instruction and doctrine have, however, other contents than what the history contains, namely, Jesus the Son of God. And so the evangelist ensures at the same time the correct understanding of the history, and thereby arms belief against attacks upon, and aspersions of, Jesus the Christ on the part of unbelief. And since the church of Jesus Christ is entirely conditioned upon Him, and has a similar form with Him, the evangelist, in the same act, teaches men how rightly to understand the form and position of Christ's church in the world, and secures those who belong to that church against the hostility especially of Jewish unbelief. The characteristic thing in the church, as in Jesus, in the former because in the latter, is that they stand in opposition to the contradiction of unbelief and disobedience, while the salvation which they give is only imparted to the obedience of belief.

Each of these has its history, the exhibition of salvation and the contradiction against it and against its offer. The part of the gospel with which we here have to deal contains both of these; the exhibition of salvation in its various essential sides, and the course of Jewish contradiction from its occasion and its first utterance, to its completion in the decree of the Sanhedrim and to the last judicial words of Jesus. Previously, his finding belief outside of Judea was not sought by him, but was ordered by God, and brought to him by God. And thus the contest with Israel's unbelief in which he now becomes entangled, is not sought by him, but is introduced without his will. Previously, the opposition to his self-witness as the Son of God found a semblance of legal foundation in his form of flesh, and this foundation will ever remain in so far as he testifies to himself as the Son of God. But still other seeming foundations for opposition will be added from the letter of the law, or from the Old Testament Scriptures in general, in so far as Jesus exhibits his divine Sonship as the fulfilment of all Old Testament revelation in its various sides. This will at once be clear to us in the fifth chapter.

The fifth and sixth chapters form the first section of this second part. For, as we saw above,[1] there is a break in the historical narrative at the sixth chapter. This section is of two parts, moreover, because Judea and Galilee are to be brought together and to be contrasted with each other, on account both of the similarity of Jesus' conduct and claim and of his experience. We here find ourselves still in the first stage of the contest, which reaches its height in chapters vii.–x. The fact that Jesus reveals himself first as the life, and then in the second section as the light, corresponds to the course of the statements concerning him in the opening of the gospel. In that opening, however, the evangelist's proclamation returns again to the true life of the new birth which is bestowed on believers, i. 12 f.; and here the revelation of Jesus returns from light to life.

The third part of the gospel has also a certain analogy

[1] Vol. i. p. 204 f.

with the third paragraph of the opening. In the latter, the glorious revelation of grace in the only-begotten Son is praised; and in the former, chapters xiii.–xx., we find at heart nothing but a magnifying of Jesus' love, or an announcement of the glory which he has revealed to his disciples in the revelation of his unending love.

Attention may further be called to still another phase of the analogy. The second paragraph of the opening moves entirely in the contrast between the revelation of Jesus and his reception in the world, between believers and unbelievers; the same is the case with the second part of the gospel. And as the evangelist forsakes this contrast in the third paragraph of the opening, and only announces the blessed experience which they, his own, have had in communion with him, in the same way the third part of the gospel passes from the contrast between Jesus and the Jews to the announcement of Jesus' love to his own, who stood in the communion of belief with him. These manifold references and analogies permit us to recognise the deep internal unity of conception, which is based upon the energetic self-limitation of the evangelist to that which is essential in the revelation and proclamation of Jesus.

V. 1–47.

The God-like Activity of Jesus the Son of God, and the Beginning of the Opposition.

This is the subject of the fifth chapter, and it is treated in three paragraphs. (1.) Vers. 1–9 report the deed which becomes the occasion of opposition; (2.) Vers. 10–18 relate the growth and intensifying of the antagonism; (3.) Vers. 19–47 contain the declaration as to himself and as to the right of his claim, made by Jesus in view of the opposition.

(1.) VERSES 1–9. *The Occasion.*

VERSE 1.

After this there was a feast of the Jews; and Jesus went up to Jerusalem. The evangelist does not say how long after. The continuation of the narrative by μετὰ ταῦτα ('after this') is quite customary in John's gospel.[1] Lücke's distinction between μετὰ τοῦτο, as denoting immediate, and μετὰ ταῦτα, as denoting more distant sequence, is entirely incapable of proof (see Meyer), and is also arbitrary linguistically.

The Feast.

A feast, without closer definition. The Sinaitic, it is true, has the article ἡ ἑορτή ('the feast'). But the authorities, A B D etc., on the other side are too strong. The addition of the article is easy to explain from the old exposition, which made this a passover; see Meyer. Jesus goes thither on account of the feast, and not, in the first instance at least, for the purpose of renewing his former activity in Judea. The latter is certain, from the fact that we after this behold him active in Galilee again. We therefore conclude that the former was the case, and hence that the feast was not the feast of Purim, celebrated on account of the deliverance from Haman's murderous plans. Purim is, however, commonly taken to be the feast meant (Hug, Olshausen, Wieseler, Bäumlein, Meyer, Godet), because it falls in March (14 and 15 Adar), and thus seems most easily to fit the last statement of time, iv. 35, and the next one, vi. 4. The worldly character of this feast, the celebration of which was not bound to the temple, makes it improbable that Jesus went to Jerusalem on account of it (see Hengstenberg, Lücke, De Wette, Brückner). And if he went for the sake of working, why should he not rather have chosen the passover, which came but a month later, vi. 4? But if it be not Purim, it is one of the great feasts, and the passover at vi. 4 falls in the next year. It is then not possible to say which feast it was (Lücke, De Wette, Tholuck, Brückner), since the evangelist has not defined it. It is labour lost to guess the passover (Lampe, Hengstenberg), or Pentecost (Bengel), or Tabernacles (Krafft,[2] Lich-

---

[1] See vol. i. p. 26.

[2] Krafft, *Chronologie und Harmonie der vier Evangelien*, Erlangen 1848, p. 98.

tenstein,[1] Riggenbach[2]), though the last is the most probable. The evangelist did not define it, because he wished to emphasize only this point, namely, that Jesus did not go to Jerusalem without being occasioned to go by a feast.

VERSE 2.

There is—it doubtless still existed after the destruction of the city—*at Jerusalem by the sheep-gate a pool*. This is at least what is commonly understood by the reading ἐπὶ τῇ ('at the'),[3] πύλῃ ('gate') being supplied after προβατικῇ ('sheep'). Meyer emphasizes κολυμβήθρᾳ, and connects it with προβατικῇ: there is at the sheep-pool Bethesda. But then the evangelist would not tell his readers what Bethesda was. The sheep-gate שַׁעַר הַצֹּאן is mentioned, at Neh. iii. 1, 32, xii. 39, as near the temple. Whence its name came we do not know. Probably it was connected with the sheep appointed for sacrifice.

Bethesda.

At this place was a *pool, called* (ἐπιλεγομένη introduces a characteristic name of this very pool) *in the Hebrew tongue Bethesda, with five porches*. Bethesda is commonly explained as בֵּית חִסְדָּא, 'domus benignitatis' · ('house of grace'). Delitzsch[4] explains it as *beth* (e) *stáw* (סְטָיֵי, אֶסְטָיֵי, στόα, porch), house of porches, which is less probable. The name, doubtless, is connected with the use of the place for poor sick people, for which purpose five porches, with vaulted arches, surrounded the little pool. Where we are to look for Bethesda now it is not easy to say. The pool may have been filled up[5] (Godet). The fountain of the pool may be identical with the present Mary's' fountain,[6] a

---

[1] Lichtenstein, *Lebensgeschichte des Herrn Jesu Christi in chronologischer Uebersicht*, Erlangen 1856, p. 198.

[2] Riggenbach, *Vorlesungen über das Leben des Herrn Jesu*, Basel 1858, p. 408.

[3] The omission of these words in the Sinaitic manuscript is evidently a correction, intended to make the sentence easier.

[4] Delitzsch, Talmudische Studien, *Zeitschrift für die gesammte lutherische Theologie und Kirche*, 1856, pp. 622–624.

[5] Ritter, *Erdkunde Asiens*, Berlin 1852, vol. viii. part 2, pp. 329, 443.

[6] Robinson, *Palästina*, Halle 1841, vol. ii. p. 148 ff.

thought which Tobler [1] discusses at length without noticing Robinson's suggestion. At any rate, we may with Tobler say, that it is doubtful whether we can find the pool again at all or not. Lieutenant Warren made excavations and found water-reservoirs and porches in the neighbourhood of Birket-Israel, a large, dry, grass and shrub overgrown, square hollow, north of the Haram, whither tradition puts the pool of Bethesda. This can hardly be Bethesda. These things are probably connected with the water-supply for Jerusalem, and for the temple-worship.[2]

Verses 3, 4.

On the floors of the porches *lay a multitude* (πολύ, 'great,' after πλῆθοσ is to be struck out, according to the testimony of the manuscripts) *of impotent folk: blind, halt, withered,* —namely, with withered limbs,—*waiting for the moving of the water. For an angel came down into the pool from time to time, and troubled the water. Whosoever then first, after the troubling of the water, stepped in, was made whole of whatsoever disease he had.* The words ἐκδεχομένων ... νοσήματι (in the English 'waiting ... he had') are wanting in א B C; the last words of the third verse in A L; and only the fourth verse is lacking in D. Besides, there are many different readings in the text. Hence this whole passage is critically more than suspicious. It is no less doubtful as to its substance. The first part, it is true,—the close of the third verse,—is a correct gloss as to the fact; this appears

---

[1] Tobler, *Die Siloahquelle und der Oelberg*, St. Gallen 1852.

[2] Instead of Bηθισδά (A C I Lachmann), א L 33, Eusebius *Onomasticon*, and Tischendorf in his eighth edition read Bηθζαθά, D reads Βιλζιθά, B Bηθσαιδά. Keim, *Geschichte Jesu von Nazara*, Zürich 1871, vol. ii. p. 177, points to the city-quarter Bezetha or New City, at Jerusalem, as if the pool were named from it. It is true that tradition places it on the northern slope of the temple, where the hill Bezetha rises and the new city begins (see Josephus, *De bello judaico*, V. iv. 2, *Opera*, Amsterdam 1726, vol. i. p. 328; V. v. 8, *ibid.* p. 336). This combination has, however, little to support it. It would be easier to find in the name a confirmation of Delitzsch's suggestion that the name is to be traced back to *beth (e) stâw*. The readings are so uncertain that it will scarcely be possible to decide upon the right one. The safest thing will be to keep to the reading of A and C. Not understanding it, they have made Bezetha, or still worse, Bethsaida, out of it.

from the seventh verse. But the conception which lies at the base of the words in the fourth verse goes beyond the bounds of the Biblical mode of viewing things. That the common and constant phenomena of nature should be called forth by the special activity of angels, finds no support in the Scriptures.[1] Although, according to the Scriptures, the spirits do rule in the life of nature, still they belong not to the sphere of the 'causae efficientes' ('efficient causes'), but to that of the 'causae finales' ('final causes'). They mediate the teleological connection of the life of nature with the kingdom of God. That is a different thing from the simple fact of an ordinary healing fountain. If this passage were genuine, it would find its analogue in no other. Besides, the later age would have been much more inclined to put in such a peculiar addition, than to leave the words out if they were genuine. The last words also, ᾧ δήποτε ('of whatsoever'), are somewhat extravagant. In short, everything speaks for the striking out of the whole passage.

Verse 5.

Among the sick people at this place there was one who was calculated to excite sympathy more than the others. The evangelist mentions the long continuance of his disease not as a merely external remark, but as the motive for Jesus' action. He desires to urge the point that Jesus worked the miracle, not for the purpose of beginning a continuous activity, but only out of pity, as an exception. This is clear, partly from the detailed way in which the place is designated, and partly from the citation of the thirty-eight years. Jesus healed the sick man at a place of suffering and of pity (Βηθεσδά 'locus benignitatis'), and among the many afflicted men, he healed one who already *had thirty-eight years in his infirmity*, that is, who had been ill thirty-eight years. But at the same time, Jesus performed this miracle both as a testimony to and as a trial for Israel. This appears from the fact that Jesus heals an infirm man, and that without having been asked, and above all on the

---

[1] Against Hofmann, *Der Schriftbeweis*, 2d ed., Nördlingen 1857, vol. i. p. 327.

Sabbath. He seems to have sought this place, and to have intended to heal one of the sick. At least the narrative gives such an impression.

Verse 6.

For Jesus, in that He himself asks the sick man a question, which must have excited a wish and a hope in him, directs his longing and hoping thoughts at once to His person. *Wilt thou be made whole?* The man did not know at all who it was that addressed him; see ver. 13. Jesus contents himself with this small measure of dawning belief. Hence the healing was not the reward of belief, but had the ground for its consummation in Jesus himself.

Verse 7.

To the long continuance of the illness was added the helpless forsaken state of the sick man, as a motive for Jesus' decision. *I have no man, when the water is troubled, to put me into the pool: but while I am going, another steps down before me.* It was an intermittent healing fountain, not enclosed by itself, and hence its water soon mingled with the rest of the pool. Therefore, if a sick man would experience its healing effect, he must hasten to come into the first flow. Perhaps, too, the way to the water, probably down steps, was narrow. The infirm man had no friends and acquaintances to care for him and put him quickly in the flowing water,—hence βάλῃ exactly: 'throw,' to cast him in,—and he himself was too helpless to be able to reach the right spot at once. All this is spoken with a certain tone of resignation.

Verse 8.

So much the more does Jesus direct His helpful, powerful sympathy to him. *Rise, take up thy bed and walk.* And Jesus' words at once fulfil themselves. The repetition of Jesus' words gives this impression.

Verse 9.

The testimony concerning himself which Jesus here

offered was easy to understand for all who saw the healed man. They could, and they should, recognize in this, that the power of a new and healing life was given in Him, a life which He offered even without being solicited. This healing was therefore a question put to Jerusalem. The question which he asked the sick man was meant for the whole nation. Thus the man is in a measure, it is true, a type of the nation. But it seems to me far-fetched to say that there is a reference to the thirty-eight years of wandering in the desert (Krafft). The emphasis rather lies on the ὅτι πολὺν ἤδη χρόνον ἔχει (sc. τὴν ἀσθένειαν, 'that he had been ill a long time'). This is also true of the nation.

If, however, the question was especially meant for the nation, we understand, in the first place, why Jesus did not demand that decided belief should come to meet Him, but Himself awakened it, and why little is said about the man, because he recedes in comparison with the general meaning.

And, in the second place, we see that Jesus offers Jerusalem a new opportunity. He makes a new trial. Yet the possibility of belief must become more difficult to the degree in which belief is refused. Israel had to believe on the Nazarene, because it would not hear of the one born in Bethlehem, and the same law repeats itself on every further stage in the history of salvation. Previously Jesus, testified to as the Son of the Father by the last and greatest prophet, came to his temple with open self-proclamation and with rich manifestation of his miraculous power. Now, Israel must believe on the simple feast-pilgrim,—which He from this time forward is and continues to be for Jerusalem,— who, moved by pity, healed that one sick man, and that upon the Sabbath, but otherwise did not testify to himself at all. He who wished to be recognized as the Saviour of Israel, seemed to offend against the very fundamental law of the government of God's church. How much more was it now necessary to hold firm to the essence which appeared in Jesus, and to free oneself from the letter of the law?

The more offensive Jesus became, the more difficult was belief, and just so much keener and more compelling grew the dilemma; that they must behold in Him a sinner worthy of death, or a man who in a God-like manner effects life in the world, unfettered by the limits which the law of the Sabbath traced. The fact of the healing by his mighty word, witnesses to his Lordship over the Sabbath as well as over the temple. What an importance must this one event have gained in this way! It is conceivable that it became the starting-point of all further transactions between Jesus and the Jews, and we shall have no occasion to be surprised when at a much later date we see that both come back to it, vii. 21 ff. The point, however, was this, how the act was viewed, namely, whether they laid stress on the healing or on the apparent breach of the Sabbath which Jesus committed and caused the healed man to commit. We see both sides of these views represented in a characteristic manner in what follows.

(2.) VERSES 10–18. *The Antagonism.*

VERSES 10, 11.

The Jews therefore said unto him that was cured, It is the Sabbath-day: it is not lawful for thee to carry thy bed. He answered them, He that made me whole, the same said unto me, Take up thy bed and walk. The healed man having been informed that it was the Sabbath, and that his deed was unbecoming the day, justifies this deed by the authority of the one who had made him whole.

VERSE 12.

Then asked they him, What man is that which said unto thee, Take up thy bed and walk? It is characteristic that the Jews only ask who had told him to do this on the Sabbath, a deed forbidden by the law. They do not inquire who had healed him, the fact to which the man had referred in the eleventh verse, and one which they might well have found worthy of the first attention.

VERSES 13, 14.

And it is again characteristic that, on the other hand, the man questioned does not reply that Jesus had bidden him do it, the answer apparently required by the Jews' question. Instead of this, he waits till he again meets Jesus, who had retired to avoid attracting attention, and learns who he is. Then in the fifteenth verse he replies to the Jews, that Jesus has made him whole. [The Jews speak of the supposed sin; the man speaks of the healing.] All this shows the mood of both.

VERSE 15.

It is true that if the announcement in this verse is a token of deep hard-heartedness and reprobation (Schleiermacher), then this difference of moods does not exist. But even the characteristic difference of utterance and of conception which lies in the words is a testimony against such a view: this was observed by Chrysostom, and Lücke unjustly calls the remark too acute.[1] Nor do we, therefore, need to leave the reason for the announcement undecided (Baumgarten-Crusius). It is to be sought, with Bengel and De Wette, in the design to justify himself before his spiritual rulers.

For, on the one hand, we meet the cured man in the temple. This is doubtless not a mere matter of chance, though most of the later exegetes (except Meyer and Godet) have failed to observe it. It was certainly for the purpose of thanking God for the healing. And, on the other hand, we perceive that Jesus is able to speak to him the words in the fourteenth verse: 'Behold, thou art made whole: sin no more, lest a worse thing come unto thee.' It is true that He reminds him of his sin, the punishment of which he should behold in his illness, and for which he had to expect heavier, probably eternal, punishment in case he renewed the sin. But this presupposes an already existing repentant and thankful disposition, and is not intended to awaken such a state of mind. These two things, the fact that the man was in the temple, and that Jesus addressed these words to him, show that the blessing he had experienced had not failed to make the proper moral impression upon

---

[1] Lücke, *Commentar über das Evangelium des Johannes*, 2d ed., Bonn 1843, vol. ii. p. 32.

him. In this the Jews are contrasted with him, since the event made the opposite impression upon them, because of the offence which it contained for the unbelief of those who clave unto the obedience to the letter.

VERSE 16.

And therefore did the Jews persecute Jesus, because he had done these things on the Sabbath-day. With this begins the conflict, which grows more ardent step by step until its final tragic issue. Ἐδίωκον ('persecuted') here means only the hostile disposition, and not a legal process yet. The healing on the Sabbath does not seem to them an isolated event (we do not read: ἐποίησεν, 'did'), but one characteristic of Jesus' general posture towards the law of the Sabbath (ἐποίει, 'was in the habit of doing').

VERSE 17.

Jesus' justification only serves to increase their antagonism. The words, *My Father worketh hitherto, and I work*, place him in his activity in such a manner on a level with God, that the opposition of unbelief, especially against the supposed Sabbath-breaker (compare ver. 18), could only be the more intense. In what sense does Jesus make himself equal to his Father? Baumgarten-Crusius and Meyer are right in declaring themselves against the explanation offered by Olshausen and De Wette, namely, that Jesus intends to say of himself, that, as God combines repose and activity in the Sabbath's rest, so he combines religious contemplation with moral, benevolent activity. The text gives as little support to this as it does to De Wette's view concerning an assault here made upon false notions as to the rest intended on the Sabbath. When Jesus called God his Father, this title only received a distinctive sense by the circumstance that he made himself equal to God in a special respect. Hence it is that the Jews draw the former as a conclusion from the latter. This is evidently the grammatical relation of the two sentences to each other in ver. 18, and not the reverse; nor are they two parallel sentences (Baumgarten-Crusius). But it is true that he can only put his activity on a level with the divine activity because he can call God his Father in a specific sense. For this is not said of, and intended to refer to, those related to God in general in the freest sense (Baumgarten-Crusius); it bears exclusively upon the relation of the one Son to his Father.

It seems to me that there has been one very common error in the explanation of this passage. They have conceived in too general a way the contrast of rest and activity, which they have placed at the foundation of the words as a religious presupposition. God did not contrast the Sabbath with his action in general. He contrasted it with, and set it at the end of, his act of creation.[1] At that point began a new activity on the part of God, and its Sabbath has not come yet. We may therefore say that a day of rest has not yet been appointed for the human activity which corresponds to that second divine activity, but only for the one corresponding to the creative. We may learn what the work of God is, which he effects from that point onwards, from the fact that Jesus came to do and to complete God's work; see for example iv. 34. Hence all the action of God since the creation, or rather since the Sabbath of God which concluded the creation, is essentially related only to Christ and his work. Therefore it is of a salvation-bringing, a redeeming kind.

The execution of the will of God unto salvation is Christ's work, because it is God's work. The gradual realisation of this saving will is the substantial contents of the divine action since its Sabbath began. And for this work there is no Sabbath either for him or for the Son, whose action wholly coincides with that work of God. In this sense, then, Jesus speaks these words. The redemptive working and executing God's saving will still continues, and is not yet at an end. Its Sabbath has not yet come. And the same is true of his corresponding action, or rather of that action of his which performs the work in question. This is similar to, though deeper in conception than, Matt. xii.

---

[1] See Hofmann, *Der Schriftbeweis*, 2d ed., Nördlingen 1857, vol. i. pp. 267, 280.

10-13, where he justifies the healing on the Sabbath in the synagogue by other acts of deliverance which they unhesitatingly allowed themselves to perform on that day. He emphasizes the right of redemption, since it has not yet reached its conclusion, but still stands in the course of its history.

The ordinary explanation is, that God's rest does not exclude his activity. This alters the specific meaning of the Sabbath. But in particular it leaves the expression ἕωσ ἄρτι ('hitherto') unexplained. We should expect, 'in spite of the rest of the Sabbath,' or something of that kind, but not an expression which evidently includes the thought that the time of rest is not yet come (against Meyer). Since God the creator rests from creating, God the redeemer works through the Son. The new Sabbath came with the day of the glorification of Christ in his resurrection. That closed the fact of redemption. That day stands as a dividing wall between the time of the redemption and of its acceptance, just as the old Sabbath stood between creation and preservation or ruling. Since then, the Holy Ghost is the active, immanent principle of sacred history, as Christ was in the time of redemption. This last thought is also contained in these words of Christ. For the connection is not intended in such a way as that the ἐργάζεσθαι ('to work') should be said of both in exactly the same sense, and that the working of the Son should only come forth at the side of that of the Father. The thing said here must be like what the context presents in the succeeding paragraph, ver. 19 ff., namely, that the action belongs to the Father in so far as it proceeds from God, and to the Son in so far as it completes itself in the world. Jesus here designates himself as the continuing organ of all divine redeeming activity.

Verse 18.

The keenness of the dilemma to which the matter is at once brought upon this first occasion of the contest, a contest intensifying and developing itself from this time onwards, calls forth also opposition at once in all its keenness.

In the sixteenth verse it says ἐδίωκον ('they persecuted'), but in the eighteenth we find μᾶλλον ἐζήτουν αὐτὸν ἀποκτεῖναι (they 'sought the more to kill him').[1] It is not as if we were so to understand it that μᾶλλον, with the meaning 'now indeed,' should indicate the advance from διώκειν ('to persecute') to ζητεῖν ἀποκτεῖναι ('to seek to slay'), as Bengel and Baumgarten-Crusius would persuade us. Μᾶλλον belongs to ἐζήτουν, and διώκειν already includes in itself the wish to slay (Meyer). Baumgarten-Crusius regards this as essentially improbable. But he did not consider the fundamental importance of the command touching the Sabbath, the strictness of the law of the Sabbath. It was the apparent offence against this law that made Jesus' words unendurable, the words in which *he called God his own special* (ἴδιον, 'proprium,' belonging peculiarly to him) *Father, in that he* at the same time *made himself equal to God*. The former point lay in the ὁ πατήρ μου ('my Father'), the latter in the making the ἐργάζεσθαι ('to work') the same for both.[2] Ἴσον ἑαυτὸν ποιῶν κ.τ.λ. ('making himself equal' etc.) is neither a conclusion from (thus Lücke), nor a presupposition for, that which precedes. If the Jews saw in Jesus a transgressor of the law, such a speech must excite them in the extreme.

There is, however, nothing here about external 'temptations' (against Baumgarten-Crusius), but only about their disposition and their inward desire (ἐζήτουν, 'they sought'), as it was made more intense by Jesus' reply. Thus, as we see, at the very beginning the issue is already settled. Of necessity, the psychological fact transplanted itself into the external reality. Previously, however, the disposition and the desire must become a persistent psychological character, and this character must grow clear and decided, so that the desire may become a settled purpose, and that purpose ripen into a formal resolution. In what follows we see the un-

---

[1] [It will be observed that the like phrase in the received text, and in the English version of the sixteenth verse, is rejected as spurious by Tischendorf, Tregelles, and Westcott and Hort.—C. R. G.]

[2] Compare Hofmann, *Der Schriftbeweis*, 2d ed., Nördlingen 1857, vol. i. p. 133; and Meyer.

belief of Israel pass through this development. Jesus' self-witness, which is to perfect the belief on miracles by making it a true belief on and in the word, is also the thing which causes the first offence at the healing on the Sabbath to grow to the peremptory death resolution.

(3.) VERSES 19–47. *Jesus' Self-Witness.*

The declaration Jesus here makes is nothing but a development of the words in the seventeenth verse, which had only increased the offence. They treat of his relation to his Father, as a relation not only of dependence, but also of equality and of union in regard to working.

VERSE 19.

Verily, verily, I say unto you, The Son can do nothing of himself, but what he seeth the Father do. It is first a relation of dependence. For a preparatory movement of the Father's precedes every act of the Son. He receives the direction and the impulse for his action, not from himself, but from the Father. But that which in the case of the prophets was a temporary influence and excitement is here a continuing essential relation, and that of communion. He is not so humanly dependent that he must first be instructed on each occasion. On the contrary, he beholds the movements of the Father's will: $\beta\lambda\acute{\epsilon}\pi\eta$ is the designation of inward direct vision—that is, of inward intercourse of life. In the first place, therefore, he speaks of a constant communion, and after that of a communion the basis and contents of which are not of a human kind and of a human origin, but lie beyond them. He is here called dependent, not as man, but because of the essential communion with the Father which is peculiar to him. $O\mathring{v}\ \delta\acute{v}\nu\alpha\tau\alpha\iota$ ('cannot') contains not an external but an internal necessity. He is conditioned upon this relation to the Father, only because that communion essentially belongs to him. The beginning of all motion of the will is not isolated in him, but proceeds from the one, the standing in communion with whom completes his being.

We therefore shall not find in $\mathring{\alpha}\phi'\ \mathring{\epsilon}\alpha\upsilon\tauo\hat{\upsilon}$ (' of himself ') a popular abstraction, namely, that the Son is considered abstractly in his human appearance,[1] or that the words are spoken with a 'dim, one-sided reference' to what is human in Christ (De Wette). The whole divine-human subject is intended (Meyer). The only thing is, that the first point in question is his earthly historical condition of being. This, however, is but the appearance and completion of a heavenly historical condition upon which he has entered, and upon the analogy of which this earthly condition is formed. Therefore this self-witness also bears upon the heavenly condition. And hence it is as well an exact as an essential declaration concerning Christ. The expression corresponds to the thing itself, and is true no less of God with God than of the man Jesus.

For these reasons we shall also not be inclined so to weaken ἀφ' ἑαυτοῦ as to refer it to knowledge (De Wette), since it really touches upon the most internal life and life-motion. Nor shall we understand by the βλέπειν ('to see') and δεικνύειν ('to show') a gift of power and a making something possible (Baumgarten-Crusius), since they denote the innermost, essential communion of life. Hence the negative statement is expressly followed by the positive as its support: *For what things soever he doeth, these also doeth the Son likewise.* Ὁμοίωσ ('likewise') is an emphasized repetition of that which lies in the ταῦτα ('these'). He does not say, I; but designedly says, 'the Son,' so as to characterize his relation to the Father. If that communion belong essentially to him, then he indeed came forth from God into the world, then he is ὁ υἱόσ ('the Son') in the exact sense.

Verse 20.

For the Father loveth the Son, and showeth him all things that himself doeth. Such exceptional equality of working does exist, and therefore he is Son in the exact sense, for the relation between the Father and him is an unlimited one. It is true the relation of the Father to the Son is desig-

---

[1] Lücke, *Commentar über das Evangelium des Johannes*, 3d ed., Bonn 1843, vol. ii. p. 37.

nated as a communion of love, such as perhaps might also occur in the case of every man (φιλεῖ, 'loveth'). But inasmuch as this is called the basis of an absolute intercourse of communion (πάντα δείκνυσιν, 'showeth all things'), it must itself be of an uncommon, unconditioned, and unlimited kind. It is therefore not the love of God to the man of obedience, between whom and God there is still ever an essential line of division. It is the love of God to the eternal person of the Son, of whom it is elsewhere said, xvii. 24, that God loved him before the foundation of the world. The fact that ἀγαπᾶν is used in that passage, and φιλεῖν in the passage before us, to express the affection of love (Meyer), furnishes no ground for understanding one thing there and another here; compare Baumgarten-Crusius' note on this passage. Hence this communion of love designates not a relation which arose in time, but one which existed eternally. And for this reason is it said that the Father showeth him all that he does, namely, that the mutual intercourse has no limit.

Stier[1] cites the Berlenburger Bible and Baader, and calls attention to the Trinitarian meaning of the notion of love, that God is no solitary unity, that the Father is not hidden from the Son, and the like. In this Stier not only goes 'beyond the possible understanding of the first hearers' of the words, but also goes entirely beyond the most patent meaning of this declaration. The thing here dealt with is the position and importance of the Son, not in the Trinity, but in the history of salvation. It is not said that he is the 'alter ego' ('other self') of God, who, aside from all revelation, is necessary for God's internal living activity; but that, on the basis of an essential intercourse of communion with the Father (in the Spirit), he has absolute knowedge of all the saving will of God, and that he stands in that essential relation to God for the very purpose of fulfilling this will. The Son, then, Christ, is spoken of only in reference to the history of salvation, only in his destined character for that history. Any further conclusions that may be drawn from this are the

[1] Stier, *Reden Jesu*, 3d ed., Barmen and Elberfeld 1870, vol. iv. p. 205.

business of systematical theological thinking, and not of exegetical discussion.

That the above is all that is intended appears further from the following future. Μείζονα τούτων δείξει αὐτῷ ἔργα, 'he will show him greater works than these,' namely, that he may do them, and thereby bring men to a willing or an unwilling recognition of him; ἵνα ὑμεῖσ θαυμάζητε, 'that ye may marvel.' These words can only point to the progressive realization of the divine saving will. Baumgarten-Crusius was right when he remarked that the ἔργα ('works') of Christ, which here appear for the first time, stand in connection with the ἔργον ('work') of Christ, iv. 34, xvii. 4. He is engaged in executing this ἔργον, namely, the act of redemption, but he has not yet reached its glorious conclusion. This furnishes us with a new confirmation of the explanation of ἐργάζεσθαι, given above at the seventeenth verse.

Verses 21–23.

We may learn of what description the new, greater, future works will be, in which Jesus executes and completes the saving will of God, from the fact that it pertains to him to give life, because the judgment is granted unto him, in order that he may share in equal honour with God. In this he comprehends all historically, not so that he treats merely of what is present or speaks of what is future, but that he tells what is essentially and always proper to him. That which is future will then consist only in the highest possible advance of these three facts. The notion of the ζωή, 'life,' or rather the work of ζωοποιεῖν, 'making alive,' comes forward as the principal and the most comprehensive. The others are conditioned afterwards upon this fact. He who had previously testified to himself as the bearer and executor of the whole saving will of God, here proclaims himself as the ζωή, 'life,' as soon as he wishes to denote the contents of this saving will. The progress is the same as that made in the opening of the gospel, where the salvation in Christ was to be expressed, a progress from λόγοσ, 'word,' to ζωή, 'life.'

Verse 21.

For as the Father raiseth up, and thereby quickeneth the dead, even so the Son quickeneth whom he will. The action of the Son is conditioned on that of the Father, and yet again is equal to it and one with it. But God is life; therefore working and giving life is his essential action. The same must then be true of the Son.

There has always been a contention about the way of understanding νεκρόσ, 'dead,' and ζωοποιεῖν, 'making alive,' as to whether they are to be understood exactly or inexactly, as the case is commonly expressed.[1] Most of the fathers and of the older commentators, as for instance Bengel, understood the whole passage to treat of the resurrection and of the judgment in the exact sense. A few later scholars, as Baumgarten-Crusius, take the whole passage in the ethical sense. And most of the later scholars follow Augustine in taking the passage as far as the twenty-seventh verse in the ethical sense, and then understanding vers. 28, 29 to refer to the future general resurrection of the dead.

If vers. 21-23 form the theme or summary of what follows, so that the development proceeds from the twenty-fourth verse onwards, as we shall see that it really does, then that which is explained in ver. 24 ff. must be comprehended in our verse. The present ζωοποιεῖ, 'quickeneth,' expresses not the work he is now doing, but that which essentially belongs to him. Hence the progress from the spiritual to the physical resurrection of the dead, if we may use this expression,—a progress which Lücke[2] declares to continue through vers. 21-28,—we shall only permit to begin at the twenty-fourth verse. But we shall then not venture to express ourselves to the effect that one is said exactly and the other inexactly. In the new birth the ζωή, 'life,' begins in the exact sense, and this finally completes itself in the future resurrection unto life. We,

---

[1] Compare Lücke, *Commentar über das Evangelium des Johannes*, 3d ed., Bonn 1843, vol. ii. pp. 38-43.

[2] Lücke, *ut supra*, vol. ii. p. 42.

therefore, must not distinguish between the spiritual and the bodily side, but understand the life in the substantial sense; a life which is one and the same for the man in his personal and natural life, and only gradually perfects itself in these two sides.

This agrees also with οὓσ θέλει, 'whom he will.' As a rule, they found upon these words the limitation to the purely spiritual life, since the future bodily quickening will be a general, not a limited one. This, however, does not limit the future resurrection, but the ζωοποιεῖν, 'quickening,' namely, the impartation of life, to the final perfection of which then only the future ἀνάστασισ ζωῆσ, 'resurrection of life,' belongs. Jesus is unto ζωή, 'life,' only to those who believe; to the others, he is unto κρίσισ, 'judgment.' To this must be added that the emphasis lies not on this point, not on οὓσ, 'whom,' but on θέλει, 'he wills.' The intention, however, is not to designate the ζωοποιεῖν as an arbitrary act, and one not supplied with a motive by the persons in question. Nor is the intention here to oppose Jewish particularism.[1] The purpose is to say, that as the Father in his perfection of power bestows life on the dead, so also the Son's will has the same power: 'nunquam ejus voluntatem destituit effectus,' 'the effect never failed his will' (Bengel). Baumgarten-Crusius paraphrases it: 'Therefore because, and as he wills it.' His will, however, is morally conditioned: he will impart life only to those who believe, because that is the necessary moral presupposition for it.

Verse 22.

That also refutes the notion that οὐδὲ γάρ ('for . . . not') confirms the preceding οὓσ θέλει (Lücke, De Wette, Meyer, Stier), namely, in so far as is contained therein that the others, whom the Son will not quicken, experience in themselves the judgment of condemnation, the preliminary analogue of the condemning judgment of the second advent, ver. 29,—thus Meyer. On the contrary, it is the

[1] Lücke, *Commentar über das Evangelium des Johannes*, 3d ed., Bonn 1843, vol. ii. p. 49.

Son's vocation to bestow life, because it is appointed to him to execute the separating of men. *For the Father judgeth no man, but hath committed all judgment unto the Son.* If he separate or distinguish between them, to what purpose is it, except to give to certain ones the saving blessing, namely ζωή, 'life,' and to grant to the rest the exclusion they have desired from the possession of that blessing?

He is set for κρίσισ, 'judgment,' that is to say, in the words of Simeon, Luke ii. 34, for the fall of some and for the rising of others. Meyer, among others, limits the κρίσισ to the judgment of condemnation, and appeals to κρίνει οὐδένα ('judgeth no man'); but that is no proof for his point, seeing that κρίνειν ('to judge') here only designates the judicial decision in general. Moreover, such a limitation is as arbitrary as Stier's[1] extension of it to the separating sin from the life of believers. This latter is by no means justified by the expression κρίσισ πᾶσα, 'all judgment.' Strictly speaking, these two words do not belong so close together. The meaning is, that the Father has committed to the Son the judgment, that is to say, the decision and the separation which is to be carried out, in all its parts or in its entire execution. The κρίσισ is intended to be designated as a well known and necessary event by ἡ κρίσισ, 'the judgment.' For it is the essential form in which the saving will of God comes to its realization upon earth. It corresponds to the φῶσ, 'light,' as the form of his revelation. Indeed, the κρίσισ is commonly brought into connection with φῶσ, see i. 5, iii. 19, 20, ix. 5, 39; and ζωή names the contents of the saving will.

VERSE 23.

It is given to the Son to bestow life, because it is given to him to execute judgment; and both with the design that all men may show him such honour as they show God. For he exercises a God-like activity. He works in a God-like manner, in such a way that God does his own work through and in him. Therefore the God-like honour is to

---

[1] Stier, *Reden Jesu*, 3d ed., Barmen and Elberfeld 1870, vol. iv. p. 210.

be thus understood; that God is honoured in him. In this sense it is added that he who does not honour the Son does not honour the Father, namely, just because he does not honour the former; of course, the contrary follows upon this, that men honour the Father in the very honouring of the Son. Such, and not the reverse,[1] is the relation to each other into which the two parts are to be brought.

It certainly is not said in the words before us that this honouring concerns not his person but his cause (Baumgarten-Crusius). Do not the words τιμᾶν τὸν πατέρα ('to honour the Father') express a posture towards the person, and then, as a result, a posture towards the cause? The other case is entirely parallel to this in language and in matter, and how can it have a different meaning? It is true that the claim Jesus here utters may point to the dishonouring on the part of the Jews (De Wette). But the thought is not exhausted in the contrast with that. It has been urged that the original Father and the Son in his image ever remain different subjects for the honouring.[2] This is not incorrect, but it rather lies beyond the thoughts touched by the text. The latter calls upon us to confess that, and to understand how, the Father is honoured in the honour which is shown to the Son.

Jesus does not, indeed, demand direct religious honour in prayer and the like, but the right, and certainly religious, posture towards him as the contents of the divine saving will in belief. So far as the historical manifestation of this goes, just so far will the τιμή ('honour') have to extend. He is always the one in whom the God of salvation is present for us. If he, however, has now been raised to a God-like existence, and if he was properly named by Thomas, κύριοσ καὶ θεόσ, 'Lord and God,' what other form of τιμή shall belief now assume than that which the Christian church shows to Jesus? That honour is designated as God's design and will, and it is quite plainly

[1] Lücke, *Commentar über das Evangelium des Johannes*, 3d ed., Bonn 1843, vol. ii. p. 50.
[2] Lücke, *ut supra*, vol. ii. p. 51.

indicated that any one would deceive himself in thinking he had the Father, if he were not willing to have and to honour Him in the Son.

Verses 24–26.

That which vers. 21–23 offered in a summary, is developed in what now follows. Jesus gives life.

Verse 24.

Verily, verily, I say unto you, He that heareth my word, and believeth on him that sent me, hath everlasting life. It is the present, ἔχει, 'hath.' With hearing and believing, having is also given. The impartation and the possession of life begin from this time forth, and perfect themselves in the future. He gives it by means of his word, because he, as the personal word of God to humanity, bears the life of God in himself. For when Jesus speaks now, his word has himself for its contents, him who is the word of God, and at the same time the life. We may draw from this, that the idea of the Logos lies at the base also of the part of our gospel with which we are now engaged, namely, in the sense in which it coincides with ὁ υἱὸσ τοῦ θεοῦ, 'the Son of God.' When Jesus, in the context of the passage before us, designates himself as the one sent by God, we need only to recall the words in x. 35, 36, to perceive that this conception of Christ forms also the presupposition of vers. 24–26. Jesus' word, which has him for its substance, corresponds to the personal word of God in Jesus to us.

The right posture to it consists, in the nature of the case, purely in belief or in receptive hearing. For ἀκούων, 'hearing,' is more closely defined by the following πιστεύων, 'believing.' Everything in the fourth gospel turns upon word and belief. If the man takes this word and its contents essentially into himself in belief, he is by that very fact in possession of life itself. It is a matter of course that this life, which is the divine life of Christ, of the one come from heaven, is ζωὴ αἰώνιοσ, 'eternal life,' a life belonging to the essential being. Therefore belief, since it is in possession of the essential life, likewise possesses the heavenly, eternal, and hence future life. As the immanence of the world to come is given in the Son of God and in his word, objectively, so is it given in belief, subjectively.

If, according to this, the notions Son of God or word and belief form the fundamental notions of our gospel, the point of immanence belongs to its fundamental conception. Indeed, it has always been observed that this thought of immanence controls the whole view of the fourth gospel. It was for the sake of this basis that Fichte also, for example, especially valued it. But it would be unjust praise to see in this an exclusive pre-eminence of this book. There is no other immanence here than that which belongs to Paul's presentation of doctrine, or than that proper to Christianity and to the general Christian conception of the universe. It merely comes out in another connection of thought, and with a different turn.

With the possession of life is granted freedom from the κρίσισ ('judgment'): *and shall not enter into condemnation, but is passed from death unto life.* 'He shall not enter into condemnation' is not exactly the same as in viii. 51: θάνατον οὐ μὴ θεωρήσῃ, 'he shall never see death' (De Wette). For the latter is a result of the former. But since the κρίσισ consummates itself chiefly in the dividing the world according to belief and unbelief, this dividing does not further affect the man who believes. He is already, by reason of his belief, an ἐκλεκτὸσ ἐκ τοῦ κόσμου ('chosen out of the world,' xv. 19). But the notion of κρίσισ goes further. It betokens the exclusion of the unbelieving world from the communion of the saving blessing offered in the φῶσ ('light'), namely, of the ζωή ('life'). This exclusion is occasioned and brought on by the revelation of Jesus as φῶσ, the 'light,' which compels to a decision.

The believer is free from the judgment which executes itself in that exclusion, because he is in possession of that saving blessing. The believer is still, however, in reality a part of the world, the living element of which world is σκοτία ('darkness'), and the fate or condition of which is θανατοσ ('death'). But he is a lover of the φῶσ ('light') within the σκοτία ('darkness'). By his belief on the word of life, it has come to pass that he has gone over from the realm of the death of this world into the realm of that life which springs from the world to come, the world of eternity; compare Col. i. 13. Hence that which really takes place with the fact of belief is designated by μεταβέβηκεν ἐκ τοῦ θανάτου εἰσ τὴν ζωήν, 'is passed from death unto life.'

Verse 25.

Jesus repeats the last thought with increased emphasis. Yes, the dead shall hear and live! *Verily, verily, I say unto you, The hour is coming, and now is, when the dead shall hear the voice of the Son of God: and they that hear shall live.* Οἱ ἀκούσαντεσ ('they that hear') shows that this is a continuation of the preceding thought, and not a transition from the sphere of spiritual death and coming to life, to the sphere of the bodily death (thus, for example, Olshausen and Hengstenberg), so that καὶ νῦν ἐστίν ('and now is') should refer to the various bodily resurrections wrought by Jesus. It does not say merely ἀκούσαντεσ ('hearing'), so that it could be explained, 'simul atque audierint,' 'as soon as they hear' (Grotius), and so that we could comprehend all dead men under it.

On the contrary, οἱ ('they that') limits the hearing to a certain portion, and ζήσουσιν ('shall live') can, as before, only designate the essential life, and not the bodily life, which is indifferent for this point. But then no one may combine the two with each other and appeal to them as a proof that those who shall in the future rise from their graves unto spiritual life shall hear the voice of Jesus differently from the others (thus my first edition). For οἱ ἀκού'σαντεσ is not more closely defined by any additional phrase. *The hour is coming,* when the apostolical preaching shall go through the world; *and now is* with the preaching of Jesus. All will hear the voice, but only a part hear in truth, those, namely, who permit themselves to be called from death unto life by the alarm-cry in the words of

Christ. It is *the voice of the Son of God*, of him who stands in absolute communion with God, and who therefore bears in himself the fulness of life. Hence, also, life is his working.

Verse 26.

For as the Father has life in himself, so hath he given to the Son to have life in himself. This presents the basis of the previously-mentioned working of the word of God: he bears the source of life in himself. For ver. 26 belongs more closely to ver. 25 than to ver. 27, since with the latter the discourse passes to the κρίσισ, 'judgment' (thus also Baumgarten-Crusius, against Lücke, De Wette, Meyer). The emphasis of the thought does not fall upon ἔδωκεν ('hath given'), so that peculiar eminence should be bestowed upon the independence of his possession of life, an independence appointed by a special event. The stress rather lies upon the making him equal to the Father, and that not in reference to the peculiar method of the possession of life, but in reference to the contents of the possession.

Baumgarten-Crusius understood ζωή ('life') of the basis of life, and therefore explained ζωὴν ἔχειν ἐν ἑαυτῷ ('to have life in himself') as equivalent to ζωοποιεῖν ('to quicken'). But he failed to observe that ζωή has not the article. It therefore cannot be explained as if it had a contrasting, opposing tone; that is to say, not as if it meant the true life over against the apparent, or the principle of life over against its result, the secondary life, and so forth. The contrast lies in the notion itself and in its whole scope. Life, and not something different, forms the substance of God; hence life forms also the essential substance of the Son. It follows necessarily from this that his workings will also have like contents.

If, then, the contrast, and therefore the emphasis, lies in the notion ζωή, it does not lie in ἐν ἑαυτῷ ('in himself'). That is to say, the thing which above all is to be brought out with particular emphasis in this phrase, is not independence or self-sufficiency, and in general not the special manner of the possession of life. Nor would the context furnish any ground for laying peculiar stress on this point. The fact that Jesus bestows life does not, in the first place, find its logical basis in his living, 'not from a foreign but from his own essence,' to use Anselm's [1] words, not in his bearing the source of his life independently in himself. It rather rests upon the circumstance that life composes also his substance and fills him, as life and nothing else dwells in God. But it is true that he would not be able to impart this his substance if he did not possess it as one which was independently his own, of which he could dispose at pleasure. This is said by the ἐν ἑαυτῷ, which is put at the end each time.

This possession, peculiar to him, however, became his own by an impartation on the part of the Father: ἔδωκεν ('hath given'). Stier [2] alludes at this point to the eternal generation of the Son within the Trinity; and according to Godet also, 'ἔδωκεν expresses an eternal act.' But if the Son be the man who went forth from the Father and came into the world, we must give up that reference. On the contrary, in that Christ went forth from the Father, he entered into human dependence upon him and his will. Since that time he finds the substance of his life, the substance essentially proper to him, in so far as he proceeded from the Father, in dependence upon his will. Hence, upon the basis of the general relation in which he stands towards the Father, he also declares that his possession of life is conditioned upon the causality of the Father's will. In this conditionality he is, however, equal to the Father, so far as the essential substance is concerned: he bears the divine life, namely, the substance of God, in himself as his essential substance, for he is the Son.

VERSES 27–30.

He bears life in himself because he is from God; judgment is entrusted to him because he became man. With this thought the discourse proceeds in these verses to

---

[1] Anselm: 'Non per extraneam sed suam essentiam vivat,' *Monologium* 44, *Opera*, 2d ed. Gerberon, Paris 1721, vol. i. p. 19 b.

[2] Stier, *Reden Jesu*, 3d ed., Barmen and Elberfeld 1870, vol. iv. p. 218.

develop that second clause of the 22d verse. Ver. 27 connects with ver. 26 only in an accidental manner, by the repetition of ἔδωκεν ('hath given').

VERSE 27.

And hath given him authority to execute judgment also, because he is a son of man. The stress does not lie on ἔδωκεν. The progress of the discourse is not found in ἔδωκεν, but in κρίσισ, 'judgment,' because it is the new point which follows upon ζωή ('life') as something further. Hofmann[1] used to think the contrary: he thought that in υἱὸσ ἀνθρώπου ('son of man') the reason was given why the judgment was entrusted to him; of himself he was unable to do such a thing, because he was man and a child of man like the rest. But the thought of dependence upon the Father is in the whole discourse not the really pervading thought. It stands merely in a subordinate relation to the other thought, namely, that his working is God-like, and is God's own working. As, in accordance with this, he imparts life, so also the judgment belongs to him. And this too he has undertaken because he has become a son of man.

Meyer also emphasizes ἔδωκεν ('hath given'), and explains the passage thus: that the Father has bestowed on him this authorization of judgment because he has become man, and because his essence for the history of salvation, or the basis of his essence for this history, rests on that fact. To this we reply, that the saving historical essence of Christ does not consist in the fact that he is man, but that he is the man of salvation, so that it must at least have said that he was *the* son of man. Others (Lücke, Olshausen, Bäumlein, Tholuck) have in like manner taken υἱὸσ ἀνθρώπου ('son of man') in the sense of ὁ υἱὸσ κ.τ.λ. ('the son,' etc.), namely, of the Messiahship of Jesus, on the basis of Dan. vii. 13. But the two are not equivalent. Nor would the circumstance that υἱὸσ ἀνθρώπου is the predicate here make

---

[1] Hofmann, *Weissagung und Erfüllung im alten und im neuen Testamente*, Nördlingen 1844, vol. ii. p. 19. He has now changed his opinion in *Der Schriftbeweis*, 2d ed., Nördlingen 1859, vol. ii. part i. p. 73.

the article superfluous, since the thing in question is a fixed term. Christ here calls himself not the son of man, but a man. When, then, he connects with that the commission of judgment to him, there is, in spite of Meyer's opposition, no other explanation left for us than this, that God willed to judge the earth by a man; compare Acts xvii. 31, μέλλει κρίνειν ... ἐν ἀνδρὶ ᾧ ὥρισεν, ' he will judge ... by the man whom he hath ordained.' This is Hofmann's view also.[1]

By this means we are likewise relieved from the forced connection (Chrysostom) of ὅτι υἱ. δ. ἐ. (' because he is a son man ') with the following μὴ θαυμάζετε (' marvel not '), a construction justly condemned by Baumgarten-Crusius. If we have hit the right point in our division, this connection is altogether impossible, as will at once be perceived. Such a fragmentary sentence as καὶ ... ποιεῖν (' and ... also,' ver. 27) cannot be the development of the second thought. It would in that case lack all reason and all analogy in and with what precedes.

At the same time, it is true that the argument cannot be ' because the Father, namely, the concealed God, cannot judge ' (De Wette). This would find its contrast, not in the Son of man, but in the Son of God. Baumgarten-Crusius[2] explains it thus: ' The human nature is demanded by the judgment,' because the judgment ' requires a direct, decided, and complete influence upon man.' In regard to this, I must confess, for my part, that I cannot obtain a clear conception of what is intended by the thought, seeing that it is not further developed. Hebrews iv. 15 has nothing to do with this thought of Baumgarten-Crusius'. And, finally, Godet's explanation is that the judgment is founded upon the incarnation, because the judgment is an act of homage towards God, and therefore must go forth from the bosom of humanity; and because by that, humanity has become the property of Christ. To me this seems to

[1] Hofmann, *Der Schriftbeweis*, 2d ed., Nördlingen 1859, vol. ii. part i. p. 79.

[2] Baumgarten-Crusius, *Theologische Auslegung der Johanneischen Schriften*, Jena 1843, p. 207.

combine things which are too widely different, and if the train of thought be clearly pursued, to lead in the end to the view given above.

VERSE 28.

Jesus, because he has become man, administers judgment for God. This saying calls forth, not a confused,[1] but an unbelieving astonishment. The thing which surprises the Jews is twofold. In the first place, it is singular that Jesus should speak of a judgment at hand. They see clearly from his words a moment before, καὶ νῦν ἐστίν ('and now is'), ver. 25, that his meaning is that the judgment is already in process of execution, and yet they can perceive nothing of the kind. And, in the second place, it is singular that he should speak of the execution of the judgment of God when he stands before them as one like them, and wishes to speak thus for that very reason. This should not seem strange to them. For, on the one hand, it will in the future be revealed and will complete itself externally. And, on the other hand, ver. 29, it will be completed in such a way that an almighty call shall proceed from him and summon the dead from their graves to the final separation.

Thus he explains both the presence of, and his words concerning his relation to, the judgment, by this reference to the future of the judgment. But the argument is of such a kind as only to increase their surprise, since it is an argument only for belief. Jesus can so little dispense the Jews from rendering belief, that his explanation is altogether based upon that presupposition. Indeed, the proof of that which they are to believe demands still greater belief. What he says of the future sounds still more wonderful than what he had said previously. These words, however, were not meant to quell their surprise by this surprising statement (thus Meyer); they are, on the contrary, a proof, one which, it is true, demands belief; compare Lücke. Jesus speaks here of the future: ἔρχεται ὥρα ('the hour cometh') without καὶ νῦν ἐστίν ('and now

[1] Stier, *Reden Jesu*, 3d ed., Barmen and Elberfeld 1870, vol. iv. p. 220.

is'). *The hour is coming, in the which all that are in the graves shall hear his voice.* John's gospel is as well aware of the future judgment as a historical fact as the synoptists are, and knows nothing merely of an internal judgment, which constantly takes place. The future judgment, however, certainly is only the completion and appearance of the essential judgment, which at present is already in process.

VERSE 29.

As it now is, so will it come to pass in the future. Jesus' call pressed its way to all of them, and excited emotion in them all, but only to life in belief for those who 'did the truth,' iii. 21. In the case of the others, it was unto the judgment of unbelief. Thus is it here said to be in the future resurrection: *and shall come forth; they that have done good, unto the resurrection of life; and they that have done evil, unto the resurrection of damnation.* It is unnecessary to prove, against Baumgarten-Crusius, that the above-given meaning is correct. The ground for the distinction is called, not in the first place belief or unbelief, but a moral doing, or rather belief is named as the real, moral posture.[1] It does not say good and bad things in general, but the article is added. He who, as one φαῦλα πράσσων ('doing evil things'), iii. 20, refuses to come to the light, has thereby done τὸ φαῦλον, 'the evil thing,' so that at last he is condemned as one τὰ φαῦλα πράσσων ('doing the evil things'), namely, for his life of unbelief. And likewise, on the other side, belief is the ground for the fact that the life-posture of the man no longer is properly called a ποιεῖν ἀγαθά ('doing good'), but a ποιεῖν τὰ ἀγαθά ('doing the good things'), namely, the right conduct.

It accordingly is a consequence of belief and of unbelief, that the resurrection is at once a resurrection of life or of judgment. For the genitive in ζωῆσ ('life') and κρίσεωσ ('judgment') is not to be resolved into εἰσ ('unto'), as

[1] Lücke, *Commentar über das Evangelium des Johannes*, 3d ed., Bonn 1840, vol. ii. p. 68.

De Wette, Lücke, Meyer, Baumgarten-Crusius, and Winer[1] think it should be. The sense is not that each will become the lot of each afterwards, but that as they had already the one or the other by belief or unbelief, so that is at once their lot, essentially, when and as soon as they rise. No regard is here paid to the question whether or not it will be assigned to them by a declarative act. Yet that is in no way excluded by the account. Even in spite of such a declaration, the resurrections remain, the one a life-resurrection, the other a judgment-resurrection. That is to say, the genitive designates what is proper to the resurrection on the one side and on the other. Σῶμα θανάτου ('body of death'), Rom. vii. 24, is not a body which leads to death,[2] but one to which death belongs. This and the meaning of σῶμα τῆσ ἁμαρτίασ ('body of sin'), Rom. vi. 6, and of σῶμα τῆσ σαρκόσ ('body of flesh'), Col. i. 22, guide us to the due sense of the passage before us. The genitive betokens not the destination of, but the character of the thing, in the cases just mentioned, of the body, in the case under discussion, of the resurrection.

VERSE 30.

Such is his judgment. Jesus, however, based his declaration, concerning the impartation of life which he exercises, upon his equality of being with the Father, given with the dependence of being. In like manner he bases this second declaration upon his equality of will with the Father, given with the dependence of will. *I can of mine own self do nothing: as I hear, I judge: and my judgment is just; because I seek not my own will, but the will of the Father which hath sent me.* In the twenty-seventh verse he established the consignment of the judgment to him as a part of the history of salvation. In the twenty-eighth and the following verse he verified the possibility of this as a matter of fact. Here he confirms his declaration, concerning his judgment, morally by repeating the statement as to his

---

[1] Winer, *Grammatik des neutestamentlichen Sprachidioms*, § 30. 2. β., 7th ed., Leipzig 1867, p. 177 f.

[2] Winer, *ut supra*.

relation to the Father in general, with which he began the development in ver. 19. The substance of the two verses is the same. In the former βλέπειν ('to see'), in this one ἀκούειν ('to hear'), is the expression for the internal communion and intercourse between the Father and the Son in spirit. He executes the will of God, as it thus becomes known to him, because the will of the Father is his will. It is true the two wills are here contrasted with each other, but that is only abstractly said; compare Baumgarten-Crusius. If it be God's will that he executes, his judgment must be a righteous one. Thus in the words καθὼσ ἀκούω κρίνω ('as I hear, I judge'), the other point, that the judgment is just, is already necessarily contained in this, and does not hereafter follow as a second point (Schleiermacher, Baumgarten-Crusius).

The dependence which he declares of himself in respect to the Father, is accordingly in every view such a one that it has equality as its substance. With this thought he closes the circle of thought. But he has formulated it to a personal declaration, and retains this form also in what follows. This, however, is no proof that 'the second part of this discourse' begins with the thirtieth verse (Stier, compare against him De Wette, Lücke, and Baumgarten-Crusius). Yet it is true that, according to the custom of our gospel, the conclusion forms the transition to that which is new. That dependent equality of working, as he described it in the impartation of ζωή ('life') and the execution of the κρίσισ ('judgment'), was the foundation of his demand for God-like τιμή ('honour'). Thus, then, he proceeds to this latter thought. The discourse is not put together in such a hap-hazard way as to pay respect only 'to objections and misunderstandings and to the unbelief of the Jews' (De Wette, Lücke, and Meyer). It is certainly the case (similarly Baumgarten-Crusius) that Jesus, after having previously treated of his relation to the Father, now in vers. 31–47 speaks of his relation to the Jews, and thereby as to substance (against Meyer), if not as to very words, he returns to the claim made in the twenty-third verse.

Verses 31–47.

By the testimony to him, lying outside of him, he establishes the right of his declaration concerning that dependent equality, and the right of his grounding upon it the claim for τιμή ('honour') or for belief. These must make up to him for the honour which the Jews will not permit themselves to be moved to give him, even upon such testimony. It is a double witness: a man's and God's; the Baptist's and the Father's. But he could cite still another, his own. He begins with this.

Verses 31, 32.

If I bear witness of myself, my witness is not true. If he should bear witness to himself, he would do it in unison with God's witness to him, or as a testimony of God himself, and therefore agreeably to the truth, viii. 14. But since the Jews do not concede to him such unity with God, and do isolate him from God, he now, according to the common rule of law, by reason of which no man can testify in his own case, cannot appeal to his own testimony in such isolation, but only to God's. *There is another that beareth witness of me; and I know that his witness which he witnesseth of me is true.* He speaks of the testimony as of one foreign to him and outside of him, which is given concerning him. It is a matter of course, that, as most commentators agree, he means God by this ἄλλος ('another'), whose testimony he knows to be true, and not John the Baptist (thus Chrysostom, Theophylact, Grotius, Baumgarten-Crusius, De Wette, and Ewald). He alone forms the true contrast to Jesus' own human testimony considered as isolated.[1] Nor does Jesus indeed wish to make the Baptist's testimony his support, ver. 34.

As to God's testimony, however, he knows that it is true. For οἶδα ('I know'), and not οἴδατε ('ye know;' Tischendorf, following the Sinaitic manuscript), is the right reading. Οἴδατε may have arisen from the following ὅτι by a slip in writing. Or some one may have corrected it purposely,

[1] Stier, *Reden Jesu*, 3d ed., Barmen and Elberfeld 1870, vol. iv. p. 225.

thinking (as De Wette did) that οἶδα was a guarantee that said very little. As a fact, however, the οἶδα is full of expression, just because of its simplicity and by its emphasizing Jesus' self-consciousness; and its impression is supported by the repetitive form of expression: μαρτυρίαν μαρτυρεῖν ('to witness witness'). The progress of the discourse is simply this: It is true I could appeal to John's testimony, but I did not refer to him, and I will not appeal to him, for I have, etc. This is found in what follows.

VERSES 33–35.

The importance of the Baptist for the history of salvation, and the posture of Israel towards him, are here strikingly characterized in two statements.

VERSE 33.

Ye sent unto John, and he bare witness unto the truth. John was nothing but a μαρτυρία τῇ ἀληθείᾳ ('witness to the truth'), namely, to the substantial truth which is offered in Christ. The Baptist's whole importance is exhausted in this; compare i. 7, 8, 23.

VERSE 34.

But Jesus does not take such testimony as a proof. He will not allow himself to receive His (τήν, 'the') testimony from *a man*, so as to rest on it. He reminds the Jews, however, of this testimony and of their embassy to the Baptist, i. 19 ff., with the purpose that they may thereby be induced to lay hold of the salvation in Christ. Λαμβάνω is to be taken in the simple meaning of reception. We are not to substitute for it 'longing after,' etc. (De Wette), or 'striving' or 'grasping' (Baumgarten-Crusius); compare also Meyer.

VERSE 35.

As such a μαρτυρία ('testimony'), the Baptist is the light which should cause the eyes of Israel to recognise the saving form of Christ. He is not τὸ φῶσ ('the light'), but ἵνα μαρτυρήσῃ περὶ τοῦ φωτόσ, ἵνα πάντεσ πιστεύσωσιν δι' αὐτοῦ ('to bear witness of the light, that all through him might believe,' i. 7). He is to place Christ in the light for Israel. If the figure of the light here has this reference, it will for that very reason, aside from the further improbability, not be intended to refer to Sirach xlviii. 1 (Bengel, Lücke, Meyer, Stier), where the sense of the figure is quite different. If the latter reference had been intended, why was λύχνοσ used instead of λαμπάσ, the word in Sirach? The article does not point out: that which was said previously in the Old Testament (Bengel), nor: that which should bring you to the way of truth (De Wette). For this light did not go before the Jews, perhaps like the pillar of fire in the desert, but before Christ.

The article, then, must be explained from that point of view. As Jesus is not a φῶσ ('light') in general, but τὸ φῶσ ('the light'), so also the Baptist is ὁ λύχνοσ ('the light'): 'which went before me,' or 'which should go before me.' This very position makes him a light in an eminent sense. Since Christ had come into the σκοτία ('darkness'), his herald had to bear the torch before Him, for Him as well as for others, to point out the way for Him, and to show Him to others. We may also perhaps recall the figure, iii. 28, 29, in which the Baptist calls Him the bridegroom before whom he goes; compare the same figure in Matt. ix. 15, and the parallel passages in Mark and Luke, see also Matt. xxiv. 1 ff. But the coming of the bridegroom there spoken of takes place at night; compare Matt. xxiv. 1 ff. Hence they bear a light before him. The fact that λύχνοσ is used instead of λαμπάσ need not cause us to hesitate. The Baptist comes under consideration, not only in so far as he moved hither in front of Christ, like a torch, but also in so far as he made it light before Him, and made Him clearly visible. It would not be particularly advisable to use the figure of the torch personally.

Instead of permitting themselves to be directed by this light, they only used it for a momentary pleasure: *He was a burning and a shining light: and ye were willing for a season to rejoice in his light.* This characterizes Israel's behaviour. It is not intended merely to say, that they took pleasure in it in a boyish way,[1] or merely that they had played with it and had followed after what was new in it (Baumgarten-Crusius, De Wette). The idea is, that they permitted the appearance of the prophet to serve the delighting of the flesh, namely, the feeding of their vanity. Besser recalls fitly Ezek. xxxiii. 30 f., where the vain joy of the people over their prophet is described; a joy which lacked obedience to his word, and moral pleasure in this particular method of God's revelation.

VERSES 36–39.

Jesus now names his own peculiar testimony, the Father's, which the Father offers doubly, in his work and in the Scriptures.

VERSE 36.

I have testimony which is greater than that of *John*—τῆσ before τοῦ Ἰωάννου is wanting, according to the so-called 'comparatio compendiaria' ('contracted comparison'); —*for the works which the Father hath given me to finish, the same works that I do, bear witness of me that the Father hath sent me.* He names the works first. In these he was superior to the Baptist, x. 41, so that no one could be in doubt as to who was the greatest. The works were both a proof of and a representation of his divine Sonship, and therefore of the δόξα ('glory') which was in him, and of his calling. They all belonged to the one great work of his life, which he must yet bring to an end, for which reason he says, not ἵνα ποιήσω ('to do'), but ἵνα τελειώσω ('to finish'); compare iv. 34, xvii. 4.[2]

But although he can only after a while bring them to an end, yet he is already doing them, ἃ ποιῶ ('that I do'). He presents himself as God's Son, he reveals and works life, he effects belief, and so forth. Such action he has as a charge from the Father, just as he has the power to do

---

[1] Lücke, *Commentar über das Evangelium des Johannes*, 3d ed., Bonn 1843, vol. ii. p. 75.

[2] See also Stier, *Reden Jesu*, 3d ed., Barmen and Elberfeld 1870, vol. iv. p. 232.

such things as an ability dependent upon the Father, though it be essentially his own in that he is God's Son. Both these points are contained in δέδωκεν ('hath given'). It is not mere commission (De Wette), and not bestowal of power (Baumgarten-Crusius). It might rather be called: empowering (Lücke). It is the Father's will, which he executes by virtue of his dependent communion with the Father. Hence they are a testimony of the Father's to him, just as they are elsewhere called the Father's own works, xiv. 10, which execute themselves by means of the Son. Substantially nothing else is said here than in the words ver. 19 ff., which betoken the relation of the Son to the Father in his activity. He testifies to himself as God's Son (ὅτι ὁ πατήρ με ἀπέσταλκεν, 'that the Father hath sent me'), in this passage as well as in that one, only from the special side.

VERSE 37.

And the Father himself, which hath sent me, hath borne witness of me. The other testimony of the Father's is given more directly, namely, in the word. Vers. 37-39 treat of this (Lücke, Maier, Meyer). Some have, indeed, wished to understand in the thirty-seventh verse, not the word, but a third thing, the voice of God at the baptism of Jesus (Bengel, Lücke, Godet), or the inward, direct drawing of the Father to the Son (De Wette, Baumgarten-Crusius, Tholuck). The last notion is urged for the sake of the climax, said to lie (De Wette) in καὶ ... αὐτόσ, or more correctly with ℵ B L ἐκεῖνοσ ('he'). But is not then the word of God, as it came to the prophets, a higher thing than the ἔργα ('works')? At least it was chiefly on account of that word that men were to believe on Jesus. Even the apostles in their preaching of Jesus as the Christ always laid the prophets' testimony as the foundation. Moreover, αὐτόσ would not be at all climactic in De Wette's sense. It would designate the contrast between the direct testimony and the testimony in the work. The latter, namely, is indirect in comparison with the former, because it itself always needed first the explaining word. This relation remains unchanged also with the reading ἐκεῖνοσ, which, with emphatic reference, lays stress on the personal testimony, as contrasted with the material testimony of the words.

Moreover, we can urge against De Wette's and Baumgarten-Crusius' view, not only the perfect, but also the second half of the thirty-seventh verse, which cannot be interpreted in a clear, simple sense in this way. Baumgarten-Crusius finds the thought: the Father has never until now made himself known as he now does. For this, the words would have to read otherwise, and be otherwise arranged and connected. The thirty-eighth verse connects too closely with the thirty-seventh, to permit us to begin the testimony in the Scriptures at this point (Baumgarten-Crusius). Besides those named above, even Stier[1] had declared himself against the arbitrary reference to the baptism of Jesus. But when he assents to the plan of those who say that the testimony of the works is still treated of here (Olshausen, for example), he only makes the matter worse. Everything goes to show that ver. 37 adds something new to what precedes; compare Lücke.

Ye have neither heard his voice at any time nor seen his shape. God's call comes to them in the word of the Old Testament Scriptures, and God gives himself to be known of them. They are sealed for both. And the word itself, which they ought to bear in themselves in believing reception as the life of their life, as their thought and their hope, is a foreign thing to them, much as they may study the letter of it. If this be a correct representation of the contents of vers. 37–39, it is clear at once that φωνή and εἶδοσ ('voice' and 'shape') are not to be explained from a symbolism peculiar to the Old Testament revelation and to a recalling it: as if, for instance, Isaiah and Jeremiah had heard the φωνή of God, and Ezekiel and Daniel beheld his εἶδοσ in spirit;[2] or as if Jehovah had appeared in the angel of the Lord (Hengstenberg); or as if Jesus brought to the view of the Jews of that day the fact that

---

[1] Stier, *Reden Jesu*, 3d ed., Barmen and Elberfeld 1870, vol. iv. p. 252.

[2] Lücke, *Commentar über das Evangelium des Johannes*, 3d ed., Bonn 1843, vol. ii. p. 83.

they lived in an age without a revelation, and that they should see a primitive judgment in that fact.[1] All this would be foreign to the connection of the thoughts. On the contrary, the whole revelation, as deposited in the Old Testament, is meant as the self-representation of God (Meyer). The point is that God's call is issued to Israel, and that his shape reveals itself to his people in the word of the Old Testament Scriptures. Israel, however, has remained deaf and blind to it.

VERSE 38.

And ye have not his word abiding in you: for whom he hath sent, him ye believe not. The revelation of God is for the Jews not the word of God, because they have it not in them. This is the relation of the third sentence, καὶ τὸν λόγον κ.τ.λ. ('and ... his word,' etc.), the thirty-eighth verse, to the two preceding sentences; hence the change of form. It is true they have the words of Scripture in their book-rolls and in the schools, but it is not living and dwelling in them.

If this silent contrast be correct, it is then plain that λόγος is simply the word, and not the spirit of the revelation (De Wette, Baumgarten-Crusius), or the revelation in the conscience (Olshausen, Frommann). Ὁ λόγος ('the word') is not contrasted with the letter, but ἐν ὑμῖν κ.τ.λ. ('in you,' etc.) with the external possession. How could this latter be said of the letter? The point in question is, the proper place for keeping the word. The emphasis does not lie upon μένοντα ('abiding'), because it is the contrast, so that the continuity of the internal possession of it should be made prominent (Olshausen, Meyer, and in part Lücke), but rather on the ἐν ὑμῖν ('in you'), so that the possession is declared not to be internal. This showed and punished itself in the circumstance that they did not believe (τούτῳ ὑμεῖς, 'him ye,' with emphatic juxtaposition) in him, who, as the conclusion of all divine messengers, is the substance of the Old Testament word. Since this word did not live within them, it could not give them

[1] Weiss, *Der johanneische Lehrbegriff*, Berlin 1866, p. 104 f.

internal testimony that Jesus was the one whom it had in view.

Verse 39.

Ye search the Scriptures. The argument adduced in the thirty-eighth verse needed a justification. This lies in the fact that He is the substance of the word. Thus one who assumes the proper position towards the word, also assumes the proper position towards his person, and contrariwise. Hence from the failure to believe in him it is possible to conclude what the relation to the word is. That justification of this conclusion is offered in the verse before us, the thirty-ninth.

Whether ἐρευνᾶτε ('search') is to be taken as an imperative or as an indicative, that is, whether the justification follows in the form of a demand, or argues 'e concessis' ('from what is granted'), is an old contested question. Almost all modern commentators regard it as an indicative. Only a few, Baumgarten-Crusius, Tholuck, Hofmann,[1] Stier,[2] and Hengstenberg, for example, hold firmly to the imperative conception of it, as most of the older commentators do. After the preceding sentence, that the Jews lacked the true inward possession of the word, and therefore lacked belief in him, ἐρευνᾶτε, taken as an imperative, would be a demand that they should obtain such a possession by a study which should force its way into the matter. They busied themselves much with the Scriptures outwardly, but wanted the true ἐρευνᾶν ('searching'); compare 1 Peter i. 11. But this emphatic conception of ἐρευνᾶν is hardly justified. The Jews had searched the Scriptures sufficiently, only not in the right sense and spirit. They made a great to-do over the letter, but they did not find the real substance of the Scriptures. Ἐρευνᾶτε, therefore, is to be taken as a concession, as the indicative, in order from that point to argue against the Jews. In this way, Jesus' words remain in unison with what precedes: ye have the Scriptures indeed outwardly,

---

[1] Hofmann, *Der Schriftbeweis*, 2d ed., Nördlingen 1857, vol. i. p. 671.
[2] Stier, *Reden Jesu*, 3d ed., Barmen and Elberfeld 1870, vol. iv. p. 236 f.

but not inwardly; ye search them indeed, but ye do not find the real kernel.

They search the Holy Scriptures because they lay great weight on them. Ὑμεῖσ—put first for emphasis—*ye yourselves think ye have*, possess, *eternal life in them;* and even *they*—ἐκεῖναι, emphatic, according to John's habit—*are they which testify of me*. Hence they ought to find him in them, and so come to him. Δοκεῖτε ('ye think') is the simple expression of a fact, and in itself implies neither approbation nor blame. We shall therefore not say, with Stier,[1] that Jesus 'rejects' the Jewish opinion 'as a proud lying fancy.'[2] Nor shall we be able to take the words directly as an approbation, for the following words show under what condition alone that meaning contains the truth. 'While they think they possess eternal life in the Scriptures, they will not come to him of whom the Scriptures testify. They therefore will not gain eternal life, although indeed it be to be found in the Scriptures, because they do not find therein him who is the essential substance of the Scriptures, and who makes them the book of eternal life.'[3] Because he wished δοκεῖτε ('ye think') to be understood in this way, Jesus chooses purposely the expression, that they thought they had in the Scriptures, not mere knowledge or the like, but eternal life.

The essential blessing of salvation, the state of being, which is filled with salvation, is in the Scriptures, in so far as they proclaim it, and impart it by their proclamation of it. But they bear it in themselves, proclaim and impart it, in so far as and because they bear in themselves, proclaim, and impart Christ. Observe, also, that this is said of the whole of the Scriptures. And the essential peculiarity and characteristic of this whole is said to be that it is a testimony to Christ, as, on the other hand, the true testimony to him is said to be contained in it.

[1] Stier, *Reden Jesu*, 3d ed., Barmen and Elberfeld 1870, vol. iv. p. 239.

[2] Similarly Hilgenfeld, *Das Evangelium und die Briefe Johannis nach ihrem Lehrbegriff dargestellt*, Halle 1849, p. 213; *Die Evangelien*, Leipzig 1854, p. 272; *Zeitschrift für wissenschaftliche Theologie*, 1863, p. 217, because the word of the Old Testament comes from the demiurge.

[3] Hofmann, *Der Schriftbeweis*, 2d ed., Nördlingen 1857, vol. i. p. 671.

Verse 40.

And ye will not come to me, that ye might have life. If, upon the condition that they assumed the proper posture towards the Scripture, they must necessarily be led to him, then the fact that they do not come to him is a sign that they do not wish to come to him, do not wish to have life in him. Οὐ θέλετε ('ye will not') has the emphasis. And the simple καί ('and') of itself makes the accusation of not wishing only the more emphatic. Instead of saying: ye will not believe, it says, 'ye will not come to me.' This is in order to lay stress on their own free action in belief and non-belief, namely, on that which is so fraught with responsibility. Jesus has brought the matter so far that the unbelief is based merely in their will, and appears merely as their guilt. In this he has stated the theme, which is now to be developed. Hence as to the thought we must connect the fortieth verse with what follows. Ye could believe on me, but ye will not believe on me; ye should give me the honour due, but ye will not. This paragraph of Jesus' discourse divides into these two sentences.

The naming of the testimonies, vers. 31–39, with which his Father gives him honour, had served to establish and develop the ability and the duty of belief. Vers. 40–47 develop the not willing. This takes place in three parts. Vers. 40–43 present their unwillingness itself, ver. 44 presents their moral incapacity to believe, and vers. 45–47 present the judgment upon their unbelief.

Verses 40-43.

Verse 41.

They will not believe. Ver. 41 also serves this thought, though its logical connection with the others has always been regarded as difficult. It does not serve to confirm ver. 40, for that verse is complete in itself, and has its keenness in the very fact that it is said purely for itself. Nor does Jesus wish to ward off the suspicion that he possibly urged belief upon them out of a vain desire for honour (De Wette, also Lücke and Meyer); for his tone is too polemical for such a consideration, although this explanation is nearer the right thing than the former one was. Nor does Jesus merely wish to contrast his disposition in reference to God and the love of that which is divine with theirs, ver. 42 (Baumgarten-Crusius); for then the contrast would lie in the fact that he did not seek human honour, while they did. How could δόξαν ('glory') be then put first? The contrast is to be sought in this.

Jesus speaks these words in a polemical tone. Hence ver. 41 serves the accusation which he brings against the Jews. That is to say, he brings this accusation against them, not, perchance, because he is concerned about empty honour from men, and because they did not show him such honour, but because he perceives from their unbelief that they are lacking in the proper disposition towards God and that which is divine. He accuses them, not because of honour which they failed to show towards him, but because of their ungodly disposition. This is the correct logical relation of vers. 40, 41, and 42 to each other. It is clear from this why δόξα ('glory') is put first. 'Honour from men, which he possibly longed for, is by no means the thing which made him say that, ver. 40, but it was the recognition and perception of the fact, that,' etc.

VERSE 42.

What he perceives in them is that they have not the love of God in them. Ἀλλὰ ἔγνωκα ὑμᾶσ[1] ὅτι οὐκ ἔχετε τὴν ἀγάπην τοῦ θεοῦ ἐν ἑαυτοῖσ: *But I know you, that ye have not the love of God in you.* If that were the 'drawing towards God, the striving after that which is divine,' as Baumgarten-Crusius explains it, would not θεοῦ ('God') stand without the article, as indeed he repeatedly writes it?[2]

---

[1] Bengel, *Gnomon ad locum*: ἔγνωκα ὑμᾶσ cognitos vos habeo; hoc radio penetrat corda auditorum. ('I know you; with this ray he pierces the hearts of his hearers.')

[2] Baumgarten-Crusius, *Theologische Auslegung der Johanneischen Schriften*, Jena 1843, vol. i. p. 222 f.

Stier demands that, in accordance with the New Testament use of language, the genitive be taken subjectively. He might also have referred to the preceding καὶ τὸν λόγον αὐτοῦ οὐκ ἔχετε, κ.τ.λ. ('and ye have not his word,' etc.). But the words taken in this sense will not give any suitable meaning. Ἡ ἀγάπη τοῦ θεοῦ ('the love of God') would have to be the revelation of God's love in the Old Testament. This turn of the thought, however, is not suggested by the context. We shall therefore have to cling to the usual conception of the passage. Τὴν ἀγάπην ('the love') is said because the love due is meant; and τοῦ θεοῦ ('of God') because it is the love due to the God of Israel.

The matter in question, therefore, is not an ungodly disposition in general, but a lack of the Israelitic religious disposition. 'They do not desire Jesus; for they are not true Israelites.' This last thought is presented first in view of the position of heart due towards God, and then later in view of the proper position towards the scriptural word of God. If the judgment of moral religious incapacity follows upon the lack of the former, ver. 44, the latter includes the judgment in itself, in so far as the book of revelation thereby becomes for them a book of accusation; see ver. 45. If this be correct, it is clear that the true ground of the seeking for honour is not meant to be given in ἀγάπη τοῦ θεοῦ ('love of God'); thus Lücke. It is likewise plain that the emphasis does not lie on ἐν ἑαυτοῖσ ('in you'), in the sense that they only boasted in their legal acts of love towards God, while this love was not the inmost spring of life in them.[1] The stress really bears upon the points, urged by the articles, of love as a due manifestation of duty, and of God as their God. Ἐν ἑαυτοῖσ ('in you') will then express the fact that such love is foreign to them.

Verse 43.

I am come in my Father's name, and ye received me not: if another shall come in his own name, him ye will receive. What wonder is it that they do not receive him in belief,

---

[1] Lücke, *Commentar über das Evangelium des Johannes*, 3d ed., Bonn 1843, vol. ii. p. 43.

since he came to them in the name of his Father, their God? For only on condition that that posture of heart towards God was theirs, only on condition that they were true Israelites, would they find again their God in him, in whose name and from whom Jesus declared that he came. In this the discourse indeed already passes over to the thought: you could not do otherwise.[1] Yet that is only a preparation for the display of this point made in the following verse. Here the λαμβάνετε and λήψεσθε ('ye receive' and 'ye will receive') give the impression that the deed is intended to be called a free one. They wish to know nothing of Jesus. For they will not have their God as he offers himself to them; and Jesus in all his actions presents himself as one, the basis and the substance of whose sending lie in the saving will of their God, his Father. This is what is meant by ἐν τῷ ὀνόματι τοῦ πατρόσ μου ('in the name of my Father'), and not mere 'divine willing, urging' (Baumgarten-Crusius).

On the contrary, he who finds the basis and the substance of his actions solely in his own will and pleasure, comes in his own name. The most fitting thing here is to think of the false Messiahs in Israel, not only on account of the relation of the ἔλθῃ ('shall come') to the ἐλήλυθα ('am come'), but above all on account of ἄλλοσ ('another'), which indicates a certain formal likeness of the one to whom they attach themselves, to Jesus whom they reject. Such a one they will receive and cleave to, because he will not demand love to God, but will satisfy their self-love, flatter their national vanity, and establish the kingdom of God in outward might and glory. Christ's words were fulfilled in Barkochba (to whom Hilgenfeld refers them, dating the gospel later), but not in him alone. Since the time of Christ, sixty-four such deceivers have been observed; compare Bengel and Meyer.

Verse 44.

How can ye believe, which receive honour one of another, and seek not the honour that cometh from the only God?

[1] Stier, *Reden Jesu*, 3d ed., Barmen and Elberfeld 1870, vol. iv. p. 244.

This is the very reason they cannot do otherwise. Of course the inability here spoken of is only a moral and self-caused inability, and not one presented by virtue of an alleged dualistic view (against Hilgenfeld and others). This moral inability is based on their whole religious and moral character. In them is found the reverse of what is found in Jesus; see ver. 41. He has only the will of God as the reason and substance of all his actions, but the Jews, on the contrary, do not care in the least to attain the glory which God's love desires to offer them. On the contrary, they with eagerness accept mutually from each other the honours by which human fancy on this side and that endeavours to glorify itself. God is here presented as ὁ μόνοσ θεόσ ('the only God')—the words are to be understood thus, and not as: God only (De Wette, Godet)—in order to indicate that he also alone can give true δόξα, 'glory' (Meyer), that we may and must seek it only at his hand. Why should that not touch the Israelites above all, since their God is indeed ὁ μόνοσ θεόσ?

With these words Jesus has again designated the essential vice and sins of the Israel of his day: the pride in the external Israelitic glory, and the unwillingness so to receive as a gift, and so to desire, the true glory of Israel, as the God of their salvation wishes to give it to them; compare Matt. xi. 16 ff. The forty-fourth verse has usually been understood in too wide a generality, 'as if it referred in general to a worthless vain state of being, as a ground of the inability to receive the true and the divine;'[1] or to satanic pride as the absolute hindrance to belief;[2] or in general to ambition (De Wette). Jesus' accusation rather aims at this: that they are not true Israelites, and therefore do not become Christians. The δόξαν παρὰ ἀλλήλων λαμβάνοντεσ ('receiving honour one from another') is therefore a designation of later Judaism, namely, of that Jewish vanity by reason of which the separate Jews displayed and attributed unto themselves boastingly the advantages of the

---

[1] Baumgarten-Crusius, *Theologische Auslegung der Johanneischen Schriften*, Jena 1843, vol. i. p. 223.
[2] Stier. *Reden Jesu*, 3d ed., Barmen and Elberfeld 1870, vol. iv. p. 244.

Jews, and thus honoured each other mutually as Jews, while they at the same time lost the true Jewish glory, which God had prepared in Jesus. In this the discourse makes the transition to the emphasizing of the judgment upon them that is contained in this their unbelief.

VERSES 45–47.

Jesus designates the judgment upon their unbelief in two ways. He denies to them the future and the present of an Israelite.

VERSE 45.

The former he presents, not by displaying to them how, instead of sharing the future of His salvation, they will fall under His judgment, but how, instead of obtaining the hope of Moses, they will fall under his accusation and condemnation. *Do not think that I will accuse you to the Father.* It is not as if he intended to say some different thing by the words about Moses; he only lends the statement by that means a greater sharpness. For, when he says of them that they have set their hopes upon Moses, the meaning is simply that they are on account of Moses sure of their share in the glory of the Messianic kingdom. This, however, is the future which Jesus gives. For, this reason they incur Moses' accusation, and therefore the condemnation of the law and of the word of the Old Testament in general; that is to say, they have no part in the future of Israel. If this be the case, Jesus does not need specially to accuse them before the Father, perhaps, for instance, in prayer: ἔστιν, *there is one that accuseth you, Moses, in whom ye have trusted,* have set and do set your hopes; observe the perfect. The reason for naming Moses is easily to be seen, when we consider the importance of his position in the Old Testament. In contrast with the son of the house, he is the faithful servant in the house, Heb. iii. 5, and therefore the representative of the entire old covenant. Indeed, zeal for Moses' law was the occasion for this proceeding, and the Jews decorated themselves eagerly by references to Moses and their discipleship in Moses; ix. 28, 29.

Verse 46.

For had ye believed Moses, ye would have believed me: for he wrote of me. Jesus had just denied them the future. He now denies them the present. They are by no means Moses' disciples. They boast themselves in him, but they do not belong to him, because they lack the religious posture of belief on his word. This belief would necessarily shape itself into a believing posture towards Jesus, since he is the contents of Moses' word. Περὶ ἐμοῦ ἐκεῖνοσ ἔγραψεν ('he wrote of me') is intended in this sense, and not simply as an allusion to various Messianic passages in the Pentateuch, such as Deut. xviii. 15 (De Wette), or to these in union with the patriarchal promises (Lücke). The words of Jesus are too general for that. On the other hand, it is true, it is not intended to designate 'the Christ-related disposition presented in the Holy Scriptures.'[1] What definite idea are we to conceive of under these words, if not the proclamation of Christ himself in the Old Testament Scriptures? And this indeed is 'nusquam non' —'nowhere lacking' (Bengel, Meyer); compare Luke xxiv. 44. Even the history written by Moses is all so conceived that it becomes a preparatory history and a preparatory presentation of Christ, because it is grasped and developed in its essential importance.

Verse 47.

But if ye believe not his writings, how shall ye believe my words? If they do not accept in belief Moses' word as a proclamation of salvation, they in truth cannot recognise, and accept in belief, in Jesus' self-witness the presence of the salvation preached by Moses. The emphasis, following the contrast, rests not on γράμμασιν ('writings') and ῥήμασιν ('words'), but on ἐκείνου ('his') and τοῖσ ἐμοῖσ ('mine'); see Meyer against De Wette, Lücke, and Stier.[2] For that Moses' words should be given in writing, and

---

[1] Baumgarten-Crusius, *Theologische Auslegung der johanneischen Schriften*, Jena 1843, vol. i. p. 225.

[2] Stier, *Reden Jesu*, 3d ed., Barmen and Elberfeld 1870, vol. iv. p. 249.

Jesus' words, on the contrary, be mouth to mouth, lay in the nature of the case. Nothing else was to be expected, and accordingly this could not form the contrast in the thoughts, or even a special point in the contrast. As far as the contrast is concerned, this distinction is a matter of chance and of indifference.

In this way Jesus has traced back to its foundation the unbelief of Israel towards his person. They are not Israel, they are not Moses' disciples, or they would become Jesus' disciples and Christ's church. By this means he has passed from the defence to the accusation,[1] and that to an accusation which corresponds to the one brought against Jesus. For they had reproached him with having sinned against the fundamental order of Israel, and they believed they had a right in that case to assume to condemn his claim. Jesus now justifies himself by his divine right. And he condemns them as having lost their claim to membership in the true Israel, and thereby also as having lost the ability to believe in him.

Summary.

The Son of God established on the part of his activity, and belief upon the basis of the divine testimony to him : such are the contents of Jesus' discourse. Moreover, he is so sufficiently divinely witnessed to as the Son of God, and accordingly the belief is so sufficiently divinely established, that the ground for unbelief can only lie in an ungodly will, and is proved by Jesus to lie therein. Through these things this first discourse of the conflict, and this first meeting, obtain a certain decisive character. As the murderous disposition of the Jews is made plain, so also is the fact that they are condemned. This is true upon the whole, though the design to save what will let itself be saved, vers. 34, 39, is not entirely shut out.

The single exceptions do not nullify the whole, nor does this under-current-like design change the character of the whole discourse. 'The endeavour to make belief more

---

[1] Lücke, *Commentar über das Evangelium des Johannes*, 3d ed., Bonn 1843, vol. ii. p. 93.

easy to the opponents from their own point of view'[1] does not dominate in it, but a tone of condemnation does. 'Ye will not, therefore ye cannot.' Hence also the evangelist needed to say nothing about 'the success of this hostile discourse.'[2] That was not the thing in point. The question touched the condemnation of the unbelief of Israel, with which Jesus closed his discourse. We shall remain more faithful to the meaning of the evangelist if we make this point prominent as the leading one, than if we follow Baur's explanation. He[3] makes the ruling thought the internal contradiction in which unbelief becomes involved with itself, or rather, which is brought about by the dialectic development of its idea, since they wish still to hold fast to Moses and yet not to believe on Jesus. For stress is laid, not so much on the fact that they wish still to cleave to Moses, as on the fact that they do not receive his word in belief.

Now the contrast is a decidedly outspoken and determined one. All that follows will but serve to display its history, namely, to show how it develops and completes itself according to the measure of Jesus' progressive self-testimony and self-presentation.

Chapter VI.

The sixth chapter[4] serves the purpose just mentioned, though in it the parallelizing with what preceded is the most striking feature. In the first place, the sixth chapter intends to place Galilee by the side of Judea, so as to close the circle and to make plain that the conduct of Jesus and of the Jews was quite the same in the one as in the other, and that it was only believing obedience to Jesus' word which caused the formation of the beginnings of the future church. At the same time, however, the history marches forwards on both sides.

[1] Lücke, *Commentar über das Evangelium des Johannes*, 3d ed., Bonh 1843, vol. ii. p. 94.   [2] Lücke, *ut supra*, vol. ii. p. 93.
[3] Baur, *Kritische Untersuchungen über die kanonischen Evangelien*, Tübingen 1847, p. 158.
[4] [On chapter vi. see curious view of J. P. Norris, *Journal of Philology*, 1871, vol. iii. pp. 107 ff.—C. R. G.]

Jesus points still more decisively to his person in so far as it dwells in the flesh, and bids them seek life in him, the one who has become flesh. By this he demands a stronger belief than before, since he now neither appeals to the divine testimony in Scripture and in work, nor calls attention to the way in which the divine life appears in his activity. He bids them believe that life is to be found in his human nature, which he nevertheless must yield up to death, and that he, who now is in the flesh, will be raised up into the essential form of life. Nothing was to be seen of all this. And so much the more was there need of the belief which believes without seeing, xx. 29, and which cleaves only to Jesus' word, vi. 68.

At the same time, this increase of the demand for belief must work critically. It must sift among those who in their belief could not yet dispense with the support of sight. And it must rebuff those who only wished to see without believing. Thus both progress together, on the one side Jesus' self-witness as the life in the flesh, and on the other side belief and unbelief. The progress of this latter twofold bearing appears at the close; the one side in Peter's confession, the other in the fact that the hostility of unbelief assumes a place in the nearest circle of Jesus' own disciples. The evangelist takes up this single event from the Galilean activity of Jesus—which he does not treat of elsewhere, though he knows it well[1]—because it is of decisive importance. Upon the one hand it characterizes the height of Jesus' Galilean work, and on the other hand it leads in the crisis and therefore the turning-point of it.

VI. 1–71. *Jesus the Life in the Flesh.*—*The Progress of Belief and of Unbelief.*

The strife has begun. Opposition advances against Jesus in Galilee as well as in Jerusalem. Jews, 'Ιουδαῖοι, are spoken of in the synagogue at Capernaum, ver. 41, as in

---

[1] Compare vi. 1, vii. 1, and see above, vol. i. p. 232, and Luthardt, *St. John the Author of the Fourth Gospel*, Edinburgh, T. and T. Clark, 1875, p. 197.

the capital. They may have assumed whatever position they pleased among the people : in their opposition they represented it. The external occasion is offered by a miracle in which Jesus shows himself as ζωή ('life'), as in the fifth chapter. Here it is joined with the approach of the feast of the passover, the last before the death-passover of Jesus ; a year later the Lord was to die. This circumstance gives the proceedings and the discourses a peculiar importance.[1] By this means the progress of the self-witness receives its temporal background, and the turn which the discourse takes receives its temporal application. Moreover, the place at which Jesus worked the miracle, and the very form of the miracle, both of which recalled the experiences of Israel on its march through the desert, give the point of departure for the discourse. There is no need to prove how easily this connection could be combined with the passover. We need only refer to i. 29, and to what was said upon that passage.

The whole falls into three paragraphs : (1) verses 1-21 ; (2) verses 22-59 ; (3) verses 60-71.

(1.) Verses 1-21.

These verses form a connected body of typical events. We shall at once perceive that vers. 16-21 belong closely to the verses preceding them, and the typical character of the events demands that we divide at ver. 21 and not at ver. 25 (De Wette, Lücke).

Verse 1.

The evangelist begins with μετὰ ταῦτα ἀπῆλθεν ὁ Ἰησοῦσ πέραν τῆσ θαλάσσησ τῆσ Γαλιλαίασ τῆσ Τιβεριάδοσ ('after these things Jesus went over the sea of Galilee, which is the sea of Tiberias'). In doing this he places us in the very midst of the Galilean activity of Jesus. Μετὰ ταῦτα

---

[1] Compare Bruno Bauer, *Kritik der evangelischen Geschichte des Johannes*, Bremen 1840, p. 222, and Baur, *Kritische Untersuchungen über die kanonischen Evangelien*, Tübingen 1847, p. 262, in spite of the opposition of Lücke, *Commentar über das Evangelium des Johannes*, 3d ed., Bonn 1843, vol. ii. p. 105 f., Baumgarten-Crusius, and Meyer.

('after these things') does not intend to join what follows directly as to time to what precedes, but only in general puts the matter in an after time. This is made clear by a glance at the other places in which this formula of continuance occurs; it is frequently used in John's gospel.[1] Ἀπῆλθεν πέραν ('went over'), namely to the eastern shore, presupposes a stay upon the western shore, that is in Galilee (Brückner, Hengstenberg, Godet). It is impossible to refer it, as Meyer does, to Jesus' stay in Jerusalem. Such language could not be used with reference to going from Jerusalem to the eastern shore of the sea of Galilee, because the two places stand in no direct relation to each other. The case is utterly different, as every one sees, in x. 40 and xviii. 1, to which Meyer refers.

The evangelist wrote for readers who knew the synoptic account, and who approached his narrative with this historical knowledge, and with such premises as were thereby afforded. We therefore may combine this account with the synoptic one. Jesus had come forward as the prophet of Galilee in the place of the imprisoned Baptist. Starting from Capernaum, he had begun to traverse Galilee in all directions. He had also already caused his apostles— whom he had chosen from the throng of his followers to a share in his calling—to try their powers in independent activity. At the very time of their return, as we learn from the synoptic account, the news came that the Baptist was beheaded. This affected Jesus so much that he withdrew himself into the desert, without the people, only with his disciples, κατ' ἰδίαν ('apart'), Matt. xiv. 13, Mark vi. 30, 31. His own end rose before his soul, and the thought of his death moved him.

The sea is doubly named: 'the Galilean sea of Tiberias.' Tiberias, built by Herod Antipas, and named after Tiberius, elsewhere gave its name to the sea.[2] Hence it is unnecessary to assume that the addition indicates the more southern part of the sea because Tiberias lay there (Meyer). This

---

[1] See vol. i. p. 26.
[2] Pausanias, *Descriptio Græciæ*, V. vii. 3, λίμνη Τιβιριάς ('lake of Tiberias'); ed. Schubart, Leipzig 1875, vol. i. p. 364 [vii. 4; 391].

closer definition was doubtless only chosen for the sake of the Greek readers (Lücke, Godet). And the designation of the sea as the sea of Galilee was too familiar to the evangelist for him to omit it as unnecessary (against Meyer).

Verse 2.

And a great multitude followed him, because they saw the miracles which he did on them that were diseased. Jesus wished to withdraw from public notice, but the people followed him into his retirement. These are the throngs who accompanied him on his journeyings, so as to be witnesses of his miracles of healing exercised upon the diseased. The imperfects show this. We are thus transferred into the middle of his Galilean activity; compare, for example, Matt. iv. 23–25.

Verse 3.

And Jesus went up into a mountain. He sought to escape the people: he went up εἰσ τὸ ὄροσ ('to the height') which ran through that place. Doubtless τὸ ὄροσ is intended to designate this in general, and not a certain mountain found there (Meyer), since no such has been previously mentioned. *And there he sat with his disciples.* Καθίζεσθαι ('to sit') is the expression for a calm, inactive sojourn.

Verse 4.

And the passover, a feast of the Jews, was nigh. In saying this, the evangelist does not, as is almost always assumed, mean to explain the gathering of the crowds of people mentioned afterwards. That gathering is already accounted for by Jesus' miraculous activity, upon which stress had been previously laid. Besides, the journey to Jerusalem to the feast of the passover would not explain how these people came to stay with Jesus in this mountain solitude by the sea of Galilee. The two do not agree together. Yet it is not a mere chronological note (Baumgarten-Crusius, Brückner); that would be contrary to the evangelist's method. The remark stands in internal connection with the whole occurrence, and with the discourse which follows (Bruno

Bauer, Baur, Hengstenberg), and is designed especially to explain Jesus' mood. Therefore it belongs, not to what follows, but to what precedes (ἐκεῖ ἐκαθίζετο μετὰ τῶν μαθητῶν αὐτοῦ, 'there he sat with his disciples'). Earnest thoughts of the future filled his soul. At the next passover he was to die. It does not necessarily follow from the ἐγγὺσ κ.τ.λ. ('the passover was nigh') that Jesus did not go to the passover at Jerusalem. It is inconceivable that these thousands, who here gathered around Jesus, should have stayed away from the celebration of the feast. Jesus also could go to it as well as they could. Of course we cannot say whether he did or not. It is possible that Jesus did not go thither; we do not know.

VERSE 5.

When Jesus then lifted up his eyes, and saw a great company come unto him, he saith unto Philip, Whence shall we buy bread, that these may eat? Meyer sees in the approaching multitudes different ones from those mentioned in the second verse. But that is not possible. It was said before that the people followed after Jesus as he went to the eastern shore, and now it is said that Jesus saw the multitudes coming, therefore the same ones must be meant both times. The note concerning the passover is only thrust between because the evangelist felt it necessary to give such a note, and yet did not wish to break the connection of the narrative by it at a later point.

According to the synoptists, Matt. xiv. 15 and parallels, Jesus did not feed the multitude until evening. Here he seems to have been prompted to this action at once upon their coming. We need, however, only to remember that five thousand men could not come at one moment, and that their very coming must have consumed a large amount of time. Jesus can hardly have filled up this time in any other way than that related by the synoptists, namely, with teaching and healing. It is urged as a difference between the accounts, that Jesus here takes the initiative, and that he does not do so in the synoptists. They say the difference is due to the fact that the evangelist here wished to direct attention more to the spiritual aim of the miracle,[1] or to the predominance of the idea of the Messianic autonomy (Meyer, similarly Brückner). The latter, however, remains the same, even if he causes his disciples to come to him with the demand that he dismiss the people. Even according to the synoptic account he could not have kept the people by him until evening without knowing what he would do, ver. 6. His reply to that demand, Matt. xiv. 16, was a word of trial for all of them, and his question to Philip, following on that reply,—'whence shall we buy bread?' ἀγοράσωμεν is better substantiated than the future,—was intended to be a word of special trial and education for that disciple.

Verse 6.

This he said to prove him, πειράζων αὐτόν: *for he himself knew what he would do.* It is unnecessary, with Bengel, to attempt to explain the question upon the hypothesis that Philip had charge of the 'res alimentaria' ('matters of food'). The question is rather to be sufficiently explained by the reflecting, thoughtful character of Philip.[2] The trial is indeed a trial of belief, and not merely a trial whether or not he knows what to do (against Meyer). The intention was, that in a position from which there was no escape in a human way, he should be led to draw security from confidence in Jesus.

Verse 7.

Philip answered him, Two hundred pennyworth of bread is not sufficient for them, that every one of them may take a little. He reckons at 200 denarii (about £6, 15s., or $33.75) the sum which was necessary on the lowest calculation, and even that would scarcely be enough to satisfy the most slender necessity of each one.

Verses 8, 9.

One of his disciples, Simon Peter's brother, saith unto him, There is a lad here, which hath five barley loaves, and two

---

[1] Baur, *Kritische Untersuchungen über die kanonischen Evangelien,* Tübingen 1847, p. 252 f.   [2] See vol. i. p. 87 f.

small fishes. Andrew, in accordance with the more hasty character of his mind,[1] answers without having been asked, and goes over what there is on hand. Besides, we perceive from this that the disciples must already have been looking around to see about food. For Andrew is aware that only a little boy—παιδάριον, in the Septuagint frequently for נַעַר, namely, a young servant; hardly a slave, because that meaning, though elsewhere found, does not suit here—and more than that, only a single one—if ἕν ('one') is to be read in spite of ℵ B D L—is there, who has food to sell (against Baumgarten-Crusius). And he knows also how much or how little the boy has. He has only five barley loaves, such as the poorer people were accustomed to eat, and two ὀψάρια—diminutive from ὄψον, a relish to be eaten with bread—commonly, and so also here: fishes. But with this small supply of course nothing can be attempted for so many, εἰσ τοσούτουσ. We see that Andrew has been searching about, and has asked that child what he had. Therefore the disciples had, even before Jesus' question, ver. 5, considered how the people were to be fed, and had found that it was not possible. Should they not have rested quietly at that? John, however, himself gives at once the point by which the demand with which, according to the synoptists, the disciples come to Jesus, is not only explained, but directly required.

VERSE 10.

And Jesus said, Make the men sit down. Now there was much grass in the place. So the men sat down, in number about five thousand. The place was a grassy one. It was in the spring, perhaps at the beginning of April, and the latter rain of March and April, which falls before the harvest of the winter fruits, was probably just over. Only the number—τὸν ἀριθμόν, accusative of nearer definition—of the men is given, and it is said only of them that they sat down to eat. This does not mean that there were no women and children there, or that these remained standing. It is simply that the rows were counted and arranged

[1] See vol. i. p. 88.

according to the men, and perhaps only the men received the food, and distributed it to the women and children. Moreover, there were probably only a few women and children; the most of them doubtless started home at an earlier hour.

Verse 11.

And Jesus took the loaves; and when he had given thanks, he distributed to them that were set down; and likewise of the fishes as much as they would. As Jesus elsewhere was in the habit, in the circle of his disciples, of offering the thanks properly uttered by the father of the family, so too he offers them here. In this place they probably had a special relation to that which Jesus was about to do. Thereupon he distributed (διέδωκε B, ἔδωκεν ℵ) the bread as much as was necessary, and of the fishes as much as was desired,—not, as Luther rendered it, following a false reading, 'as much as he would.' The words τοῖσ μαθηταῖσ, οἱ δὲ μαθηταί ('to the disciples, and the disciples') of the received text are, according to the manuscripts, to be struck out; they are only transferred from Matt. xiv. 19. The thing they express is a matter of course.

Verse 12.

When the multitudes were fully satisfied—this is expressly noted — Jesus orders the remains to be gathered up, so that nothing should be lost.

Verse 13.

They gathered of the fragments that remained twelve baskets, one for each disciple. These were travelling baskets, such as they were accustomed to carry with them. Whether each disciple himself carried one such basket, or whether they got them from others, must be left undecided. The bread alone is spoken of, because only the bread obtains a symbolical meaning in what follows.

There is no question that the feeding, according to the representation of the evangelist, is to be regarded as a miracle in the most exact sense. And if we do not intend to make a myth of the narrative, we must let it stand as it reads. Neither the quickened process of nature (Olshausen), nor the increasing the nourishing power of the bread (J. P. Lange), is of any service here. Of course we cannot explain it by a mere human kindliness, which excited others to follow his example (Paulus). The idea of a myth is opposed by the fact that this very event maintained its position in the consciousness of the early Christianity, as we perceive by the four evangelical accounts; compare also the frequent representation in the catacombs. Jesus gives, with divine completeness in unlimited fulness, that which serves unto life.

This is the fact which is to be translated into the sphere of the spiritual life. Moreover, it must be added that, though he does indeed connect it with that which is existing and visible, yet that which was earthly had to experience a new creative exercise of power, by which it was raised to the endless fulness. Thus, then, something visible will also in that other sphere form the foundation which, raised by an exercise of God's power into the life that has no limit, will serve the true life in an inexhaustible manner. But although his power is an endless one, he nevertheless gives forth of his fulness only according to need. It will then be the same there also. At the end, that which remains is gathered up;—it was left over, not because Jesus gives above what is needed, but to carry a special meaning. The twelve apostles gather each a basket, not merely for their own needs, nor as a memento, nor merely to point out the fulness of his grace, but to indicate that they should gather from his fulness, in order themselves to possess something they can give. This aims at the future of their mission to the world.

Even if it be true that 'no standpoint and no mode of thought to-day feels satisfied and joyful at this material, magical, miraculous activity,'[1] that is not enough to determine us to take the event in a different sense from the one in which it is related. So far from its being the fact that

[1] Baumgarten-Crusius, *Theologische Auslegung der johanneischen Schriften*, Jena 1843, vol. i. p. 229.

'the succeeding discourses themselves turn away from it,'[1] they really are altogether based upon it. Only they do indeed direct us to view the event as a σημεῖον ('sign'), and not in the externality of its first appearance and effect. If we follow this direction, we shall certainly find something much more definite than merely 'the expression of that unconditioned feeling of security, satisfaction, fulness, which the disciples bore in themselves, which they continually developed, and in which no object was too petty for them.'[2] How much better Baur understood the meaning of the gospel, when he made this narrative stand entirely in the service of the thought treated in the subsequent discourse, as a sensible image of that thought! We hold fast to this: Jesus, the one existing in the flesh, possesses, because he is the life, in his flesh, namely in his human nature, that wherewith he is able to bestow upon man the power and fulness of life. This was what he desired to represent, for he knew what he intended to do, ver. 6. Why should not that, which he did with such a conscious and determined purpose, serve his self-witness as the Son of God, in the unfolding of his various characteristics?

Verse 14.

It is indeed true that the sign did not serve unto this knowledge for the Jews. On that account they receive blame from Jesus, ver. 26. This blame shows that the miracle was not to them a σημεῖον ('sign') in the true meaning, but that they only clave to its sensible appearance and effect, which suited them. Still it made but the greater impression upon them externally, and carried them away in the most lively expression of enthusiasm: *This is of a truth that prophet that should come into the world.* It is uncertain how the prophet, whom they expected on the ground of Deut. xviii. 15, was related to the Messiah in the Messianic conceptions of the nation; compare what was said i. 21. Here the crowd of the people clearly

---

[1] Baumgarten-Crusius, *Theologische Auslegung der johanneischen Schriften*, Jena 1843, vol. i. p. 229.
[2] *Ibidem.*

meant the prophet in a Messianic sense. According to the Jewish opinion, Elias was to anoint the future Messiah to be the Messiah. They desired to aid in bringing about this object.

VERSE 15.

When Jesus therefore perceived that they would come and take him by force and make him a king, he departed again into a mountain himself alone. They wished to seize Jesus and make him a king, that is, they thought they would lead him in triumph to Jerusalem and proclaim him at the feast of the passover as the Messianic king. Thus they would establish the Messianic empire, of the blessings of which they conceived they had experienced a feeble prelude in the miraculous feeding. They desired even then to carry out that which, according to Jesus' will and ordering, took place a year later on his entry into Jerusalem. We encounter the same trait as before of Jewish behaviour towards the future salvation of Israel. They wish to determine the form of the salvation themselves, instead of accepting it, and they desire a Messianic glory by the way of sensible exercise of power, not of ethical preparation. The more decidedly, therefore, it must more and more appear that the form of salvation needs in the first place to be a purely moral one, and one which mediates itself in a purely moral way. And hence the more the contradiction between the claim of the Jews and the claim of Jesus was revealed, just so much the more decidedly must the relation of the nation to its Messiah become a hostile relation.

On this account the approbation he here met with, was to Jesus a sign of his rejection and of his death. The fact that he did not permit himself to be led by them to the throne by their way, ver. 15, led him to the way unto the cross. Even there he was lifted up for the salvation of Israel and of the nations, but lifted up only for belief, for a belief which would not let itself be distracted by the seemingly contradictory visible phenomena. He must therefore also now proclaim himself as the life in a way which demanded a belief that seemed to be contradicted by the outward appearance. The contradiction in this place and in the other could only be removed by an exercise of God's power, exerted upon his flesh. Doubtless such thoughts of the future were revolving in his mind. Hence he again ($\pi \acute{a} \lambda \iota \nu$, back where he was before, with his disciples) withdrew to the loneliness of prayer (Meyer); compare Matt. xiv. 23; Mark vi. 46. It is true he did at first withdraw, ver. 15, to avoid the zeal of the people, namely, to cause that the way of the salvation should not be disturbed, but that was not the only reason; for he withdrew even from his disciples ($a\mathring{v}\tau\grave{o}\sigma$ $\mu\acute{o}\nu o\sigma$, 'himself alone') until towards morning.

In the feeding the thousands and in the enthusiasm of the people, we behold the climax of Jesus' Galilean activity. From that time onward it sinks downwards. Temporally also it is the middle of the Galilean year. The former half, until Easter, goes upon an upward course; the latter half, until the late autumn, a downward course. In the midst of, and because of, the enthusiasm of the people, earnest thoughts of the future occupy Jesus, just as, a year later, at the entrance into Jerusalem in the midst of the shouts of the people, tears burst from his eyes at the thought of the future.

VERSES 16–21.

The next occurrence is also entirely sustained by the thought of the future, and, in correspondence with this, is full of typical meaning. Baumgarten-Crusius and Bleek[1] are indeed unwilling to find the least thing miraculous here, to which we have only to say that the event is, on the contrary, entirely of a miraculous, and that of a symbolically miraculous, character.

VERSES 16, 17.

And when even was come, his disciples went down unto the sea, and entered into a ship, and went over the sea towards

---

[1] Bleek, *Beiträge zur Evangelien-Kritik*, Berlin 1846, p. 102 ff.; see, against him, Baur, *Theologische Jahrbücher*, Tübingen 1847, p. 100 ff., and Hilgenfeld's review of Bleek in the *Allgemeine Literatur-Zeitung*, Halle and Leipzig 1847, No. 82, col. 650.

Capernaum. And it was now dark, and Jesus was not come to them. The disciples waited for Jesus till late in the evening (ὀψία), and Jesus did not come. So they went into the boat. According to the synoptists, Jesus had told them to do it. Although this is not expressly said here, it is quite a matter of course that the disciples would not have left Jesus alone, and have sought the western shore without orders. If we are to read εἰσ τὸ πλοῖον ('into the ship') with the article (which it is true is wanting in ℵ and B), then the ship in which they had sailed across is meant. The evangelist presupposes it to be known or to be a matter of necessity that they had gone over in a boat. Thus the article refers to the journey thither, reported by the synoptists, Matt. xiv. 13, and at the same time proves (against Meyer) that in the first verse we are to think, not of Jerusalem, but of the hither-shore in Galilee as the point of departure. They return to that place. Perhaps they expected Jesus on the next day.[1] The fact that they sailed directly towards Capernaum to wait for Jesus there, is most simply explained by the synoptic account, according to which Jesus had moved thither from Nazareth and had made this city his city. It had grown dark, and Jesus had not come to them. So they start off without him.

VERSE 18.

And the sea arose by reason of a great wind that blew. The storm they had to endure, made them feel more deeply the separation from Jesus.

VERSE 19.

So when they had rowed about five and twenty or thirty furlongs, they see Jesus walking on the sea, and drawing nigh unto the ship: and they were afraid. They had not gotten much more than half-way across, 25 or 30 stadia (according to Matt. xiv. 24, less exactly μέσον, 'middle'), since the sea is 40 stadia, or about two leagues wide.[2] It is

---

[1] Against Wieseler, *Chronologische Synopse der vier Evangelien*, Hamburg 1843, p. 275, note.

[2] Josephus, *De Bello Judaico*, III. x. 7 ; *Opera*, ed. Bekker, Leipzig 1856, vol. v. p. 281.

arbitrary to assume, with Godet, that the disciples had been thrown back again into the middle of the sea from the western shore; in spite of all their pains, they had come no farther. The thought of meeting could not possibly occur to them under such circumstances. Hence it is no wonder that they were afraid, when they saw a shape advancing upon the water and approaching the ship. It is necessary that ἐπὶ τῆσ θαλάσσησ ('on the sea') be taken thus. Baumgarten-Crusius, indeed, appealing to ver. 21, ἐπὶ τῆσ γῆσ ('at the land'), and xxi. 1, ἐπὶ τῆσ θαλάσσησ ('at the sea'), explains ἐπὶ τῆσ θαλάσσησ as 'on the shore,' so that everything uncommon falls away. On the one hand, Lücke,[1] and Meyer on Matt. xiv. 25, have refuted this explanation. And, on the other hand, it refutes itself of necessity by the whole narrative, although it would in itself be philologically possible.

VERSE 20.

Only Jesus' voice in his call: *It is I; be not afraid,* calms them. These words are preserved in all the accounts. We may thence conclude what an impression they made on the disciples. Matthew inserts here the incident with Peter. There, the disciples and the position of their believing knowledge form the decisive point of view; here, it is the self-revelation of Jesus that the evangelist has in view. What follows also serves this standpoint.

VERSE 21.

Then they wished to receive him into the ship: and immediately the ship was at the land whither they went. This latter is a variation from the synoptic account, and is intended as a miraculous event. The evangelist could not have written εὐθέωσ ἐγένετο κ.τ.λ. ('immediately . . . was,' etc.) if the disciples had perchance only deceived themselves as to their distance from the shore. On the contrary, he must there have remarked, that they found that they were already at the land, only they had not known it.

---

[1] Lücke, *Commentar über das Evangelium des Johannes*, 3d ed., Bonn 1843, vol. ii. p. 119.

This as well as Jesus' walking on the water is meant to be considered as miraculous. Moreover, we are probably not to suppose that they now really took him into the ship. Ἤθελον ('wished') is not to be understood in an adverbial sense: they received him willingly, in contrast with a previous not willing (Tholuck); in that case the evangelist would have written it so. It rather stands in contrast with the following sentence καὶ εὐθέωσ ('and immediately'), to show that it stopped at wishing, and did not reach the full deed (against Hengstenberg).

Still it was not merely a wish, but an action that did not arrive at the carrying out of the desire, and therefore it was a beginning. From the circumstance that Jesus spoke the words to them, ver. 20, we see that he must have been quite close to the ship. How else could they have heard his words, since the wind and the waves were raging? We shall therefore have to understand the twenty-first verse thus, namely, that they had already stretched out the hand to him, and he had stepped upon the ship towards them: and immediately, even before he stepped into their midst, the ship was at the land. Meyer's objections to this way of conceiving it are refuted by a consideration of the whole situation. Godet also calls attention to the fact that it is said, not ἀλλά ('but'), but καὶ εὐθέωσ ('and immediately'). This point, touching the miraculous arrival at the land, was left unnoticed by the synoptists, because it lay distant from the purpose of their account. Hence in their narrative it seems as if the rest of the way had only been passed over after a considerable sail. The reading of the Sinaitic, however, ἦλθον: they came to him, to receive him, etc., appears to be a correction, to avoid the difficulty found in ἤθελον. Besides, the ship did not need to come to Jesus, but Jesus came to the ship.

The meaning of these events is made clear to us by their likeness to that occurrence which is involuntarily brought up to our thoughts, namely, the meeting of the Raised One with his disciples, Luke xxiv. 39. There, forsaken by Jesus, anxiously tossed about in sorrow and fear, they perceived the appearance of the glorified One at first only with fright. Thus, too, it was here. Their storm-tossed, nightly sail is a type of those days between death and resurrection. The fact that Jesus is released from the law of earthly limitation by the supernatural working of the Spirit, is here sensibly imaged. As he here came, so was he also to come again at another time to the forsaken and fearful ones, though again only as if standing upon the threshold, and not externally sojourning in their midst. But his coming is an effective help out of all need, and unto rest and security. That which is true of those days is true in general for the time of the church. It is a time of distress and of violent storms; but Jesus is near his own, and his nearness is their deliverance. Probably the disciples did not recognise the meaning of this occurrence until afterwards. Yet they should and could gain from this appearance of Jesus an impression as to the possible freedom and spirituality of him who had become flesh, which impression then would enable them more easily to pass over the stumbling-block in the following discourse.

We therefore do not need, with Lücke,[1] to let the riddle remain unsolved, since even John gives expression to no specific purpose for the miracle. Nor need we, with Olshausen, think that Christ's body was different from that of other men, since the intention is only to report a passing event as a sign of the working of the Spirit upon Jesus. Nor need we satisfy ourselves with the general aim of the development of the disciples in belief (Olshausen). As little is it necessary to 'solve the riddle by making new puzzles' (Lücke); or finally, to own that Baur's[2] and Hilgenfeld's[3] discovery really is a correct one, namely, that the fourth gospel wishes Christ's body to be regarded docetically. On the contrary, the whole bearing of this narrative betrays

---

[1] Lücke, *Commentar über das Evangelium des Johannes*, 3d ed., Bonn 1843, vol. ii. p. 120.

[2] Baur, *Kritische Untersuchungen über die kanonischen Evangelien*, Tübingen 1847, pp. 254 f., 373 f. [See Hilgenfeld, who refers to Baur, p. 166 f., but incorrectly. He may have some other passage of Baur's in view than the one here noted.—C. R. G.]

[3] Hilgenfeld, *Das Evangelium und die Briefe Johannis nach ihrem Lehrbegriff dargestellt*, Halle 1849, p. 244.

plainly enough how uncommon, and how contradictory to the remaining experience of Christ's corporality, this event was.

(2.) VERSES 22-59.

This section, following upon the above occurrences, offers a discourse which has often been falsely spiritualized, to the same degree that men have, from a false fear, believed it was necessary to avoid a true spiritualization of the historical events. The relation of the words of Jesus in question to the preceding historical notes is especially fitted to teach us on what very equal ground the history and the discourses stand in the fourth gospel, and how careful we must be to grasp the former in their spiritual meaning, and the latter in their concrete reality.

It has been said that the discourse did not fit the preceding miracle. For how could the Jews make the demand in ver. 30 f. if they had but the day before had that miraculous experience (Bruno Bauer, Schweizer)? Baumgarten-Crusius answered this satisfactorily, namely, that the Jews' demand had that very experience as its presupposition, since that alone offers the explanation for the special form of their speech. Jesus came to them with a far higher claim than Moses. Therefore a much higher miracle must establish his claim. And the immediately preceding one, as well as the earlier ones, in their view by no means equalled the miracle of the manna. What now is Jesus' claim.

The various words, from one side and from the other, fall into three paragraphs: (*a*) vers. 22–40; (*b*) vers. 41–51; (*c*) vers. 52–59.

(*a*.) VERSES 22–40.

These verses open with a period which is characteristic for the unperiodological style of the evangelist, and especially for his Hebraic tendency to co-ordinate sentences which logically stand towards each other in a relation of dependence.[1]

---

[1] See vol. i. p. 37 ff.

Verse 22.

The people had observed that Jesus had not entered into the ship in which his disciples sailed away, and there was no other boat upon which he could possibly have gone.

Verses 23, 24.

Therefore as many of them as were left, seeing that they found at that place neither Jesus nor his disciples, took ship and sailed to Capernaum, where they might hope again to meet with Jesus. They went upon ships which had in the meanwhile come over from Tiberias,—come, probably, in order to use this opportunity of ferrying the multitude over. Hence ver. 23 is said with reference to ἐνέβησαν αὐτοὶ εἰσ τὰ πλοιάρια ('they took shipping') in ver. 24; and in turn this latter is preceded by the new reason, ὅτε οὖν εἶδεν ὁ ὄχλοσ ('when the people therefore saw'), in ver. 24. The twenty-third verse therefore does not intend to say that the disciples had not come back upon these ships, upon which they might have returned (Meyer). And much less does ver. 24 merely take up ver. 22 again, since it adds a new point. If, however, they cause themselves to be taken by these boats, which had come from Tiberias, to Capernaum, on the north-western shore of the sea,[1] because they hope to find Jesus there, then this must have been Jesus' place of abode. Thus we are directed to a Galilean activity, and must assume that he went from Capernaum to the eastern shore. The evangelist in this way everywhere presupposes the synoptic narrative and a knowledge of it, and desires to be understood from its standpoint.

Verse 25.

At the close, in ver. 59, the synagogue is given as the place of the meeting and talking. Here, on the contrary, it merely says: πέραν τῆσ θαλάσσησ ('on the other side of the sea'), because the emphasis lies upon the fact that they are surprised to find him on the western shore (Meyer). Their question, 'when' he came to Capernaum, contains also

[1] See Furrer, *Wanderungen durch Palästina*, Zürich 1865, p. 323 f.

the question as to 'how,' even although the word is πότε ('when') and not πῶσ ('how') (Baumgarten-Crusius). The time is inexplicable to them because the 'how' is. If he had taken the way by land, he could hardly have reached there yet; and he had not sailed across the sea—that they knew. Therefore the one question is not to be separated from the other, and they must have hoped, in the answer to the expressed question, to have the unspoken question likewise answered. This shows, moreover, that they expected to hear something wonderful. They did not know how to explain Jesus' arrival in an ordinary way. Hence we shall not venture to find in the question either curiosity (Schleiermacher, Meyer) or desire after Jesus (Baumgarten-Crusius). Nor shall we perceive in the seeking, the intention to try again to make him a king.[1] Nothing of that is to be seen. On the contrary, just as the Athenians busied themselves with hearing or telling something new every day, so did the Jews rejoice in miraculous divine revelation. The latter were as greedy of miracles as the Greeks were of wisdom. In this we see their old character, and perceive how little moral the motive for their coming was.

Verse 26.

That is what Jesus now holds up before them. For his words are not to be taken rudely, as if they were only anxious about the bread, but to the effect that they sought him only because of the miraculous satisfying of hunger. It does not say merely: ye have eaten and have become full. The ἐκ τῶν ἄρτων is added, to say: 'of the few loaves.' This shows that the chief thing for them was the miracle in the satisfying their hunger, and not the satisfaction itself and alone. The plural σημεῖα ('signs') does not refer to the healings of the sick (Bengel, Lücke), but is the plural of category (Meyer).

Verse 27.

In contrast with this, Jesus presents a claim of a moral

[1] Lücke, *Commentar über das Evangelium des Johannes*, 3d ed., Bonn 1843, vol. ii. p. 125.

kind: ἐργάζεσθε, 'labour.' The gift is conditioned on their own activity. They must do something that would secure for them the enduring meat unto everlasting life, which he the Son of man desired to give them. Τὴν βρῶσιν τὴν μένουσαν εἰσ ζωὴν αἰώνιον is commonly explained as: the meat which endureth unto everlasting life. But the contrast to the preceding τὴν βρῶσιν τὴν ἀπολλυμένην ('the meat which perisheth') requires us also to take τὴν μένουσαν absolutely: the enduring meat, which does not perish, which does not consume away, and which therefore also suffices unto eternal life. Hence εἰσ ζωὴν αἰώνιον ('unto eternal life') belongs not simply to μένουσαν ('enduring'), but to the whole conception, 'enduring meat.' They are to obtain such meat for themselves. How shall they obtain it? The Son of man will 'give' it to them. This, therefore, is their ἐργάζεσθαι ('labour'), that they come to him, believe on him, and let him give them such meat. He gives it to them in his character as the Son of man. For this purpose he has become man, and bears this blessing of eternal life in his human nature. By a moral conduct they are to bring themselves into a relation to him, the one who has appeared in the flesh, a relation which has for its gain the meat of eternal life.

A relation unto the one who has appeared in the flesh is demanded, *for him hath God the Father*—the highest authority, hence put emphatically at the end—*sealed*, that is, accredited as the one who bears in himself, and imparts, this blessing. Hence, accordingly, among all men, this very one (τοῦτον) is made known by God unto all who are willing to see him, as the one who has God's vocation unto men, and who therefore has also received the right to demand a moral bearing and relation of men to his person. The meat of the higher life, which he designates as the gain of this, is the higher miracle with which he answers their silent demand. But he names a moral condition which they have to perform.

Verse 28.

The Jews think of a number of moral, God-pleasing

methods of conduct. He is to name and describe these to them, so that they may know what they have to do to fulfil these performances which correspond to the will of God. We may not, however, on account of this their reply, believe that the evangelist wished to place them higher (Baumgarten-Crusius). They had in thought merely legal deeds, which did not need to be of a really moral character, and by which they hoped to be able to place themselves in the condition agreeable to God. The connection shows that the genitive τοῦ θεοῦ ('of God'), ver. 28, is intended to designate the works, not as wrought of God, but as willed by God, and therefore as agreeable to God, and hence such as would give them the capacity or the right to share in the kingdom of God.

VERSE 29.

But then also in Jesus' answer: *This is the work of God, that ye believe on him whom he hath sent*, the genitive τοῦ θεοῦ must be taken in the same way. The common exposition of the church theology, however, takes the other view, and finds God herein designated as the author of belief. The view stated above by us is the right one. For the correction which lies in Jesus' words extends only to the change of the plural into the singular, to the contrasting πίστισ ('belief') with the expressed opinion of the Jews, that legal deeds were in question. Therefore the relation of the genitive to τὸ ἔργον ('the work') remains the same.

Jesus opposes, to the variety of conduct, one in itself simple and united, ver. 29. It is ever a doing, but one which comprehends the whole man and determines the whole shape of his life. Jesus names as this action, belief on his person. It is true it says not τοῦτό ἐστιν ὅτι, but ἵνα, with the aorist subjunctive. We may not, however, conclude from this that the two, ἔργον and πίστισ ('work' and 'belief'), are meant to designate different things; it is merely that belief is named in the form of a demand. It is in such a shape the work agreeable to God, that we must believe in order (even thereby) to do it. In this sense I think I must correct my treatise upon ἔργον and πίστισ.[1] But certainly the matter remains essentially as it is there presented, namely, that τὸ ἔργον τοῦ θεοῦ (' the work of God ') designates the true condition of life, and here denotes belief as such, in which all action must be comprehended, if on the part of its variety it may be designated as ἔργα τοῦ θεοῦ (' works of God '), or as ἔργα ἐν θεῷ εἰργασμένα (' works wrought in God '), iii. 21. All true morality is only the development of belief. In all action agreeable to God, it is belief which exercises itself. Jesus' demand points to the proper conduct of man. Moreover, he demands the essential conduct, by demanding belief in his person as the one come from the Father.

VERSE 30.

The Jews turn back upon him this his demand: *What sign doest thou then, that we may see and believe thee? What dost thou work?* They say with emphasis: σύ, thou on thy part. And they reply to his demand for ἐργάζεσθαι (' work ') with the same demand upon him: τί ἐργάζῃ; what dost thou work? He must first prove the right of his demand? Thus they hope they will still at last reach their aim and see a miracle done by him, upon which they will believe, that is, offer a belief which is no belief.

VERSE 31.

They base their claim upon the legitimation of Moses in the manna miracle in the desert. *He*—God through Moses —*gave them bread from heaven to eat*, Ps. lxxviii. 24, cv. 40; Ex. xvi. 4. If he makes a claim so much higher than Moses, he must legitimatize himself accordingly. In this point is contained the refutation of the objections which have been raised. It is said, namely, that the claim on the part of the Jews stands in contradiction with the miracle of the preceding day, and therefore is not historical (for example, Weisse), or proves the non-Johannean origin (Schweizer), or the non-miraculous character of the narrative of the feeding (Schenkel). On the contrary, this event is

---
[1] Luthardt, *Theologische Studien und Kritiken*, 1852, p. 334.

brought to their thoughts by the very miracle of the feeding on the preceding day. But Moses is the type of the Messiah, and the manna miracle is his highest legitimation. Hence the question lay near to them, what Jesus had to put by the side of this miracle. His miracle of yesterday did not seem to them sufficient if he raised such a high claim as he had a moment before presented. Jesus cannot dispense from belief. He can only so accredit himself as to demand and to presuppose belief.

VERSE 32.

Verily, verily, I say unto you, not Moses gave you the bread from heaven; but my Father giveth you the bread from heaven, the true. Since the article is not repeated after ἄρτον ('bread'), ἐκ τοῦ οὐρανοῦ ('from heaven') is to be connected in both places with the verb and not with ἄρτον. Not Moses had given them down from heaven the bread; so also in Ex. xvi. 4, מִן הַשָּׁמַיִם ('from heaven') is to be connected with the verb מַמְטִיר ('causing to rain'), not with the substantive לֶחֶם. Jesus does not intend to deny that the manna was a food miraculously caused and given by God. But it was not the real bread which God gives from heaven; this, τὸν ἀληθινόν ('the true'), namely, the reality of the idea, is only given to them by the Father of Jesus. It does not say: God, but ὁ πατήρ μου ('my Father'), which contains the fact that God gives it to them in Jesus, and indeed δίδωσιν ('gives'), for in him it is present and existing. This, moreover, the Jews must believe. Jesus could not relieve from that belief. Thus throughout, over against the Jewish demand for sensible proof, which should compel to belief, and therefore really make belief unnecessary, he sets up the claim for belief, which should be a free moral act. In this he ever remains the same. As to expression, he allows himself to be decided by that demand.

VERSE 33.

Hence he characterizes the bread, which is the true bread, namely, the bread of God: *For the bread of God is that which cometh down from heaven and giveth life unto the world*. We must translate thus, and not: is he who, etc. The whole context compels us to refer ὁ καταβαίνων κ.τ.λ. ('that which cometh down,' etc.) to ὁ ἄρτοσ ('the bread'). This is accepted and established by most of the later exegetes, against Olshausen, Fritzsche, and Godet. To spring from heaven, and to bestow life: such is the character of the bread which in truth deserves the name of 'the bread of God.' It is true that these words find their application in Jesus, since in what follows he is designated as this very bread. But to understand them of Jesus here would be an anticipation of what follows. In regard to the construction, it is a question whether ὁ ἄρτοσ or ὁ καταβαίνων is the subject; whether we should say: 'for no other than the bread bestowed by God is it, which comes down,' etc. (thus Meyer), or: 'that which comes down, etc., is the bread of God.' The logical connection demands the second explanation. The words are intended to establish the point that Moses did not give the true bread of God, but that only Jesus or his Father gives it. What Moses gave was not in the exact sense from above, and able to bestow life. But only such bread is God's bread. These two points: from above, and bestowing life, constitute in John's gospel the conception and the importance of the Son of God. When Jesus speaks of the bread, he has himself in view. Hence the addition: τῷ κόσμῳ ('unto the world'), for he is in the world, and has come for it, to bestow the life from God upon it, the one given up to death; compare iii. 16.

VERSE 34.

The Jews understand very well that Jesus names in this a desirable gift. Πάντοτε, *in every way give us this bread*, so that we may always have it to eat. Their case is similar to that of the Samaritan woman. The hope, the fulfilment of which Jesus places in prospect, is, in their thoughts, formed entirely upon the analogy of the present life. The request is not ironical (Calvin, Lampe, Bengel), nor is anything to be said concerning a dim suspicion of the higher gift (Lücke, Baumgarten-Crusius). The request is seriously intended, but in an earthly and sensible way. They well believe that he who fed them so miraculously yesterday is able to give them this higher manna (Meyer). Whatever it may be, it seems to them worth wishing for. They are busied with this thing as they imagine it to themselves, and not with the person of Jesus. Therefore Jesus turns them from the moral to the spiritual, and from the thing to his person. He demands a moral conduct, that of belief: to this he promises satisfaction.

VERSE 35.

In this verse we must observe, above all, the emphatic and therefore contrasting position of the ἐγώ ('I') at the front. Everything depends upon his person. The thing which they seek is given in him. They cannot have the thing, salvation, Christianity, etc., without him: *I am the bread of life*, ζωὴν διδοῦσ τῷ κόσμῳ ('giving life unto the world') (Meyer), ver. 33. They must then make him their own. This is a moral bearing. Hence we read: *he that cometh to me;* as much as: he who believes on me, but purposely thus expressed in order to emphasize the point of free self-activity. The following: *he that believeth on me*, is entirely synonymous with it, and is only repeated for the sake of the rhetorical parallelism. This belief shall receive satisfaction: *shall never hunger;* and that this is full satisfaction is shown by the parallel: *shall never thirst.* Only by this is the new feature in the picture occasioned; but it at the same time serves to prepare for what follows. 'Never:' it is a lasting satisfaction, ζωὴ αἰώνιοσ ('eternal life'). Compare iv. 14: πηγὴ ὕδατοσ ἁλλομένου εἰσ ζωὴν αἰώνιον ('a fountain of bubbling water unto everlasting life'). That is the reward of belief. Such belief was made possible for them.

VERSE 36.

But I said unto you, That ye also have seen me, and believe not. The mediation or the empowering of belief lies in the ὁρᾶν ('to see'). The recognition of Jesus is mediated by perception. That which is to be perceived is Jesus' self-presentation as the one who he is, namely, as the Son of God. This same thing is also the object of recognition, and, as accepted by a moral act into the special life of the man, is the object of belief. The Jews now have seen him, namely, the revelation and testification of himself, and yet do not believe. He has already had to upbraid them with this: εἶπον ὑμῖν ('I said unto you'). The former was in the miracle of the preceding day, the latter in the words of salutation, ver. 26 (for example, Grotius, Baumgarten-Crusius). It is not pertinent to recall v. 37–44 (Lücke, De Wette), for the evangelist did not forget so far that the situation is an entirely different one. Nor is it necessary, with Meyer, to take εἶπον ('I will have it said to you'), in a manner foreign to the New Testament, as an announcement of what follows καὶ ἑωράκατε ('ye also have seen'). Even in xi. 42, to which Meyer appeals, εἶπον refers to the εὐχαριστῶ ('I thank') spoken immediately before. Moreover, the two, ἑωράκατε and οὐ πιστεύετε ('ye believe not'), are connected with each other by καὶ ... καί ('also ... and') to make the contrast thoroughly appreciable; in opposition to ver. 30, ἵνα ἴδωμεν καὶ πιστεύσωμέν σοι ('that we may see and believe thee,' Bengel).

Verse 37.

It is neither necessary nor correct to assume, with De Wette, 'a pause in the conversation.' What follows is closely connected with what preceded. From their behaviour, it is easily to be seen that they do not belong to those whom the Father gives to him, for: *All that the Father giveth me shall come to me; and him that cometh to me I will in no wise cast out.* Christ withdraws himself from no one. Πᾶν ('all') is neuter, as in iii. 6. Bengel says: 'Pater filio totam quasi massam dedit, ut omnes quod dedit unum sint: id universum filius singulatim evolvit, in exsecutione.' ('The Father gave the Son, as it were, the whole mass, so that all whom he gave may be one: the Son developes this whole one by one, in execution.'[1]) Ὅ δίδωσιν ('that he giveth') is not said in the sense of absolute

---
[1] Compare also Bengel on xvii. 2.

predestination as the election of certain persons (Augustine), or of a natural 'zeal for piety' ('pietatis studium,' Calov, against Grotius), but of a giving by means of that 'drawing of the Father' ('tractum patris,' ver. 44, Bengel), by the inward moral working of the word, to which a man must yield himself, but from which he can also free himself. This is the inward moral presupposition of the coming to him, namely, of belief. Where the former exists, there also the latter occurs—$\pi\hat{a}\nu$. But it occurs only where the former exists. 'Tantummodo omne illud ad me veniet' ('Only all that will come to me'), Bengel. Therefore the guilt of their unbelief rests only on them, not on him. For those who come to him he will in no wise ($o\dot{v}\ \mu\acute{\eta}$) cast out: 'It is *litotes:* I will not cast out, but I will in every wise protect,' x. 28 f.[1] 'Cast out,' namely, out of the communion of eternal life, which he mediates, and of the kingdom of God, which he establishes.

Verse 38.

He has come for that sole purpose, to execute this blessed will of God. The expression $\kappa\alpha\tau\alpha\beta\acute{\epsilon}\beta\eta\kappa\alpha\ \kappa.\tau.\lambda.$ ('I came down,' etc.) designedly recalls what was said above concerning the bread. He came not to do his will, as one different from the will of God, but the will of the Father.

Verse 39.

This will, moreover, is deliverance, not destruction, and that of all whom the Father has given him. $\Pi\hat{a}\nu\ \delta\ \delta\acute{\epsilon}\delta\omega\kappa\acute{\epsilon}\nu\ \mu\omicron\iota$ ('all which he hath given me') is put first, and in the nominative absolute, because the emphasis lies on it; compare ver. 31. Bengel says: 'Credentes dantur, credentibus datur' ('believers are given, to believers is given'). What Jesus gives them is expressed after John's manner, by contrast:[2] $\mu\dot{\eta}\ \dot{a}\pi o\lambda\acute{\epsilon}\sigma\omega\ \dot{\epsilon}\xi\ a\dot{v}\tau o\hat{v}$—namely, from that which the Father has given me—*scilicet* $\tau\iota$, that I may lose nothing of it, so that it should fall a prey to eternal death in contrast with eternal life. Eternal life is here

---

[1] Bengel: 'Est Litotes: non eiiciam, sed omni modo tuebor.'
[2] See vol. i. p. 44 f.

designated by ἀναστήσω ('I will raise up') from the side of its completion. Bengel writes: 'Hic finis est, ultra quem periculum nullum' ('here is the end, beyond which there is no danger'). Hence also, because this is the final security of the state of salvation, it is impressively repeated in vers. 40, 44, and 54.[1]

There is no need of proving that this ἀναστήσω τῇ ἐσχάτῃ ἡμέρᾳ ('I will raise up again at the last day') is meant really and not figuratively. It cannot allude to something which happens to the believer in his death.[2] How could dying be called a resurrection, and the last day of the life of each separate man be called ἡ ἐσχάτη ἡμέρα ('the last day') in general? Nor can ἀναστήσω ('I will raise') denote an event that at once coincides with the impartation of life which takes place in the present (Baumgarten-Crusius). The change of form shows this. That possession of life is always expressed as a present one in our gospel. This event, on the contrary, is a future one, whether ἀναστήσω be taken as a subjunctive depending on ἵνα (for example, De Wette, Meyer), or as an independent indicative future. I should prefer the latter, with the Vulgate, Luther, and Hengstenberg, partly because of ver. 54, and partly because of John's way of writing. The evangelist breaks the construction, in order to name with the loosely added future the final development of the new life which he bestows.

VERSE 40.

At least that is true, if not for ver. 39, for ver. 40, which explains, confirms, and emphatically concludes what precedes. Instead of τοῦ πέμψαντός με ('of him that sent me'), τοῦ πατρός μου ('of my Father') comes in, since Jesus intends to designate himself expressly and beyond the possibility of misunderstanding as Son; compare immediately afterwards τὸν υἱόν ('the Son'). Instead of ὃ δέδωκέν μοι ('that which he giveth me'), it is here said, rather

---

[1] As to these repetitions, see vol. i. p. 30 f.
[2] Reuss, *Beiträge zu den theologischen Wissenschaften von den Mitgliedern der theologischen Gesellschaft zu Strassburg.* Erstes Heft. Jena 1847, p. 81 f.

depicting the internal moral process, πᾶσ ὁ θεωρῶν τὸν υἱὸν καὶ πιστεύων εἰσ αὐτόν ('every one which seeth the Son, and believeth on him'): beholding and believing. 'Beholding,' for θεωρεῖν more than ὁρᾶν betokens the beholding of that which is essential in Christ, with the eye of the soul; and then 'believing,' that is, the uniting with him. This belief therefore 'hath' the living possession of Christ, and this present possession is to be made complete in the future. How can belief, which is moral bearing, and therefore also in the first instance only an appropriation of moral possessions, have as its consequence resurrection, an effect on the natural life? With this problem closes the first paragraph, the essential contents of which are the development of the thought: Jesus gives unto belief the true bread unto everlasting life. It is unfolded in these three periods, the demand of right moral bearing, the designation of the heavenly gift, and the appropriation by the moral reception of Jesus' person. The mediation of that contrast will now lie in the person of Jesus, which belief appropriates to itself. The Jews also in the first place take up the question of his person.

(b.) VERSES 41–51.

Jesus is the bread of life. That is the chief thought of this second paragraph. It starts with the person of Jesus, and closes with laying stress upon his flesh. For this second paragraph passes through these three thoughts: how one attains to recognition of His person in belief, what the saving blessing for this recognition is, and how this saving blessing is imparted to belief.

VERSES 41, 42.

The first thought is connected with the hesitation, or rather, the discontented murmuring (Meyer), of the Jews—purposely οἱ Ἰουδαῖοι. How could he call himself one come from heaven, the bread come from heaven, when they knew him to be Joseph's son? In the words ἐγώ εἰμι κ.τ.λ. ('I am,' etc.) they combine the various statements Jesus had made in what went before. This they do to contrast with them Jesus' earthly descent, which they think they know exactly, and with which a being come from heaven did not consist. Πῶσ οὖν λέγει οὗτοσ (' how is it then that he saith'), with a scornful tone. From the fact that they do not know Jesus to be other than the son of Joseph, it does not follow that the evangelist also knew him to be nothing else. His καταβαίνειν ἐκ τοῦ οὐρανοῦ (' descending from heaven') stands in contradiction with that. Hence he must have spoken this in an exactness which was irreconcilable with that view. In no other place, and not even in this place, does Jesus strive to make belief possible by removing this obstacle to it upon the external way of historical disclosures. These would have been even less believed than the obstacle itself. And had they in appearance reached their design, such belief would not have been formed in an internal way, and thus been of moral value. Why should Jesus do this? Even Philip believed without being farther on in his historical knowledge as to Jesus' descent than these Jews were. The way of belief is that of inward sincerity.

Verse 43.

Jesus calls their attention to this in the following verses, after reproving them for their murmuring. A man must have experienced the internal divine working, and have accepted it, in order to join himself to Jesus in belief, and to become a partaker in the hope of salvation.

Verse 44.

Jesus designates the divine working which men must accept as a drawing of the Father to the Son. 'Drawing' is not a forcing or a compelling with the additional notion of that which is irresistible (Calvin, Lampe[1]), but in its conception it excludes beforehand the possibility of refusal. It is an inward urging and leading of the human will to Christ (Meyer). Before, the word was 'give,' vers. 37, 39, rather from the side of the result; here, it is 'draw,' from the side of the internal psychological process. Accordingly, this

---

Lampe, *Commentarius analytico-exegeticus tam literalis quam realis evangelii secundum Joannem*, Amsterdam 1726, vol. ii. pp. 237-239.

drawing is to be understood of the working of the word, as διδόναι ('giving') is above. There is doubtless, even in the sphere of the natural life outside of the revelation of salvation, a certain drawing of the Father to the Son: the internal urging of the Spirit of God the creator in the conscience. It brings the man to a consciousness of the unsatisfactory nature of the relation in which he by nature stands towards God, and by this means it strives to urge him beyond that into the truth of the relation constituted in Christ. This, however, is but a preliminary to the peculiar saving efficiency which is here spoken of. Jesus is not speaking of the general divine working, but of the working of the 'Father, who hath sent him.' He does not tell how a man comes to a desire for salvation and the like, but how a man comes to Him in His historical appearance, so that this is presupposed.[1] To the beginning of the saving work, Jesus contrasts its completion in the promise of the resurrection.

Verse 45.

This verse explains what precedes. Ver. 44: One comes to the Son only by means of the drawing on the part of the Father. For, ver. 45: one must be internally taught of God, and listen unto the Father. But this teaching, ver. 46, completes itself only in the testimony of Jesus. Ver. 45 therefore tells how that drawing effects itself, namely, through the inward teaching. The teaching is not the drawing itself, but the means to it. Teaching is a working upon the consciousness, drawing is a working upon the will. The former working is accompanied by one of the latter kind. It is written in the prophets, that is, not: in several prophets, but only in general: in the prophetical books; compare Acts xiii. 40: 'they shall be all taught of God.' This is a free rendering of Isa. liv. 13, where the direct knowledge of God is named among the blessed results of the Messianic salvation. The connection in both passages shows that the emphasis does not lie on πάντεσ ('all'), but on θεοῦ ('of God'): taught of God himself. But one must be a pupil of God's. *Every man*—οὖν is right as to the matter, but is an addi-

[1] See Luthardt, *Die Lehre vom freien Willen*, Leipzig 1863, p. 420.

tion to the text—but only such a one, *that shall have heard from the Father,*—for according to the manuscripts, including ℵ and B, we are to read ἀκούσασ, not ἀκούων, against Meyer—*and learned, cometh to me.* A man must have perceived God's voice in Jesus' word, and have accepted his testimony, in order to join himself to Jesus in belief. It is included in this, of course, that he is to place himself aright towards it inwardly, that he is not to close but open himself, so as to take the word of God into himself (μαθών).

Verse 46.

But we see and hear the Father only in the Son. *Not that any man hath seen the Father*—the thing in question is not about a direct divine revelation which we might wait for—*save he which is of God,* namely, the Son—a designation of his historical, not his supra-historical, relation of origin to God—*he hath seen the Father,* namely, in the condition of pre-existence. This cannot be the expression of a mere internal relation and intercourse on the part of the man Jesus with God in heaven, which would be something belonging to the present, and not to the past (ἑώρακεν, 'hath seen'). It stands in connection with ὢν παρὰ τοῦ θεοῦ ('being from God').[1] Therefore, he had such a vision with him from whom he comes. All saving relation to God is conditioned upon him, and accordingly we must cleave to him in belief. This closes the first thought of this paragraph: Jesus as the Son of God is an object of belief; of a belief which is mediated, not outwardly, but by internal divine efficiency, and by free devotion of will on the part of man; it has the resurrection for its reward.

Verse 47.

The last point forms the transition to the second period

---

[1] The Sinaiticus reads: εἰ μὴ ὁ ὢν παρὰ τοῦ πατρός, οὗτος ἑώρακεν τὸν θεόν ('save he which is of the Father, he hath seen God'). The Vatican, on the other hand, reads: εἰ μὴ ὁ ὢν παρὰ τοῦ θεοῦ, οὗτος ἑώρακεν τὸν πατέρα ('save he which is of God, he hath seen the Father'). The second reading is the more correct one logically. The first reading seems to have been occasioned by the immediately preceding πατρός, it being easy to continue with πατρός instead of with θεοῦ.

of this paragraph, which treats of the saving blessing bestowed upon belief in Jesus' person. In the first instance, the saving blessing is designated by the comprehensive expression of ζωὴ αἰώνιοσ ('eternal life'). *He that believeth hath everlasting life*, even now.

VERSE 48.

This is given in his person: *I am that bread of life;* bearing life in himself, and imparting it. All depends on him, and therefore on the personal relation to him; an entirely different gift and effect from the gift and effect in the case of the manna of their fathers.

VERSE 49.

They had appealed to the manna, ver. 31; hence ὑμῶν, not ἡμῶν ('your,' not 'our'). *They did eat manna in the wilderness.* Jesus returns upon them their own words, ver. 31, and then adds impressively: καὶ ἀπέθανον, 'et tamen mortui sunt,' 'and yet are dead' (Bengel).

VERSE 50.

On the contrary, the true bread of heaven is of an entirely different nature and working. Οὗτόσ ἐστιν ... ἵνα ('this is ... that');[1] it is of such a character that he who eats thereof shall not die (ἵνα ... μὴ ἀποθάνῃ). Instead of placing the two members of the period, eating and dying, in the correct logical relation of subordination, the evangelist has resolved the logical relation into the more convenient juxtaposition. According to the thought, φάγῃ ('eat') should not be dependent upon ἵνα ('that') (against Meyer), but only ἀποθάνῃ ('die'). The dying, previously mentioned, was meant in the bodily sense; here it is meant in the first place in the spiritual sense. Hence these unlike notions could only be placed in a contrasted relation to each other, upon condition that an efficiency removing the bodily death be regarded as at once included in the 'not dying' due to the heavenly bread.

[1] Compare vol. i. p. 39 f.

Verse 51.

Thus, in the application of the bread to Jesus' person, we find, instead of the above, the words: *he shall live for ever*. The previous discussion is closed by the words which sum up what precedes: *I am the living bread which came down from heaven; if any man eat of this bread, he shall live for ever*. Jesus now transfers to himself what he previously said with regard to the right belief. He is this bread, come down from heaven; hence he bears the life of God in himself, and imparts it to those who appropriate him to themselves. He speaks of his person; not of a doing. Eating, therefore, is appropriation of him himself. In this he has chosen the strongest expression that he has thus far used touching the relation to his person. Although he has likewise constantly put all upon this relation, yet he has not before spoken of it with such force as he does here: to eat of the bread which is he himself. The reading of ℵ: $\dot{\epsilon}\kappa$ $\tau o\hat{\upsilon}$ $\dot{\epsilon}\mu o\hat{\upsilon}$ $\ddot{\alpha}\rho\tau o\upsilon$ ('of my bread'), would not suit this view: of the bread which he gives. In what goes before, he placed and united the bread and himself as identical; only in what follows does he separate the two, by speaking of a gift which he gives.

With this we have already passed to the third period of this paragraph: how that saving blessing of eternal life mediates itself to belief on his person; namely: in that he gives himself to the believing one to eat as the bread come from heaven. When Jesus names himself as bread, he means by it himself in the exact sense, and not merely an utterance of his, whether his doctrine, or his activity, or his death. Exegetes are accustomed, for the most part, to limit the sense to one of these three points. Jesus, however, does not speak of a doing, but of his person, as it is in its very self. He will give himself to belief, and thus become unto it a means of participation in the saving blessing. We are therefore not to think of something which the belief as a psychological act has and effects in itself. The thing in question is an influence which, proceeding from Jesus, effects belief, namely, Jesus' yielding up of himself unto belief. Nor does this impartation of himself limit itself to one side or utterance of Jesus; it is an impartation of his true person. How now can this self-impartation exercise that influence also upon the natural life of man (ἀναστήσω κ.τ.λ., 'I will raise,' etc.), unless it is at the same time an impartation of his own natural life, of his life in the flesh?

In this way, then, this paragraph closes in ver. 51 by his defining the bread of heaven more closely, and explaining it as his flesh. Καὶ . . . δέ here is not the ordinary 'moreover . . . also,' which adds something new in an emphatic way to what precedes. As in 1 John i. 3, it is only intended to define what precedes by a new turn, in which case καί connects in the way of explanation, and δέ characterizes the explanation as something new. *And the bread that I will give is my flesh for the life of the world.* It is true the reading is contested. The Sinaitic manuscript reads: 'Ο ἄρτοσ ὃν ἐγὼ δώσω ὑπὲρ τῆσ τοῦ κόσμου ζωῆσ ἡ σάρξ μου ἐστίν ('the bread that I will give for the life of the world is my flesh'). The Vatican reads: καὶ ὁ ἄρτοσ δὲ ὃν ἐγὼ δώσω ἡ σάρξ μου ἐστὶν ὑπὲρ τῆσ τοῦ κόσμου ζωῆσ ('and the bread that I will give is my flesh for the life of the world'). After ἡ σάρξ μου ἐστίν, the received text, in agreement with E G H K M and various fathers, as Clement, Origen, Cyril, Chrysostom, and Theodoret, adds ἣν ἐγὼ δώσω ('which I will give'). Tischendorf had taken it up again in the seventh edition of his Greek Testament. Meyer, Godet, and other exegetes demand these words as necessary. They are lacking, however, not only in ℵ and B, but also in C D L T, Itala, Vulgate, Syriac. Hence, like Lachmann, Tischendorf omitted them in 1849. In his eighth edition he has adopted the order of the Sinaitic. This, however, appears, in the putting ὑπὲρ τῆσ τοῦ κόσμου ζωῆσ earlier, to be merely a correction to make the passage easier; moreover, the asyndetic connection with the preceding is here not Johannean. It is true the reading of the Vatican is difficult, but it is too strongly accredited to be safely given up.

The addition of the second ἣν ἐγὼ δώσω ('which I will give') to ἡ σάρξ μου is intended to make the meaning easier. It rests, nevertheless, on the old and still ruling misunderstanding, that Jesus is speaking of his death. He is not speaking of his death, but only of his flesh, that is, of his human nature. As a matter of course, ἡ σάρξ μου ('my flesh') is the subject, and ὁ ἄρτοσ ('the bread') the predicate.

His flesh is the bread which he gives,—of course, not to death, but to be eaten. He named himself before this as the bread of life. Now, however, he distinguishes himself the giver, from the gift which he bestows. 'Τπὲρ τῆσ τοῦ κόσμου ζωῆσ ('for the life of the world') refers to this. His flesh serves the world unto life. Therefore he makes his flesh bread, so that he imparts life with it. He speaks of his flesh as a gift to be enjoyed ('bread'), and not of anything that happens to him, not of his death, although most exegetes take it so.[1] But the development thus far given refutes this view.

For the flesh comes under consideration as a gift and as a matter of enjoyment, and not as the expression of an event in Jesus' life, namely, his death. Hence De Wette extended this saying to the expression of 'the self-denying dedication of his life to the salvation of the world in general,' which, moreover, also includes his death. But here also the fact is not observed, that the matter spoken of is not a deed, but a gift on behalf of enjoyment. Hitherto Jesus had designated himself as the life-bestowing bread, in so far as he bears eternal life in himself. When he now calls his flesh this bread, and flesh denotes the sensible human nature, he thereby says that he bears eternal life decreed in this; and therefore that they can find and gain that life in this alone; and therefore that if they wish that, they must appropriate this to themselves. 'They eat and drink the Godhead in the human nature.'[2]

---

[1] Augustine, Luther,—though not without exception,—Calvin, Grotius, Calov, Lampe, Tholuck, Ebrard in his *Das Dogma vom heiligen Abendmahl und seine Geschichte*, Frankfort-on-the-Main 1845, vol. i. p. 78 ff.; Lücke, Meyer, Godet, Kahnis in his *Die lutherische Dogmatik historisch-genetisch dargestellt*, 1st ed., Leipzig 1861, vol. i. p. 624; and De Wette, at least as the completion of his yielding himself up for the salvation of the world.

[2] Luther, *Werke*, Erlangen ed., 1851, vol. xlvii. p. 387. Compare Hofmann, *Der Schriftbeweis*, Nördlingen 1860, vol. ii. part ii. p. 245 ff.; thus also Brückner and Hengstenberg.

The question arises, how and where this eating of his flesh unto eternal life takes place. Many fathers, as Chrysostom, Cyril, Theophylact, and Cyprian, the Catholic commentators, and Calixt, in spite of Calov's violent opposition, understood it of the Lord's supper. Among later scholars, Scheibel, Olshausen, Kling,[1] Köstlin,[2] Kahnis,[3] and Stier[4] understand it of the Lord's supper, or at least of the idea of it; Bengel, in view of the future Lord's supper. Negative criticism[5] has used this exegesis to combat the genuineness of this discourse; and even Meyer decides that 'it can only stand upon condition of giving up the authenticity of John.'

Luther, the Formula of Concord, and the Lutheran exegetes and systematic theologians, on the other hand, were so much the more opposed to this exposition, because it was employed by the Reformed exegesis and systematic theology in favour of the merely symbolical conception of the words of institution in the Lord's supper. In any case, the form of the Lord's supper is not the matter in question, for the bread is only meant figuratively. Nor is the act of the Lord's supper in question, since the eating is not meant as an external act, but only as an internal process. Nor is the discussion about the case of the Lord's supper in the exact sense, since what Jesus says of his flesh is not different from what he says of his person, just as he after this, ver. 57, makes ὁ τρώγων με ('he that eateth me') alternate with this.[6] For this very reason, it stands upon the same footing with what he had said from the beginning about belief on his person; for example, ver. 35. The eating of the bread, which is his flesh, takes place in belief

---

[1] Kling, *Studien und Kritiken*, 1836, p. 140 ff.
[2] Köstlin, *Der Lehrbegriff des Evangeliums und der Briefe Johannis*, Berlin 1843, p. 265 ff.
[3] Kahnis, *Die Lehre vom Abendmahl*, Leipzig 1861, p. 104 ff.
[4] Stier, *Reden Jesu*, 3d ed., Barmen and Elberfeld 1870, vol. iv. p. 232 ff.
[5] Bretschneider, Strauss, Weisse, Baur in his *Kritische Untersuchungen über die kanonischen Evangelien*, Tübingen 1847, p. 262 ff.; and Hilgenfeld in his *Das Evangelium und die Briefe Johannis nach ihrem Lehrbegriff dargestellt*, Halle 1849, p. 308 ff.
[6] Compare Hofmann, *Der Schriftbeweis*, Nördlingen 1860, vol. ii. part ii. p. 250.

on him. To this extent the Formula of Concord is right in the sentence: 'manducatio est credere,' or, more correctly, 'credentis' ('eating is to believe,' or, 'is the right of the believer'). Belief itself is not the eating of this bread, that is, of his flesh, but the Lord gives it to belief to enjoy. Belief is not a merely rational relation to Christ, but constitutes a relation of communion, and Christ became flesh so that belief should enter into communion with him in his human nature, and thereby obtain a share in the eternal life. This, however, is not a single act, like the Lord's supper, but a constant relation, like the 'unio mystica' ('mystic union').[1]

The words, nevertheless, do involuntarily recall the Lord's supper. Hence Bengel says: 'Jesu verba sua scienter ita formavit, ut statim et semper illa quidem de spirituali fruitione sui agerent proprie, sed posthac eadem consequenter etiam in augustissimum s. coenae mysterium, quum id institutum foret, convenirent' ('Jesus wittingly so shaped his words, that at once and ever they should properly treat of the spiritual enjoyment of him, but after this that the same should naturally fit also the most august mystery of the holy supper, when it should be instituted').[2] As Jesus, in the conversation with Nicodemus in the third chapter, does not speak of Christian baptism, but of that influence of the Spirit which forms the presupposition of the institution of baptism, so here in the sixth chapter he does not speak of the Lord's supper, but of that personal communion with the incarnate One in belief, which communion forms the presupposition of the Lord's supper. Thus, therefore, the evangelist could dispense with an account of the institution of baptism and of the Lord's supper, just as he dispenses with telling about Gethsemane by giving the scene in xii. 27 ff.

The concluding words offer the transition to, and the theme of, the third division of Jesus' discourse. Jesus

---

[1] Compare Hofmann, *Der Schriftbeweis*, Nördlingen 1860, vol. ii. part ii. p. 250; and Delitzsch, 'Die Rede des Herrn von dem geistlichen Genuss seines Fleisches und Blutes, aufs Neue erwogen,' *Zeitschrift für die gesammte lutherische Theologie und Kirche*, 1845, Heft 2, p. 24 f.

[2] Compare also Delitzsch, *ut supra*, p. 29.

gives to the believer the bread of life; Jesus gives himself to the believer as the bread of life; Jesus gives his flesh to the believer as the bread of life,—thus the thoughts proceed, not sharply distinguished, it is true, but yet in a gradual progress. He has now reached the last turn of the thought, and the offence the Jews take at it serves him as an occasion, not merely to develop it further, but also to repeat and develop it directly in the offensive form.

(c.) Verses 52–59.

He had named his flesh as the means of the impartation of life, and that his flesh in the exact sense and as a thing; not as the fact of his life or of his death, but in the sense of his human nature, though in a future manner.

Verse 52.

His words, however, are an offence to the Jews, just because they take them in the exact sense. It seems to them absurd that οὗτοσ, this one who stands before them, should be able to give them his flesh—this relation lies in the article, even without αὐτοῦ, which is lacking in א, but not in B—to eat. They add φαγεῖν ('to eat'), so as to make that perfectly clear. They try to explain it to themselves, but in contradictory ways: ἐμάχοντο, 'non jam solum murmurabant uti ver. 41' (Bengel) ('they strove,' 'now they do not merely murmur as in ver. 41'). The futurity in Jesus' discourse (δώσω, 'I will give') has not helped them over the difficulty, for they can hardly have noticed it. We have no reason to believe that the disciples perhaps might have suspected the answer to the riddle from the future. But they submit themselves to his word in the obedience of belief. Thus they become worthy of receiving afterwards from Jesus a view of the answer at least in the distance. On the other hand, Jesus is not inclined so to remove the difficulty for the Jews as to make believing obedience unnecessary. On the contrary, he increases the assumption. And, indeed, he heightens not only the necessity of the appropriation, but also the expression for the reality of the appropriation and of the one to be appropriated.

Verse 53.

Yes, it is true, ye must eat my flesh and drink my blood. Previously he had only spoken of eating the bread, and had designated the bread as his flesh. The Jews had combined both to the eating of his flesh. Jesus accepts this, and confirms this offensive thing. Indeed, he increases the offence by adding to the eating of his flesh the drinking of his blood. Accordingly, the second contains, not something different, but only the strengthening of what precedes. We cannot, therefore, give the flesh and the blood such different applications as Godet does. He refers the former to the holy life of Jesus, which we must behold in belief, by which we must allow ourselves to be pervaded, and which we must imitate. The latter he beholds in the death of Jesus, which we must appropriate in belief, and the atoning power of which we must taste. This view is like Lücke's; he referred both to the human life and death of Jesus. But, neglecting the *quid pro quo* ('equivalent'), which Godet puts for eating and drinking, flesh and blood here come under consideration, not as separated, but as associated points, and blood is not meant to offer something new, but to strengthen the old. Both, moreover, are a paraphrase for himself in his human nature. Hence Jesus connects participation in eternal life with the partaking of these; this life is deposited in him, the incarnate One—'Son of man.' The fact that Jesus speaks of an absolute necessity of eating and drinking his flesh and blood, does not, it is true, agree with the application of this to the Lord's supper, but is a sheer matter of course, if we are to understand by it the communion with the incarnate One which is imparted to belief.

Verse 54.

Hereupon follows the unconditionality of the effect. From this point onwards, instead of φαγεῖν ('to eat'), the more sensuous τρώγειν ('to eat eagerly') comes forward and remains, vers. 56–58. Although τρώγειν is elsewhere also used as synonymous with φαγεῖν, this use of it is doubtless for a certain purpose (against Meyer). In any case, the constantly renewed repetition of the same offensive speech about eating and drinking is designed. Jesus intends to speak offensively for those who do not believe, and does not purpose to facilitate or dispense with belief by removing the offence. On this account he here connects with the eating and drinking the same effect which he had previously, ver. 40, connected with belief, namely, the possession of eternal life and the resurrection at the last day, as the completion of the possession of life even for the natural side of the believer.

Verse 55.

He lays stress on the strictness and exactness in which he desires his words about eating and drinking to be understood. His flesh is ἀληθὴσ βρῶσισ ('true meat'), his blood is ἀληθὴσ πόσισ ('true drink')—this reading is, with B C L, to be preferred to the other ἀληθῶσ ('indeed'), which is easier, and, to be sure, supported by ℵ (ℵ is, moreover, confused in this passage), and as well to the still easier ἀληθινή ('true'). Jesus therefore designates his flesh and blood as true meat and drink. He intends the words to be taken in the exact understanding of them.

Verse 56.

In consequence of this, such eating and drinking bestows true communion with him. Bengel says: 'Qui edit et quod editur, re ipsa intime conjunguntur' ('he who eats, and that which is eaten, are in fact intimately joined together'). It is an internal and mutual communion: he *in me, and I in him,* and a lasting one: μένει ('remains'). This is a peculiarly Johannean expression. Although the similar ἐν Χριστῷ ('in Christ') is characteristically Pauline, yet this more intimate and personal sounding expression for the internal mutual communion: I in them, they in me, is characteristically Johannean; compare xv. 4 ff., xvii. 23, 1 John iii. 24 (iv. 16). This means what systematic theology calls the 'unio mystica' ('mystical union'). Lutheran theologians define it as the: 'realis et arctissima substantiae sacro sanctae trinitatis et Christi θεανθρώπου cum substantia fidelium conjunctio' ('real and most compact union of the substance of the sacred and holy Trinity and of Christ the God-man with the substance of the faithful').[1] More particularly, the 'unio mystica Christi cum homine fideli' is defined as 'conjunctio vera et realis atque arctissima divinae et humanae Christi θεανθρώπου naturae cum homine renato . . . ita ut Christus cum homine renato unum spirituale constituat et in ipso et per ipsum operetur,' etc. (the 'mystical union of Christ with one of the faithful' is defined as 'a true, real, and most compact union of the divine and human nature of Christ the God-man with the renewed man, . . . so that Christ forms one spiritual object with the renewed man, and works in and by him,' etc.). And among the consequences of this 'unio mystica' they reckon especially the 'desponsatio Christi cum fidelibus, qua sese aeternum copulat credentibus per fidem' ('espousals of Christ with the faithful, in which he joins himself eternally unto believers by faith').[2]

VERSE 57.

Upon the basis of the fact that Christ is the constant meat of such a one, that person has life, as Christ upon the basis of his relation to the Father has life: *As the living Father hath sent me, and I live because of the Father: so*—for it is beyond question that the latter clause begins here—*he that eateth me, he shall also live because of me.* That he is sent by the Father, says as much as that he is God's Son. This, moreover, is not merely a fact of a single moment, but a lasting relation, in which he, the incarnate One, now stands towards the Father. The Father is ὁ ζῶν, that is: he bears the life in himself; compare v. 26. Hence Christ also has life (ζῶ; see v. 26; therefore hath

---

[1] Quenstedt, *Theologia Didactio-Polemica*, part iii., Wittenberg 1685, p. 622 b.

[2] Calov, *Systema Locorum Theologicorum*, Wittenberg 1677, vol. x. pp. 526, 527. [The latter quotation not verbal.—C. R. G.]

he also given unto the Son to have life in himself) διὰ τὸν πατέρα, not 'through' the Father, but 'on account of' the Father—διά with the accusative denotes not the cause (De Wette), but the reason.[1] That means, not: because the Father lives, but: because he has the Living One for his Father;[2] the middle notion is that the Father bears life in himself.

Jesus, upon the basis of his relation of sonship to the Father, has part in the life of God. He at all times nourishes himself upon and out of this: the Father is his meat. So then also, upon the basis of the relation to Christ—δι' ἐμέ, because they have me for their food—believers have part in his life. Ὁ τρώγων με ('he that eateth me'), accordingly, must indicate in a similar manner a lasting relation, such as is given with the Sonship in the other case:[3] not a single act, or one repeating itself now and then, such as the Lord's supper would be, but an enduring relation of internal communion and intercourse of life. Christ the Son of God is the constant meat of believers. He became man, and bears life in his human nature, in order that we may enter into such communion with him, by means of which communion he is the food of our souls.

Verse 58.

Instead of flesh and blood, the person of Jesus himself now comes in, and is at once named the bread. With this the discourse returns to its beginning again, and even reaches back to the contrast with the manna from which the whole discourse started: *This is the bread which came down from heaven: not as your fathers did eat and are dead: he that eateth of this bread shall live for ever.* Οὗτοσ ('this') glances back to what he had said of himself or of his flesh and blood, namely, that it imparts the essential life. He

---

[1] Winer, *Grammatik des neutestamentlichen Sprachidioms*, sec. 49 c, 7th ed., Leipzig 1867, p. 372.
[2] Hofmann, *Der Schriftbeweis*, 2d ed., Nördlingen 1860, vol. ii. part ii. p. 251.
[3] Hofmann, *ut supra*, p. 252.

does not speak directly concerning himself thus: 'this one,' who gives life to the one eating (Lücke); for, aside from everything else, there would be no reason why Jesus should speak of himself in the third person instead of in the first, since he immediately before had said δι' ἐμέ ('because of me'), and earlier still had even named himself the bread. Nor is οὗτος to be taken in this way: 'this,' namely, my flesh and blood (De Wette); for the context, as what follows shows, demands a statement concerning the character of, and not a mere naming of, the bread (Meyer). That which lies in οὗτος is then taken up and developed in the following words: ὁ τρώγων κ.τ.λ. ('he that eateth,' etc.). He describes the bread as come from heaven, remembering and connecting it with what had been said before about the bread from heaven; compare ver. 32. He does not say of his flesh and blood, that is, of his human nature, that they are come from heaven; but that his human nature is the bread come from heaven, that is, the meat, springing from God and imparted to men, which bestows eternal life.

VERSE 59.

The evangelist adds that Jesus spoke these things while teaching in the synagogue at Capernaum. Before, in ver. 25, it is said in general, πέραν τῆς θαλάσσης ('on the other side of the sea'); it is defined more clearly by way of conclusion. We perceive from this that the fourth gospel also knows, and presupposes as well known, the stay of Jesus in Capernaum. The fact that Jesus taught this in the synagogue does not require a Sabbath; they gathered as well at other times in the synagogues. Moreover, this whole addition is certainly not merely an external historical note (against Meyer), but the evangelist desires to lay stress on the point that Jesus demanded belief as unflinchingly in Galilee and in Capernaum as in Judea and in Jerusalem, and that he spoke not less, but rather still more, offensively at the former than at the latter place—at the former in the synagogue, at the latter in the temple. He remained the same throughout.

Summary of the Discourse.[1]

After the details we have gone through, there will scarcely be any doubt as to what is intended by this discourse. We have convinced ourselves that the death of Christ is not the thing treated of, because we find nothing about the giving up of the body to death, but about the offering his human nature as food. Yet it does not have in view the offer in the Lord's supper; for neither is bread meant exactly, nor is the eating and drinking meant as an external act. It is a process of belief, in which belief enters upon such communion with the incarnate One that it becomes a partaker of eternal life which is deposited in Christ's human nature, and is there alone to be found and to be obtained. Christ desires to emphasize the fact that eternal life is joined to him, the one who has become man, and to this his human nature, and that in such a way that the personal relation to him shall thereby be brought to decision.

And such a decision was brought about by this discourse. It worked critically. The crisis in Jesus' Galilean activity is connected with it. This the evangelist reports in what follows.

(3.) VERSES 60-71. *The Crisis.*

The third division of this chapter depicts the effect of the speech, and at the same time the progress made both by unbelief and by belief.

VERSE 60.

The first effect was the surprise and the offence which Jesus' words excited in many, even among the circle of his

---

[1] On the history of the exposition of this discourse at Capernaum, compare Lücke, *Commentar über das Evangelium des Johannes*, 2d ed., Bonn 1834, vol. ii. Anhang B. pp. 727-735; Lindner, *Die Lehre vom Abendmahl nach der Schrift*, Hamburg 1831, pp. 241-266; Tischendorf, *Disputatio de Christo, pane vitae, sive de loco evang. Joann.* c. vi. vv. 51-59, *coenae sacrae potissimum ratione habita*, Leipzig 1839, p. 15 ff.; Mack, *Theologische Quartalschrift*, Tübingen 1832, Heft i. p. 52 ff.; Kahnis, *Die Lehre vom Abendmahle*, Leipzig 1861, p. 114 ff., and *Sächsisches Kirchen- und Schulblatt*, 1856, Nr. 51 ff.; and Rückert, *Das Abendmahl*, Leipzig 1856, p. 273 ff.

disciples. The μαθηταί ('disciples'), distinguished from the twelve in ver. 67, are here meant in the wider sense. Perhaps the followers of Jesus were more numerous in Capernaum than elsewhere. As we see, the evangelist presupposes the synoptic account of Jesus' Galilean activity, and particularly his stay at Capernaum.

The generality of the expression in ver. 61 shows that the offence which they took was a general one: ὅτι γογγύζουσιν οἱ μαθηταὶ αὐτοῦ ('that his disciples murmured'). They find Jesus' discourse σκληρόσ, that is, not dark (Chrysostom, Grotius, Olshausen), but, in contrast to μαλακόσ, 'suavis' ('mild'), rough, hard; then as used of conduct: inconsiderate; compare Matt. xxv. 24. This does not mean the thought of Jesus' death (for example, Meyer), which is not in question, and which also could not be called wounding. Nor does it mean the apparent assumption of Jesus, by reason of which he makes salvation dependent upon his person (Tholuck, Hengstenberg); for he had done that elsewhere, and he who could not stand that was no disciple of Jesus. What is meant is the inexorableness with which Jesus ever returned to the eating and drinking of his flesh and blood, and connected the true, eternal life, with that partaking of his sensible corporality. That was what they found offensive and unbearable. Τίσ δύναται αὐτοῦ ἀκούειν; who can persuade himself to listen to it?—αὐτοῦ is to be referred to λόγοσ ('saying'). And, indeed, they must believe that all was decreed in the One who became man, if they were not to find such a discourse unbearable, and be led astray in their belief.

Verse 61.

Jesus recognised the mood, ἐν ἑαυτῷ ('in himself'), without needing an external communication about it. Τοῦτο ὑμῖν σκανδαλίζει; 'hoc vos offendit?' 'Doth this offend you?' Σκανδαλίζειν is meant of an offence to belief, in the full sense, as also in other passages; compare Luke vii. 23. It is not in this place the σκάνδαλον τοῦ σταυροῦ ('offence of the cross;' Bengel says: 'passio Christi, scandalum Judaeis,' 'Christ's passion, an offence to the Jew'), but the above-mentioned offence at the emphasizing the corporality of Jesus.

Verse 62.

Jesus opposes to this offence the words, *What if ye now see the Son of Man ascend up where he was before?* These words can be taken either as an increasing of the offence, so that we must understand as an unspoken second clause: τοῦτο ὑμᾶσ οὐ πολλῷ μᾶλλον σκανδαλίσει; ('will not this offend you much more?')[1] or as a reference to an event in the future which shall bring the understanding of Jesus' words, and thus remove the offence (thus, besides Hofmann, Hengstenberg, Godet, and even Ewald and Brückner). The continuing the discourse by οὖν ('therefore'), instead of by ἀλλά ('but'), does not bear against the second explanation (against Meyer), since the discourse did not intend to mark the contrast, but to proceed from the present to the future. The decision lies in the way ἀναβαίνειν ('to ascend') is taken. If this is to be understood of Jesus' death (Meyer), it of course designates the increase of the offence. But if, as we saw, in general the saying about the death was not what gave offence, then also the 'seeing' of the death cannot be the more offensive thing. Moreover, ἀναβαίνειν, and above all ἀναβαίνειν ὅπου ἦν τὸ πρότερον ('to ascend up where he was before'), is nowhere in our gospel the expression for the death on the cross. The passages about the going away to the Father, ὑπάγειν πρὸσ κ.τ.λ., vii. 33, xiii. 3, xvi. 5, 28, or about being lifted up from the earth, xii. 32, to which, for example, Meyer appeals, do not permit of application here, since according to that view the thing in question here must be neither the going away to the Father, nor the lifting up, nor death in so far as it is a return to God, but death in so far as it is a sorrowful and, for a Jew, an offensive dying of the Messiah. Or

---

[1] Compare Winer, *Grammatik des neutestamentlichen Sprachidioms*, 7th ed., Leipzig 1867, p. 558; Meyer, De Wette, Lücke, *Commentar über das Evangelium des Johannes*, 3d ed., Bonn 1843, vol. ii. pp. 169-171, and Baumgarten-Crusius.

how can that expression denote the way, since it stands in contrast with the 'terminus a quo' ('starting-point')? Ἀναβαίνειν is in contrast with καταβαίνειν ('to descend'), which was spoken of so often in the preceding discourse.

Hence the old explanation of the church, the ascension, is the one called for by the words as well as by the context (thus also Olshausen, Ebrard, Kahnis, Hilgenfeld, Hofmann, Hengstenberg, Godet). It is not a fair objection to this to say that John then must have related it also. He certainly does speak of it, xx. 17,—whether before or after the death makes no difference (against Meyer),—and further xvi. 5, 7, 28, xvii. 11, 13, etc. The fact that he does not relate the external view of the event, corresponds to the manner of his historical narrative in general, which directs its gaze at the inner essence and the substance of the history.[1] Besides, the externality and the visibility of the event did not compose its essence, but was only a sensible figuring of what was essential, done for the sake of the disciples. The exact thing which is here emphasized, namely, the return ὅπου ἦν τὸ πρότερον ('where he was before'), had not been seen by the disciples. So much the less importance belongs to Meyer's objection, which lays all the stress on θεωρῆτε ('if ye see'), that the Galilean disciples to whom Jesus here speaks were not witnesses of the ascension. On the one hand, θεωρῆτε is not to be emphasized, but the last words on which all depended are to be emphasized. And, on the other hand, Jesus does not here distinguish between various disciples, but takes them all combined. The five hundred also on the Galilean mountain, who saw the glorified one upon the passage from this to that world, there saw him ascend where he was before, that is, upon his return to the heavenly spiritual existence which before was proper to him.

Beyschlag sees, in the fact that this is said of the Son of Man, a confirmation of his Christology, according to which Christ pre-existed as the Son of Man, namely, in the divine idea of the image. It follows, however, from this that

---

[1] Compare Luthardt, *St. John the Author of the Fourth Gospel*, Edinburgh, T. & T. Clark, 1875, p. 209 f.

pre-existence is here predicated of the Son of Man, but not that he pre-existed as the Son of Man (compare Meyer against Beyschlag[1]); what is expressed is merely the identity of the subject in the variety of the periods of his life. The post-earthly existence of the one who became man returns into the spiritual manner of being of his ante-earthly existence; save that even now, as the one who has become man, he is a partaker of the same. But this pneumatic manner of being is what offers the solution of the preceding problem and the possibility of eating and drinking, which was spoken of. His future is the solution of the riddle of his present. Thus Jesus directs them to it as the removing of the offence, but it is true he does it in such a way as to demand belief in the future, in order to make the belief of the present possible. That is his manner throughout. The event of that night, vers. 16-21, might serve the disciples as a type of the future in which they should believe.

Verse 63.

If the explanation given be correct, it will also afford at once a clear understanding of these next words: *It is the Spirit*—ℵ omits τό before πνεῦμα ('the' before 'spirit')—*that quickeneth; the flesh profiteth nothing: the words that I have spoken*—λελάληκα, with ℵ B C D L, Itala, Vulgate, instead of λαλῶ ('I speak')—*are spirit and are life.* If, therefore, he has spoken of his σάρξ ('flesh'), and has joined life unto the partaking thereof, he has in that had τὸ πνεῦμα ('the spirit') in mind; for this, not the σάρξ, is the power of life. The σάρξ, accordingly, has life only through the πνεῦμα, and for itself alone profiteth nothing, 'scilicet, ad vivificandum' ('namely, for quickening;' Bengel). It is a general truth—τὸ πνεῦμα, ἡ σάρξ without μου ('the spirit, the life,' without 'my')—that Jesus expresses, and that he wishes to have applied only to himself and to his words.

It is a matter of course that this cannot be understood of spiritual and fleshly understanding of Jesus (thus Chrysostom, Theophylact, Luther, Lampe). The σάρξ of Christ has just before been spoken of, and therefore here also

[1] Beyschlag, *Die Christologie des Neuen Testaments*, Berlin 1866, p. 85.

σάρξ and πνεῦμα must be taken in the objective sense. Hence σάρξ cannot be referred to the nature of men (Hengstenberg), much less to the hereditarily depraved nature;[1] for the thing in question is not the σάρξ of men, but of Christ. Nor is the Lord's supper meant, so that the spiritual partaking of the Lord's supper would be taught (Augustine, Calvin, Olshausen); nor the death of Christ, in which 'the corporality of Christ must be yielded up' (Meyer). The matter concerned is Christ's human nature, the life of which lies not in the σάρξ, but in the πνεῦμα which fills and rules in the σάρξ. When he speaks of his σάρξ, they are not to stop at this σάρξ which they see, but to fasten their gaze upon the πνεῦμα, which dwells in it, forms its life, and thus makes it able to impart life.

Jesus does not intend by this absolutely to deny what he previously said of his σάρξ, for that would have been to contradict himself; it is only that he desires to have it conceived, not for itself, but as the bearer of his πνεῦμα. When his human nature ceases to be fleshly in order to become spiritual—in the glorification—then they will understand it. Now, while it is still fleshly, they must believe on the πνεῦμα which dwells on him. The πνεῦμα is his internality, the σάρξ his externality, as the present manner of his human nature. The latter, the σάρξ, has its life in the former, but the former imparts itself only through the latter, for 'interna non dantur nisi per externa' ('internal things are only given through external'). He spoke of this πνεῦμα. The ῥήματα ('words') are not to enter upon its place and remain after his death, as a compensation (Lücke, De Wette, Baumgarten-Crusius), but they have πνεῦμα and ζωή ('life') as their contents; in this sense they are it. Ζωή is the effect of the πνεῦμα, and hence put last; life is conditioned on the participation of his σάρξ, because πνεῦμα dwells in it. That they should have said themselves. For it is indeed 'he' who spoke those words—ἐγὼ λελάληκα ('I have spoken') with emphasis—the bearer of eternal life. Therefore, if they have taken offence at his words,

---

[1] Wieseler, *Commentar über den Brief Pauli an die Galater*, Göttingen 1859, p. 446.

the fault is not in him and his words, but in them and in their concealed unbelief.

VERSE 64.

The circumstance that Jesus directly in this connection speaks of the concealed unbelief in the circle of his disciples, is due to the influence which Jesus' discourse had in bringing to view the unbelief which was veiled under the form of belief. It was intended to lead in this crisis. Nothing unforeseen occurred to Jesus. Hence the evangelist adds the remark, that Jesus knew from the beginning who those would be that did not believe, and who it was that should betray him. 'Eξ ἀρχῆσ ('from the beginning') stands contrasted with the revelation of unbelief and of the treasonable disposition. It cannot therefore point to the beginning of Jesus' Messianic activity (against Meyer), since it is not opposed to the issue of that; it refers to the beginning of the union with Jesus on the part of the person in question (De Wette, Baumgarten-Crusius, Tholuck, Hengstenberg). Jesus did not choose Judas with the design that he should betray Him (thus Augustine), but probably, according to the evangelist's words, with the consciousness whom he chose in Judas. This knowledge, however, is not to be thought of as a historical, but as a psychological one, by which Jesus could not let himself be determined as to whom, of those who followed him as disciples, he should receive into the narrower circle of disciples. The choice of Judas as an apostle was thus, then, an act of obedience to the will of the Father which was made known to him inwardly, and not an act of his own pleasure. Perhaps we may also recall the fact that, according to Luke vi. 12, Jesus spent the night, before the choice of the apostles, in prayer.

This view disposes of Strauss' and others' objections to the historical character of John's account. It is not hard to see how Jesus' discourse could serve to further the internal estranging of Judas. He had joined himself to Jesus, but that was for him only the means to the end of participation in the glory of the Messianic reign. Jesus, however, throughout designated as the way, that they must accept his person and seek the blessing of salvation only in it. Far from this moral communion, Judas must have been only the more estranged from Jesus, the more paradoxically He expressed that demand. Nor could it well be put in a more paradox-like way than it here is. The fact that Jesus chained men so to His person, and that as He actually was in His very self, and that He demanded such a comprehensive communion with Himself, must have made His person only the more strange to Judas, His person of which Judas wished to know nothing.—Judas' feeling rose to enmity.

Verse 65.

This verse connects closely with Jesus' words in the last verse: *Therefore said I unto you,* vers. 37, 44, *no one can* —moral possibility is the point—*come unto me,* that is, believe on me, *to whom it is not given of my Father,* namely, through that internal spiritual influence of the ἑλκύειν ('drawing,' ver. 44, 'per tractum gratiae,' 'by the drawing of grace,' Bengel) which men must accept.

An increase of belief, moreover, occurred in correspondence with this increased self-witness on the part of Jesus. This we perceive in Peter's confession, ver. 68 f. The importance of this confession, namely, lies not merely in its contents, but also in its historical situation. For in spite of the estrangement which Christ's words had excited, and in spite of the opposition which they saw raised and actually urged by men whom they had until now been able to reckon upon as one with themselves, the eleven make this confession through the mouth of Peter.

Verse 66.

'Εκ τούτου ('from that'), it says, many of Jesus' followers withdrew themselves. It is not 'from then onwards' (Lücke, De Wette), but 'in consequence of this discourse'. (for example, Meyer), that we are to understand this. The offensive character of Jesus' words was what brought about this withdrawal. The change of the internal posture towards Jesus manifested itself in the external leaving of his fellowship: οὐκέτι μετ' αὐτοῦ περιεπάτουν ('they walked no more with him').

VERSE 67.

Thereupon Jesus calls forth the decision of the apostles, and in such a way as to show that he was certain what it would be: μὴ καὶ ὑμεῖσ κ.τ.λ. *You also do not wish to go away?* Θέλετε ('wish'), 'Jesus neminem cogit, atque hoc ipso arctius sibi suos jungit' ('Jesus compels no one, and by this very fact joins his own more closely to him,' Bengel). The question is so put, that it makes us expect a negative answer. He directs the question to the twelve, not for his own sake, so that he should not be left alone, but for their sake, that he might bind them more closely to him. The crisis is to have as its consequence a progress in belief and in fellowship with him.

VERSE 68.

Peter, as the mouth of the rest, whose gift it was to say the right word at the right time,[1] denies the forsaking for all time: *to whom shall we* ever (this lies in the future) *go?* There is a double reason for the denial, in Jesus and in them. Thou alone *hast words of eternal life,* that is, thou hast and therefore also canst impart words, which have eternal, namely essential, life as their substance, and which, in consequence of this, if they are believingly received, have it as their effect. In this Peter looks back to ver. 63, and to the emphasizing of ζωὴ αἰώνιοσ ('eternal life') in Jesus' discourse in general. Although the disciples do not as yet fully understand the words of Jesus, they are nevertheless, by reason of what they have found in Jesus, certain of this, namely, that in him and in his words eternal life is decreed. 'Nobilissimum fidei implicitae in explicita exemplum' ('most noble example of implicit faith in explicit,' Bengel).

VERSE 69.

Corresponding to the objective reason for the disciples'

[1] See vol. i. p. 80.

remaining, which reason lies in Jesus, we next see the subjective reason, resting in their experience: *And*—corresponding thereunto—*we* on our part. This ἡμεῖσ ('we') is not to be taken in contrast with the apostates (thus Meyer), but, since it corresponds to the σύ ('thou'), in reference to Jesus. *Have believed and known:* the perfect intends to designate the belief and the knowledge as now existing. Peter adds after πιστεύκαμεν ('we have believed'), ἐγνώκαμεν ('we have known'), while elsewhere, xvii. 8, 1 John iv. 16, γινώσκειν ('to know') precedes πιστεύειν ('to believe'); this is to show that the knowledge here meant is one conditioned upon belief, and therefore to show that the knowledge has made progress. They have become quite sure of the matter. Πεπιστεύκαμεν looks back at the first belief which the disciples offered at their first meeting Jesus (Meyer); ἐγνώκαμεν, on the other hand, is that knowledge which since then has been allotted to them by reason of their belief, and as the reward of it. The expression of the confession shows this. For we are to read, with ℵ B C D L, ὁ ἅγιοσ τοῦ θεοῦ ('the holy one of God'). The received text, ὁ Χριστὸσ ὁ υἱὸσ τοῦ θεοῦ ('the Christ the Son of God'), with the addition τοῦ ζῶντοσ ('the living'), is transferred from Matt. xvi. 16. But Matt. xvi. 16 is half a year later, and therefore is fuller in its expression; here, moreover, though as to the matter it is identical with the other (against Ewald), the confession is of a more general character.

Some say the ὁ ἅγιοσ τοῦ θεοῦ is a name of the Messiah from of old (for example, Baumgarten-Crusius), but that is of little avail. Where did this designation for the Messiah come from, and why was just this one used here? Does it mean 'devoted to God' in the sense of an offering, which then might have the appearance of a connection with the discourse of Jesus? This is opposed by the remaining use of this designation of Jesus. In Mark i. 24 and Luke iv. 34, the demon addresses Jesus thus; and of course he means Jesus not as the offering of the world, but as the One separated from all men and fully belonging to God, the One who, because sin does not dwell in his flesh, and because his flesh is the organ of holy life, therefore has power over the realm of death. Hence it is that he there terrifies the demon. In like manner, Rev. iii. 7, he attributes to himself, the holy one, the power over death. In Acts iv. 27, this designation is brought into connection with the anointing of the Spirit; he is the Son of man, drawn from the sinful human race, and his human nature, because holy, can be the organ of the Spirit. And at 1 John ii. 20, accordingly, the anointing is traced to the holy one.

When, however, it is said in our gospel, x. 36, that the Father has sanctified him, the fact is simply expressed, that he, because the Son of God, has been as the Son of man separated from the race of sinful humanity, and appropriated to God, in order to be capable of becoming the bearer and the imparter of the divine blessing of salvation. This, too, is what Peter here means. He is the holy one of God, in so far as he, the only one among men, not only as to his personal will, but also as to his nature, is removed from the communion of human depravity, and as to his nature, therefore, can serve as the means of the impartation of the divine blessing of salvation, namely, of eternal life in its full extent.

Peter has gained this knowledge from Jesus' words. These his belief has recognised and experienced as words of eternal life. Thus, as we see, belief bases itself purely on the word, unmindful of the contradiction of the sensible appearance, and it takes what the word gives it as an earnest and pledge of the future possession. The certainty, however, to which he, led by the progress of Jesus' self-witness in the word, has advanced even in belief, is this: that Jesus' human nature, because that of the holy God, serves as the means of imparting the essential blessing of salvation, and accordingly, that there is an appropriation of eternal life, which appropriation is the reward of belief. From this time forward, belief knows that the human nature of the Son of God is the place of salvation, and therefore that this nature ever endures, because it is the eternal mediation of salvation, and rewards belief by self-impartation.

Verse 70.

But at the side of this word of belief, the strongest we have thus far read, appears in tragical contrast the strongest demonstration of the most hostile unbelief, as the point of the other side of the crisis. It is true that he, Jesus, has chosen the twelve; and yet one of them is a devil. Ἐγὼ ὑμᾶσ ('I, you'), designedly placed beside each other: *I*, I myself, no other, *have chosen you*—thus greatly are you distinguished—*for myself.* In ἐξελεξάμην the middle must be observed: 'chosen for myself.' Ἐξ ('out of') emphasizes, not so much the various other persons whom Jesus did not choose, as, in agreement with xv. 19, ἐκ τοῦ κόσμου ('from the world'), the opposite condition, to which they previously belonged.

And of you—put first with emphasis: the ones thus chosen by me—*one is a devil;* not *the* devil; not, on the other hand, merely devilish, but what the devil is for God, that Judas is for Jesus. The same relation of opposition in which God has come to stand, should also take place in the case of Jesus. And as little as God excluded Satan from the fellowship of the universe, so little was Jesus to exclude his opponent from his fellowship. The latter, like the former, must serve the saving will of God. The possibility of salvation is offered to the disobedient one. But this very offer must effect the opposite in the case of the unwilling one, and God then takes the divinely-ordered form of the sin of the hardened man into his service for the execution of his loving will. This the Scriptures teach us throughout, and this also is to be recognised here.

The purposely chosen expression διάβολοσ ('devil') bids us think of that parallel with Satan. It is utterly insufficient for the strength of the word to render it merely by denouncer (De Wette), or opponent, or betrayer (Lücke, Baumgarten-Crusius), or the like. It is meant to be taken in the strict, exact understanding (compare Meyer). This is required both by the Scripture usage in general, and by the use of this word in John's writings in particular (compare viii. 44, xiii. 2; 1 John iii. 8, 10). Baumgarten-

Crusius thinks it must mean Satan's child, but he entirely misunderstands the design of this designation. Jesus desires to say, not that Judas has apostatized to Satan, but that he is the representative of Satan for Jesus, because he is Satan's organ.

Verse 71.

The evangelist remarks by way of explanation, that Jesus spoke of (λέγειν τινά, 'to speak of a certain person;' compare ix. 19; Mark xiv. 71) Judas the son of Simon the Iscariot. According to B C, we are to read 'Ἰσκαριώτου (Sinaitic: ἀπὸ Καρυώτου, 'from Karioth'), so that it belongs to the name of his father Simon, as also in xiii. 26 (here א too). Like his father, so also was he thus named, xiv. 22. 'Ἰσκαριώτησ, אִישׁ קְרִיּוֹת, the man from Karioth, a town in the tribe of Judah, Josh. xv. 25, south from Hebron, in the neighbourhood of the Baptist's home. He seems to have been the only Judean among the twelve. Perhaps the Baptist had directed his attention to Jesus, and caused him to follow him.

Jesus names him διάβολοσ. This the evangelist explains (γάρ, 'for') by ἤμελλεν αὐτὸν παραδιδόναι, not: 'he intended to betray him'—he had not yet gone so far as this, compare xiii. 2,—but: 'traditurus erat,' 'he should betray him, according to divine ordering.' For God orders the circumstances and effects the form in which the sin of disobedience on the part of man comes to utterance and view.

Εἷσ ὢν (א too) ἐκ τῶν δώδεκα: *he who yet was one of the twelve.* With these words of tragic contrast the evangelist closes this piece of the narrative from Galilee. It forms a climax in the progress, both of Jesus' testimony to himself as the essential life, and of belief on the one hand, as well as of unbelief on the other hand.

Chapters VII.–X.

Jesus the Light.—The Struggle at its Height.

The self-witness of Jesus as the life, closed with the sixth chapter. Jesus had proclaimed himself, even according to his human nature, yes, directly according to his human nature, as the means of the impartation of life. The evangelist now adds the next part, how Jesus testified to himself also as the light.[1] For this purpose he brings forward the announcements which belong here. The most decided testimony of this kind falls exactly at a time in which the contention between Jesus and the Jews appeared in its greatest keenness, during his presence at the feast of tabernacles at Jerusalem. The evangelist therefore can, at one stroke, effect both designs to depict the progress of the historical relation between Jesus and the Jews, and to present Jesus' self-proclamation. To the degree in which the opposition becomes more keen, the self-witness of Jesus as the light of the world becomes clearer. We may therefore conclude that there is a relation between the two.

Life is the essential blessing of salvation, and thereby comes to meet the essential need, in order to satisfy it. Light, on the other hand, is the essential form of salvation, and thereby comes to meet the life-form of a salvationless condition, in order to put itself in its place.[2] That, however, cannot take place without correction of, or rather condemnation of, the opposite form of life. In consequence of this, with the proclamation of salvation as light, there is necessarily presented an opposition to the real state of life, which this proclamation finds to be existing,—an opposition which does not arise in this way at the proclamation of salvation as life. It is therefore said of the light, that it punishes the works of darkness; compare iii. 20. Where, now, this proclamation of salvation strikes upon an unprepared and unwilling state, the former must call forth the opposition of the latter in a constantly stronger way, because the former contains in itself a condemnation of the reality which comes to meet it. And according to the measure in which the actual character of life opposes itself to that proclamation, the latter constantly assumes more decidedly the form of the punishing light. By this means

---

[1] Compare Stier, *Reden Jesu*, 3d ed., Barmen and Elberfeld 1870, vol. iv. p. 324 f.

[2] On these conceptions, compare vol. i. p. 269, on i. 5.

it receives to an entirely peculiar degree, a deciding and dividing power.

Upon the ground of the consideration of these practical relations, the peculiar character of the section with which we now have to deal explains itself very readily. We are at once brought into this connection of thought in the seventh chapter, as is proved by Jesus' words at vii. 7, that he testifies to the world the salvationless condition of its actual life, and that he is on that account the object of their hatred. These words, which strongly recall iii. 19 ff., allow us at the same time to perceive the mood of Jesus, and show that he was aware of the situation and of the station to which the history had advanced.

We have seen[1] that this middle section of the second part is threefold: chapter vii.; chapter viii.; chapters ix.-x. It is again a drama in miniature. The seventh chapter shows us the new resumption of the conflict. The eighth chapter depicts it at its height. And from the ninth chapter onwards, Jesus, not without speaking a word of judgment upon his opponents, withdraws more and more, at first from the dispute, and soon from Jerusalem itself. Thus, externally viewed, the Jews remain upon the field of battle. But they are condemned, while the church of Jesus forms itself in the distance.

VII. 1-52. *Jesus' Meeting with the Unbelief of the Jews at Jerusalem.*

This chapter falls into three parts: (1.) vers. 1-13; (2.) vers. 14-39; (3.) vers. 40-52.

(1.) VERSES 1-13.

This first division leads us at once into the situation. Jesus stands in the midst of a world of unbelief; even his brethren do not believe on him. But the centre of the unbelief is Jerusalem. Since, then, the evangelist desires to show us the development of the conflict, he draws forth, from the mass of historical material, the encounter of Jesus

[1] See vol. i. p. 205 f.

with the unbelief of Israel at Jerusalem. With such presuppositions we shall be able to appropriate to ourselves the good remarks with which Baur introduces his discussion of chapters vii.-x. It is impossible to see why, because of that purpose, these events in Jerusalem must have been invented and could not have been picked out—we have here no occasion to enter more closely into the relation to the synoptic account. Moreover, Baur's declaration is refuted by the one fact, that Jesus before this had already appeared in Jerusalem, and, according to our evangelist, worked after this in Jerusalem.[1]

VERSE 1.

The narrative intends to call attention to the fact that Jesus did not seek the conflict, but let it come to him. The imperfects περιεπάτει and ἐζήτουν ('walked' and 'sought') show that both his activity in Galilee and the hatred and the murderous purpose of the Jews were something lasting. Herewith the time of a longer activity in Galilee is hinted at by the evangelist himself. In this clear manner he betrays that he has only made a choice, and knew quite well other gospel material from the Galilean residence. If Jesus, moreover, selected Galilee in order to avoid the hatred of the Jews, he would probably not have remained at Jerusalem after the feast. He merely made a festal visit to Jerusalem. Why should he at such an early point entirely break off his Galilean activity? Therefore he first of all returned again to Galilee. If, however, this visit was only a temporary interruption of the Galilean activity, the synoptists could well let it pass in silence. Towards the latter part of the year, then—we shall have to assume—he left Galilee for ever, because his time approached its end. At the middle of the winter, towards the close of the year, he appears in Jerusalem, x. 22 ff. From there he withdrew to Perea, where he spent the quarter of a year until the last passover.

According to his custom, the evangelist opens this account

---

[1] Compare also Hauff, *Studien und Kritiken*, 1849, p. 124 ff. ; and Beyschlag, *Studien und Kritiken*, 1874, pp. 650, 669 f.

with μετὰ ταῦτα ('after these things').[1] For μετὰ ταῦτα is not to be put after περιεπάτει ὁ Ἰησοῦσ ('Jesus walked'), as the received text has it, but before, as ℵ B C D have it. We may hesitate as to whether we should read καί ('and') before μετὰ ταῦτα, with B and the majority, or whether we should erase it, with ℵ. If we read καί, then the subsequent mention of the Galilean residence is thereby knit more closely to the preceding report. But for that very reason it was an easy matter for copyists to add it. The evangelist is content with the general formula: μετὰ ταῦτα, and leaves it to the reader to perceive, by a comparison of what precedes and what follows, that half a year of Galilean activity is comprehended in it. As we see, the evangelist knows well, and presupposes as known to his readers, such a residence; but he does not desire to make it the object of his narrative, because he hastens to the decision of the fate of Jesus.

In each case, for Galilee as well as for Judea, the evangelist writes περιπατεῖν ('to walk'), which is a frequently used designation of his for Jesus' activity in His calling; compare Baumgarten-Crusius on i. 36. *For he would not walk in Judea* — this assumes or implies that his most natural sphere of work would have been in Judea (Baumgarten-Crusius, against Meyer). The evangelist thereby recalls the fact that Jesus first appeared there, and was only compelled to leave Judea by the hostility of the Jews. Hence, then, every new presence in Judea will have as its result a renewal of that hostility, and will finally bring about the catastrophe. Jesus, however, wished to put it off as long as possible. Therefore: he did not wish to walk in Judea, *because the Jews sought to kill him*. This does not mean a practical conduct, but their continuing disposition, from v. 16, 18 onwards. 'The Jews' are, according to John's manner, those who represent the people in its opposition to Jesus, and for the most part the official heads of the people are intended by the phrase, and they were to be sought in Jerusalem as the hearth of the opposition.

[1] See vol. i. p. 26.

Verse 2.

This verse leads to what follows (δέ, 'now'). It was the approach of the feast of tabernacles which gave occasion both to the demand on the part of Jesus' brethren and to Jesus' subsequent journey to Jerusalem. The feast of tabernacles—חַג הַסֻּכּוֹת, Lev. xxiii. 34–36, 39–43; compare Ex. xxiii. 16; Deut. xvi. 13-15, σκηνοπηγία; also in Josephus — lasted seven days, from the fifteenth to the twenty-first of the seventh month, Tisri, October. An eighth day, the twenty-second, was further celebrated as a closing festival (עֲצֶרֶת), like the first day, with a sabbath rest and a holy convocation. The feast served as a thankful remembrance of the gracious protection afforded by Jehovah to the nation upon its wanderings through the desert, and at the same time it was a joyous celebration of the harvest then completed with the gathering in of the fruit and wine. It therefore was considered by the Jews after the exile to be the greatest and most glorious feast, and its celebration was distinguished by various customs: (1) By an arbitrary interpretation of Lev. xxiii. 40, those who visited the feast carried in the left hand a lemon, and in the right hand a palm-branch (לוּלָב), bound with sprays of willow and myrtle. (2) At every morning-offering, a priest, amid music and songs of praise, poured into two perforated vessels on the west side of the altar, water which he had drawn in a golden pitcher from the fountain of Siloah; compare Isa. xii. 3. (3) On the evening of the first day of the feast— according to later rabbinic accounts, on each of the seven days—there was an illumination in the court of the women by means of great golden candelabra, accompanied by a torch-dance before them.[1]

Verse 3.

The more joyful this feast was, at which the people were always accustomed to gather in great multitudes at Jerusalem, the more easy it is to understand why Jesus' brethren

---

[1] Compare Keil, *Handbuch der biblischen Archäologie*, § 85, Frankfort-on-the-Main and Erlangen 1858, vol. i. p. 412 ff.

called upon him to go also to the feast. As to the brethren of Jesus, compare what is said at ii. 12. In directing that call to him, they support it with the words: *that thy disciples also may see the works that thou doest.* They do not deny that he does wonderful works, or consider it a mere report (Baumgarten-Crusius), or problematical (Tholuck). On the contrary, it is just because he does them that he ought to go thither, so as to do them there too, and win for himself recognition. Jesus has not ceased his miraculous activity; he is rather in the very midst of it, as the present ποιεῖσ ('doest') shows. But he works in such a way that his disciples do not see it. Hence at that time he cannot have wrought in such publicity as would otherwise have been expected (Meyer also). This agrees with the picture which we gain from the synoptists, according to which, after the crisis of the passover of that year (compare what was said at vi. 66), Jesus withdrew himself from the public stage more towards the border lands, and devoted himself to his disciples, in the narrower sense, exclusively; we see him in the north-west, in the neighbourhood of Tyre and Sidon, Matt. xv. 21, Mark vii. 24; and in the north-east, Mark vii. 31.

If we may here presuppose these circumstances, the appeal of the brethren gains from this point of view so much the more light. They do not find the proper publicity in Jesus' working. His 'disciples' see too little of it. By this must here be meant, not the twelve, but the wider circle of disciples, all followers of Jesus. It does not refer to the followers he had won for himself in Judea, recalling iv. 1 (Godet, similarly I also in the previous edition). The evangelist might perhaps think of these, but the brethren of Jesus would not, because they proceed from their Galilean observations. If it be said that they thought of vi. 66 (Godet), and made a malicious (Brückner), or at at least a contemptuous (Stier) allusion to it, we must remember that Jesus had found 'disciples' in Galilee, and kept them in spite of the defection of so many. We need not therefore think of the Judean disciples merely (thus most frequently understood), and by no means of those yet to be acquired (Baur). Nor need we supply in thought an ἐκεῖ ('there'), and assume that the expression is not exact. Still less do we have to suggest that the reading is false (Lücke). His followers are, however, now all in Jerusalem, with the rest of the nation. He therefore is to transfer to that point the scene of his activity. They say: *into Judea*, for that is the chief province. Doubtless at the same time they think of the heads of the nation. It is the approval of these leaders alone that finally gives the decision. Hence he must seek for recognition there, and not in the out of the way corners of Galilee.

Verse 4.

The brethren of Jesus urge their demand by pointing to the internal contradiction in which Jesus' actions and claims stand towards each other: *For no man doeth anything in secret*—as seems to them to be the case with Jesus—*and yet himself seeketh*, for his person (αὐτό, B, can only be a mistake in copying for αὐτόσ), *to be known openly.* Παρρησία, from πᾶν and ῥῆσισ, in contrast with ἀρρησία, 'silentium,' 'silence,' designates primarily an openness in speaking which keeps nothing back; compare xviii. 20, x. 24; from this it is transferred to a manner of conduct in which a man does not keep himself back, but comes forward freely; compare xi. 54; Wisdom v. 1. It does not denote that which is undaunted and bold in contrast with that which is shy (Meyer), but that which is open in contrast with that which is concealed. Christ does not desire, as to his person, to be a hidden man, but to be one known in the recognition of all men, and therefore he should make his action to be, not a hidden one, ἐν κρυπτῷ, but an open one. It is true that αὐτόσ names the person in contrast with the action (Meyer), and does not merely resume the subject again (Lücke, Tholuck). Jesus' brethren call upon him to remove that contradiction.

From this it follows that εἰ ταῦτα ποιεῖσ is intended, not problematically or doubtingly (Tholuck, Lücke, De Wette, Brückner), but logically. *If thou do these things*, if thy action consists in such deeds as thou executest,—ταῦτα ποιεῖσ ('do these things') looks back unmistakably to τὰ ἔργα σου ἃ ποιεῖσ ('the works that thou doest'),—*make thyself and thy person known to the world.* Bengel says : 'Maius, inquiunt, theatrum quaere' ('Seek, they say, a greater stage'). The whole world is assembled there at Jerusalem at the feast; what occurs there has general importance. The 'world' is to be understood according to the sphere of vision of Jesus' brethren. The motive for their appeal is not to be sought in an ordinary selfishness and desire of gain (Lücke), although they may nevertheless have thought that, in case of the public recognition of their brother, some advantage would accrue to them and to the whole family. The fact is, that they also are like the rest of the Jews. They desire the revelation and communion of the kingdom of heaven by means of a sensible display of miracles, and not of moral belief upon the person of the salvation. The former, not the latter, is their aim in their appeal.

VERSE 5.

Hence the evangelist can say of them that they did not believe, although they owned the miracles of Jesus. Οὐδέ, *not even his brethren believed in him,* though it must have been the most easy thing for them. But doubtless they did not believe, just because they stood so near to him. They must first be convinced of the essential distinction between him and them. After the resurrection of Jesus we find them among the believers, Acts i. 14. Their unbelief, moreover, offers us no conclusions as to 'the condemnation of the miraculous account, in Matthew and Luke, of what happened before the birth of Jesus and during his childhood' (against Meyer, ver. 3), for these events were not the subject of common family speech. Jesus' glory wore at first still the purely moral form, and hence demanded for its recognition a moral posture towards it. That they lacked. What the evangelist here says of their unbelief does not denote merely weakness of belief or a temporary lack of belief (Hengstenberg, Lange), but an enduring position towards Jesus. We are not to read, with D L, ἐπίστευσαν, but ἐπίστευον [the former a momentary, the latter a

continuing state of (un)belief]. By this the possibility of
their being disciples is absolutely excluded, because discipleship calls for the opposite position towards Jesus. On the
contrary, they belong to the world, they condemn Jesus
after the manner of the world, and they wish to lead him
into the ways of the world.

Through this phase, their suggestion obtains for Jesus
the form of a temptation. It is put before him, that, in
order to win recognition for himself and realization for the
kingdom of heaven, he should enter upon a way which is
not the divinely intended moral way, but which would be
like the way into which, according to the synoptic representation of the story of the temptation, Satan also wished to
lead him. In the next place, he is to go his way upon his
own responsibility, without waiting for the time which the
Father should determine for his public self-witness. This
explains Jesus' answer in the following verse.

Verse 6.

He will indeed cause himself to be saluted at Jerusalem
as the king of the kingdom of God; but, on the one hand,
he will appear in a different manner from what they think;
and, on the other hand, it is not yet the time for that appearance. *My time is not yet come, your time is alway ready.*
His 'time' is not merely the time to journey to the feast,—
the word is much too emphatic for that,—but the right
point of time (ὁ καιρόσ) to reveal himself to the world, that
is, to present himself as the one whom he is. Hence it is
not the time of his passion, although that self-presentation
brought the passion upon him: Palm Sunday was followed
by Good Friday (Godet). But upon that very account he
must wait for the time appointed by God. His brethren
need make no such distinction of time. They can at any
time present themselves to the world as that which they are,
for they stand in unison with the essence of the world.

Verse 7.

They therefore do not have to expect the hatred of the
world. Οὐ δύναται ('cannot') is put first: it cannot at all;

it is a moral impossibility for the world, for it would hate its own. The discourse passes involuntarily over to the ethical notion of ὁ κόσμος. It is a matter of course that the world, spoken of in the fourth verse, bears in itself this ethical character. Jesus, on the contrary, is not only not of the world, but he punishes it even for its corresponding moral conduct. Its works are πονηρά ('evil'), because it is ἐκ τοῦ πονηροῦ ('of the evil one'); compare 1 John v. 19. Μαρτυρῶ, 'insigne opus Christi' ('I testify,' 'a special work of Christ's,' Bengel), which has passed over from him to his spirit of testimony, xvi. 8, and to his witnesses. Hence these also have the same lot to expect. Bengel says: 'Christianos quoque aut summo amore prosequuntur homines aut summo odio. Qui omnibus semper placent, sibi merito suspecti esse debent. . . . Mundi opera mala esse, ipsi mundani fatentur omnes; at se ipsum excipere nemo non conatur' ('Men follow Christians also either with the greatest love or with the greatest hatred. Those who always are acceptable to every one should justly be suspected by themselves. . . . Even men of the world agree that the works of the world are evil, but no one attempts to attend to his own case').

Verse 8.

They therefore are to go to the feast (without ταύτην, ℵ B D, etc.): *I go not up to this feast; for my time is not yet full come.* Most of the manuscripts, including B, have οὔπω ἀναβαίνω ('I go not up yet'), while ℵ D and others have οὐκ ἀναβαίνω ('I go not up'), as also the most of the versions, Epiphanius, Cyril, Chrysostom, Augustine, Jerome, and even Porphyrius, read; the last-named accused Jesus of 'inconstantia' ('inconstancy') on that very account (related by Jerome). Probably they changed οὐκ into οὔπω ('not' into 'not yet'), in order to ward off this reproach. Meyer thinks that Jesus did indeed change his purpose, and so think Bleek[1] and Baumgarten-Crusius. But aside from the fact that it is true here, no less than in

---

[1] Bleek, *Beiträge zur Evangelien-Kritik* (also: *Beiträge zur Einleitung und Auslegung der heiligen Schrift*, vol. i.), Berlin 1846, p. 106.

vi. 6, that he knew what he would do, Jesus' words, 'I go not up to this feast,' sound entirely too decidedly like a refusal, to be used to designate only a purpose, which in a few days would perhaps be exchanged for another. We must entirely refuse, as too nearly bordering on sophistry, the explanation which emphasizes the present and supplies in thought a νῦν ('now'): not now, but in a few days (Chrysostom, Bengel—'non jam vobiscum,' 'not now with you,' although he adds the more correct point: 'uti vos suadetis ut specter,' 'as you are urging that I may be seen,' —Lücke, Olshausen, Tholuck, Stier[1]); the explanation which takes οὐκ in the sense of οὔπω (De Wette); and the one which emphasizes the feast: Jesus did not visit the feast itself (Lange), or not in the legally prescribed way (Ebrard).

The answer is determined by the appeal. Jesus' brethren had not called upon him to a festal visit as such, but to visit the feast with public Messianic self-presentation. Jesus refuses this, repeating the preceding words,[2] yet in such a way as not merely to say: εἰσ τὴν ἑορτήν (' to the feast '), but he adds with emphasis ταύτην (' this '); compare also Godet. He will not at this feast go up to and enter into Jerusalem in the way they suppose. The context affords necessarily this 'in the way they suppose.' And ταύτην contains the contrast, that it will probably occur at another feast, though even then not exactly in the sense they think of. ' Unus jam proprie ascensus, ad pascha passionis, Domino erat propositus: de hoc per aenigma loquitur' (' One ascent in especial, unto the passover of the passion, was in the Lord's view; he speaks of this in an enigma,' Bengel). This disposes of Porphyrius' objection cited above, and as well of Bruno Bauer's suggestion of Jesuitry, and of Baur's of invention, in order to save the appearance of Jesus' independence. That the future festal visit stands before Jesus' soul, the visit which is to bring about the decision, is clear from the reason given: *for my time is not yet full come;* these words point to that decisive future. Godet recalls

---

[1] Stier, *Reden Jesu*, 3d ed., Barmen and Elberfeld 1870, vol. iv. p. 332.
[2] See vol. i. p. 25.

fitly Jesus' answer to the demand of his mother at Cana. There also, by the 'hour,' Jesus means the time of the decisive revelation in the future.

VERSES 9, 10.

Jesus therefore let the feast-pilgrims and his brethren go up to the feast, while he himself (αὐτόσ, ℵ; αὐτοῖσ, B) still remained in Galilee. Only after that did he also start off to fulfil his religious duty, but in such a way as to avoid all observation.

The first point, then, to be remarked in this report is, that Jesus attempts as far as possible to avoid a conflict with Israel. The next point is, that he for this reason does not yet testify to himself publicly in Jerusalem as the one whom he is, because this testifying would excite conflict. The third point is, then, that for this reason he is led to go to Jerusalem silently and in concealment, and that in this very thing it is shown that Israel has fallen under condemnation for unbelief. Because they would not recognise him, they shall also not be able to recognise him.

This οὐ φανερῶσ ἀλλ' ὡσ (ὡσ is lacking in ℵ D, but is elsewhere preponderatingly attested) ἐν κρυπτῷ ('not openly, but as it were in secret,' ver. 10) has been explained by Baur[1] and Hilgenfeld[2] in a singular exegesis, as a docetic change of form, or at least one bordering on docetism.[3] They believe they can extend it also to the stay in Jerusalem, and for this refer, besides, to the alleged traces of it in vi. 19, viii. 59, x. 39. This is utterly arbitrary. The extension of the alleged docetic veiling or changing of form to his stay in Jerusalem is in no way confirmed by the text, nor is the explanation itself at all to be drawn philologically from these words: 'He went to Jerusalem, not openly before the eyes of men, but as one journeys when

---

[1] Baur, *Kritische Untersuchungen über die kanonischen Evangelien*, Tübingen 1847, p. 166 f.

[2] Hilgenfeld, *Das Evangelium und die Briefe Johannis nach ihrem Lehrbegriff dargestellt*, Halle 1849, p. 244.

[3] Baur, *Vorlesungen über neutestamentliche Theologie*, Hamburg 1864, p. 367.

he desires to travel and to arrive in concealment.' He therefore doubtless avoided meeting people on the road, and took care not to enter the city in the day-time. The text says nothing about another way (De Wette), perchance through Samaria (Wieseler and Hengstenberg, according to Luke ix. 51 f.).

The combination of this journey with Luke ix. 51, where Jesus sends disciples before him, or above all with Luke x. 1, where Jesus sends out the seventy, is entirely untenable. These journeys were φανερῶσ ἀλλ' οὐχ ὡσ ἐν κρυπτῷ ('openly, and not as it were in secret'). This combination is based upon a failure to understand the alleged account of journeys in Luke ix.–xviii. In fact, this middle third of Luke's gospel is not an account of travels, but a collection of discourses, with the addition of the historical circumstances under which the various words were spoken.

Nor is this journey to the feast of tabernacles identical with Matt. xix. 1 (against Meyer). For we have no reason to assume that Jesus did not return again from Jerusalem to Galilee, and that he did not first leave this province for ever in order to pass the winter at Perea. For Jesus does not transfer his activity from Galilee to Jerusalem with the journey to the feast of tabernacles, but only interrupts it, merely in order not to remain entirely at a distance from the feast. His secret going up and arrival—what else is this than a sign of the judgment under which Israel has already begun to fall by its unbelief? The king of the kingdom of heaven comes to them; but their unbelief compels him to come secretly.

Verse 11.

The utterances which follow in vers. 11–13 serve to make us acquainted with the importance of this situation. I do not consider it, as most exegetes seem to do (compare De Wette, Lücke, Baumgarten-Crusius, Stier, Meyer), a settled thing that the seeking on the part of the Jews was a decidedly hostile one. The Jews, indeed, are, as elsewhere, meant in the sense of the hostile opposition, and not of the whole people (Hengstenberg). But the seeking was occasioned only by the fact that they were accustomed before to see Jesus at the feast in Jerusalem, and this time he was not at hand. 'Where is that one?' Ἐκεῖνοσ ('that one') bears a contemptuous accent: 'he does not dare to let himself be seen any longer.'

VERSE 12.

While 'the Jews' are settled in their decision about Jesus, the ὄχλοσ ('multitude'), especially the Galilean throngs, are wavering. They have all been busy thinking about him,—πολύσ ('much'),—but they did not know what they ought to think of him. Some declare him to be ἀγαθόσ ('good'), one who means all honourably, in contrast to the seducer of the people, which the others take him to be, that is, one who seeks only his own honour, etc. But it was only a γογγυσμόσ, compare ver. 32, a low murmur, 'sermo non audens erumpere,' 'speech not venturing to break forth,' Bengel.

VERSE 13.

Howbeit no man spake openly of him, on account of the fear of the Jews, which ruled in them. 'No one,' therefore not merely those judging favourably (so commonly), but also those judging unfavourably (Baumgarten-Crusius, Brückner, Tholuck, Hengstenberg, Godet, Meyer). So long as the authorities have not declared themselves officially, and the people are not certain of the definitive decision of the authorities, it seems prudent to refrain from every judgment, even from an unfavourable one. This position of affairs, the hostility of the authorities, the uncertainty of the decision, and the fear on the part of the people to come out with their decision,—all this shows that Israel advances to the judgment.

(2.) VERSES 14–39.

This section is to be extended to ver. 39, and not, as is usual (Godet also), to ver. 36. For ver. 37 ff. belongs to the preceding proclamation, and ver. 40 ff. belongs to the utterances mentioned in ver. 45 ff.

We perceived, from the fact that the Jews expected him

at the feast, that it was his custom to go to Jerusalem to the feasts. For this reason he went up now also. He dared not prepare for his enemies the triumph, that they might be able to represent him to the masses as one who was afraid to come, and who therefore had no good conscience, and no trust in God and in His support of his cause.

Verse 14.

Now about the midst of the feast, therefore perhaps on the fourth day; compare above, ver. 2, the description of the feast. If this journey belongs to the year 782 'ab urbe condita,' or 29 'aerae Dionysii,' the feast fell upon the 11th to the 19th of October, and the fourth day upon a Sabbath.[1] It is, however, not necessary to assume this, since at the time of the feast offerings were made in the temple, and the people were gathered together, every day.[2] It is hardly to be supposed that Jesus had even earlier than this been present in Jerusalem, concealed, and that he only now first appeared in the temple (Meyer, appealing to ver. 10). There would have been no reason for an earlier presence in concealment. The evangelist shortens the account by leading Jesus at once into the temple. Jesus could not stay in Jerusalem and be silent. He desires to use the opportunity of teaching, yet so that he does not directly provoke the conflict, and at the same time does not avoid it through fear.

In consequence he did not offer a direct self-witness, but gave his preaching a more general form, as we see from ver. 15. The Jews, here too the representatives of the opposition, wonder that he knows γράμματα, that is, not the Old Testament Scriptures, but 'literas,' 'letters,'—theological,—learning, Acts xxvi. 24, which was, it is true, Scripture learning, without having enjoyed learned instruction. We perceive by this that his teaching limited itself to exposition of the Scriptures, yet probably from the side of its

---

[1] Wieseler, *Chronologische Synopse der vier Evangelien*, Hamburg 1843, p. 309.

[2] Compare Lichtenstein, *Lebensgeschichte des Herrn Jesu Christi in chronologischer Uebersicht*, Erlangen 1856, p. 294.

prophetic contents. He thus avoided what he wished to avoid, and yet fulfilled his calling as a prophet of Israel; at the same time he made way for his self-witness.

Three periods of self-proclamation form the contents of what follows. Vers. 15–24: his doctrine is from the Father; he merely executes the Father's will, and is therefore blameless. Vers. 25–31: he himself is also sent by the Father, and comes from him. Vers. 32–39: he returns again to the Father, and that soon, by reason of the guilt of the Jews; his departure will be, to those who now will not accept him, unto judgment; to those who believe, unto blessing. Thus this section divides itself in a simple way both as to contents and as to outward form. Each of these declarations is called forth by a certain act of questioning on the part of the Jews.

Verse 15.

The words of the Jews, which led Jesus to his first declaration, may not be taken as an ill-meant questioning of his right to teach (Brückner). Were that so, why should we have ἐθαύμαζον ('marvelled') and πῶσ οἶδεν ('how knoweth'), instead of ἐγόγγυζον ('murmured') and διδάσκει ('teaches')? It is the power of his words which compels this sign of involuntary astonishment even from his Pharisaical opponents (Meyer). The scribes, at any rate, knew that he had not passed through their schools, as Paul later did with Gamaliel, and they saw it also in his method of teaching; compare Matt. vii. 29. Bengel says: 'Non usus erat schola. Character Messiae' ('He had not used a school. Mark of the Messiah'). And yet they must recognise him as learned in the Scriptures! Their wonder, however, is a morally worthless one. It does not permit itself to be affected by the contents of his teaching, but merely puts before itself the riddle of its origin. Instead, therefore, of allowing that recognition, wrung from their conscience, to be a leader to the recognition of the spirit and of the person of Jesus, it only serves them as a means of most thoroughly barring themselves off from this one who is not qualified to speak. The progress of the history to which we are at once brought, is the gradual hardening of the Jews against the truth which accredited itself to their knowledge and conscience; with this belongs the judgment of hardening. This explains to us how the Lord in the course of events can call them directly the children of the devil.

Verse 16.

Jesus connects his reply with the involuntary recognition, that is to say, with the manifestation of conscience, in order to lead it over to the positive recognition of his doctrine and of himself. By the effect of his exposition of the Scriptures, they are even now made capable of understanding and accepting the words of his doctrine, ver. 16, because this is the only possible solution of the problem at which they have arrived. Jesus' οὐκ ἔστιν ἐμή ('is not mine') is explained by the contrast to their question. They had conceived him in the conditionality of human being, which conditionality he shared with all. Jesus takes himself now also in the same way, and denies that this human nature is the source of his doctrine. If he had not learned from others that which he taught, he could, humanly, only have invented it. What essential change would that make, and how would the impression of his words be sufficiently explained by that? Jesus places the divine origin over against the human, even in the form of originality; compare viii. 28, xiv. 24. For Jesus speaks in the first place of the origin and not of the 'substance and character of his doctrine' (De Wette). But, of course, the latter also is determined by the former. 'Pater me docuit,' 'The Father hath taught me.' 'If we may speak humanly about it, his heavenly Father read to him a "collegium privatissimum," and that upon no authors.'[1]

---

[1] Bengel in Wächter, *Beiträge zu J. A. Bengel's Schrifterklärung . . . aus handschriftlichen Aufzeichnungen mitgetheilt*, Leipzig 1865, p. 125.

['Collegium privatissimum' is a technical term for the most private exercises at a German university. 'Public' lectures may be visited, and that without paying, by any matriculated student. 'Private' lectures, by any matriculated student who pays the fee for them. 'Most private' lectures or exercises are, as a rule, only open to such as receive permission on personal application to the professor, and are often, in the case of small

Verse 17.

The moral way alone aids in securing such knowledge. The θέλειν ('willing') of men must correspond to the θέλημα ('will') of God. 'Suavis harmonia. Voluntas caelestis excitat primum voluntatem humanam deinde haec illi occurrit' ('Delightful harmony. The heavenly will first arouses the human will: thereupon the latter hastens to meet the former,' Bengel). The way of knowledge is that of conscience, for it rests with the will.[1] The will, the heart, is throughout decisive. We do not will as we think, but we think as we will. We must desire to do the will of God, if we wish to come to sure knowledge concerning the question of Jesus' doctrine and its origin.

What will of God is it that Jesus here means? It has been referred to the will of the Creator as it is known in the conscience to all men, Rom. i. 19 ff., as the presupposition of the revelation of salvation and of the relation of salvation — thus my first edition, Godet, and at least included by Meyer and Stier. Others refer it to the revelation of God in the Old Testament (Bengel, Tholuck, Hengstenberg); or to the demand for belief made by Christ —'fides praecedit intellectum' ('faith precedes understanding')—(thus Augustine, Luther, Lampe: 'lex fidei,' 'law of faith'), as it were a 'belief on trial.' But belief cannot be the presupposition of the certainty of the divine origin of Jesus' doctrine, since it cannot exist at all without this. Those explanations are opposed by the fact that the question here is not as to God in general, but as to Him who 'sent' Christ, therefore as to the New Testament revelation. Hence we have no right to understand it generally of all

---

classes, held in the professor's own study. The 'upon no authors' refers to the custom, in such societies, of studying a particular author; as, for example, here at Leipzig in the last semester, winter 1876-77, Professor Harnack's society dealt with the *Muratori Fragment* and with *Eusebius' Church History*, and in the present summer semester, 1877, is dealing with the *Letters of Ignatius*. Men of high rank have at times taken 'collegia privatissima' as more consistent with dignity than lectures heard in class.—C. R. G.]

[1] Compare Stier, *Reden Jesu*, 3d ed., Barmen and Elberfeld 1870, vol. iv. p. 338.

grades and forms of revelation together (thus especially Meyer). Moreover, the thing treated of is not the definite religious contents of the New Testament revelation, as it is the object of belief, but of this revelation merely as the utterance of God's will to men, with which the posture of the will of men must correspond.

The emphasis does not rest on θέλημα ('will'), but on θέλειν ('to will'); we must 'will,' we must assume inwardly the right moral posture towards the revelation of God in Christ, if we desire to attain unto the certainty and knowledge of belief. Jesus here emphasizes the moral origin of belief, as in the corresponding passages before; compare on iii. 21, vi. 44. 'Here also the matter in hand is an inner moral posture of will towards the revelation of salvation, and not aside from it and outside of its sphere; therefore this is a posture of will, which has this revelation of salvation as its presupposition, in which it is true there is no consideration of the way in which such a direction of will is reached.'[1] Such a one will know whether (πότερον . . . ἤ classic, only found here in the New Testament) God or he himself, considered as isolated in himself, is the source of his doctrine.

Verse 18.

This verse proves that the former is the case. For the aim and the origin correspond to each other. He who speaks only from himself, has also only himself in thought and for his aim. 'Syllogismus: qui a se ipso loquitur, suam quaerit, falsus et injustus, gloriam; atqui Jesus non suam, sed enim Patris, a quo missus est, gloriam quaerit. Ergo Jesus non loquitur a se ipso, sed verus et fide dignus est' ('Syllogism: he who speaks of himself, false and unjust, seeketh his own glory; Jesus, however, seeketh not his own glory, but that of the Father by whom he was sent. Therefore Jesus speaketh not of himself, but is true and worthy of belief,' Bengel). Every one who desires to see perceives in him his pure devotion to his calling, which shows that he is concerned not for vainglory, but exclu-

---

[1] Compare Luthardt, *Die Lehre vom freien Willen*, Leipzig 1863, p. 420.

sively for God's cause. That is the point in which his brethren wronged him; they held him to be a φιλόδοξοσ ('one desirous of honour'), whereas they might easily have perceived the opposite in him. Jesus utters a general proposition (ὁ δὲ ζητῶν κ.τ.λ., 'he that seeketh,' etc.) in order to draw the conclusion, yet in such a way that this conclusion can only be applied to him. Ὁ ζητῶν τὴν δόξαν τοῦ πέμψαντοσ αὐτόν ('he that seeketh his glory that sent him'): 'duo hic includuntur: missum esse, et gloriam eius qui misit quaerere. Hoc illius criterium. Οὗτοσ, hic demum, ἀληθήσ verus et pro vero habendus' ('two things are included in this: to be sent, and to seek the glory of him who sent. The latter is the criterion of the former. "This one," this one at length, "true," true and to be held as true,' Bengel). This fact, that he seeks only the Father's δόξα ('glory'), is undeniable: hence the other point follows necessarily, namely, that he speaks the truth, and in general that there is nothing unrighteous in him.

Verse 19.

He now contrasts with this, the conduct of the Jews towards the will of God revealed to them in the law. It is unnecessary to assume a discourse or a transaction occurring in the meantime (Olshausen). How much less right have they, then, to wish to express and even to execute a sentence of condemnation against him! *Did not Moses give you the law? And none of you doeth the law.* This is the right punctuation, with the first mark of interrogation after the first τὸν νόμον ('the law'). This makes the second clause more important. Jesus turns from the defence to the accusation. 'Moses' is said with emphasis: the servant of God, by whom they therefore received the law as a revelation of the will of God. 'The law' here means the whole law, and not merely a part of it, say the sixth commandment, or the command about the Sabbath (thus Godet). He declares it as an unquestionable fact, that no one of them fulfils the legal will of God. How, therefore, can they, the transgressors of the law, place themselves as officers of the law against him the alleged Sabbath-breaker, whose acts are nevertheless the fulfilment of the will of God? *Why do ye seek to kill me?* It is an act of love when Jesus thus speaks straight out to the Jews their murderous purpose. Perhaps they may be horrified at their own thought, and so may give it up.

VERSE 20.

But those who are occupied with this purpose now desire to know nothing of it, and hence they let the others, who really know nothing of it, speak for themselves. This speech seems to the crowd the words of madness, only explicable on the supposition that a demon is presenting to his fancy horrible pictures, which in reality are nothing at all: *Thou hast a devil: who goeth about to kill thee?*

VERSE 21.

Jesus' answer apparently leaves out of consideration the words of the ὄχλοσ ('multitude,' ver. 20), but replies to them indirectly, by reminding the surprised people of the transaction, v. 2 ff., which had called forth the astonishment of all of them, and the murderous thought of the Jews, v. 16, 'Hierosolymis videntur alii fuisse insidiatores, alii id scisse, ver. 25, et ii qui hic loquuntur ab iis fuisse remotiores, nec tamen intus meliores. Jesus ostendit, se profundius eos nosse, et hoc radio eos penetrat' ('at Jerusalem some seem to have been plotters, others to have known that, ver. 25, and those who here speak seem to have been more remote from them, and yet not to have been be ter at heart. Jesus showed that he knew them very thoroughly, and pierces them with this ray,' Bengel). He has done only *one* work in Jerusalem, namely, since he had left this and Judea, and, on the other hand, made Galilee the scene of his activity; previous to that he had done more, ii. 23. This ἕν ('one'), therefore, is contrasted with the many in Galilee. The healing the sick man on the Sabbath is meant. They could neither forget nor forgive this supposed breach of the Sabbath. It formed the starting-point for the hostility.[1] Θαυμάζετε is

---
[1] See above, p. 93 f.

to be understood accordingly; it is not wonder, but indignant surprise, estrangement, and offence, that he could do such a thing on the Sabbath. This was general: πάντεσ ('all'). Ἐν and πάντεσ correspond to each other. The 'one' deed called forth such general surprise. But they should only think what position circumcision holds towards the Sabbath; then they will understand aright the relation of his miracle of healing to the Sabbath.

Verse 22.

This verse develops the thought. According to John's usual manner, compare v. 16, 18, vi. 65, viii. 47, x. 17, διὰ τοῦτο ('therefore;' improperly omitted by ℵ) is to be connected, not with θαυμάζετε ('marvel;' thus almost all later commentators connect it, Hengstenberg and Godet also), but with what follows (Chrysostom, Bengel, Meyer). In the former connection it would drag in a superfluous way. Moreover, ver. 22 is not then to be taken as a question, so that διὰ τοῦτο would refer back to θαυμάζειν: 'was it for this purpose, namely, that you should assume such a position towards my Sabbath-healing, that Moses gave you circumcision, and ye circumcise,' etc.? in which οὐχ ὅτι ... πατέρων ('not because ... fathers') is a parenthesis (thus Meyer earlier). On the contrary, the sentence proceeds in an entirely simple way, οὐχ ὅτι being the correlative of διὰ τοῦτο (Cyril, Bengel, Meyer). The reason is given doubly, after John's method, first negatively and then positively.[1] The circumcision which Moses appointed was given by him not as an outflow from the Mosaic legal order, but as an ordinance from the fathers. 'Amplificatur dignitas circumcisionis, respectu sabbati, quo illa fit antiquior adeoque potior' ('The dignity of circumcision in comparison with the Sabbath is enlarged, in that the former is more ancient and so more excellent than the latter,' Bengel). Jesus, moreover, names the fathers, not Abraham; for he does not wish to compare Abraham with Moses, 'but the economies themselves, the Mosaic and the patriarchal, with each other. The matter dealt with is not the prero-

[1] See vol. i. p. 44 f.

gative of persons, but of the time.'[1] Hence circumcision stands higher than the Sabbath.

The intention is not merely to emphasize the more exact holiness of that custom (for example, Meyer). Still less is it to call attention to the slight holiness of circumcision, because that rite 'was only an old tradition' (Godet, even Baumgarten-Crusius, Ewald), which is entirely impossible. As little is it merely a historical remark on the part of Jesus (Tholuck, Hengstenberg) or of the evangelist (Lücke), which would be altogether superfluous. Nor is the relativity of the Sabbath commandment to be proved by the one exception (thus commonly). The two economies, the old patriarchal and the Mosaic, therefore probably (against Meyer) that of the promise and that of the law, are contrasted by Jesus, as by Paul, Gal. iii. 17. Circumcision is the sign of the covenant of promise, which precedes the sign of the Sinaitic covenant, the sign of saving communion with God. For only 'by means of circumcision is a man received into the covenant, within which alone the blessing of the Sabbath rest can be imparted to him' (Besser and Burger in their popular expositions, following Lampe). Hence circumcision, taken up into the law, precedes the Sabbath.

Verse 23.

Accordingly, when the eighth day falls on a Sabbath, the circumcision is performed on the Sabbath (as Schürer says:[2] 'One of the numerous features which prove that the fourth evangelist knows the Jewish circumstances exactly'), so that the law of Moses, which commands the circumcision on the eighth day, may not be broken. For ἵνα μή ('that not') is to remain in its proper meaning, and not, against the language, to be changed into 'without that' (for

[1] Lampe, *Commentarius analytico-exegeticus evangelii secundum Joannem*, Amsterdam 1726, vol. ii. p. 328: 'sed ipsas oeconomias Mosaicam et patri-archalem inter se conferre. Non hic de personarum, sed de temporis agebatur praerogativa.'

[2] Schürer, *Lehrbuch der neutestamentlichen Zeitgeschichte*, Leipzig 1874, p. 489. See also Luthardt, *St. John the Author of the Fourth Gospel*, Edinburgh, T. and T. Clark, 1875, p. 172 f.

example, Bengel, Bäumlein). How can they then be angry because he has made an entire man sound on the Sabbath day?

Jesus compares with circumcision his deed, that he ὅλον ἄνθρωπον ὑγιῆ ἐποίησεν ('made an entire man well'). This cannot be intended as a contrast of wounding and healing,[1] for Jesus puts his act into one category with circumcision. On the same account, the contrast of the legal and of the human interest (Baumgarten-Crusius) is not admissible. The category intended is shown, not by the healing which follows upon circumcision (Lampe), since not it but the circumcision is the thing spoken of; nor by the medicinal aim (Lücke), of which neither law nor Jew thought;[2]— but by the importance and meaning of circumcision in the history of salvation. It has a relation to the salvation of man, but only as to one special side of it, namely, in so far as his body serves for propagation, and directly in this place needs purification.[3]

Jesus, on the other hand, has made the entire man well, that is to say, has brought his whole bodily life into the proper condition. Ὅλον ἄνθρωπον ('entire man') is to be thus referred to the body, and not to body and soul (for example, Bengel, Olshausen). But this bodily healing is to be taken in its correct meaning. It was a true health in so far as it could and would be to the man the mean of appropriating the essential salvation (compare on v. 11, 14 f.), and in so far as at the same time it should be a representation of this essential salvation itself. Accordingly, this healing stands in one category with circumcision, and therefore also belongs to the saving revelation of God, to the sphere of the gospel, which is above the law. Hence it is admissible on the Sabbath, indeed it is a duty, as much as circumcision.

---

[1] Kling, *Studien und Kritiken*, 1836, p. 157 f.

[2] Compare Keil, *Handbuch der biblischen Archäologie*, Frankfort-on-the-Main and Erlangen 1858, vol. i. pp. 309, 310 f.

[3] Compare Hofmann, *Weissagung und Erfüllung im alten und im neuen Testamente*, Nördlingen 1841, vol. i. p. 100; Baumgarten, *Theologischer Commentar zum alten Testament*, Kiel 1843, vol. i. p. 200 f.; Delitzsch, *Genesis*, 4th ed., Leipzig 1872, p. 327 f.; and Keil, *ut supra*, vol. i. pp. 309, 310 f.

Verse 24.

Jesus can therefore reproach the Jews with judging the matter only according to the external appearance, and not according to its essence and its meaning. Κατ' ὄψιν ('according to the appearance') does not designate the countenance of Christ, 'without form and comeliness,' in contrast to the beaming face of Moses (Hengstenberg). Aside from the arbitrary suppositions brought in, this is disproved by the fact that ὄψιν stands without the article (as at xi. 44, Rev. i. 16, to which therefore Hengstenberg is wrong in appealing). The meaning is the ordinary one: that which lies before the eyes, forms the external appearance. As to this external side, Jesus' healing might seem to be a breach of the Sabbath, but they must judge quite otherwise if they took the thing itself into account. *But judge*, that which is due in this case, *righteous judgment*. Κρίσιν κρίνειν ('to judge judgment') is after the familiar Hebrew manner of repeating the noun in the verb.[1] If the aorist κρίνατε (ℵ) is to be read instead of the present κρίνετε (B D L), a doubtful point, the expression becomes somewhat peremptory. The aorist denotes that which takes place at once.[2] This, however, seems less suitable here.

The fact that Jesus and the Jews think of a transaction which had occurred a considerable time before, can only surprise one who, in the first place, fails to observe to what extent the appearance and the action of Jesus busied the thoughts of the Jews, and how single acts of his in Jerusalem must retain their place in memory the more easily the more rarely he appeared at Jerusalem; and who, in the second place, does not consider that in the eyes of an Israelite a breach of the Sabbath was no less than a crime worthy of death.

Jesus therefore, as we have seen, in his whole exposition proceeds from the principle, that both in his doctrinal preaching and in his actions it is exclusively the Father's will that he is executing, and that accordingly his whole self-

---

[1] See vol. i. p. 53.
[2] Winer, *Grammatik des neutestamentlichen Sprachidioms*, § 43. 3. *a*, 7th ed., Leipzig 1867, p. 293 f.

presentation in both relations is determined by and has its origin in God. He then turns this in such a way as to convince his opponents of the unjustifiable character of their conduct and of their disposition towards him.

Verse 25.

Thus the discourse passes from his actions to his person. Some take occasion (οὖν, 'therefore') of his bold self-vindication to express their thoughts about him. They are characterized as residents of the capital, distinguished not only from the heads of the people, whose murderous plans they know without sharing in them, but also from the Galilean crowds, who are not acquainted with those plans of the authorities. Thus clearly, as we perceive, does the situation stand before the eyes of the evangelist in his memory.[1]

Verse 26.

Since they know the thoughts of their authorities, they wonder that Jesus is permitted to speak so openly and freely, without any one contradicting him. *Have, then, the authorities*, the rulers, that is, the members of the Sanhedrim, *perhaps really perceived that this is* — ἀληθῶσ ('truly') after ἐστιν ('is') is to be struck out—*the Messiah ?* Μή in questions for which a negative answer is presupposed: it is not so, is it ? This question is only raised, to be at once cast aside as an impossibility.

Verse 27.

Howbeit we know this man whence he is; but when the Messiah cometh, no one will know whence he is. According to Jewish opinion, the descent of the Messiah, namely, not his Davidic ancestry, but his closer family connection, was to be unknown. He was to go forth from concealment.[2] Doubtless this view was based on Mal. iii. 1: ' shall suddenly

---

[1] See vol. i. p. 230, and Luthardt, *St. John the Author of the Fourth Gospel*, Edinburgh, T. and T. Clark, 1875, p. 178.

[2] See Schürer, *Lehrbuch der neutestamentlichen Zeitgeschichte*, Leipzig 1874, p. 585; and Luthardt, *ut supra*, p. 172 f. Schürer refers to Justin Martyr, and to the Targum Jonathan on Micah iv. 8.

come,' etc. They thought they knew Jesus' descent from Mary and Joseph too well for him to be the Messiah.

VERSE 28.

This gives Jesus occasion to raise his voice instructing in the temple, crying aloud—ἔκραξεν—for a weighty testimony was now to be dealt with. Bengel says: 'clamores quos edidit magnas habuere causas' ('the cries he put forth had great causes'). Such an introduction of Jesus' testimony by the evangelist is intended to enforce the impression of the παρρησίᾳ λαλεῖ ('he speaketh boldly'), ver. 26. The Lord had come into his temple, Mal. iii. 1. *Ye both know me, and ye know whence I am.* They did not know his doctrine, whence he got it, though they imagined to themselves that he perhaps might himself have invented it. In like manner, they did not know as to his person whence it was, though they fancied that they did know. On account of that imagination they did not receive the former, and on account of this supposed knowledge they did not accept the latter. They think they know Jesus' footsteps back to the very beginning; while the Messiah introduced by the raised Elias will appear so suddenly, that they will merely be able to say he is there, but not by what way he came.

Should we say that Jesus now concedes to them that knowledge which they suppose themselves to possess? How can he say in one breath, that they knew his origin, and that they do not know the Father from whom he has come? Jesus' reply, therefore, cannot in any case be 'simple earnest' (compare De Wette), and just as little a real 'concession' (Meyer, and also Bengel). From Luther and Calvin to Lücke, Tholuck, Stier,[1] and even Godet, the predominant explanation is that the words are ironical. For myself, with Grotius and Lampe, I think I must prefer the interrogative way of taking it. Bengel says: 'Ironia nunquam usum invenias dominum' ('you nowhere find that the Lord used irony'). It is true (Baumgarten-Crusius) that this meaning does not lie in καί ('and'),—an assumption neither applicable nor necessary,—but κἀμέ, on the

[1] Stier, *Reden Jesu*, 3d ed., Barmen and Elberfeld 1870, vol. iv. p. 354.

other hand, does not hinder this way of taking the passage, as Stier declares. The two clauses are placed in a causal relation to each other by the close connection of the double καί. They think they know the one thing in and with the other. Hence Jesus can turn it round, so that with the second he also denies the first.

He first turns himself against the πόθεν (' whence '), Baumgarten-Crusius. Καὶ κ.τ.λ., ' et tamen a me ipso non veni, ut vos putatis' ('and yet I did not come of myself, as ye think,' Bengel); that characteristically Johannean καί.[1] His vocation comes from another, from one who is a right one, not: a true one, ' verax,' ἀληθής (against Cyril, Chrysostom, Theophylact, Euthymius, Lampe, Baumgarten-Crusius, Stier), but a real one (ἀληθινός denotes the reality of the idea), namely, a real sender. For the subject belonging to this attribute lies in the ὁ πέμψας (' he that sent '), and is therefore πέμπων (' one sending'), Meyer. Ἀληθινός is meant as an attribute, and not absolutely, so that it might be a designation of God as the true (Olshausen, Hengstenberg), in which case it must at least have the article. This one they do not know, in spite of all their fancied knowledge of and propriety in God, because they do not stand in ethical fellowship with him. Hence they also do not know Jesus himself.

Verse 29.

He, however, knows him on the basis of the relation of fellowship in which he stands towards him. *For I am from him, and he hath sent me.* He is from him, as to his person, and as well as to his vocation. His relation to God, therefore, is not merely the relation contained in his sending, but an essential one. Παρ' αὐτοῦ εἰμί (' I am from him') must denote something beyond the limits of that which follows, something going before it as a presupposition, and lying at its foundation. He has received the absolute vocation of God to humanity, only because he is the one who is from the Father. That, therefore, is the right knowledge of the πόθεν ('whence'). He is from the Father, both as to his being and as to his vocation. In

[1] See vol. i. p. 43 f.

these two phrases, then, Jesus comprehends, in the most concentrated way, his entire self-witness.

Verse 30.

This and the next verse depict the whole situation in a few words. The more the Jews are convinced by the internal testimony of their conscience, the more (οὖν, 'then') their opposition, hatred, and murderous desires grow. In this appears the judgment of hardening, to which they become more and more subject; and at the same time the fact appears that they dare not do what they wish to do, but that Jesus' history proceeds according to the saving will of God: *Because his hour was not yet come.*[1] It was not conscience (Hengstenberg, Godet) that held them back, but fear in the presence of the respect that Jesus enjoyed. But in this the hand of God ruled, which still put off the last decision.

Verse 31.

The belief of the masses stands opposed to the enmity of the Jews. The received text reads: πολλοὶ δὲ ἐκ τοῦ ὄχλου ἐπίστευσαν ('many of the multitude believed'). ℵ D read: π. δὲ ἐπίστ. ἐκ τ. ὀχ. ('many believed from among the multitude'). In distinction from these orders for the words, B puts the last words first: ἐκ τ. ὄχ. δὲ πολλ. ἐπίστ. ('of the multitude many believed'); this brings out more distinctly, in correspondence with the situation, the contrast between the Galilean popular masses and the leaders. According to ℵ B D L, the introductory ὅτι ('that') before 'Χριστός' ('Christ') is to be omitted. Instead of μήτι, according to the manuscripts, we must read μή ('not'); and we must strike out τούτων ('these') after σημεῖα ('miracles'), as an unnecessary explanatory addition. Ποιεῖ ('does'), instead of ἐποίησεν ('hath done'), the reading of B, is not sufficiently attested (ℵ D), and seems to be a correction, which is easily to be explained by the fact that Jesus' miraculous activity still continued. Part of them had probably also seen his Galilean miracles.

Even the Messiah, they think, cannot do more miracles.

[1] On this, see vol. i. p. 131 f.

Therefore Jesus must be the Messiah. We may perceive with sufficient clearness the small moral value of this Messianic belief of the Galileans, by the fact that they base it on the number of Jesus' miracles. Hence it was a matter of course that this belief of the masses should not grow to be a power which made the hostile operations of the spiritual authorities impossible. The execution of the hostile plans could only be delayed somewhat; at last the wavering ones must bow themselves to the issue.

Verse 32.

Thereupon follows the paragraph of Jesus' proclamation, vers. 32–39, which becomes a proclamation of judgment. At the urging of the Pharisees, a decree of arrest was determined on by the Sanhedrim. That is what we are to understand by ἀρχιερεῖσ καὶ οἱ Φαρισαῖοι (' the chief priests and the Pharisees'). It is true the members of this highest court of judgment, seventy-one in number, are commonly called ἀρχιερεῖσ, πρεσβύτεροι, and γραμματεῖσ (' chief priests, elders, and scribes'). Here, aside from the high priest, the members in question are characterized, not according to their rank, but according to their religious or theological party, in correspondence with the occasion (at the suggestion of Pharisees) and with the aim, to find support among the people, before whom the Pharisees enjoyed much greater respect than the Sadducees, to which latter party the ἀρχιερεῖσ (' high priests') belonged. By the last named, as Schürer[1] has proved, we are to understand, not, as is usually assumed, the presidents of the twenty-four orders of priests, but the real high priest, both the previous one and the one acting, and the remaining members of the high-priestly families who were members of the Sanhedrim. Before the evangelist relates the issue of the attempt at an arrest, he lays before us two utterances of Jesus, which were occasioned by the position of the matter, and in particular by the presence of the servants of the court, which servants we must regard as being near him.

[1] Schürer, *Studien und Kritiken*, 1872, pp. 593–657, *Lehrbuch der neutestamentlichen Zeitgeschichte*, Leipzig 1874, p. 420 f.

Verse 33.

First comes Jesus' declaration that he goes unto the Father who hath sent him. He goes to the Father because he came from him. The latter must be as exactly meant as the former. The meaning of it for the Jews is, however, that he then is taken away from them, and thus the way of salvation is withdrawn from them.

Verse 34.

This he tells them in the words: ζητήσετέ με καὶ οὐχ εὑρήσετε κ.τ.λ. ('Ye shall seek me, and shall not find,' etc.). At the time of the judgment, which must come upon Israel on account of the rejection of Jesus, they will in anxiety of soul seek Jesus—not merely the Messiah—and not be able to find him. Thus Meyer explains it rightly, against Lücke and De Wette, who take the whole merely as a characterization of the complete separation. They will seek him, but will not be able to reach him—Jesus continues. For he will be (εἰμί, not εἶμι, as Bengel says; the latter is foreign to the New Testament) with God, and they will be not merely on earth, but also in a state of condemnation, forsaken of God, far from God. These words are a proclamation of the judgment, full of tragedy.

Verse 35.

The Jews do not understand Jesus' words. This is the predominant evil mind, which is determined not to understand and own the judgment plainly enough announced to them. They were capable of knowing what πρὸσ τὸν πέμψαντα ('unto him that sent me') meant, ver. 33. We have no right, for the sake of ver. 35, to consider this as an addition of John's, since the evangelist would thereby himself have made his account unintelligible, and would have spoiled it. Therefore the question on the part of the Jews cannot be a seriously intended conjecture (Meyer). This is confirmed to us by a comparison with viii. 22, which is only an intensifying of the passage before us. It is not yet open scorn, as in that place, but dissembling, which acts as if they 'could' not understand Jesus' words.

Whither will he—οὗτος, scornfully: this fellow here—*go, that*—for thus is ὅτι to be understood simply, with Meyer—*we*—ἡμεῖς, with B, against ℵ, not without a contrasting emphasis over against Jesus—*shall not find him,* shall not be able to find him? *He will certainly not go to the dispersion*—of the Jews—*among the Greeks*—thus is the genitive τῶν Ἑλλήνων to be taken of the external, local relation, since "Ηλληνες in the New Testament never means the Hellenists, that is, the Greek-speaking Jews, and therefore the 'diaspora,' but only the Greeks, namely, the Gentiles—*and* there perchance also *teach the Greeks* themselves, because he can succeed in nothing among us? In this they must unconsciously declare the future of the gospel proclamation. It proved to be so, just because they would not know anything of him: an involuntary prophecy, like the later one of Caiaphas (compare Godet, Meyer).

VERSE 36.

Or—they proceed—if he does not mean that, as is not in the least likely, what do his words mean? *What saying is this that he said, Ye shall seek me, and shall not find: and where I am, ye cannot come?*

VERSE 37.

To the above the evangelist now adds an utterance of Jesus, because it properly belongs here. Vers. 40 and 45 look back to vers. 31 and 32. The fact that the time is mentioned in ver. 37 does not necessarily prove that the following words were spoken on another day. It simply intends to say: in the loudest festal joy of the last most gladsome day he cried publicly and openly, εἰστήκει καὶ ἔκραξεν, his message. The 'last great day,' according to Bengel, the seventh, is doubtless more correctly usually regarded as the eighth day, which, like the first, had a sabbatical character; compare on ver. 2. When we observe that Josephus[1] calls the feast of tabernacles in general σφόδρα ἁγιωτάτην καὶ μεγίστην ('most especially holy and great'), we can easily imagine that the joy rose to the highest pitch on the last day. It is true that the libation, the pouring out of the water, to which Jesus' words referred, no longer took place on that day. But Jesus may well have let his words concerning the higher fulfilling of that type follow upon the type itself, so that they entered upon its place.

By the pouring out of the water at the side of the altar, see ver. 2, to which Jesus' words referred, they represented in a figure the promise, Isa. xii. 3: 'with joy shall ye draw water out of the wells of salvation.' As Israel in its passage through the desert was miraculously supplied with drink by God, so in the Messianic age salvation was to go forth from Zion like a living stream; compare Ezek. xlvii. 1; Joel iv. 18; Zech. xiv. 8. This is now fulfilled in Jesus. Jesus cried these words, standing—thus the more invitingly:—*If any man thirst, let him come unto me* (א omits πρὸσ ἐμέ, 'unto me') *and drink;*—compare Matt. v. 6: grace fills up human emptiness. Bengel says: 'sitire prima animae ad salutem aspirantis proprietas et character certissimus' ('thirsting is the first property and the most sure mark of a soul longing for salvation'). Ἐρχέσθω ('let him come')—compare Rev. xxii. 17: καὶ ὁ διψῶν ἐρχέσθω, ὁ θέλων λαβέτω ὕδωρ ζωῆσ δωρεάν ('and let him that is athirst come. And whosoever will, let him take the water of life freely'). The coming takes place in belief. Hence ὁ πιστεύων ('he that believeth') afterwards enters in its stead. Belief has a double promise: for itself and for others.

Verse 38.

The evangelist purposely places by the side of the future judgment upon unbelief, ver. 34, the promise of the future blessing which is given to belief. The promise, however, is a double one. He who believes shall not merely himself

---

[1] Josephus, *Antiquitates*, VIII. iv. 1; *Opera*, ed. Bekker, Leipzig 1855, vol. ii. p. 174.

find satisfaction in the Spirit which will fill him ($\pi\iota\nu\acute{\epsilon}\tau\omega$, 'let him drink'), but shall also mediate this blessing of salvation to others: *He that believeth on me, as the Scripture saith, streams of living water shall flow from his body.* 'He that believeth on me,' that is, not: he that thirsteth, but: he that cometh to me and drinketh. This is made to precede in the nominative absolute, in order to be taken up again by $α\dot{v}τοῦ$ ('his'), in the Hebrew manner.[1] It is hence unnecessary, with Bengel, to supply the copula: 'he who believeth, he is such a one as the Scripture saith,' etc., that is, an analogue of the Messiah;—this explanation is needlessly forced.

Further, $\dot{o}$ $\pi\iota\sigma\tau\epsilon\acute{v}\omega\nu$ $\epsilon\dot{\iota}\sigma$ $\dot{\epsilon}\mu\acute{\epsilon}$ ('he that believeth on me') does not belong to $\pi\iota\nu\acute{\epsilon}\tau\omega$ before it, so that then the following $α\dot{v}τοῦ$ ('his') could be referred to Christ.[2] What followed in $\dot{o}$ $\pi\iota\sigma\tau\epsilon\acute{v}\omega\nu$ would in that case be already contained in $\dot{\epsilon}\rho\chi\acute{\epsilon}\sigma\theta\omega$ ('let him come'), and would therefore drag on behind in a superfluous way. Moreover, the one who believes cannot be called upon to drink, since the drinking is already included in the believing. It is the thirsty one who is invited to drink, as the parables show (Meyer). $\dot{O}$ $\pi\iota\sigma\tau\epsilon\acute{v}\omega\nu$ takes up both: $\dot{\epsilon}\rho\chi\acute{\epsilon}\sigma\theta\omega$ $\kappa\alpha\grave{\iota}$ $\pi\iota\nu\acute{\epsilon}\tau\omega$ ('let him come and drink'), in order to add the further promise according to the Scripture. The words $\kappa\alpha\theta\grave{\omega}\sigma$ $\kappa.\tau.\lambda.$ ('as,' etc.) do not intend to define more closely $\dot{o}$ $\pi\iota\sigma\tau\epsilon\acute{v}\omega\nu$ $\epsilon\dot{\iota}\sigma$ $\dot{\epsilon}\mu\acute{\epsilon}$, and emphasize the fact that belief is in agreement with the Scriptures (thus Chrysostom, Theophylact, Calvin). This is neither necessary nor possible, since $\kappa\alpha\theta\grave{\omega}\sigma$ $\kappa.\tau.\lambda.$ is a form of citation, and therefore must relate to what follows, not to what precedes (so most commentators).

What passages of Scripture are meant can only be drawn from the due understanding of what follows. In this it is clear that the thing spoken of is not, as before, the blessing which the believing one receives for himself (thus Baumgar-

---

[1] See vol. i. p. 55 f.
[2] Thus Stier, *Reden Jesu*, 3d ed., Barmen and Elberfeld 1870, vol. iv. p. 366 f., appealing to various practical expositions; Hahn, *Die Theologie des Neuen Testaments*, Leipzig 1854, vol. i. p. 229 f.; Gess, *Die Lehre von der Person Christi*, Basel 1856, p. 166; Steinmeyer, *Beiträge zum Schriftverständniss in Predigten* [2d ed. Berlin 1859 ?], vol. ii. pp. 123, 129.

ten-Crusius: 'his soul will hence for ever have enlivening and satisfaction from the deep'). This is at once refuted by the ἐκ τῆσ κοιλίασ αὐτοῦ ('out of his belly'). For this implies that from his fulness, the blessing now streams forth to others. What follows is said of the believer, not of Christ so that αὐτοῦ were to be referred to the latter (thus Bengel, Hahn, Gess, see above). The expression κοιλία ('belly') is occasioned by the figure of drinking, and therefore is in the first place to be taken corporally, and not as identical with καρδία ('heart,' Chrysostom). Yet it is not to be limited to the abdomen (thus Meyer), but designates the 'interior of the body' in general.[1] By the working of the Spirit, even the bodily nature of the believer is to become a holy place, an abode and fountain of the Spirit, and a means of its impartation. In comparison with the foregoing, this unmistakably contains a progress.

If the words concerning the new beginning of the personal life were followed by the promise of the blessed influence, which even the nature of the man should experience, chap. vi., nevertheless this is now placed not merely in a receptive, but also in an active relation to the Spirit. Here is promised something analogous to, the analogue of, what was imparted to Jesus himself at his baptism. As the Spirit-filled streams of the living and enlivening water proceeded from him in the word of his mouth, so shall it be in the case of those who believe on him. In this their sensible nature they shall be the fountains of life for others.

It is true that no such passage is found word for word in the Old Testament. But it is not necessary upon that account to think of an apocryphal or lost saying.[2] It is far-fetched, with Hengstenberg, to think of the Song of Solomon iv. 12, 15, and utterly wanting in taste to refer to vii. 3, where the Shulamite's navel is compared to a round goblet. Nor does the citation depend on the κοιλία

---

[1] Compare Delitzsch, *Biblische Psychologie*, 2d ed., Leipzig 1861, p. 266.

[2] Compare Weizsäcker, *Untersuchungen über die evangelischen Geschichte*, Gotha 1864, p. 518; Bleek, *Beiträge zur Evangelienkritik* [*Beiträge zur Einleitung und Auslegung der heiligen Schrift*, vol. i.], Berlin 1846, p. 234, note, and *Studien und Kritiken*, 1853, p. 331 f.

('hollow'), so that the comparison were to be sought, with Olshausen, in the κοιλία of Mount Moriah, out of which the fountain Siloah proceeds; or, with Godet, in the rock in the desert, from whose inner parts the water streamed. The point is the streams of living water, under which figure the Old Testament often presents the blessing of the Messianic period of salvation, both in the prophecy as to the stream of life, which proceeds from the sanctuary, Ezek. xlvii. 1-12, Joel iv. 18, Zech. xiv. 8, and in the pictures of the Messianic revival of life, Isa. xliv. 3, lv. 1. Here, however, throughout, the thing spoken of is only the Spirit which proceeds from the Messiah. Hence we should, with Hofmann,[1] refer to Isa. lviii. 11, where the one who is supplied with drink by Jehovah is compared to a well of water מוֹצָא מַיִם, whose water does not fail. This is like the passage in the conversation with the Samaritan woman, iv. 14, where it is said that the water 'will be in him a fountain of bubbling water;' compare on that passage.

Verse 39.

But this he spake of the Spirit, which (οὗ, attraction) *they that believed* (B: πιστεύσαντεσ; ℵ: πιστεύοντεσ) *on him should receive; for the* (*Holy*) *Ghost was not yet* (B: πνεῦμα ἅγιον δεδομένον; others: δοθέν, 'Holy Ghost given;' this is an addition; moreover, ἅγιον, 'holy,' is omitted by ℵ K T, in opposition to the majority of the uncial manuscripts, and apparently for dogmatical reasons, in order to avoid the apparent denial of the third hypostasis, since πνεῦμα, 'spirit,' alone could be understood of the effect of the Spirit, of spiritual life); *for Jesus was not yet glorified.* The evangelist's explanation has been objected to (Lücke) because he explains ῥεύσουσιν ('shall flow') by the pentecostal outpouring of the Spirit, which no one could have thought of then, and of which Jesus cannot have spoken. But aside from the fact that the canon here expressed cannot be conceded, it is to be answered that ἤμελλον λαμβάνειν ('should receive') does not explain the ῥεύσουσιν itself,

---

[1] Hofmann, *Der Schriftbeweis*, 2d ed., Nördlingen 1860, vol. ii. part ii. p. 13.

but is intended to name the fact which necessarily preceded it, on which that ῥεύσουσιν is conditioned.

The fact which the evangelist names began with the 'breathing' of the Raised One upon the disciples, xx. 22, and with the reception of the Spirit at Pentecost,—and the evangelist speaks from this his experience,—but it continued itself in the Christian church, in that the believers were filled with the Holy Ghost by word and sacrament. The effect, however, which Jesus names, ver. 38, is all the Spirit-moved activity of believers in the service of Jesus and of his church, in which they made their nature a means of this service. It appears, for example, even in every Spirit-moved and Spirit-breathing word, in which the loosened, healed tongue of the Christian poured itself out. From this we may perceive in what sense οὔπω ἦν πνεῦμα ἅγιον ('the Holy Spirit was not yet') is to be understood. It does not mean merely 'the activity' (Tholuck), or 'the ruling and enduring appearance and working of the Holy Ghost' (De Wette), or the dwelling of the Spirit in the heart (Godet). Nor is the intensified presence and activity of the Spirit merely absolutely expressed instead of relatively (Hengstenberg), for this would always presuppose the existence of the Holy Ghost, and therefore stand in contradiction with the words. What is meant, is the Spirit in this—New Testament—specificness (Meyer), which is to be recognised from the effect named: a specific character, which the Spirit could not receive until it had become the Spirit of the glorified Son of Man, and thereby had also as such become free, while it previously was shut up in Jesus.[1]

It is true the Spirit was already present and active in the Old Testament, as the Spirit of prophetic illumination and so forth, and as the Spirit of a divinely-conformed willing and living. But in its New Testament specific character it was a new thing, even for the consciousness of the disciples; compare, for example, 1 John iv. 13. It was promised by Jesus as such, and was experienced in its working as the Spirit of regeneration, of adoption, and the

---

[1] Compare Hofmann, *Der Schriftbeweis*, 2d ed., Nördlingen 1857, vol. i. p. 195.

like. This specific character and working of the Spirit was dependent on Jesus' completion of his work of salvation, and on his glorification.

Jesus' first words, ver. 33 f., had told the result his lifting up was to have for unbelieving Israel. The next words, ver. 37 f., told the results for his own. Yet even these words are a judgment for Israel: it thereby loses the future of salvation, which is attached to the person of Jesus as the fulfilment of all Old Testament pre-representation of the future of salvation.

(3.) VERSES 40–52.

This third section describes to us the effect of Jesus' words. The first confessions out of the midst of the people show what impression Jesus' self-testification made on those who let themselves be determined by it, without bringing in other considerations and thereby changing its impression. We can here perceive the testimony of the conscience in its sincerity.

VERSE 40.

They took him for the expected prophet; compare on i. 19: *Many of the people therefore, when they heard this saying, said, Of a truth this is the Prophet.*

VERSE 41.

Others even take him to be the Messiah himself. Upon this follows the utterance of the impression, which allowed its simplicity to be rendered turbid by the consideration of external circumstances which seemed to contradict it. To the people, he was only the Nazarene, and was to be the Nazarene.

VERSE 42.

But according to prophecy the Messiah was to spring from David's race and from Bethlehem; compare Micah v. 1; Isa. xi. 1; Jer. xxiii. 5. They knew nothing of this in the case of Jesus. The conclusion that the evangelist also knew no better (De Wette, Keim), is an entirely unsupported conclusion. He simply reports, so as to characterize the situation. Why should he correct what his readers knew at any rate correctly (Meyer)?

VERSE 43.

The evangelist closes: *So there arose a division among the people because of him;* compare ix. 16, x. 19. As long as they do not allow Jesus' self-testification to work purely upon them, but permit themselves to be at the same time determined by all kinds of presuppositions and critical thoughts of their own, they come to no surety and consistent certainty in regard to Jesus. We see how the right belief had to be begotten exclusively by Jesus' word. It dared not base itself on what is visible, but had to content itself with a certain contradiction of the visible. But we perceive of what description Israel was, in the fact that it could not free itself from its hold upon externals.

VERSE 44.

The mood just displayed was, upon the whole, a favourable one, and now the opposite mood is contrasted with it. The point of their being condemned now appears much more decidedly. It shows itself at the very first in the feebleness of the hostile will. The person of Jesus affects them with a certain awe, which involuntarily binds their hands. Τινέσ ('some') doubtless means some of the people who were desirous to help the servants to seize Jesus (De Wette, against Meyer). This, and not an act of mob-law (Meyer), is the thing suggested by the following reference to the servants of the court. But they could not persuade themselves really to do it. They were, of course, not merely held back by respect to the multitude who confessed Jesus as the Christ, or who were at least favourably disposed towards him. The reason was doubtless the same as in the case of the servants themselves.

VERSE 45.

These, the servants, as they return, without executing their orders, are called to account by those designated by ἐκεῖνοι, 'they,' as inwardly distant from the evangelist who had despatched them: *Why have ye not brought him?*

VERSE 46.

The servants allege that the power of his word was what made it impossible for them to carry out the command of their chiefs. The received text reads: οὐδέποτε οὕτως ἐλάλησεν ἄνθρωπος ὡς οὗτος ὁ ἄνθρωπος ('never man spake like this man'), with E G H K, etc. The reading of ℵ is οὐδέποτε οὕτως ἄνθρωπος ἐλάλησεν ὡς οὗτος λαλεῖ ὁ ἄνθρωπος ('never spake man as this man speaks'). On the other hand, B L T have only οὐδέποτε ἐλάλησεν οὕτως ἄνθρωπος ('never spake man thus'). Is the omission of the words perhaps an oversight (Meyer)? The last words may also be an addition, and that addition have been completed in ℵ by λαλεῖ ('speaks'). Bengel says: 'Character veritatis etiam idiotas convincentis, prae dominis eorum' ('the stamp of truth convincing even simple men before their masters'), and in another place: 'haud raro facilius rudiores virtutem verbi Christi, quam sagacissimi, persentiscunt' ('not seldom ignorant men perceive the virtue of Christ's word more easily than the wisest men do').

The power which Jesus' personality exercised even upon the hostile minds, and which displays thoroughly how Israel never could have seized and slain Jesus if the will of God and of Jesus had not itself permitted it, and which then, moreover, finds its actual confirmation in the story of the arrest, xviii. 6,—this power is at the same time a condemnation of the enmity. This hostility appears as condemned. If it reaches its desire in the end, that is only a sign that God has given it up entirely to the judgment of unbelief. They will fall into this judgment, because they have hardened themselves in unbelief.

VERSE 47.

This hardening is distinctly portrayed. The judgment of hardening shows itself in both the directions in which the hostility declares itself, both towards the conscientious utterance of their servant, and towards the legal requirement held up to them by Nicodemus. Against the excitement of the servants' consciences, they bring to bear their authority. *You are not deceived too, are you?* As the servants of the Sanhedrim, ye have no right to entertain any other conviction than this.

Verse 48.

Have any of the rulers—that is, the members of the Sanhedrim—*believed on him, or of the Pharisees,*—the representatives of orthodoxy ? These are the official authorities on the two sides, of office, and of moral respect. Bengel says: 'Simili argumentatione ac fremitu utuntur, zelotae hodierni praesertim Romanenses' ('zealots of to-day, especially Romish zealots, use similar reasoning and murmuring').

Verse 49.

But this—οὗτοσ, 'iste, ad contemptum pertinet' ('*this,* is contemptuous')—*people, who knoweth not the law—they are cursed.* For we must understand the sentence in such a way that ἀλλά ('but') brings the contrast to what precedes: but only this ignorant people believe on him; so that ἀλλά is 'sed' ('but'), and simply continuing, not 'at' ('but'), 'interrupting' (Meyer). Then, however, at last the speech does break off and turns to the cursing of the people.

The received text has for 'cursed:' ἐπικατάρατοι, not classical, after Gal. iii. 10, 13. The reading of ℵ B L T is ἐπάρατοι, classical, but not found elsewhere in the New Testament, Septuagint, or Apocrypha. They called the people cursed, but we must not forget that in the first place they do not mean the people in general, but the multitude inclined to follow Jesus (Baumgarten-Crusius), and that in the second place they utter ἐπάρατοί εἰσιν in the strict sense. It is not intended as a conclusion; that they concluded from the inclination of the people to follow Jesus, that it stood under the curse (Ewald, Hengstenberg). That would be entirely too much a matter of reflection for the passionate excitement of the moment (compare Meyer). But in their passionate excitement they declare the curse upon the people. It is not that they thereby excluded these persons at once from the religious body; but in their passion they uttered the inconsiderate words which they then only needed to formulate as a decree, and probably did formulate at once; compare ix. 22 and Baumgarten-Crusius.[1] Of course it was merely a conditional cursing, namely, for the followers of Jesus (against Meyer).

According to their view, this following of Jesus is only to be explained from ignorance. They look down upon the people with proud contempt. Nowhere was the pride of scholars greater than in Israel.[2] They called the common people עַם הָאָרֶץ ('people of the land'), even שְׁקֶץ, abomination. So much the less do they hesitate to utter the curse on the unlearned people. According to the word of God, the curse of the law affected only the transgressor of the law, Deut. xxviii. 15 ff., but they utter it against those who believe on the fulfilment of the promise in Jesus. In this act they show how, on account of their unbelief, they were given over by God, to do that which is against God's word.

VERSE 50.

In like manner they also show themselves as condemned in the reply by which they strike down Nicodemus' objection. Scruples were raised by Nicodemus, out of their own midst—as the evangelist says emphatically in the words εἷς ὢν ἐξ αὐτῶν ('being one of them'). Nicodemus is mentioned three times in our gospel. This passage forms the transition from his first timidity in the third chapter, to his final joyful confession, xix. 39. The fact that he here lifts up his voice for Jesus, is, especially for one of his peculiar nature,[3] a great step. Bengel says: 'Saepe ii qui timidi fuerant extra discrimen, in ipso discrimine veritatis defensores evadunt' ('often those who have been timid when not

---

[1] Baumgarten-Crusius, *Theologische Auslegung der johanneischen Schriften*, Jena 1843, vol. i. p. 314.

[2] Compare Gfrörer, *Das Jahrhundert des Heils* [*Geschichte* (not *Kritische Geschichte*) *des Urchristenthums*, part i.], Stuttgart 1838, vol. i. p. 140 ff.; Schürer, *Lehrbuch der neutestamentlichen Zeitgeschichte*, Leipzig 1874, p. 442.

[3] See vol. i. p. 104 f.

tried, prove defenders of the truth in the very time of trial'). The received text has an explanatory clause, ὁ ἐλθὼν νυκτὸσ πρὸσ αὐτόν ('he that came to Him by night'), with E G H M. The reading of D is ὁ ἐλθὼν πρὸσ αὐτὸν νυκτὸσ τὸ πρῶτcν ('which came to him by night at the first'), from xix. 39. And B L T read better, ὁ ἐλθὼν πρὸσ αὐτὸν πρότερον, without νυκτὸσ ('he that came to him before;' omit 'by night'). The codex Sinaiticus leaves this clause out. Certainly the difference of readings makes the addition suspicious, especially as its insertion is more easily to be explained than its omission.

VERSE 51.

Nicodemus is not yet, however, so far on as to stand up for Christ openly. He clothes his defence of Jesus in a defence of the law. *But our law does not judge the man*—τὸν ἄνθρωπον, the man coming under consideration—*before it* (to wit, the law, namely, in the person of the judges) *has heard him, and known what he doeth*, what he is about; compare Deut. i. 16.

VERSE 52.

His comrades see quite clearly that this is a mere pretext, and they ridicule him: *You are not from Galilee too?* A Judean cannot believe in Jesus. He is good enough as Messiah only for the Galileans. Jewish theology looked upon Galilee in a careless, contemptuous way.[1] If, with the received text, and with Meyer, Hengstenberg, and Godet, we are to read ἐγήγερται ('has arisen'), the Sanhedrists utter a historical error. It is useless to try to avoid the difficulty in the sentence by understanding it thus: 'no chief prophetic figure, and no greater number of prophets, have proceeded from Galilee' (Hengstenberg); that is an entirely arbitrary limitation of the general sounding phrase. Godet's explanation, that in Jesus the Galilean no true prophet has arisen in Galilee, brings in an addition arbitrarily. It must, in the case of this reading, be acknow-

---

[1] See Winer, *Biblisches Realwörterbuch*, 3d ed., Leipzig 1847, vol. i. p. 339.

ledged that the Sanhedrists in their passionate zeal overlooked the prophets born in Galilee, to which at least Jonah belonged, according to 2 Kings xiv. 25, probably also Nahum from Elkosh (hardly in Assyria),[1] and perhaps Hosea from the kingdom of Ephraim.[2] To ascribe the error to the evangelist, in order to roll it off from the Sanhedrists (Bretschneider, Baur), makes the matter no better, but worse.

But according to the manuscripts א B D L, we are to read ἐγείρεται. Then this saying does not point to the past but to the future, and puts itself in contradiction to the promise. The promise, they think, does not refer to despised Galilee, but to Zion and Jerusalem—from this place shall the light arise, according to the unanimous testimony of the Old Testament. Therefore the Messiah cannot be a Galilean, but must be a Judean. This conclusion is apparently one to which they are compelled. But Isaiah had indeed seen the light of salvation arise from Galilee, and spread over Israel; Isa. ix. 1 ff. Hence the prophetic proclamation, and as well the prophet of salvation, will go forth from Galilee. In consequence, their hostile mind, which does not wish to believe and to be obedient, must blind itself against the Scripture word of promise.

Through the fault of unbelief, it came to pass that Jesus appeared in Israel not as the Bethlehemite, but as the Galilean. This must, however, become to the Jews a great support for their unbelief. In this way first the letter of the law, and then the letter of the promise, serves them as an occasion for taking offence at Jesus' actions and appearance. They lose two things thereby: the fulfilling of the law or the righteousness which is in Jesus,—compare Acts ii. 27, iii. 14, iv. 30, vii. 52,—and the fulfilling of the promise or the spirit of the new life of Jesus.

If we have not altogether failed in the attempt to show the meaning this chapter has in the progress of the historical development in the fourth gospel, then we have in the

---

[1] Keil, *Lehrbuch der historisch-kritischen Einleitung in die . . . Schriften des Alten Testamentes*, 3d ed., Frankfort-on-the-Main 1873, p. 327.

[2] Keil, *ibid.* p. 304 f.

same act refuted Baur's unhistorical view, a view which does not stand even in details; compare Brückner's closing words upon this chapter. Baur's idea is, that this chapter is intended to show the dialectic self-refutation of unbelief. Our conception of the chapter also disposes on the other side of Brückner's meagre view, that it was intended to depict the σχίσμα ('division') between the people and the rulers.[1] That is an external 'historical character' over against which Baur will always assert a relative right. Baur, however, sees a merely subjective and dialectic process, where an objective and ethical one takes place. The self-refutation of unbelief does not here complete itself in a dialectic way. But the events of the feast of tabernacles are so chosen and grouped, that, with the beginning of the conflict, the judgment of unbelief, which judgment lay in Jesus' actions and words, and in the involuntary evidence of their consciences, should also present itself clearly to view.

VII. 53–VIII. 11. *The Paragraph about the Adulterous Woman.*

The following paragraph concerning the adulteress is a fragment of very old tradition, but is not from the hand of John, and is wrongly inserted here. It is true the paragraph is found in D F G H K U, in the most but not in the best manuscripts of the Itala, and, according to Jerome: 'in multis et Graecis et Latinis codicibus ('in many both Greek and Latin manuscripts'); but it is wanting in the chief manuscripts ℵ (A) B C L T, in the Peshito, and in the better manuscripts of the Itala. In other manuscripts it is designated as doubtful; in still others it stands in a different place, at the end of the gospel or after Luke xxi. Origen, Theodore of Mopsuestia, and Chrysostom do not mention it. Euthymius calls it an insertion. Theophylact strikes it out. Moreover, the text has remarkably numerous various readings. A peculiar recension is found in D.

---

[1] Brückner in De Wette, *Kurze Erklärung des Evangeliums und der Briefe Johannis*, 5th ed., Leipzig 1863, p. 161.

Yet the narrative seems to be a piece of genuine tradition. The spirit of mildness which reveals itself in Jesus' conduct is too foreign to the later church for any one to have invented such behaviour on the part of Jesus. The whole is so characteristic and original, and so little copied after another narrative, that we may venture to regard it as historical. The story is not, as Hengstenberg declares, morally offensive, and even irritating. On the contrary, properly understood, it offers correct and healthful moral instruction. It is therefore not 'unscientific indecision' to see in this a fragment of the oral tradition, and it is entirely unnecessary to decree only 'a clear "either ... or :"' either 'the Johannean composition or a partisan invention.' These are purely arbitrary statements[1] of Hengstenberg's. Eusebius[2] mentions, as in the gospel of the Hebrews, a story of Papias, περὶ γυναικὸσ ἐπὶ πολλαῖσ ἁμαρτίαισ διαβληθείσησ ἐπὶ τοῦ κυρίου ('concerning a woman accused of many sins before the Lord'). Whether this be identical or not with our story, is doubtful, since here the question is as to one sin, not as to many. In any case, the story is an old one; that explains its reception into so many manuscripts.

But it is not Johannean. The very language is different from John's. Thus, for example, the characteristic Johannean οὖν ('then') is wanting, and δέ ('and') occurs very frequently in place of it. Οἱ γραμματεῖσ καὶ οἱ Φαρισαῖοι ('the scribes and Pharisees') is, moreover, not Johannean, but synoptic. If the story springs from a Johannean circle, it has at any rate taken upon itself a synoptic stamp. Even the theme, a question as to the law, which was laid before Jesus with the design to tempt him, belongs to the synoptic, not to the Johannean sphere of narration. In no case does it belong to the context in which it stands. The question treated of in John is the person of Jesus and the relation to his person; here, the question touches the law.

The reason for putting the piece of tradition into this

---

[1] Original: 'Trumpfe.'
[2] Eusebius, *Historia Ecclesiastica*, III. xxxix. 17 ; *Opera*, ed. Dindorf, Leipzig 1871, vol. iv. p. 136.

particular place was, that the legal question viii. 5 recalls the appeal to the law in vii. 51, and, moreover, that previously as well as here the matter in hand is the conviction of conscience, viii. 9. They might have thought of viii. 15 too. But it is perfectly plain that these are merely external points of contact, not an internal connection. Hence this paragraph is almost universally acknowledged by critics and exegetes not to belong here, and not to be Johannean. It is defended only by a few; as in the old church by Augustine,[1] who explained the omission as caused by the anxiety of those who feared that 'peccandi impunitatem dari mulieribus suis' ('impunity in sinning would be given to their wives'); and among later commentators by Bengel, Hug, Catholic exegetes like Maier, further also by Ebrard,[2] Lange, and Stier.[3] Hilgenfeld[4] also insists that it belongs where it is. Even in his 'Introduction'[5] he declares the pericope concerning the adulteress to be 'overwhelmingly attested.' 'In the context it is indispensable. If it be struck out, not only have we no due occasion for the claim, viii. 15, ἐγὼ οὐ κρίνω οὐδένα (" I judge no one "), and no due occasion for Jesus' appearance in the temple, but we also in no wise get out from the last day of the feast, vii. 37.'

VII. 53–VIII. 11.

The paragraph begins with the closing of the last and the introduction of a new scene. ἐπορεύθη κ.τ.λ. ('went,' etc.) cannot refer to the Sanhedrists, but only to the people gathered in the temple. For the Mount of Olives, whither Jesus went, is contrasted with the οἶκοσ ('house') of the others, and therefore they are thought of as together with Jesus. The scenic representation is conceived as in the

---

[1] Augustine, *De conjugiis adulterinis*, lib. ii. 6; *Opera*, ed. Benedictin., Antwerp 1701, tom. vi. col. 299a.

[2] Ebrard, *Wissenschaftliche Kritik der evangelischen Geschichte*, 3d ed., Frankfort-on-the-Main 1868, p. 502 ff.

[3] Stier, *Reden Jesu*, 3d ed., Barmen and Elberfeld 1870, vol. iv. p. 375 ff.

[4] Hilgenfeld, *Die Evangelien*, Leipzig 1854, p. 284 ff.; *Zeitschrift für wissenschaftliche Theologie*, 1860, p. 317.

[5] Hilgenfeld, *Historisch-Kritische Einleitung in das Neue Testament*, Leipzig 1875, p. 701.

case of Jesus' last stay in Jerusalem; compare Luke xxi. 37.

VERSE 2.

This verse transfers us to the day next following upon the feast, on which day there might easily still be many non-Jerusalemites present and crowding around Jesus in the temple. Ὄρθρου ('early in the morning') does not occur elsewhere in John—on the other hand, see Luke xxiv. 1 and Acts v. 21, ὑπὸ τὸν ὄρθρον ('early in the morning'); instead of it we find the commoner πρωΐ (especially frequent in Mark) or πρωΐα. Λαόσ ('people') also occurs elsewhere in John only at xi. 50 and xviii. 14, though very frequent in the synoptists and in Acts; John usually has ὄχλοσ ('multitude'). In like manner καθίσασ ἐδίδασκεν ('he sat down and taught') is rather synoptic than Johannean. Jesus therefore prepared himself for a long discourse, for which it was customary to sit,—in distinction from vii. 37, εἱστήκει ('stood'),[1]—see Luke iv. 20.

VERSE 3.

'The scribes and Pharisees' is the synoptic expression for the party hostile to Jesus, and does not occur elsewhere in John's gospel. The scribes are also called νομικοί ('lawyers') or νομοδιδάσκαλοι ('teachers of the law') in the New Testament, and הַכָמִים, 'the learned,' in the Mishna. Their ordinary title was רַב, or רַבִּי, or רַבָּן, hence, Mark x. 51 and John xx. 16, ῥαββουνί ('master').[2]

VERSE 4.

The Pharisees who bring the woman to Jesus do it, not in commission of the Sanhedrim, but of their own motion, before they place her in the court. They have caught the woman in the very act. Αὐτοφώρῳ ('in the act') refers in the first instance to theft, from φώρ, 'fur,' 'thief.' Then

---

[1] See Schürer, *Lehrbuch der neutestamentlichen Zeitgeschichte*, Leipzig 1874, p. 474.

[2] As to the position and activity of the scribes, see Schürer, *ut supra*, p. 441 f.

it is used in a wider sense in prose, commonly ἐπ' αὐτοφώρῳ, 'in the very act,' in general.

VERSE 5.

The command of the law for such a sin was stoning, and that for both parties. Perhaps the adulterer had fled. Stoning, it is true, is in the law, Deut. xxii. 23 f., only given as the death-penalty for the special case, when a betrothed bride submits herself to a seducer in the town where she could have called for help. For ordinary adultery, on the other hand, the death-penalty is left indefinite, Lev. xx. 10. In the Talmud and in Maimonides strangling is named, but that proves nothing for the time of Jesus. It was an easy matter to interpret and use this general command in accordance with that special definition, although no support for this can be drawn from Ezek. xvi. 38, 40, or from the story of Susanna. Michaelis, however, referred justly to Ex. xxxi. 14, xxxv. 2, compared with Num. xv. 32–34. If this be not agreed to, there lies in μοιχευομένη ('committing adultery') no hindrance to placing the present case, with Meyer, in that special category which is spoken of in Deut. xxii. 23 f. In no event can anything against the historical character of the account be concluded from this point.

VERSE 6.

The accusers lay stress upon the legality of the question; hence the object of the tempting question was not this legality itself, but its instant execution. Πειράζοντεσ ('tempting'), because if Jesus ordered the execution, they could at once have made use of his order to bring him into suspicion before the Roman authorities as a dangerous man. When the old painters—as, for example, Cranach—represent the accusers as' having stones ready in their hands, they catch the sense of the accusation rightly, even though not the external event. If Jesus said no, he appeared as one who overthrew the law. If he said yes, he could be held up as one who laid hands upon the office of the authorities, by suggesting to the people a tumultuous execution of justice. A reference to the authorities did not seem to offer any escape from that dilemma. For the Sanhedrim had lost the right of the death-penalty, and the Roman officers would with difficulty have agreed to decide according to that decree of the Mosaic law (Meyer). Hence this would have been equivalent to a negative answer, and the result have remained the same.

Accordingly, Jesus seemed compelled to decide either against the law or against the authority of the government. The emphasizing of the law, and as well the fact that they say οὖν ('then') and not δέ ('and'), show that these accusers expected the latter alternative. Bengel says: 'haec particula quaestionem exhibet magis captiosam quam si aperto antitheto dixissent; vero' ('this particle makes the question appear more captious than if they had spoken in open antithesis; but'). That emphasizing combats the assumption that they had expected a negative answer, and had laid their plan upon that (Bengel, Tholuck, Hengstenberg). Their design to gain a ground for an accusation against Jesus, likewise combats the supposition that they desired to lead him either to an inconsistency in regard to his mildness, or to a decision against Moses (for example, Calvin).

We do not need to ask what Jesus wrote upon the earth, —some say the contents of ver. 7 (thus also Godet),— because this action was only intended to show that he did not desire to answer. That does not make the action a mere play (against Hengstenberg and Godet), but a very decisive dismission. Either Jesus intends to say that this transaction does not concern him at all, 'id negotii ad se nil pertinere significans' (Bengel), and that he does not desire to interfere in the governmental domain (Meyer); or, in agreement with the whole situation, he desires by neglect of their question to make them understand that by reason of their impure disposition they do not deserve any answer.

Verse 7.

Yet, since they insist upon an answer, they shall have it. Looking up into their faces, he saith: *He that is without sin among you, let him first cast the stone at her.* Ἀναμάρτητοσ, only here in the New Testament, 'faultless,' is here, of course, to be understood only of actual, not of possible, faultlessness. Lücke, Meyer, and Ebrard limit it, but without reason, to the special class of sins against chastity. There is no ground for assuming that all the accusers were guilty of just these sins. The intention is simply in general to awaken the consciousness of sin. The point is this testimony of the conscience, and not 'the consciousness of one's own sinfulness, which breaks the power of every sin.'[1] From that consciousness of one's own sin the position towards the sins of others results as a matter of necessity. He does not altogether deny the right of punishment. 'Let him first cast the stone at her,' leaves the decree of the law standing in its right. But this is true of the authoritative use of law.

The question here is the personal position towards the sins of others. It was the method of the Pharisaic theology and morals, as we see from the sermon on the mount, to form rules of moral conduct from the prescriptions of the law, thereby reducing morality in the exact sense to legality, and making a matter of disposition a matter of external action. Jesus, on the contrary, separates the two spheres, and thus restores the internal independence and dignity of the moral sphere. In a similar way he here also transfers the question as to the relation to the sins of others from the sphere of law into that of the moral consciousness, from the sphere of official treatment in which the men before him have no authority, to that of personal condemnation of the sins of others. In this regard, moreover, he strikes down their assuming self-righteousness by the testimony of the condemning conscience which he awakens. He will remind them that they should rather seek forgiveness for their own sins than desire to judge others.

VERSE 8.

Where a vivid consciousness of one's own sins exists, the correct posture towards the sins of others offers itself as a matter of course. Hence the accusers need no further

---

[1] Baur, *Kritische Untersuchungen über die kanonischen Evangelien*, Tübingen 1847, p. 170.

advice, and they do not deserve it. Jesus therefore repeats his former action. *And again he stooped down, and wrote on the ground.*

VERSE 9.

Jesus' words touch their consciences, and convince them of their unjustifiable desires, so that they withdraw. The imperfect ἐξήρχοντο ('went out') is descriptive (Meyer). The older ones begin: 'hi maxime perculsi erant' ('these had been especially struck,' Bengel). So they go out unto the last, who went out; thus Meyer, and rightly, against the ordinary interpretation of it as to rank (for example, Lücke, De Wette, Baumgarten-Crusius). They leave Jesus alone behind: 'relicti sunt duo, miseria et misericordia' ('the two are left, misery and pity');[1] μόνοσ ('alone') here does not exclude the presence of disciples and people. The woman had not withdrawn herself from Jesus: ἐν μέσῳ ἑστῶσα ('standing in the midst') is said of her; therefore she stands there as if waiting for Jesus' decision as judge.

VERSE 10.

Jesus looks up: *Hath no man condemned thee?* 'No man' is emphatic. They had all withdrawn.

VERSE 11.

Then will not Jesus condemn her. By this he does not deny the competence of the court. That has not been treated of in the whole occurrence. The popular dealing with law remains fully untouched (against Hengstenberg). The only thing concerned is personal estimation of the sins of others. Jesus as the ἀναμάρτητοσ ('sinless one') would have had the right to utter words of condemnation against her. But he does not wish to do it. For his office is not judging, but saving, in that he calls sinners to repentance. The words are not in themselves a declaration of the forgiveness of sins,— they run not affirmatively, but only negatively,—they are a call to repentance by the fact that they are words of forbearance.

---

[1] Augustine, *In Johannis Evangelium*, tractatus xxxiii. 5; *Opera*, ed. Benedictin., Antwerp 1700, vol. iii. part ii. col. 386d.

'Ergo et dominus damnavit, sed peccatum, non hominem'
('therefore also the Lord condemned, but the sin, not the
person,' Augustine). To the woman, therefore, if she lets
repentance work in her through these words, they may
become to her words of the forgiveness of sin. And they
doubtless did become such to her. Her waiting on Jesus'
decision shows that she was in the preparatory frame for
this. She is to show by her deeds whether the change of
mind now begun is earnestly meant or not. Jesus does not
let her go freely—πορεύου ('go')—without the admonition:
μηκέτι ἁμάρτανε ('sin no more'). 'Non addit: in pace,
neque dicit: remissa sunt tibi peccata tua, sed: posthac noli
peccare' ('he does not add: in peace, nor does he say: thy
sins are forgiven; but: hereafter be unwilling to sin').
The sinning of course here points, in the first place, to the
sin in question. For μηκέτι ('no more') glances back.

We perceive that Jesus' words and bearing are fully
worthy of him, and in unison with his teachings elsewhere.
We therefore here have before us a fragment of genuine
tradition, for the preservation of which we may be thankful.
But the narrative does not belong to the present context.
On the contrary, viii. 12 ff., which follows, connects directly
with vii. 52, and transfers us to the conflict between Jesus
and his opponents at the visit to the feast of tabernacles in
the last year before the death of Jesus, and in such a way
that we see that conflict here attain its greatest keenness.

VIII. 12–59. *The Antagonism between Jesus and the Jews
in its Greatest Sharpness.*

Lücke questions whether so many speeches could be
exchanged on one day. Against this we might point to the
farewell discourses, chapters xiii. 31 to xvii. But nothing
forces us to the assumption that the discourses all were
held on the same day. The evangelist, not being a writer
of history in the ordinary sense, is not concerned so much
about the time, but much more about the relation of Jesus
and the Jews, as it shaped itself at this feast. He desires
to make it stand out very sharply and characteristically. On
this account, and from this point of view, he puts together

the speeches as they were exchanged upon occasion of the feast. We may not therefore venture, with De Wette, to say: it looks as if the evangelist had not known how to hold securely the historical thread. He had an entirely different historical thread upon his heart than that of days and hours. And he demands of us that we cause our attention to be directed to this thread, and to no other which he did not wish to hold fast to and to follow.

From the fact that the ὄχλοσ ('multitude') is not mentioned, and from the way in which the 'Ιουδαῖοι ('Jews') come forward, Lücke desires to conclude that the feast was over. But if Jesus, who had only come to Jerusalem to visit the feast, remained there one day or a few days longer, so also could other Galilean visitors to the feast have given up a few days, in order to hear Jesus, or to await the development of the conflict. The reason the evangelist does not mention the ὄχλοσ lies in the matter itself. For if he wishes to make the conflict come before our eyes at its height, and in all its sharpness, he will only bring forward the scenes in which Jesus met exclusively with 'Ιουδαίοισ ('Jews'). Why should not such meetings have occurred? The twelfth and twenty-first verses show evidently that the evangelist proceeds by the way of selection and combination.

When likenesses to earlier passages are found, as in ver. 21 to vii. 34, they do not permit us to hold the eighth chapter to be a supplement to the seventh chapter. Points of contact with the foregoing are natural, since the situation is essentially the same, and the antagonism is only increased. As to time and place, the relation to what precedes is to be so considered as that viii. 12 connects with vii. 44, and we must imagine ourselves in the same surroundings. Since the attempt at Jesus' arrest had missed its object, in ver. 12 we read: *Then—οὖν—spake Jesus again to them.* The evangelist does not define this relation more closely, as little as he does afterwards in ver. 21, so that in fixing the time of the occurrence we have a certain freedom of supposition.

Baur,[1] from his point of view, has made very striking

[1] Baur, *Kritische Untersuchungen über die kanonischen Evangelien*, Tübingen 1847, p. 174 ff.

remarks upon the importance and meaning of this chapter, as it forms the climax to the previously described development of the conflict. His view is, that this chapter serves especially to place in sharp relief the internal nature of belief; that it is at root a lack of religiousness; that in it the entire contrariety between above and below comes to sight, vers. 12–29; and that he who is not a child of God through belief, must thereby necessarily be a child of the devil, vers. 30–58.

Even the outward form betrays the progress in the contrasted position of Jesus and of the Jews. In the sixth chapter Jesus' discourses are upon the whole only seldom interrupted, and that more by murmuring than by contradicting speeches. The interruptions grow stronger in the seventh chapter; yet longer discourses on Jesus' part are at least hinted at; compare ver. 14, ἐδίδασκεν ('he taught'); ver. 15, πῶσ οὗτοσ γράμματα οἶδεν ('how knoweth this man letters?'); ver. 37 ff., ver. 40, τῶν λόγων τούτων ('these words'). But in the eighth chapter it soon goes so far that Jesus can hardly speak a single word without the Jews at once contradicting him. Thus the discourse passes almost entirely into the form of the dialogue, with a constantly increasing keenness of reply. Ἐγώ and ὑμεῖσ ('I' and 'ye') are the theme of the whole conversation.

The manner and method of teaching which is here ascribed to Jesus has been considered improbable and inconceivable, and by a hasty conclusion from this judgment the whole account has been regarded as unhistorical.[1] They say that Jesus nowhere comes down to the level of his opponents, nowhere lifts them up to himself, and does not give them the means to understand his words, but simply estranges himself from them; they complain that the method of pedagogical wisdom and love appears nowhere, but only punishing, judging, rebuffing: no wonder, then, that at the end both parties have to stand hostilely opposed to each other. But if they do at the end really stand in such exclusive antagonism towards each other as the synoptists

---

[1] Baur, *Kritische Untersuchungen über die kanonischen Evangelien*, Tübingen 1847, p. 297 ff., especially p. 300.

report to us, must not this antagonism have formed itself, and must it not have let itself be recognised even before the end? Jesus showed in the case of the Samaritan woman, he showed towards his disciples, chap. xiii.–xvii., that he understood very well how to descend and how to lift up to himself. And the same thing is reported at this feast also. For when it is said of him that he explained the Scriptures, and that they wondered at his learning in the Scriptures, vii. 14, 15, it must have been an instructing and the like, not a judging and a rebuffing.

But what if they rebuffed him? How could he then do anything else? The words viii. 31, 32, at which the contradiction begins, are words of love. No one ought to wonder that his Galilean discourses sound so entirely different. They are just as different from these words, as the forsaken, hungry, salvation-desiring people of Galilee from the satisfied, proud, constantly contradicting Pharisees of Jerusalem. It lies in the nature of the thing, that through the antagonism the words of Jesus received more and more the form of sharp, decisive, and divisive self-witness. The eighth chapter begins: ἐγώ εἰμι ('I am'); and it closes with ἐγώ εἰμι. In between it passes continuously through 'I' and 'ye.' As necessary also is it, that this did not make belief easier for the Jews, but harder; this has often enough met us as a divine ordering. And finally, the fact that by this Jesus' testimony constantly grows more entirely a testimony to the light, has already become plain to us.

The three parts of this chapter are recognisable at a glance: (1) vers. 12-20; (2) vers. 21-29; (3) vers. 30-59. At ver. 20, we see the hostility still held in check. At ver. 30, the mood has decided more in his favour, but in that very act has been divided. At ver. 59, the hostility breaks out openly in a tumultuous attempt at murder. The contents of the separate sections agree with this. In the first, Jesus gives testimony concerning his saving calling as the light of the world. In the second, he places himself and the Jews over against one another in their antagonism. In the third, he traces this antagonism back to its last roots.

(1.) VERSES 12–20.

VERSE 12.

I am the light of the world. Ἐγώ εἰμι stands at the head emphatically. Jesus begins with this—if we may so speak—proud expression of his self-consciousness: I am. All depends on his person. In it is given all which is now in question, and all the world needs. He gives himself a relation not merely to Israel, but also to the whole world; he has a value for it: he is the light of the world.

It is unnecessary to seek the occasion for this form of Jesus' self-witness in some external thing, a festal custom, as for instance the lighting of the two great candelabra in the court of the women,—thus Olshausen,—which, however, only occurred on the evening of the first day of the feast, and at any rate no longer on the eighth day.[1] Nor need we refer it to the brilliancy of the rising sun.[2] The symbol of light was not merely generally familiar through the Old Testament prophecy, but was also placed in special connection with the Messianic hope. For Jesus, moreover, this designation of himself was as easily suggested as was that of life. Here it was, besides, induced by the progress of the self-witness. Upon the self-testification of Jesus as the life, follows his self-testification as the light. He is the one as much as the other, and because he is the other, the light because he is the life, and not the reverse (against Kübel;[3] compare on i. 5).[4] The symbol of the light belongs to the oldest religious conceptions of the divinity in the East.[5] Having become a view of nature in the heathen religions, it sustained itself in the sacred Scriptures in the ethical sense. As God is life in the absolute sense, so also it is true of him, in the absolute sense that he is light

---

[1] Compare Keil, *Handbuch der biblischen Archäologie*, Frankfort-on-the-Main and Erlangen 1858, vol. i. p. 419, note 11.

[2] Stier, *Reden Jesu*, 3d ed., Barmen and Elberfeld 1870, vol. iv. p. 394.

[3] Kübel, *Das christliche Lehrsystem*, Stuttgart 1873, p. 24.

[4] See vol. i. p. 270 f.

[5] Compare Roth, 'Die höchsten Götter der arischen Völker,' *Zeitschrift der Deutschen Morgenländischen Gesellschaft*, 1852, Heft 1, pp. 67–77.

and in the light; Ps. xxxvi. 10 (English version, ver. 9): 'With thee is the fountain of life, and in thy light we see the light.' As, then, all life springs only from God, so too is all experience of and fellowship in light connected with God.

Light is that which is transparently pure, which excludes all mixture. Thus even in the Old Testament it stands in the closest connection with the notion of holiness, whether the root קדש, 'to be holy,' come from דש, 'to be pure,' or 'to shine forth,' or from קד, 'to be separate.'[1] And in the same manner in the New Testament, 1 John i. 5, God is light —not a light, but light as to his kind; to be full of light is his constitution.

The Scriptures do not distinguish, as we are in the habit of doing, according to the various sides of the spirit's life, and least of all in such a way that light would be to be referred only to the side of knowledge (against Weiss:[2] light in 1 John i. 5 designates the fact of God's having become intelligible through and through). To the Scriptures the intellectual is also an ethical thing. God, who as to his being and essence is life, is as to his constitution light, that is, sincere transparent purity, which excludes from itself all foreign disturbing elements. As we should let ourselves be filled with the life of God, so should we bear in ourselves this light as our constitution. For this purpose this light, which is God, has disclosed itself to the world, and has entered into it, in Christ Jesus. He is both the life, namely of God, and as well this light of God for the world. In itself the world is darkness, for sin is that reality which shuts itself off from God, which shuts itself up in itself, and which will not permit God to shine through itself. This, however, is the condition which lacks salvation.

Hence, when the light enters upon this world, salvation dawns for it. In consequence, in the Old Testament, light

---

[1] Compare Delitzsch on Isa. x. 17, *Biblischer Commentar über den Propheten Jesaia*, 2d ed., Leipzig 1869, p. 176 ; and Oehler, *Alttestamentliche Theologie*, Tübingen 1873, vol. i. p. 160.

[2] Weiss, *Die biblische Theologie des Neuen Testaments*, 2d ed., Berlin 1873, p. 629.

often denotes salvation, not in so far as 'light' alone might be identical with 'salvation' (against Hengstenberg), but in so far as the light brings salvation. Hence also the opening of the Messianic period of salvation is entitled the dawn and the rising of the light, especially in Isaiah, Isa. ix. 1, xlii. 6, xlix. 6, lx. 3. The Messiah is the light of the heathen, Isa. xlii. 6, xlix. 6; that does not mean merely that he will bring them more correct thoughts with regard to God, but that he transfers them to the light, brings them a new constitution of life, by drawing them from the night of their unsaved condition unto the new day of the saved condition. In a like way Jesus also calls himself here the light of the world, not simply in so far as he is the teacher who enlightens men and offers them more correct thoughts of God and so forth, but in so far as with him a new day of salvation dawns for the world.

He puts the divinely-ordered reality, in the first instance in his own person, into contrast with the God-hostile reality in the darkness of sin. That condition of being ordered by or agreeable to God is at once the judgment of the hostility to God, and the deliverance from that hostility. It is in connection with this circumstance that Jesus' testimony to himself as the light obtains a specially keen polemical character. For the light is at the same time the critical, distinguishing, and judging potency.[1] If Jesus be the light of the world, and thereby its salvation, then participation in that is connected with him. That which is spoken generally—τοῦ κόσμου, 'of the world'—is also meant exclusively: ἐγώ, 'I,' and therefore only He. Hence, where there is no fellowship with him, there is exclusion from his salvation.

Both the condition—ἀκολουθῶν, 'following'—and the promise—ἕξει, 'shall have'—show that the point in question is not merely knowledge: *He that followeth me shall surely not walk in the darkness, but shall have the light of life.* A following, ἀκολουθεῖν, that is, an active posture towards him, is demanded as a condition. It is the disciple's union with him in belief. He as the master goes before, the disciple follows him in belief. It is doubtful

---

[1] See above, p. 198 ff.

whether or not we should at this think of the pillar of fire which went in front of Israel (Lampe, Stier,[1] Godet), since the conception here is not so much the designation of and the illumination of the way, but rather the union of the disciple with Christ. We might more fitly think of the parable of the shepherd in the tenth chapter.

The result is: he shall not walk in darkness. Manuscript authority attests the subjunctive περιπατήσῃ (א B L T) rather than the uncommon future περιπατήσει, which may well have arisen because of the following ἕξει. It does not say: in darkness, but in 'the' darkness, in which he is, namely, by nature. He will be taken from this, not merely in order to see the light of life, to follow it, and the like, but to 'have' it, to possess it. Therefore what is meant is not simply an 'illustrari,' a 'being enlightened' (Lampe: 'non solum Israelem sed omnes gentes mundi erat illustraturus,' 'he was about to illuminate not only Israel, but also all the nations of the world'), but a possessing and having for one's own—not merely having with oneself (Weiss). For Baumgarten-Crusius was right in rejecting Grotius' view of ἕξει τὸ φῶσ τῆσ ζωῆσ, 'shall have the light of life,'—Grotius says: 'habebit sibi praeviam illam lucem,' 'he shall have that light going before him,'—and in accepting Nonnus' view—ἔχων ὁμόφοιτον ἐν αὐτῷ ζωῆσ ἀπλανέοσ φάοσ ἔμπεδον, 'habens comitem in ipso vitae non errantis lucem firmam,' 'having as a companion within himself the constant light of an unwavering life.'

The belief of following knits fellowship. Having Jesus, it has his 'light of life.' As death and darkness belong together, so do life and light. The former one of the two is not light, but life. Compare i. 4: the life was the light of men. So as the life he is also the light. In this sense he calls himself the light of life, in so far as light is the constitution of the life. Jesus therefore promises a new constitution of life, the correct one, conditioned upon the fellowship with him, which fellowship is given (ἕξει, 'shall have') in belief (= 'following,' ἀκουλουθεῖν). He ascribes

[1] Stier, *Reden Jesu*, 3d ed., Barmen and Elberfeld 1870, vol. iv. p. 396.

to himself this absolute importance towards the whole world. The question arises, with what right he can do this.

VERSE 13.

The Pharisees question the justness of his self-witness. They do not attack it materially—they have not the courage for that—but formally. They press the ordinary legal rule, according to which no one can be a witness in his own case. But they conclude from that, sophistically, not the lack of justification,—which might indeed consist with the truth of the cause,—but the incorrectness of the testimony: οὐκ ἔστιν ἀληθήσ ('is not true'). Jesus replies to this connectedly. Baumgarten-Crusius names correctly the three thoughts of which the answer is composed: first, ver. 14, he has a right to testify to himself as the light, because he 'knows' himself to be it, because he knows himself to be the Son of God (that is a better way of putting the first thought); secondly, ver. 16, he can give a just and true witness to himself because he does it in the society of his Father; and thirdly, ver. 17 f., it is also legally valid because he unites his Father's testimony to his own.

VERSE 14.

The ordinary rule of law does not hold for him. His self-consciousness, different from that of ordinary men, is of divine infallibility. He 'knows' himself to be the light of the world, for he knows himself to be the Son of God. Κἂν ἐγὼ κ.τ.λ., *even if I*, even in case that, etc. Not: if I also (Lücke), or although I (Baumgarten-Crusius); both of these would be ἐὰν καί (compare Meyer). Even in case he does testify of himself, his testimony is true, because he knows whence he comes and whither he goes. His witness as to himself may be taken as true, if it can be presupposed that he knows himself. Now, however, he knows the beginning and the goal of his earthly life, and accordingly, also its middle, that is, his importance, his calling, and his mission. If his self-witness differ from the testimony of men concerning him, that is but natural, because his knowledge of himself differs from the knowledge other men have of him.

He alone knows that he had a being with God before he became man, and that he also as such a one, because come from God, has a vocation to the whole world, and a saving vocation to the world, since God is the God of the world in general and the God of salvation. This they, his opponents, do not know: *Ye know not whence I come and whither I go.* πόθεν ἔρχομαι ('whence I come') is in the present, while before we had ἦλθον ('came'). This is not to express his constant coming as God's messenger (Meyer), since the coming in ἔρχομαι must be understood in the same sense as in ἦλθον. In this present he frees his coming from the historical act, and considers it in itself aside from time: the origin of his coming and its aim are alike unknown to them. But with both, Jesus designates himself as the Son of God, and thereby lays the foundation for the rest of his self-witness, because the saving vocation mentioned is deduced from this.

VERSE 15.

If they have rejected his testimony—Jesus continues—they have thereby condemned him. But if he accredits himself as the only saving mediator for all the world, and they refuse him, then his testimony becomes a word of judgment which he utters over them. Hence, by the nature of the case, the two parties stand over against each other, each condemning the other. But there is a difference. If they judge him, they do it κατὰ τὴν σάρκα ('according to the flesh'), that is, because his σάρξ, his earthly appearance, does not seem to agree with what he says about himself. This exact conception of ἡ σάρξ ('the flesh') is to be held fast, with Lücke, Meyer, and Godet, in contrast to the subjective reference given it by other exegetes (as early as Chrysostom; among modern scholars, De Wette, Baumgarten-Crusius), and in contrast to the union of the two, contended for by Stier.[1] Thus they cleave to his fleshly form, in order thereby to have the desired occasion to be able to pass a judgment of condem-

[1] Stier, *Reden Jesu*, 3d ed., Barmen and Elberfeld 1870, vol. iv. p. 400 f.

nation upon him. On the other hand, when Jesus, by his self-witness to himself, utters a sentence of condemnation upon all those who do not receive it, in that he thereby consigns them to the unsaved condition, he does not do it in the first instance in order to judge. For he witnesses to himself, in order to witness to himself unto salvation, not unto judgment.

We are not, therefore, to supply a κατὰ τὴν σάρκα ('according to the flesh') after ἐγὼ οὐ κρίνω οὐδένα ('I judge no man'); most commentators urge such a supplying, as for example Lücke, Stier.[1] This is impossible in connection with our explanation of κατὰ τὴν σάρκα, and, aside from that, is excluded on account of the repetition of the thought in καὶ ἐὰν κρίνω ἐγώ ('and if I judge'); compare De Wette. The last-mentioned, in fact, really first adds the actual point thought of (compare Meyer). Nor are we to add anything of that kind, as for example νῦν ('now') (Augustine, Chrysostom), or μόνος, 'alone' (Storr, Godet, who wishes ἐγώ, 'I,' to be emphasized, as if it read αὐτὸσ ἐγώ, 'I myself'). The thought is simply this: he has not come unto judging, but unto saving; compare iii. 17 (Meyer, Brückner, Hengstenberg). His self-witness has this aim.

Verse 16.

But his testimony as to himself can have a different result: *And if I also judge, my judgment is a true one.* In καί ... δέ, καί connects, 'and,' while δέ puts in relief the word in question, here κρίνω ('I judge'). We would express this by 'also,' indicating an emphasis and not an increase.[2] Jesus does not in this name an exception to that general maxim (thus Meyer), but the shape and effect which his self-witness obtains without his will: I do not testify to myself in order to judge; but if by means of unbelief my testimony be unto judgment, this is then a true judgment

---

[1] Stier, *Reden Jesu*, 3d ed., Barmen and Elberfeld 1870, vol. iv. p. 401.

[2] This is against Krüger, *Griechische Sprachlehre für Schulen*, § 69. 32, Anm. 10, 3d ed., Berlin 1852, p. 559. Compare Winer, *Grammatik des neutestamentlichen Sprachidioms*, § 53. 7. b, 7th ed., Leipzig 1867, p. 412 f.

that I exercise, because I do it in fellowship with my Father.

The notion which lies in κρίσισ κ.τ.λ. ('judgment, etc.') is that of self-witness. Hence, when they judge him in his self-witness, they do it κατὰ τὴν σάρκα ('according to the flesh'). And when he judges them by his self-witness, he does it according to the truth (ἀληθήσ, thus ℵ), or it is a genuine, real judgment (ἀληθινή, thus B D L T, and to be preferred), and not merely one that bears the name of a judgment, as theirs—his judgment is such for the very reason that it goes to the essence of the matter, and therefore is agreeable to the truth. He confirms this by the fellowship of the Father. *For I am not alone, but I and the Father that hath sent me.* This is a justifiable confirmation, since that fellowship, if an essential one, exists also in his judging, and hence the judgment must be right and true. It follows from this that it is not merely his act, but his Father's also. This therefore forms the third thought, in which again the μαρτυρία ('witness') enters in place of the κρίσισ ('judgment'), which latter, indeed, only meant the former, simply in a definite direction.

VERSES 17-19.

His testimony is twofold, his and his Father's. By this he satisfies their law.

VERSE 17.

And also it is written in your law, that the testimony of two men is true. Καί . . . δέ is used as above in ver. 16. Jesus does not say ὑμέτεροσ νόμοσ ('your law') from the standpoint of the evangelist (Baumgarten-Crusius, De Wette), and still less in a condemning sense (Schweizer, Baur), hence being a sign of later origin and of unhistorical narrative. He speaks thus because the Jews identified themselves with the law as contrasted with Jesus, and so claimed it exclusively for themselves over against him, in order to base their claim against Jesus upon it, v. 16, vii. 23 f.; Meyer.[1] The prescription of the law, Deut.

[1] See vol. i. p. 125 f.

xvii. 6, xix. 15, is quoted freely by Jesus. In the Old Testament μάρτυρεσ (' witnesses ') are spoken of; here, ἀνθρώπων (' men ') is used designedly, in order to hint at the surplus offered by Jesus—by a conclusion from the less to the greater, 'a minori ad maius': 'duorum hominum; quanto magis Dei et filii Dei?' 'of two men; how much greater of God and of the Son of God?' (Bengel)—in that he brings forward not merely the testimony of two men, but his and his Father's.

VERSE 18.

The man Jesus testifies to his divinity, and the Father who sent him does it, namely, by legitimating Jesus as His ambassador in his actions. This reasoning, again, it is true, has as its presupposition, first, that they accept as valid his, the man's, testimony concerning his divine origin and vocation; and second, that they own as a testimony to him, though borne by him, the testimony of the Father, which again lies only in his, Jesus', deeds.

VERSE 19.

Hence, when the Jews desired to see this testimony shown outside of the sphere of his self-presentation, in that they asked after this his Father to whom he appealed, Jesus can only again point to himself. *Ye neither know me, nor my Father: if ye had known me, ye should have known my Father also.* He himself is always the presupposition for the knowledge of his Father. He cannot point to a testimony of the Father's, which may stand over against him, independently of him, and so legitimate him, that they might first through that obtain a relation to him. They can reach that testimony only by starting from him. Jesus thus, exactly considered, does not go beyond a certain 'petitio principii,' ' begging of the question;' nor can he; for they must believe in him simply on account of himself.

In this I have presupposed that the Jews do not mean his bodily father (thus De Wette, Olshausen, Brückner, and approximately Lücke, following Augustine's example; on the contrary, Meyer). There was no reason for their assuming such an awkward position, for he had spoken of him who sent him, and they were already accustomed to the fact that he called God in a special sense his Father, v. 18. Besides, the answer becomes much sharper and bitterer, when they call upon him to bring forward also the invisible witness and his testimony, to which he appeals. They do not speak thus 'to a certain extent in an honest purpose' (Godet), but in a hostile sense.

It is as if they would give him to understand that any liar could appeal to God. If he wishes to appeal to God in a particular way, and thereby prove his special claim, he must in some way show that; he must not merely stop at the assertion, but bring the testimony to the spot, and show the testimony. They do not speak thus, as if they desired to hear his Father as a witness;[1] but Jesus is to show him in his testimony. To this Jesus can only answer, that he can only show him in his own self-presentation. He can therefore name no other way by which they can come to a knowledge of the testimony of the Father, than by understanding him himself. Since this is not the case, since they will not condescend to this, the other is also made impossible for them.

Verse 20.

These words spake Jesus as he taught in the temple, ἐν γαζοφυλακίῳ, at, by, the treasure chests, if we understand by γαζοφυλάκιον the actual receptacle for the treasure, which according to the rabbinic accounts consisted of thirteen trumpet-shaped brazen chests, designed for the reception of voluntary contributions for the temple as well as for the temple tax (Mark xii. 41; Meyer). But as this use of ἐν is foreign to the New Testament, we should perhaps understand by γαζοφυλάκιον the space in which those treasure chests stood (Winer,[2] Brückner). This would be quite possible in view of the further use of

---

[1] Lücke, *Commentar über das Evangelium des Johannes*, 3d ed., Bonn 1843, vol. ii. p. 290.

[2] Winer, *Grammatik des neutestamentlichen Sprachidioms*, § 45. a. 1. c, 7th ed., Leipzig 1867, p. 360.

γαζοφυλάκιον (compare 1 Macc. xiv. 49 and Keil on that passage), and is in this case the more probable interpretation. This treasury was in the court of the women. The evangelist names the place, not only for the sake of local exactness, but, like the addition of διδάσκων ἐν τῷ ἱερῷ ('teaching in the temple'), to make it noticeable, that Jesus, as he did, spoke at a place where many men went backwards and forwards (Meyer).

Jesus therefore testified to himself thus freely and openly (Baumgarten-Crusius, Stier[1]), and without timidity (Bengel: 'eo loco ubi aliquis facile potuisset capi; ubi maxima erat hominum frequentia,' 'in that place where any one could be easily seized; where the thronging of men was the greatest'). So much the more is it unto judgment for the Jews. *And no man seized him,*—how triumphantly said by the evangelist (Meyer)! They probably wished to seize him, but they did not dare to do so. *His hour was not yet come,* according to God's will.[2] Even this possibility of belief, which was offered to Israel, became a judgment for them. Their hostility could have no other result than to withdraw entirely from the Jews the possibility of salvation. The following paragraph begins with this.

(2.) Verses 21–29.

A good connection with what precedes is found in the fact that, in the first place, the subject concerns the final issue for both, for Jesus and for the Jews. This is based upon the origin of both, and the latter is again connected with the former by the present time, especially the present of Jesus' word. The development falls into three periods: vers. 21, 22; vers. 23, 24; vers. 25–29.

Verse 21.

Πάλιν ('again') opens a new discourse. Whether on some following day (Meyer), or on the same day (thus commonly), must be left undecided. The evangelist, utterly abstracted from the temporal relations, let himself, in the

---

[1] Stier, *Reden Jesu,* 3d ed., Barmen and Elberfeld 1870, vol. iv. p. 406.
[2] See vol. i. p. 131 f.

combination of the discourses, be decided only by consideration of the thoughts; he did not trouble himself about external historical exactness. Since Jesus' hour was not yet come (οὖν), he turned himself anew towards his opponents (αὐτοῖσ, 'unto them'), but with words which became ever more earnest and more keen. This appeared in the very beginning: *I go my way, and ye shall seek me, and shall die in your sin; whither I go, ye cannot come.* For when he says that he goes his way, the first thing that supplies itself is: to his Father. But that has less emphasis—and is therefore also not especially named—than the fact that he thereby is withdrawn from the Jews. His departure to his Father is the judgment upon Israel. They will seek him, namely, as deliverer in the severe distress which will come upon them; compare vii. 34; but in vain—that is a matter of course. Although οὐχ εὑρήσετε ('ye shall not find,' vii. 34) is here omitted, the fact is contained in ὅπου ἐγώ κ.τ.λ. ('whither I, etc.').

This negative side is, however, not without a corresponding, and that a much stronger positive side, which is designated by ἐν τῇ ἁμαρτίᾳ ὑμῶν ἀποθανεῖσθε ('ye shall die in your sin'). They will die 'in,' not 'of' (Hengstenberg), their sin. They will go unto death with the sin which forms their moral condition, and which is especially determined by lack of belief in Jesus Christ. In death, they will be determined in sin by their unbelief, and not freed from sin by belief. From this follows necessarily what they have to look for beyond death. For by unbelief, and because they are in sin, they stand under judgment. Ὅπου ἐγώ ὑπάγω κ.τ.λ. ('whither I go, etc.') thus obtains an essential definiteness. It is said in contrast to what precedes. Over against the judgment, into which they enter through death, because they were previously in it, stands the perfect fellowship with God, into which Jesus enters. De Wette opposes this explanation by referring to xiii. 33. To this we reply, that in that passage, in the first place, we must observe the appended ἄρτι ('now'); and, in the next place, that Jesus nevertheless it is true will only at a later period take his own unto him, xiv. 3, xvii. 24.

This is not yet true of the disciples, and is not true of the Jews at all, because they go unto death in sin. They understand well whither he goes, and therefore whither they will not be able to come. They feel the condemnatory force of Jesus' words. But they desire to ward off the impression from themselves, by turning his words back against him in a question of scorn.

Verse 22.

This speech is to be conceived as scornful (against Hengstenberg). If Jesus denies to them the future of salvation because it lies alone in him, the one they despise, they on the other hand deny to him the future of salvation, because he by an act of most grievous sin will free himself from them who yet are sure of the blessed future. Doubtless in despair—so they wished it to be conceived—that he finds no favour with them, he will kill himself. This reply shows clearly the progress of antagonism. Previously, they had assumed the appearance of willingly desiring to accept his words, if he only would fulfil the proper conditions for his legitimation. Now, their disposition and their posture appear without any mask, as an opposition of scorn, as simple not-willing. Therein, however, the judgment shows itself, the judgment which in their unbelief accomplishes itself in and over them. It thus becomes ever more certain: they have forfeited the future of salvation.

Verse 23.

Ye are from beneath; I am from above: ye are of this world; I am not of this world. These words trace the contrariety of destiny, back to the contrariety of origin. The ground for the former lies in the latter. Jesus in these words does not give the reason for their being able thus to exercise scorn (Meyer), but the reason for the issue. He ignores the scorn; that alone is worthy of him. Nor does he characterize 'their low nature' (Meyer), but their moral character in general. It is true that ἐκ τῶν κάτω, ἐκ τοῦ κόσμου ('from beneath, of this world'), do not in the first instance denote disposition and inclination (Meyer), but neither does ἐκ τῶν ἄνω ('from above') denote the supersensual inclination, or οὐκ ἐκ τοῦ κόσμου ('not of this world') the supramundane disposition (Baumgarten-Crusius). In the first place, τὰ κάτω ('below') and κόσμοσ ('world') do not express things substantially different (against Baumgarten-Crusius, Stier[1]), and least of all so that τὰ κἰτω means hell (Stier and also Godet, at least in part); but in the previous expression, the formal point of diametrical opposition comes more to view, and in the latter expression the reality of the designation comes more to view. In the second place, τὰ κάτω names the sphere as much as ὁ κόσμοσ does, only that in the former respect is paid to the extent and the variety of the elements constituting it, and in the latter to the fact of their belonging together, of the physical and ethical oneness.

'This world,' in its entire actuality and concrete constitution, stands in contrast to the renewed world, which is to realize itself from him, the one who has come from above. In each case the origin is meant in the first instance. Now, moreover, τὰ κάτω or ὁ κόσμοσ has its definite ethical stamp, and the destiny which is determined by that (οὖν, ver. 24). He also participates in this destiny who comes from that κόσμοσ. The designation thus becomes in its earliest phase a designation of all men in contrast to Christ, who comes from heaven, and not from the earth in the same exact sense in which the contrary must be said of men, and who hence has the corresponding ethical stamp (φῶσ, 'light') and the corresponding future (ζωὴ αἰώνιοσ, 'eternal life'). If, however, that statement be true in the exact sense for all men, how can it here be true for the Jews in a special sense? It is clearly so intended. The explanation is to be found in what Jesus, xv. 19, says of the disciples: Ἐγὼ ἐξελεξάμην ὑμᾶσ ἐκ τοῦ κόσμου ('I have chosen you out of the world'). They therefore are really ἐκ τοῦ κόσμου ('of the world') as well as the others, or else they could not be taken out of the world. But by reason of an event which has befallen them, they are taken from the world, so that it now can and must be said of them: ἐκ

---

[1] Stier, *Reden Jesu*, 3d ed., Barmen and Elberfeld 1870, vol. iv. p. 410.

τοῦ κόσμου οὐκ ἐστέ ('ye are not of the world'). It is therefore not, as Hilgenfeld[1] would persuade us, a natural difference of various classes of men which determines this division of humanity, but a divine act.

Is this, however, not mediated humanly? The fifteenth chapter says of the disciples, in connection with that thought, that they have become disciples, servants of Jesus, as their Lord. How else than by belief? In belief the objective blessing of salvation becomes immanent in the individual. Hence, in belief, ζωή ('life') has assumed the place of θάνατοσ ('death'), which forms the essence of the world; and φῶσ or ἀλήθεια ('light' or 'truth') has assumed the place of sin, which forms the life-shape of the world in its unsaved condition. Therefore, because the Jews do not believe, it is said of them that they are from below, or of the world. If they be this, then the element of their life is death, the form of it is sin. The next verse says this concerning them, upon the ground of their unbelief.

Verse 24.

We perceive, therefore, that the difference between men is conditioned on their personal behaviour in belief or unbelief. Only in this way that which is by nature, fixes itself by the personal act, or is removed for the personal life; removed by the grasping of and the possession of the contrary principle of life and form of life which is in Christ. This is what is said by ἐὰν μὴ πιστεύσητε ὅτι ἐγώ εἰμι, '*If ye believe not that I am.*' They are to believe that he is. What is he? What else can it be that he is, and that they are to believe him to be, than the entire, full salvation which formed the contents of all God's promises, the hope and the belief of Israel from the very beginning? He is the life, the light, the way, the truth, and so on; in short, he is One and All as absolutely decisive. We are here to think, not of this or that side, not at all of ὁ Χριστόσ ('the Christ') alone (De Wette, Meyer). When they appeal for this to iv. 26, they overlook the fact that

---

[1] Hilgenfeld, *Das Evangelium und die Briefe Johannis nach ihrem Lehrbegriff dargestellt*, Halle 1849, p. 146 ff.

there the definite thing to be supplied is necessarily given by the question. In this passage, on the contrary, the context at first offers nothing definite.

The predicate must therefore be taken in the utmost generality. Whatever they may think of, when they think of the future of Israel, that they are to know and believe in him. The very fact of not naming the predicate, and yet of its being a matter of course, 'lends to it a calm majesty.' 'As God in אֲנִי הוּא ("I am he") comprehends the sum of the Old Testament belief, Deut. xxxii. 39, Isa. xli. 13, xliii. 10, so does Christ in ὅτι ἐγώ εἰμι ("that I am") comprehend the sum of the New Testament belief' (Meyer).[1] The emphasis, moreover, as in אֲנִי הוּא, lies on the 'I :' the contents of belief are that 'He' is. 'What' he is, Jesus does not say, for the Old Testament says that. He, therefore, is its substance. The new point which his preaching, which the New Testament, has furnished is, that 'He' is it. Hence the first thing in question is not new knowledge, but a fact in the history of salvation ; this is to be expressed, this is to be believed. The new knowledge, then, consists only in the application of the old knowledge to this actual present. If they do not make this saving fact their own in belief, they forfeit salvation : *Ye shall die in your sins.* In ver. 21, ἀποθανεῖσθε ('ye shall die') was put at the end. Here it stands at the beginning with energetic emphasis : ye shall die (Meyer). Herein lies the whole thought and its tragic character. He alone is the deliverance, and belief in him as the only salvation is the way of deliverance.

Verse 25.

This is taken up by the Jews in their answer, which gives occasion to the whole period, vers. 25–29. To his ἐγώ εἰμι, they reply with the scornful question : σὺ τίσ εἶ ; '*Who art thou ?*' Hofmann is certainly right in designating the Jews' question as a question of unbelieving scorn.

---

[1] Compare Hofmann, *Der Schriftbeweis*, 2d ed., Nördlingen 1857, vol. i. p. 63 f. As to the relation of the Johannean ἐγώ εἰμι to Jesus' self-testimony in the synoptists, see Luthardt, *St. John the Author of the Fourth Gospel*, Edinburgh, T. and T. Clark, 1875, p. 237 ff.

They are the same who opposed him in ver. 22 with that scornful question. They had understood Jesus' statement in ver. 21, and they understood the ἐγώ εἰμι in ver. 24 just as well. It is not seeking doubters that speak thus, but proud opponents. This is to be seen from the σύ ('thou') which stands at the front, and which has the emphasis of contempt (Meyer). Jesus' reply determines itself by this. He does not give them a round answer to their question. They do not deserve it. But he refers them to his word, which he speaks in their midst.

The great question here concerns the difficult and extremely variously explained words: τὴν ἀρχὴν ὅτι καὶ λαλῶ ὑμῖν, that which I say unto you at the beginning. We must proceed step by step in order not to lose the right track in the confusion of the many expositions. Τὴν ἀρχήν is caused to precede in such a way that it must not be taken substantively, but adverbially; it is true that this is the only passage in the New Testament where it is to be thus taken, but elsewhere it often occurs in this sense. It then really appears in the place of a sentence, whose verb is to be supplied; it denotes 'the beginning,' either the one which has or had been made, or which is now made, or which is to be made.

In the former sense—in the meaning: 'at the beginning' —it occurs for example at Gen. xliii. 18, 20; Dan. viii. 1. Something earlier is emphasized and contrasted with that which is later. This might point either to his being or to his speaking. Referred to his being, it would mean 'from the beginning onward,' that is, 'from eternity,' I am that which, etc. Cyril, Lampe, Fritzsche: 'sum a rerum primordiis (i. 1) ea natura, quam me esse profiteor' ('from the first beginnings of things I am that nature which I profess that I am'), Hengstenberg, Stier.[1] Τὴν ἀρχήν means, however: at the beginning, 'initio,' 'ab initio,' but not from the beginning onwards, in the exact sense. Moreover, this reference to his eternal being would not fit into the context here, where he is speaking of the fact that the salvation of the Jews is knit to his person. Finally, λαλεῖν

---

[1] Stier, *Reden Jesu*, 3d ed., Barmen and Elberfeld 1870, vol. iv. p. 417.

('to speak') emphasizes less the contents than the action of speaking. It is no better when they refer τὴν ἀρχήν, in the sense of ἀπ' ἀρχῆσ ('from the beginning'), to his speaking: I am that which I from the beginning onwards speak to you; thus Tholuck, Baumgarten-Crusius. But aside from the way in which τὴν ἀρχήν is made to precede, we should in that case have to read, not λαλῶ ('I speak'), but λελάληκα ('I have spoken'). The fact that he still says what he said at the very beginning, does not justify this manner of expression. It must in that case read ὅτι ἀπ' ἀρχῆσ λελάληκα.

If, then, τὴν ἀρχήν does not designate a far distant beginning, whether of being or of speaking, it must denote the beginning in the sense of that which lies before him. It does not denote the present in contrast with the future, so that τὴν ἀρχήν means 'for the present.' Hofmann[1] says: 'at the beginning, namely, for the present, because this is the time in which he speaks to them, he has much to say concerning them, and to judge with words.' This is not correct. 'At the beginning' and 'for the present' are two things. Nor does it mean the first member of a series: firstly, I am the one, etc. (Luther), or in the first place (Olshausen), or above all things, I am, etc. (De Wette).

The meaning is this. The fact that he designates something as the beginning, and puts it at the front, serves to lay stress upon something as the chief thing. Connected with negations, or in negative sentences, it obtains the sense of 'throughout,' 'altogether,' by which what is denied is denied absolutely. It is, however, not allowable to apply this meaning here in the sense of 'in general' (Lücke), or 'entirely' (Maier, Winer,[2] Godet), or 'certainly' (Bäumlein), because there is no negative sentence here (compare the proofs in Brückner). But that which Jesus says in the following words is by him put at the head and designated as the chief thing, as that which is true 'from the outset.'

[1] Hofmann, *Der Schriftbeweis*, 2d ed., Nördlingen 1857, vol. i. p. 65, vol. ii. part i. (1859), p. 178.
[2] Winer, *Grammatik des neutestamentlichen Sprachidioms*, § 54. 1, 7th ed., Leipzig 1867, p. 432.

He makes the beginning of his answer with this; this is true from the first, when he treats with the Jews; this is the Alpha and Omega: I am that which also I speak to you.

In this it is presupposed that ὅτι is to be taken in the sense of ὅ τι ('that which'), as also it is commonly understood. 'That' [conjunction] he speaks to them (thus I earlier), cannot well be the answer logically to a 'What?' or 'Who?' We should in that case have to take ὅτι καὶ λαλῶ ὑμῖν as a middle clause, and connect τὴν ἀρχήν with ver. 26, πολλὰ κ.τ.λ. ('many things'). Following older commentators, Bengel takes it in this way, and says: 'principio quum etiam loquor vobis—dat. comm.: de me quis sim loquor, ut credatis et salvemini—multa habeo,' etc. ('In the first place, since also I speak for you—dative of advantage: I speak concerning myself, who I am, that ye may believe and be saved'). Hofmann[1] says: 'the very calling in which Jesus for the present stands, namely, to speak to them, brings with it that he also has much to say about them.' But, aside from the fact that Jesus would not answer thus to that question, for this explanation καί would have to be with πολλὰ κ.τ.λ. and not in the confirmatory sentence. Moreover, the words: 'because I speak to you,' would not suffice to express the much farther-reaching thought, that his vocation now is to speak to them. This weighty point of his calling would be herewith brought in. Olshausen and Bäumlein treat ὅτι κ.τ.λ. as a middle clause, and take the relative in the sense of ὅ τι; against this the former objection still holds good, and we should expect λέγω in place of λαλῶ.

Further, it is presupposed in the explanation presented, that ὅτι κ.τ.λ. is to be understood neither in the sense of questioning reflection, nor of an astonished question. Lücke, for example, took it in the former sense: In general, then, why do I yet speak to you? We saw above that τὴν ἀρχήν is not to be justified in this sense, and even if ὅτι permits of justification (as equivalent to τί ἐστιν ὅτι; 'why

---

[1] Hofmann, *Der Schriftbeweis*, 2d ed., Nördlingen 1859, vol. ii. part i. p. 179.

is it that?'), the thought itself is too singular and too inappropriate a reflection in the mouth of Jesus. Meyer took the words in the sense of a surprised question: What I even from the outset speak to you, do ye ask me that? They had not, however, asked him that, but only who he was. When Jesus here substitutes: what he speaks, that is exactly an answer to the question, and not a question itself; hence it is not to be treated as a question.

If, however, ὅ τι καὶ κ.τ.λ. is an answer to the question, λαλῶ offers a difficulty,—as we must concede to Hofmann,[1]— since ὅ τι is the statement of the contents, which would seem to demand λέγειν rather than λαλεῖν. For λαλεῖν denotes speaking as an act. But by καί ('and') Jesus puts his speaking in a parallel with his being. He not merely 'is' what he is, but he also testifies to himself as such in his activity of speaking to them. These two points, that he also speaks to them, and that in this his speaking he accredits himself to them as the one whom he is, Jesus combines together. This is true of all his speaking, whatever he says,—hence the choice of the more generalizing ὅ τι instead of the simple relative.

Their question is sufficiently answered by this reference to his testimony, which he ever and anon gives concerning himself, against them. They deserve no more; he will do them no further honour (Luther). He, who is the word of God to humanity, desires therefore to be recognised only from his word. 'I am your preacher: if you first believe that, you will doubtless learn who I am, and otherwise not' (Luther: marginal note).

Verse 26.

Over against that which his testimony says about him, he places—without 'a punishing delay' (thus Meyer)— that which he has to say about them: *I have many things to say and to judge of you.* They must agree to that, if they are to be helped. He that is the light is also the judge. He can witness to himself as the light, only in

[1] Hofmann, *Der Schriftbeweis*, 2d ed., Nördlingen 1859, vol. ii. part i. p. 178 f.

such a way that his testimony becomes a criticism of the world standing opposed thereunto. Indeed, πολλά ('many things') is emphatically placed at the head. He is far from being done with it yet: 'I have to say,' etc. To the degree that their opposition remains and increases, his judicial testimony against them must continue and grow more severe. They can attain to a recognition of him only on condition of bending before it. When, however, he thus speaks to them judging them, it is not He, for himself, that so judges, etc., but he speaks forth from the fellowship of his Father. The connection is conceived in this way by most commentators (Lücke, De Wette, Tholuck); compare also Hofmann:[1] 'The comparison of viii. 16 confirms the opinion, that, in the face of the offence which the Jews take at his judgment upon them, Jesus withdraws himself to and appeals to the fact that the truthfulness of him who sent him, and the nature of his own discourse, as that which is purely a declaration within the world, of what he before received from God's mouth, are a perfectly valid pledge for the justification of his judging and punishing.'

This is no 'artificially formed contrast' (Meyer), but a perfectly appropriate thought. Nor do ἔχω λαλεῖν ('I have to say') and λέγειν ('to speak') stand in such a contrast to each other, that the former denotes a discourse which Jesus does not bring forth, while the latter denotes his testimony to the truth of salvation, which testimony he really gives (Meyer). For it does not say: he would have, but: he has much to speak; and he means this very thing in the following λαλῶ, which corresponds to the preceding λαλεῖν —not λέγω (Meyer), but λαλῶ is to be read, with ℵ B, etc. Therefore ταῦτα ('those things') are not, as Chrysostom, and following him Meyer, explains, τὰ πρὸσ σωτηρίαν ('the things unto salvation'), but τὰ πρὸσ ἔλεγχον ('the things unto judgment'). With this also agrees the emphasizing directly the truthfulness of God, so that hence his judging testimony is in place, as well as the addition of εἰσ τὸν

[1] Hofmann, *Der Schriftbeweis*, 2d ed., Nördlingen 1859, vol. ii. part i. p. 179.

κόσμον ('unto the world'), for they belong to this; compare ver. 23.

VERSE 27.

In the justification of his judging testimony, he appealed to his peculiar relation to the Father. The evangelist adds a remark concerning this: *They understood not that he spake to them of the Father.* This certainly sounds strange. It is too improbable that the Jews did not know of whom Jesus spoke (De Wette); and it will not do to attempt to make such a thing more credible, by saying that we are to suppose that after ver. 21 the Jews are different ones from those before (Meyer); all the Jews might know that. As little can we make out of the not understanding, a not owning (Lücke), or a covert not wishing to understand (Tholuck, Stier). The evangelist does not say τὸν θεόν ('God'), but τὸν πατέρα ('the Father'): Jesus' relation to the Father, in what sense he is his Father, they might have learned from what Jesus had said previously, which he had heard from him who sent him.[1] He therefore directs them to this his word. From it they are to understand him, his relation to God, and his vocation to the world. There is no other way.

VERSE 28.

But his word does not serve that purpose for them. They do not now understand. An event of the future must occur to bring them to understanding, namely, his lifting up on the cross. Then will they recognise him. Bengel says: 'Cognoscetis ex re quod nunc ex verbo non creditis' ('Ye will recognise from the fact that which you now will not believe from the word'). In this sense the evangelist makes the transition to this new saying of Jesus' by the word οὖν ('then'): *When ye shall lift up the Son of man, then shall ye know that I am.* It is true that ὑψοῦν does not directly mean crucify; it means in the first place merely Jesus' lifting up. Since this, however, is designated as a deed of the Jews (ὅταν ὑψώσητε, 'when ye shall lift

[1] Hofmann, *Der Schriftbeweis*, 2d ed., Nördlingen 1859, vol. ii. part i. p. 180.

up '), we perceive clearly that his death is intended as the first step of the lifting up. Thus it took place historically, that he first was lifted up by men to the cross, and after that by the Father into heaven. What else was it that brought him to the cross, than that he declared of himself that He was, namely, that he was the salvation promised to Israel, although he seemed to be a man like other men. They could not forgive him that. This explains to us the scornful question, ver. 25: σὺ τίσ εἶ; ('who art thou?'), and Jesus recalls that here when he says with design τὸν υἱὸν τοῦ ἀνθρώπου ('the Son of man'). But the knowledge which his death will effect is even this, that He is: τότε γνώσεσθε ὅτι ἐγώ εἰμι ('then shall ye know that I am'). In how far will his lifting up at first on the cross serve them as a means to recognise him? Because he exactly then will be proved to be the one whom he is, at first on the cross, and then in the glorification. 'Eventum legimus' ('we read the issue'), Matt. xxvii. 54; Luke xxiii. 47 f.; Acts ii. 41, xxi. 20; Bengel.

It is hardly likely that what follows still depends on ὅτι ('that,' Meyer, Godet), since it would stand to ὅτι in a different relation from ἐγώ εἰμι ('I am'). On the contrary, the only thing that will properly correspond to the repetition of the previous thought, ver. 24, which is ὅτι ἐγώ εἰμι ('that I am'), is to close the sentence with it, and not give the ὅτι a further relation. And it is entirely in accordance with John's method of speech, that the next thing should free itself from the construction, and take an independent place at the side of what precedes. Jesus goes back to what he said before, ver. 26, about his fellowship with the Father.

I do nothing of myself; but as my Father hath taught me, that I speak. He defines the action more nearly as a speaking. Acting and speaking are not to be conceived as two parallel functions, so that in the first we should have to add in thought 'speaking,' and in the latter 'acting' (Bengel, De Wette). Jesus here has in mind only his business as teacher. Καθώσ ('as') ought to call for οὕτωσ ('so') and not ταῦτα ('that'). Hence Meyer takes ταῦτα demonstratively: that which I teach—being even occupied in this his business as teacher—I teach as, etc. But especially after the interruption in ver. 27, ταῦτα cannot well be taken demonstratively; it probably brings in again the ταῦτα λαλῶ of ver. 26. On this account the evangelist, with his liking for the use of the retrospective pronoun,[1] might well, incorrectly, make a ταῦτα correspond to the καθώσ (thus also commonly).

VERSE 29.

As his fulfilling of his vocation stands in the fellowship of his Father, so also does he himself: *And he that sent me is with me: he hath not left me alone; for I do always that which is well-pleasing to him.* He has not merely sent him at some time or other, and then perchance left him alone; his fellowship with God is a lasting one, because his posture of will also is that agreeable to God, the moral consummation of his divine fellowship. Οὐκ ἀφῆκεν ('hath not left'), namely, thus far. The divine fellowship is in its historical reality one morally mediated. Jesus has made to be the moral act of his life, that which essentially belongs to him. They will learn that also hereafter in the issue of his life: the Father will confess him, because he, Jesus, at all times confesses him. Thus does Jesus give testimony concerning his fellowship with God. The Jews, therefore, are referred to this his word if they desire to know him. Only upon the basis of it will his future help them to the saving knowledge.

What follows is most closely connected with this.

(3.) VERSES 30–59.

This paragraph contains the most cutting expression of the antagonism. Particularly in the middle part, the opposition rises to the greatest keenness. With ver. 48 the discourse turns itself unmistakably to Jesus, and thereby becomes a declaration concerning him. Before that, the statements essentially treat of the Jews. Vers. 38 and 41 (first half) and 47 denote a climax in that. Each of these three

---
[1] See vol. i. p. 32.

statements is called forth by a declaration of the Jews: ver. 33; ver. 39; ver. 41 (second half). Hence, as a rule, commentators begin a new division of this conversation with ver. 33. But it is not to be mistaken that with ver. 37 the tone of the discourse becomes different from what it is in vers. 33–36. In the latter verses, statement predominates; in the former verses, ver. 37 f., attack. Vers. 33–36 are rather a promise of the blessing which he will experience who lets himself be transferred by the Son into the Son's freedom of the truth. First with ver. 37 does Jesus begin to hold up to the Jews that for which their declaration that they are σπέρμα 'Αβραάμ ('Abraham's seed') offers the occasion. Hence he here takes up again these words of theirs. On this account it seems to me that this conversation should be divided into the three sections: vers. 30–36; vers. 37–47; vers. 48–59.

This also answers the question, who the speakers, ver. 33, are. There are difficulties in each case, whether we understand that the ones speaking are believers (Bengel, Olshausen, Baumgarten-Crusius, Meyer, Stier, Godet), or whether we understand that they are the opponents of Jesus (Lampe, De Wette, Lücke, Tholuck, Maier, Hengstenberg). The former is opposed by the continuing of the discourse, ver. 37 f.; the latter, by the change of persons, without a token of the change being given. Jesus directed ver. 31 f. to the believers, who surrounded him, mingled with his opponents. From this crowd now comes to him the remark in ver. 33: doubtless it was at first from his opponents, but the believers also, for lack of understanding, joined in with them, and perhaps in part went over to their side again. Jesus, in the first place, turns to these latter, instructing them, giving them promises. With ver. 37, on the other hand, he directs himself towards the others, judging, condemning. The strong opposition therefore begins first with ver. 37, while ver. 34 f. still belongs to the discourse to the believers. In ver. 33, moreover, the subject could not change, because it in fact did not change entirely. It is kept indefinite, because those words, taken as an utterance of all together, were also indefinite, since they had proceeded from a twofold disposition: 'turba erat promiscua' ('the crowd was a mixed one'), Bengel.

Verses 30–36.

The thing emphasized here is the decisive importance of Jesus' word. Upon this word depend discipleship to Jesus, truth, and freedom.

Verse 30.

Jesus' word brought many to believe on him. The circumstance that it was his word which called forth the belief, shows that it was a right beginning of belief. But of course it was only a mere beginning. The point was, that the progress should also correspond to it. And these were, even though many, yet only single ones out of the mass of unbelievers. It was requisite that they should free themselves entirely from that mass, and enter upon fellowship with Jesus. This was especially true for those who originally belonged to the opposition party.

Verse 31.

Jesus directs himself especially to those of that party who had become believers. Hence the evangelist makes particularly prominent the Ἰουδαῖοι ('Jews'), who *had believed him* (πεπιστευκότασ αὐτῷ), that is, his word, his self-witness, and in consequence of that had believed on him (εἰσ αὐτόν). To these, then, Jesus turns himself in chief: ὑμεῖσ ('ye') is not superfluous, but is said purposely, to distinguish them from the unbelieving Ἰουδαῖοι.

The continuation must correspond to the beginning: *if ye continue in my word*. All depends upon the continuing (compare Acts xiii. 43), and, especially in John's gospel and first epistle, μένειν ('to remain') plays an important part; compare for example v. 38, vi. 56, xv. 4, 5, 6, 7, 9, 10, etc.; 1 John ii. 6, 10, 14, 17, 24, 27, 28, iii. 6, etc. To remain in the word: the word formed the foundation of the new relation toward Jesus upon which they had entered. And the word must continue to be that foundation if the relation is to come to its truth and completion. Thus, in agreement with that which the former paragraph taught us, the word of Jesus, the personal word, appears everywhere as the foundation and mediation of the state of salvation. For it is the means of fellowship with him : *then are ye in truth my disciples.* They have now only begun to turn themselves towards him. Only on the condition mentioned will their discipleship to Jesus obtain truth and reality. 'Non satis est coepisse' ('it is not enough to have begun'), Bengel.

Verse 32.

And ye shall know the truth, and the truth shall make you free.[1] The truth is, in the first place, literally the denial of concealment, hence the manifestation, the knowledge, the expression which corresponds to the fact. The truth, therefore, is agreement with one's own self in being, knowing, speaking. In this way we name a word or a knowledge or a doctrine true, if it agrees with the fact. But ἀλήθεια ('truth') cannot refer to that in the case before us. It could not be said of the truth in the merely theoretical sense : ἐλευθερώσει ὑμᾶσ ('shall make you free'); compare Brückner also. Bengel reminds us that here the same thing is said of the truth that is afterwards said of the Son. 'Filius est veritas' ('the Son is truth'), he adds. And the question here certainly is not merely as to a truth of thought, but of being. The true relation to God has been revealed in Christ. In so far he is the truth. Because he is the life, he is also the light, that is, the right saving form of life ; on this account he is called the truth, namely, the truth of the saving relation to God. Therefore it can make free, because it is a new powerful reality. And in this we also know from what this truth will make free, namely, from the contrary, the salvationless form of life, that is, from sin. The next words tell us in how far this is necessary even for the Jews, and how it comes to pass.

Verse 33.

The Jews deny that that is also necessary for them.

[1] Upon the Biblical notion of truth, compare Hoelemann, *Bibelstudien*, Leipzig 1859, vol. i. p. 1 ff.; see also our comments upon iii. 21, p. 39.

Οὐδενὶ δεδουλεύκαμεν πώποτε ('we were never in bondage to any man'), they say, and they confirm it by the fact that they are σπέρμα Ἀβραάμ ('seed of Abraham'). If, however, the logical relation of these two sentences be the one stated, then no one has a right to take the bondage in a political (De Wette, Meyer) or civil (Lücke, Godet) sense. It is indeed true that it is promised unto the seed of Abraham, that it shall possess the gate of its enemies, Gen. xxii. 17, xxiv. 60, and the Jews expected the fulfilling of this promise, as we know, from the Messiah. But they waited for it, for the very reason that it was not yet come, and that, on the contrary, not merely before this time; but even directly then the opposite was the case. Or how should they be able only to pretend that that was not the case? It is therefore of no use to say, with Bengel: 'loquuntur de sua aetate' ('they speak of their age'), which, moreover, does not fit at all on account of δεδουλεύκαμεν πώποτε ('been in bondage at any time'). They had heard of a freeing through the truth. They answer accordingly. No one has a right to suppose that they had failed to hear the word 'truth' (Stier,[1] 'with all other exegesis' except Lange). On the contrary, they answer both points. The truth, that is, the true saving relation to God, they already possess, namely, in the fact that they are Abraham's seed; for thereby they stand in the relation of children towards God, Deut. xiv. 1.

This answer is a perfectly natural one for Jews, since they ever confound the historical position in the history of salvation with the actual possession of the essential blessing of salvation itself. So then, as belonging to God, they have, even though externally, yet never essentially, been dependent on men. They mean, it is true, spiritual dependence, not indeed in respect to sentiments (Baumgárten-Crusius) but in respect to their religious position. They are, among all men, the privileged ones of God, so that in respect to the mediation of salvation all other nations are dependent upon them. They have never lost this position in favour of another nation, so as to be in a dependent relation towards that nation. How then shall they be made free only through

---

[1] Stier, *Reden Jesu*, 2d ed., Barmen and Elberfeld 1870, vol. iv. p. 430.

Jesus? This seems to them an encroachment on their honour as Jews.

Verse 34.

Jesus' answer remains now also in the sphere of thought of spiritual dependence in a religious relation, namely, in that this answer recalls the power of sin and the condition of dependence on sin. Salvation is effected, not by means of merely belonging to that nation which forms a part of the history of salvation, but essentially by ethical means. *Every one who commits sin is a servant of sin.* Jesus says πᾶσ ('every one') designedly; the general law of the moral order of the universe suffers no exception for them. Ποιεῖν τὴν ἁμαρτίαν ('to commit sin'), moreover (the article intends to lay stress upon the fact that we are to think, not of single sins, but of the whole ethical life-character; thus also Baumgarten-Crusius), is that ethical constitution of life which contradicts the idea of the σπέρμα Ἀβραάμ; compare ver. 39. He thus also gives herewith the answer to σπέρμα Ἀβραάμ, ver. 33, and with δοῦλοσ εἰσ τὴν ἁμαρτίαν ('servant of sin') to οὐδενὶ δεδουλεύκαμεν πώποτε ('we were never in bondage to any man'). It is hence not quite correct when Bengel (and Stier) says: In ver. 34, Jesus replies to their declaration about freedom, and then, in ver. 37, he passes over to their being the children of Abraham. On the contrary, vers. 34–36 offer a complete reply. As Abraham's seed, they are God's children, in view of the external historical position alone. Actually, because ethically servants of sin, they are only like servants in the house of God, in which they stand because of their historical position. In consequence, they have only the vocation of servants in God's house; they do not stand in part possession of the property of the house, namely, of the blessings of salvation. They therefore remain in the house only so long as the master of the house needs them; their position is only a historical one. The position of one who is in the house as son is the contrary of this.

Verse 35.

The servant abideth not in the house for ever; the son

abideth for ever. Since the son stands contrasted with the servant, ὁ υἱός ('the son') is just as generically intended as ὁ δοῦλος, 'the servant' (De Wette, Lücke, Stier), and is not at once to be referred to Christ (thus Bengel, Meyer, Godet). Only in its further progress does the discourse pass over to Christ. He is a son in the house, namely, God's house, who stands not merely in a historical, but in an essential, because ethically mediated, relation to God. Such a one has a share in the possession of the essential blessings of salvation, namely, of the ζωὴ αἰώνιος ('eternal life'). He has it through the ἀλήθεια ('truth'), that is, by the fact that he stands in the right relation to God, because in the saving relation, because in the proper ethical constitution of life. This relation to God, this ἀλήθεια, withdraws him from dependence upon all other and not-divine power. Now, however, that relation is in an absolute way existing in him who in the absolute sense is ὁ υἱός, and therefore also ἡ ἀλήθεια. Where, therefore, in a manner the copy of this, it with its blessed influence is to be realized, there it is conditioned upon this υἱός κατ' ἐξοχήν ('son by way of eminence'); but then also, if wrought by him, it is not apparently but actually, not externally but essentially, existing.

VERSE 36.

If the Son make you free, then ye shall be really free. The article here gives the ὁ υἱός ('the Son') a strong emphasis. Above it was said: the truth makes free; here: the Son makes free; for he 'is' the truth. Such freedom is then real, and it alone; all other freedom is only appearance and deception.

We see, therefore, that the word of Jesus is the means and the lasting foundation for the right relation to God, even for Israel; Jesus' word, because he is that relation in an absolute way in his own person, and therefore he also alone can mediate it.

The words have a double meaning. They are instructive, and they point forward for those of the seed of Abraham who, through the beginning of belief, have also begun to enter upon the right saving relation to God. They are condemnatory for them, if the beginning in them should not grow to a progress in the relation to Jesus, but they should withdraw again from it, and associate themselves with those who, as servants of sin, choose to be mere servants in the house of God. Jesus' word now addresses itself directly to these latter.

Verses 37–47.

It was remarked above that this section falls into three periods: vers. 37, 38; vers. 39–41 (first half); vers. 41 (second half)–47. If we compare their beginnings and their ends (ver. 47 to compare with ver. 44) with each other, the progressive climax is evident. That which is at first conceded, ver. 37, is soon brought into question (ver. 39: εἰ τέκνα τοῦ Ἀβραάμ ἐστε, 'if ye are children of Abraham'), and this is then extended to the last conclusion, ver. 42. In a similar manner, in the ends of the periods, that which at first is only hinted at, is declared ever more directly, both positively and negatively.

(a.) Verses 37, 38.

They are merely historically the seed of Abraham. In consequence, they are it in such a way that at the same time they are not it, namely, essentially. This shows itself in their behaviour towards him, who nevertheless is the fulfilment of the beginning which was in Abraham.

Verse 37.

I know that ye are Abraham's seed; but ye seek to kill me, because my word hath no entrance in you. Jesus tells them to their face their murderous thoughts; thereby they practically deny their relation as children to Abraham. Their murderous disposition is occasioned by the fact that his word does not so enter into them as to have its abode in them. Thus χωρεῖ ἐν ὑμῖν is to be taken pregnantly, with De Wette, against Meyer: it has no progress in you; against another explanation which is widespread, but which is contrary to the rules of the language, namely: it finds no room in you (for example, Baumgarten-Crusius); or against Lücke and Hengstenberg's conception of ἐν ὑμῖν as 'inter vos' ('among you').

It is true that χωρεῖν means: to have progress. If we understand it as Meyer does: the word had its progress in their souls, then it is therein presupposed that it indeed had entrance. It would then be said of the πεπιστευκότεσ ('those who had believed'). But this is no explanation of the murderous disposition. For that, instead of the lacking progress, the transition into the opposite internal mood against Jesus must have been named. Οὐ χωρεῖν therefore denies not the progress, but the entrance. The meaning 'to move oneself forward' for χωρεῖν is, as Meyer also owns, a very common one; ἐν ὑμῖν then denotes the result, as so often with verbs of motion.

This statement of the reason is a logically correct one only in case the word, even if not received, still has a positive influence in the man, namely, the influence opposite to the other. The word affects either the willingness of belief or the hostile contradiction of unbelief. To such a degree, then, is the word the decisive thing, and to such a degree is the κρίσισ ('judgment') given in it. This opposing relation to him is determined by their moral constitution.

Verse 38.

In consequence, there exists an absolute contrast between him and them. B reads: ἃ ἐγὼ ἑώρακα παρὰ τῷ πατρὶ λαλῶ, καὶ ὑμεῖσ οὖν ἃ ἠκούσατε παρὰ τοῦ πατρόσ ποιεῖτε; ℵ reads: ἃ ἐγὼ ἑώρακα παρὰ τῷ πατρί μου λαλῶ, καὶ ὑμεῖσ οὖν ἃ ἑωράκατε παρὰ τοῦ πατρόσ ὑμῶν ποιεῖτε ('I speak that which I have seen with the Father [ℵ: my Father], and ye then do that which ye have heard [ℵ: seen] with the father [ℵ: your father]'). The plural ἅ is found also in C D, and is therefore to be preferred to the singular ὅ, which E F G H read. The placing ἐγώ in front is, indeed, commended by the majority of the manuscripts; yet it was such an easy thing to put it there, that this, rather than the putting it afterwards, is to be explained as a correction. Any one could be easily tempted to put a μου ('my') after πατρί, 'father' (besides ℵ, in D E F G H); while it seems less necessary than ὑμῶν ('your') in the second phrase, which is supported by C D E F G. In the second clause, ἑωράκατε, 'ye have seen' (besides ℵ, in E F G), and above all, the dative (D E F G), are to be rejected for material reasons, and are evidently only an imitation of the first clause. We may therefore follow essentially the reading of B, only perhaps with the insertion of ὑμῶν ('your').

What I have seen with the Father, I speak; and ye then, what ye have heard from your father ye do. When Jesus says of himself ἃ ἑώρακα παρὰ τῷ πατρί ('what I have seen with the Father'), and of the Jews on the other hand, ἃ ἠκούσατε παρὰ τοῦ πατρὸσ ὑμῶν ('what ye have heard from your father'), the double change is occasioned by the different kind of fellowship in which he stands with his Father, and in which they stand with their father. He was 'with the Father' (Meyer); what he speaks, arises from such direct fellowship. And although this his knowledge is in time mediated by his constant internal intercourse with the Father, still it is nevertheless that supertemporal vision which mediates itself to him for his temporal consciousness. The fellowship in which he stands with the Father, and which forms the foundation and the kernel of his ethical and historical fellowship, is an essential fellowship.

The Jews stand differently towards their father: they have entered into moral dependence upon him (compare the aorist ἠκούσατε with the preceding perfect ἑώρακα). Ἀκούειν ('to hear') is intended to designate the fact that, in obedience to their father, they have received into their soul the utterance of his will. He does not here say who this their father is, but he hints at it plainly enough. To him is traced back the moral opposition to the revelation of God in Christ. There is nothing in these words of physical conditionality, or of dualistic views. On the contrary, this discourse about the Jews moves exclusively in the sphere of the will and of the disposition. 'And ye therefore:' this οὖν does not say in 'painful irony' (Meyer, Godet): following my example of dependence, etc.; but it refers to the preceding words touching the moral opposition in which they stand towards Jesus: ye seek to slay me, etc. Their conduct, therefore, is determined by an entirely different association from that of Jesus. By this relation of drawing a conclusion, the imperative conception of ποιεῖτε (Hengstenberg) is excluded. It is a simple statement touching their regular course of action, which includes that desire to slay him, but is not exhausted in it (Meyer).

By what means he who is their father has become such, is not definitely said, at first, in the words before us. But the most fit thing, is to understand the word according to the analogy of similar designations. A man is not called τέκνον ἀπωλείασ ('child of destruction') because he perchance from the outset was determined by the ἀπώλεια ('destruction'), so that he could do nothing else but bear the character and fate of τέκνον ἀπωλείασ; but because he has given himself up into the hands of the ἀπώλεια, and hence is its own. Thus the Jews, who physically indeed, but not ethically, are Abraham's children, are in the latter sense called children of the Father whose will they as such do, because they have given themselves up to him, and therefore belong to him. What follows confirms this.

(b.) VERSES 39–41a.

If we combine the facts that they on the one hand are indeed children of Abraham, ver. 37, and on the other hand not, but the children of another, we shall evidently perceive that the latter relation in its entire extent is to be understood as an ethical one. If, moreover, it be ethical, it is then a free one as to its establishment, and is only a limited one upon the basis of this establishment.

VERSE 39.

The Jews appeal to the fatherhood of Abraham. But, Jesus replies, their actions must correspond to this. Ἐστέ (εἰ τέκνα Ἀβραάμ ἐστε), 'ye are,' is too strongly confirmed by the manuscripts ℵ B D L, against ἦτε, to be possibly rejected, and that the less the more striking the reading is. Meyer compares Luke xvii. 5 f. The sonship in Abraham is at first put forward ('εἰ ... ἐστέ') in order then to be refuted by their deeds. In the second part of a period ἄν is lacking more frequently in later Greek, especially with the imperfect, without there always being an intention to show thereby the decision, which originally was to be expressed by the omission of the ἄν.[1]

VERSE 40.

Their actions, however, stand in the sharpest contradiction to the disposition and posture which agree with Abraham. The course of thought forms a syllogism: ver. 39 the major premise, ver. 40 the minor premise: *But now ye seek to kill me, a man that hath told you the truth.* Ἄνθρωπον in itself has no emphasis (against Godet), but only introduces what follows: not any chance man, but a man who tells them the truth, and that the truth he has learned from God. The fact that ἀκούειν ('to hear') enters in place of ὁρᾶν ('to see'), depends upon the idea of the truth, and the same holds good for the genitive, παρὰ τοῦ θεοῦ ('from God'). *This did not Abraham,*—this way of conceiving it, directly by the form of the 'litotes,' makes the contrast very emphatic. That which Jesus here has in mind is not Abraham's hospitable reception of the angels (thus Hengstenberg and Lampe), which would be very distant and be too isolated. It is the entire bearing of Abraham: he was a man of believing obedience; they are men of opposition to God's saving revelation.

VERSE 41a.

In consequence, an utterly different person is their father, whose works they do; not: they are to do: in the imperative sense (Hengstenberg); 'Your father's,' to whom they have given themselves up; their posture is determined by this. The relationship itself was freely taken up by them, but they are now bound by it in their action. The reason for the ποιεῖν τὰ ἔργα ('to do the works') lies in πατήρ ('father'). Designedly, the action or the mental utterance,

---

[1] See Winer, *Grammatik des neutestamentlichen Sprachidioms*, § 42. 2, 7th ed., Leipzig 1867, p. 286.

and not the original character of mind, is named as the necessary result of their relationship. The latter, therefore, the character of mind, which is the basis of their mental utterance, coincides with the fact of the relationship. Hence it is the same whether it says, they are the children of the devil, or they have the same disposition as he. For Jesus soon names the devil to them directly as their father. The Jews themselves offer the occasion for this.

(c.) VERSES 41b–47.

Jesus, namely, had led the discourse to God. He reproached them with a murderous disposition, combined with a contempt for the truth, and that, the truth coming from God. This shows who their father is. Thus the discourse passes over to the relation to God. It is a question whether this is done in a direct way in the next words.

VERSE 41b.

We be not born of fornication. This is commonly understood in a figurative sense of idolatry (for example, Lampe, Lücke, Tholuck, Hengstenberg, Stier): our relation of sonship to God is not rendered impure by the worship of false gods, (or thus I earlier); we do not spring from the relation of Israel to another god, but are children of Israel as the wife of Jehovah—thus agreeably to frequent Old Testament conception and designation. But the preceding denial of their relationship as children to Abraham requires the contrasted reference to this as the nearest conception of the word. Therefore it is: not from whoredom of Sarah's with some one else (thus Meyer). Indeed they boast themselves, with emphasis, of their relation of descent to Abraham: ἡμεῖσ ('we').

They proceed: *We have one father, God.* They can pass from Abraham to God, not by now letting Abraham fall out of consideration (Meyer), but, on the contrary, by reason of the fact that their sonship in God is mediated by their sonship in Abraham. For Jehovah was the God of Abraham, Isaac, and Jacob. Were they then not the sons of Abraham, but of some other human father, they would also not be the children of God. They are the latter, because they are the former. They say, moreover: One, because in the other case they would be God's sons only nominally, not really. They profess to be the latter. In the former case, they would have no right or propriety in the claim; they would have two fathers, a real one—not God—and an alleged one. All this other view they deny: they have only 'one,' Jehovah, in name and in fact. Such is the due understanding of ἕνα πατέρα ἔχομεν ('we have one father'). These words do not mean: God alone, and no strange god, is our father (De Wette), which must read μόνον τὸν θεὸν πατέρα ἔχομεν. Nor do they mean: we have all the one father (Baumgarten-Crusius, Stier), for the second clause is only a positive repetition of the first, and is intended to exclude πορνεία ('fornication'), and to portray the speakers as children of pure marriage. This expresses the same opinion as what preceded. Because they, as part of the history of salvation, are children of the covenant, they think they also actually are such.

Verse 42.

Jesus offers them the actual, that is, the ethical test. The token of relationship is lacking; for they do not love him, who is from God. He proceeded forth from God— ἐγώ ('I') with emphasis and consciousness of his right— essentially and personally; καὶ ἥκω ('and I come') is the result: and am now here; he had his vocation also from God. Thus, in agreement with the New Testament use of ἔρχεσθαι ('to come'), ἐλήλυθα ('I came') is distinguished from the preceding ἐξῆλθον ('I proceeded forth'). From this also is οὐδέ ('neither') to be explained; not from the twofold possibility, of having come from a third person or from himself (Meyer). It is occasioned by the correspondence of ἐξέρχεσθαι ('to proceed forth') with ἔρχεσθαι ('to come'), of the going forth from God with the coming out in his calling. These two points, moreover, constituted the idea of sonship. Jesus therefore designates himself as the Son of God in the full extent of the notion. They reject his self-revelation in the word, and can do nothing else, because they are the children of the devil. This is the progress of the next verse.

VERSE 43.

Because they are both so foreign to each other, it is no wonder that they do not understand his discourse. *Why do ye not understand my speech? Because ye cannot hear my word.* The form of question and answer is an expression of the increasing animation (Meyer). $\Lambda a\lambda\iota\acute{a}$ designates the speech more from the side of the act and the form, without the sense of contempt it had at an earlier period; $\lambda\acute{o}\gamma o\sigma$ designates the word from the side of the contents. They do not understand the former,—$\gamma\iota\nu\acute{\omega}\sigma\kappa\epsilon\tau\epsilon$ in the sense of the internal appropriation, according to the Biblical use of language,—that they had shown clearly enough. For they cannot. All the emphasis rests on $o\dot{v}$ $\delta\acute{v}\nu a\sigma\theta\epsilon$ ('ye cannot'). Jesus denies to them the inward moral possibility. They lack the moral presupposition for it, namely, the right inward moral relation to God and to his messenger. Our whole previous treatment of the context, and the words themselves, show that this is the subject treated of, and not a natural necessary incapability in the sense of dualism (Hilgenfeld). If a dualistic view lay at the foundation of these words, the non-understanding would be more correctly named as the first result, and the thereby conditioned non-reception of Jesus' word as the further result. The more physical point would have necessarily preceded the more ethical one. The case, however, is exactly the opposite.

VERSE 44.

They cannot, because they are the children of the devil, so that accordingly their willing stands in analogy with this their association. '$T\mu\epsilon\hat{\iota}\sigma$ ('ye') in contrast to $\dot{\epsilon}\gamma\acute{\omega}$ ('I') in ver. 42: 'I proceeded forth from God; ye have the devil for your father.' It is arbitrary to refer this word to Israel in general, and thence to determine the relation of John's gospel to the Old Testament and to Judaism;[1] or to

[1] Baur, *Vorlesungen über Neutestamentliche Theologie*, Hamburg 1864, p. 391 f.

explain it from Gnosticism, and thence to conclude that John's gospel holds the view of a ruling dualism (Hilgenfeld, Volkmar, Keim). The words are completely explained by the progress of the discourse, and by the Old Testament view which lies at its base.

Since ὁ διάβολος ('the devil') is here contrasted with ὁ θεός ('God'), it is a matter of course that the former is meant by Christ quite as exactly as the latter (against Baumgarten-Crusius,[1] Schleiermacher[2]). It is true, however, that the Old Testament does not give the thought this expression. The Jews are in many passages called children of whoredom or idolatry, or children of Belial, Deut. xiii. 14; children of transgression, and seed of lying, Isa. lvii. 3, 4. The moral sphere, the spiritual power to which the Israelites belong, is at first still named neutrally and not yet designated personally. The fact that ὁ διάβολος regularly appears for this in the New Testament, depends upon the progress in the history of salvation. The personal manifestation of lying in sin, stands opposed to the personally revealed word of God.[3] Substantially, then, what Jesus here says and what the Old Testament says do not differ. But there is, by reason of the progress of the history, a greater definiteness of knowledge, and conditioned upon this a greater definiteness of expression.

These words no more rest on Gnostic dualism than do like statements and reproaches in the Old Testament. It is the complaint of all the prophets: God has brought up children for himself; but they have fallen away from him. Thus they have become the children of another. They have done this by a fellowship of will, into which they have entered, and from which their willing and their conduct now has received its necessary ethical character. In this sense, therefore, it is said: *Ye are of the father, namely, the devil.* The view that τοῦ διαβόλου ('of the devil')

---

[1] Baumgarten-Crusius, *Theologische Auslegung der Johanneischen Schriften*, Jena 1843, vol. i. p. 359.

[2] Schleiermacher, *Das Leben Jesu*, Berlin 1864, p. 338 f.

[3] Compare Hofmann, *Der Schriftbeweis*, 2d ed., Nördlingen 1857, vol. i. p. 441.

depends upon τοῦ πατρόσ ('of the father'), and that the evangelist shared the Gnostic notion that the god of the Jews is the father of the devil (Hilgenfeld, also Volkmar), needs no refutation, in spite of Lachmann's authority. The evangelist knows only two potencies: God and the devil. If the Jews are not God's children, they are the devil's children, for they have chosen him for their father. Some middle thing would, besides, not fit at all into the context.

Their relation as the devil's children reveals itself also now in the actual result: that they act according to the will of the devil, not in consequence of an external compulsion or of one arising from necessity of nature, but of their own free will: θέλετε, ye will. With conscious determination they put themselves at the service of his ἐπιθυμίαι ('lusts'): the will of the devil is thus designated, in order to designate it as one consisting in the motion of desire, namely, in the desire which is hostile to God. In this the hostility to Jesus is thought of. Hence murderous disposition and hatred of the truth are named as the two characteristics of Satan. From the very beginning, through the whole history of salvation, these two factors proceed in union with each other, against God, whose meat and whose gift is the life, and whose revelation is the truth. Thus have the two united against Jesus, who is the appearance of the life and of the truth. The church of Jesus must also have the same experience (compare 1 John iii. 13 ff., ii. 22, iv. 1 ff.), and in the Revelation hostile power and delusive lying are throughout named as the characteristics of the diabolic opposition to the church, or of anti-Christianity.

When it is said that he is a murderer from the beginning, the necessary thought to supply is: namely, since there were men (against Baumgarten-Crusius and Brückner). That also was his doing, that he brought man into death. In this is named a lasting conduct towards men (Baumgarten-Crusius), which he began with the beginning of the history of humanity. For this reason we are not to point to Cain's fratricide (thus Lücke, De Wette, Hilgenfeld), but to the first man. For it is said that he was a murderer since men have existed. Therefore we are here reminded that he brought the very first man by sin into death (Origen, Chrysostom, Augustine, Olshausen, Tholuck, Maier, Meyer, Hofmann,[1] Godet, Lechler,[2] Hahn[3]). Such is the manner of conduct of the Jews towards Jesus. It proves that they belong to the devil.

The other point is his hatred for the truth. Here too ἔστηκεν ('he stood') does not in the first instance denote a fact, but a continuing state of being. It is true that since Augustine (Vulgate: 'stetit,' 'he stood'), especially on the part of systematic theologians, and even also, at least approximately, of Martensen,[4] Thomasius,[5] and Philippi,[6] it is common to see in these words the declaration of the fall of Satan. Luther's translation also: 'has not stood against,' includes as contrast: but has fallen before it, as if it said εἱστήκει. Ἕστηκα has an intransitive and present meaning: I stand; compare Acts xxvi. 22—this is erroneously cited by Stier[7] as a confirmation of the preterite explanation, and explained: I have held myself, maintained myself, whereas it only says: I stand; Rom. v. 2; 1 Cor. xv. 1; Rev. iii. 20. So then also here. It is not: he continues not in the truth, as if he should be again won unto it by God (Olshausen), or as if his fall were to be thought as a continuous one (De Wette). It is simply: he has not his station in the truth, to which we must add: but in falsehood. The fall of Satan is then only the necessary presupposition of this his present state (Meyer).

The two sentences with ἀλήθεια ('truth') are so distinguished that the former denies the 'status in veritate' ('position in truth,' Bengel); the latter, the truthful disposition (De Wette). The former, that his dwelling-place is not in the realm of objective truth, is confirmed by the latter, that he lacks the truth inwardly and ethically.

---

[1] Hofmann, *Der Schriftbeweis*, 2d ed., Nördlingen 1857, vol. i. pp. 418, 478 f.
[2] Lechler, *Studien und Kritiken*, 1854, p. 814 f.
[3] Hahn, *Die Theologie des Neuen Testamentes*, Leipzig 1854, vol. i. p. 355.
[4] Martensen, *Die Christliche Dogmatik*, Berlin 1856, p. 182.
[5] Thomasius, *Christi Person und Werk*, 2d ed., Erlangen 1856, vol. i. p. 294.
[6] Philippi, *Kirkliche Glaubenslehre*, Stuttgart 1859, vol. iii. p. 296.
[7] Stier, *Reden Jesu*, 3d ed., Barmen and Elberfeld 1870, vol. iv. p. 458.

After our previous remarks as to ἡ ἀλήθεια, there is no question how we are to take it. It is not so much the truth as a rule (De Wette), as the truth as the rightly-formed correct state of being. It is therefore the right relation to God.

Hence ἀλήθεια, the first and the second time, though one thing, is still of necessity as different (against Stier[1] in spite of his supplementary excuse) as that which is external and that which is internal. The first time the devil is considered as being in it, and the second time it is considered as being in him. In the former, it is the form and the condition of life in which one stands; in the latter, it is the internal, ethical state of being, as character and conduct. The fact that he lacks the second is the reason for his necessarily going without the first. This, therefore, is not based on the condition in which he perchance from the outset was created, but in his direction of will, and hence in his own conduct. From this it can be seen how much right Frommann and Hilgenfeld have to declare that a fall of the devil is excluded by the passage before us. Yet his fall certainly is not taught here, since the interest in hand was a different one. In this the Jews are like him. They must lose the ἀλήθεια which is in Jesus, because they lack the proper inward bearing towards God.[2]

The lying habit of the devil in his utterances is something necessary, because it is his substance: ἐκ τῶν ἰδίων ('of his own') with emphasis. Lying is not for him something accidental, external, foreign, but his own contents. It is essential to him to be a liar; and accordingly, whosoever is a liar is his son. He is 'pater cuiusvis mendacis' ('of every liar'). This is certainly the due understanding of the passage, with Bengel, Baumgarten-Crusius, Meyer, Stier, Hengstenberg, and against both Hilgenfeld's adventurous and grammatically impossible reference to διάβολοσ ('devil'), and Brückner's reference to ψεῦδοσ ('lie'). The same thing accordingly will now also be the case with the Jews.

---

[1] Stier, *Reden Jesu*, 3d ed., Barmen and Elberfeld 1870, vol. iv. p. 459.

[2] Compare on this passage, Hofmann, *Der Schriftbeweis*, 2d ed., Nördlingen 1857, vol. i. p. 418 f.

Verse 45.

If moral obliquity has become their inner nature, it is essential and necessary for them to reject Jesus' word for the very reason that it is a word of truth. For it is 'his' word. Ἐγὼ δέ ('and I'), he begins, emphatically (Bengel, Meyer), in contrast to the devil: he is the liar; I, on the other hand, speak the truth. In this the height as well as the certainty of his self-consciousness expresses itself, which had no reply to fear. He knows that his person has not a merely relative importance, but that it forms the contrast to the universal principle of evil. But for this very reason they do not believe in him. In these words Jesus utters a word of judgment against them. For herein it appears that they have fallen under judgment. At the same time, it is a word of the strongest reproof: it should and could be otherwise. Their unbelief and their hatred for the truth has no justifying reason in Jesus. They must bear him witness that they cannot bring against him any moral reproach.

Verse 46.

Ἁμαρτία means sin, as it always does, not untruth, error (for example, Bengel), or frivolous deception (Baumgarten-Crusius). Commonly, it is thus explained: because he is without sin, he speaks the truth, because he then also is without lying (for example, Meyer); or also because he then is a certain organ of the knowledge and of the impartation of the truth (Lücke); or because the knowledge of the truth rests upon the purity of the will (De Wette). The two latter explanations are beyond doubt erroneous; for both would be as foreign to this passage as they would be foreign to the ruling habit of the fourth gospel to trace Jesus' preaching back to his ante-temporal and constant relation of fellowship with the Father (compare Meyer and Brückner). Against the former explanation, however, Hofmann[1] also rightly emphasizes for the understanding of

---

[1] Hofmann, *Der Schriftbeweis*, 2d ed., Nördlingen 1859, vol. ii. part i. p. 33.

these words the whole context of the discourse; Jesus appeals to the bearing of his opponents themselves towards him: 'you do not oppose to me a charge of sin. I say rightly therefore, that ye do not believe on me, just because I speak the truth.' It does not, however, follow from this that ἁμαρτία 'can only mean sin of word and not sin of deed.' The word reads as general, embracing the whole genus of sin, from which then in the application with ἀλήθεια the denial of the species is made especially prominent.

The discourse therefore proceeds, not in the form of drawing a conclusion (thus commonly), but of distinction in the application. If, moreover, Jesus, because without sin, is also without lying, if his word therefore be irrefutably the truth, then the difficulty is in them alone, and in their moral impurity. Thus they are convicted, they who boast their property in God as Abraham's children, of lacking entirely the ethical fellowship of God, and accordingly of being the property of the realm and the prince of the contrary moral principle. It is proved to them that in this alone lies the reason for their unbelief and for their hostility to Jesus. Hereby they are completely condemned, since Jesus, directly by their unbelief, is proved to be the absolute truth.

I say absolute truth. For the notion that his sinlessness was only relative and not absolute (Meyer), is a thought that at least may be misunderstood. The fact that he was tempted and could have sinned—which, however, is but an abstract possibility—shows only that his morality, which consisted in full obedience, was at the same time his own free act. If, moreover, in that which he suffered he 'learned' (Heb. v. 8) obedience, he learned it even in the fact that he exercised it, without at any time or in any way failing to exercise it. As in him, who became man, the absolute life appeared, so in him, who was compassed with infirmity (Heb. v. 2), appeared absolute sinlessness. That is the peculiarity of Jesus: absolute substance in earthly and human reality. If any one appeals to Mark x. 18, we reply, in the first place, that Jesus does not say: I am not good; and, in the next place, that the saying is a pedagogical one.

With the words τίσ ἐξ ὑμῶν κ.τ.λ. ('which of you, etc.'), Jesus appeals to their own conduct; they know of no reproach they can lay upon him; and even now they are silent at the provoking question. Yet this their ignorance or silence is in itself no sufficient proof that he and his word are sacred truth. It is true, he appeals to their conscience, which must give testimony for him. But the thing he bases himself on is still always his absolute consciousness. In the case of Jehovah in the Old Testament, all proof, all assurance, in the last resort rests only on his 'I';—the case is the same with Jesus. When he, in ver. 42 above, proves that they have not God as their Father, by the circumstance that they do not love him, for he is the Son, the demonstration rests entirely upon the truth of this declaration. Jesus has no higher place of appeal than his self-testification, and can substantiate it only by it itself. Nothing further can be done for him, who will not and cannot believe in him on account of his word and of his self-witness in general.

Verse 47.

Hence: if they were from God, they must have heard and understood God's word, namely, as such. The circumstance that they do not understand and accept it, serves as a proof that they are not God's children. 'To be from God' designates the inner moral propriety. This statement has as its presupposition the thought that his word is the very word of God, that he is God's Son, and hence cannot offer a proof outside of himself, but only in himself and from himself.

Verses 48–50.

Jesus has thus uncovered the last ethical root of their unbelief. From this he will now pass to the future, which they have to expect upon the ground of this their present. For if he, because absolutely the fulness of the blessing of salvation and the truth of life, in consequence therefore bears all the future decreed in himself, and if they reject him, then, with the present blessing and relation of salvation, they also reject all the future of salvation.

Verse 48.

The Jews had understood very well, that he in the last resort appealed for the truth of his declarations solely to himself. That seems to them an unbearable assumption, one that deserves alike scorn and indignation. Their passionate words in this verse combine these two feelings; and both refer to the assumption of Jesus. When they call him a Samaritan, it is hardly in the sense of 'heresy' (thus commonly, also Meyer, Hengstenberg), but in the thought that unbearable assumption is the special quality of the Samaritan. It was an assumption when the Samaritan rejected Jerusalem and Abraham's pure descent, and put Gerizim and himself in its place. And Jesus acted in the same manner, in that he rejected them all and esteemed himself alone. Jesus' assumption, however, is so much greater than that of the Samaritans, that it can only be explained on the ground of insanity, which flows from diabolic influence: δαιμόνιον ἔχεισ ('thou hast a devil'). And they are right in this, if Jesus be not God's son. But if he be God's Son, the Jews have reviled him. They did it, because according to their opinion he reviled in Abraham's race God their Father, by his diabolical, God-hostile assumption.

Verse 49.

He justifies himself against this charge. Ἐγώ ('I') and ὑμεῖσ ('ye') stand opposed to each other, but not as if Jesus returned the Jews' charge of being possessed with a devil. That would have to be, not ἐγώ ... οὐκ ('I ... not'), but οὐκ ... ἐγώ ('not ... I'); Meyer against Lücke. But ἐγώ introduces the twofold sentence with a negative and a positive side, and then ὑμεῖσ is put over against this: *I have not a devil, but I honour my Father, and ye dishonour me.* He is not actuated by a God-hostile spirit, but his speaking and action are directed alone to the purpose of defending the cause of God his Father. He did this even in the thing for which the Jews revile him. For in that he confesses himself to be the Son of God, and on the other hand denies to them the being children of God, he defends God's honour.

In return for such honouring of God, he receives from them the reward, that they dishonour him. $Kaί$ ('and') is intended to designate this contrast,[1] and not to serve the pure opposition between 'I' and 'ye' (against De Wette). Since, moreover, they revile him, who yet seeks only God's honour, their reviling strikes at God himself. Thus they only show again how right he was, when he said that they were not the children of God.

VERSE 50.

If he be thus reviled unjustly, he will still be justified in contrast with those who revile him. But it is not He who will procure justification for himself. God will do it, and will judge between him and them. This is the course of the thought, and not, as De Wette wishes: I have complained of dishonouring, not perchance from ambition, etc. A turn like that would require a contrast to 'ambition' and not to 'I.' That $ἐγώ$ ('I'), however, is emphasized, is clear even from its precedence: I seek not my own glory, etc.; another will do that. $Ἔστιν ὁ ζητῶν$, *there is one that seeketh and judgeth.* The discourse proceeds by means of a middle thought which at once supplies itself. If they revile him, namely, with injustice, that must be revealed, a $δοξάζεσθαι$ ('being glorified') must be granted to him. He can leave this $δοξάζεσθαι$ safely to his Father; He will care for it, because Jesus is leading His cause alone. God will judge. Thus too Baumgarten-Crusius.

VERSE 51.

Wherein will this justification consist? Wherein else than in its being revealed that the blessing and the future of salvation are decreed in him, and attached to his person?

---

[1] See vol. i. p. 43 f.

Baumgarten-Crusius (and Meyer) also rightly takes the relation of the sentences in this way, against the majority of commentators, who do not connect this thought directly with what precedes (Lücke), but let it be addressed after a pause either to the believers (De Wette, Godet) or to the multitude in general (Tholuck). If, moreover, this issue of his calling be his glorification and his justification, it will at the same time be unto judgment for those over against whom he is thus justified. They forfeit this future of salvation.

On the other side, however, Jesus in this places the blessing of belief before the eyes of those to whom his word has served to begin a relation to him, and will serve as the foundation of a lasting relation. Jesus introduces this saying with emphasis: ἀμὴν ἀμὴν κ.τ.λ. ('verily, verily, etc.'), and with stress upon his person: τὸν ἐμὸν λόγον ('my word')—it is his word that they must have kept (τηρήσῃ), not merely in heart (Tholuck), but also with their deeds. The reward for it is: They shall, although they must suffer death, yet in their real life, the element of which is belief, have no experience of death. *He will in eternity not die;* not perchance: 'he will not in eternity die' (Käuffer, compare Meyer). It is the first negative turn of the previous saying concerning the ζωὴ αἰώνιοσ ('eternal life'). He therefore is the light of life, τὸ φῶσ τῆσ ζωῆσ, ver. 12. He who accepts him as φῶσ ('light') will have ζωή ('life') as the fruit of it.

VERSE 52.

Jesus is the future of salvation in his own person. But salvation and life are given in his person also for the believers of the Old Testament: vers. 52–56. The Jews hold up to him the men of God in the Old Testament as an argument against his declaration that salvation is absolutely bound to his person, and that it consists in not dying. This argument seems to them so palpable, that they can see in Jesus' words only a senseless overweening pride, and therefore a confirmation of their charge that he is possessed of a demon: νῦν ἐγνώκαμεν κ.τ.λ. ('now we know, etc.'). Abraham and the prophets are dead. They understand or misinterpret Jesus' promise of the bodily life. When they put the verb γενέσθαι ('to taste') in the place of θεωρεῖν ('to see'), there is no substantial difference: the latter designates the outward experience, the former the inward life in the feelings.

VERSE 53.

Senseless, they desire to say, is the lifting up of Jesus above all of these. Hence come the emphatic σύ and σεαυτόν ('thou' and 'thyself'), and in contrast therewith the separate emphasizing of the fact that Abraham and that the prophets are dead.

VERSE 54.

Jesus' reply now follows, and first his reply to τίνα σεαυτὸν ποιεῖσ; ('whom makest thou thyself?'). He does not make himself anything. Then in ver. 56 f. we find the reply to the holding up Abraham before him. The latter, therefore, is the beginning of the real answer, as Baumgarten-Crusius rightly saw; ver. 54 f. only forms an introduction to it. When he ascribes to himself such a position in contrast with Abraham, etc.—Jesus replies at first—it is not he, as they see him in the flesh, thought of for himself (ἐγώ . . . ἐμαυτόν, 'I . . . myself'), who perchance witnesses boastingly unto himself. In that case (ἐάν . . . δοξάσω, according to א B, subjunctive aorist) his honour would be nothing. But it is the Father who, in his whole manifestation in word and deed, gives testimony to him, and they would and must recognise the Father in this testimony, if He really, as they suppose, were their God (θεὸσ ἡμῶν) in the exact sense. They, however, only say that; in truth, they have not entered into that relation of fellowship with Him which could justify them in calling Him their God.

VERSE 55.

Καὶ οὐκ ἐγνώκατε αὐτόν ('yet ye have not known him'). These words certainly do not refer to the Jewish nation in general and of all ages,[1] but refer merely to those to whom

---
[1] Stier, *Reden Jesu*, 2d ed., Barmen and Elberfeld 1870, vol. iv. p. 473.

Jesus here speaks, because they at once denote not simply theoretical knowledge, but the knowledge given with the fellowship. The notion that Jesus denies to them his Father as God, because the demiurge is their God, may be left to Hilgenfeld,[1] who thinks he must despair of a natural exposition of our gospel. Those Jews therefore have not known God upon the basis of a fellowship with him (οὐκ ἐγνώκατε, 'have not known'): he, Jesus, on the contrary, knows the Father, not in the sense of a merely historical knowledge, but in the sense of essential fellowship. When the Jews declare that they stand in such a close relation to God, they lie; Jesus would, like them, lie if he should not say this of himself. This expresses his absolute self-certainty. It rests, however, on the fellowship of knowledge and of will, with God, in his calling. When Jesus says of himself, οἶδα ('I know'), and not ἔγνωκα, it is perhaps intentional. For his knowledge does not rest on a fellowship appointed at a certain time, but is a thing absolutely existing and certain. The one who is so absolutely sure in himself calls them liars; they say they are God's, and are not his, but the devil's. Thus he vindicates himself against them in judgment and in self-testification. Upon this now rests the answer which he has to give them.

VERSE 56.

Jesus now turns himself to the other point, the one really intended. The Jews appealed against him to the patriarchs and prophets of the Old Testament covenant. To this now he replies, as we have seen, that also for the believers of the Old Testament, salvation was connected with his person. This is the substance of ver. 56: *your father Abraham*, of whom you boast, and to whom you appeal against me, compare ver. 39, *rejoiced that he should*[2] *see my day*. Jesus' day is the day of his appearance—Luke xvii. 22, of the second coming, because looking from the New Testament time of salvation into the future;—here, in the first instance, of the

---

[1] Hilgenfeld, *Das Evangelium und die Briefe Johannis nach ihrem Lehrbegriff dargestellt*, Halle 1849, p. 158.
[2] On ἵνα, compare vol. i. p. 39 f.

New Testament appearance, because looking from the Old Testament.

The day of Christ the promised one was Abraham's joy, because the promise of the salvation, the fulfilment of which He brought, was his joy. The thing in question is this spiritual joy. We therefore have to think of the promises which were imparted to Abraham, and which connected the salvation of the future with his seed. When Jesus in ἠγαλλιάσατο ('rejoiced') speaks of this joy as a historical fact, we are not simply to assume it as a fact, but to expect its express testification in the Scriptures (against Meyer). In that case, we must, with Hofmann,[1] refer to Gen. xvii. 17. The laughing there mentioned is certainly the expression of his joyful surprise at God's promise. For the promised son was to him not merely a son of his flesh, but the beginning and the pledge of the fulfilment of the promise. In the beginning his belief had the whole thing promised, in Isaac the Messiah. Thus he rejoiced at the day of salvation, in that he rejoiced at the day of the birth of his son.

When the discourse proceeds: *and he saw it, and was glad*, should this transfer us to an entirely different sphere, into the time of the post-terrestrial life of Abraham, seeing that it is only the fulfilling of what had just been said, and expressly refers back to it? Most later commentators understand it of an event in the post-terrestrial 'paradisaic' condition of Abraham, concerning which Jesus has, and here gives, information (Lampe, Lücke, Tholuck, De Wette, Meyer, Ebrard, Godet, I earlier), and they appeal at the same time, say to the appearance of Elijah and Moses on the mount of transfiguration. It is, however, in itself improbable, because without analogy, that Jesus should speak of such a supra-terrestrial single occurrence; and the words correspond too exactly to what directly precedes, for us not to keep to the same reference, if it only be possible. Before this the thing treated of was a joy which was awakened in

---

[1] Hofmann, *Weissagung und Erfüllung im alten und im neuen Testamente*, Nördlingen 1844, vol. ii. p. 12 f.; *Der Schriftbeweis*, Nördlingen 1860, vol. ii. part ii. p. 303 f.

Abraham by the promise of his son as the seed of salvation; now, the realization of the joy must have as its object the realization of that promise in the birth of his son. Most of the older commentators remained firm in this reference to an occurrence within his earthly life (Chrysostom, Theophylact, Melanchthon, Calvin, Calov), and Hofmann, as above cited, has rightly returned to this view.

We are not, however, to think of a mere inward certainty of belief (Luther,[1] and similarly Bengel), or of the appearance of the angel of the Lord, Gen. xviii. ('the Logos,' Hengstenberg), or of the sacrifice of Isaac as the type of the sacrifice and of the resurrection of Christ (Chrysostom, Grotius); this is all arbitrary. We must refer to the birth of Isaac (Hofmann[2]), in which Abraham saw (εἶδεν) the promise of the seed of salvation fulfilled in a way at once a foundation and a pledge, and which Abraham hailed joyfully (ἐχάρη); this his joyful mood expressing itself in the giving of the name Isaac. Εἶδεν καὶ ἐχάρη ('saw and rejoiced') does not imply that it was the full realization of the hope which Abraham knew, and therefore after his death (thus I earlier); but it is simply the beginning of it which is meant by this, just as the preceding joy of Abraham referred to that beginning. Jesus does not intend to prove that Abraham found full life in him, but that he connected salvation with his person. Yet he proves it in such a way that he displays how Abraham's joy referred to the promise of the Messianic salvation in the promise of his seed. In this Jesus presupposes that this Messianic salvation is given in his, Jesus', person, that he, Jesus, is the promised Christ. It is the same 'petitio principii' ('begging of the question') that we meet so often in Jesus' self-testification.

Verse 57.

What he has said of himself, he can say of himself, because

---

[1] Luther, Sermon on Genesis xxii. 18; *Werke*, Erlangen edition 1829, vol. xix. p. 14.

[2] Hofmann, *Weissagung und Erfüllung im alten und im neuen Testamente*, Nördlingen 1844, vol. ii. p. 12 f.; *Der Schriftbeweis*, Nördlingen 1860, vol. ii. part ii. p. 303 f.

he has come into the world from a state of being with God. In thus at the close coming to speak of this point, he has thereby completed the circle of the points lying in the idea of the υἱὸσ τοῦ θεοῦ ('Son of God'). The verse before us offers the occasion given him for this in the manner in which the Jews wrested his words. If Abraham saw the day of the Messiah, and therefore of Jesus, then Jesus, they argue, must have lived at that time. And yet he is not fifty years old. This statement does not give any basis for a conclusion as to his age (Irenæus,[1] following the tradition of the 'presbyters' concerning the 'aetas senior,' 'more advanced age,' of Jesus, which, as Irenæus interprets, begin 'a quadragesimo et quinquagesimo anno,' 'at the fortieth and fiftieth year'[2]) or as to his appearance (Lampe). The Jews merely name the round number which closes off the mature age, Num. iv. 3, 39, viii. 24 f. (Meyer).

They thus wrest Jesus' words, because thereby, as they think, the insane lack of understanding in his pride is most speedily refuted. Jesus spoke, it is true, only of his typical representation in the beginner of the seed of Abraham. But it was, nevertheless, a typical representation which he himself had effected. Hence, therefore, he can reply to the indignant speech of the Jews—for indignation seems to me to be the mood in which they oppose this argument to Jesus, victoriously, as they think—with still stronger words, surpassing their words with his own.

VERSE 58.

Before Abraham came into being, I am. Ἀμὴν κ.τ.λ. ('verily, etc.') announces and introduces it emphatically. If a becoming, a coming into being, be true of Abraham, of Him a being is true,—that πρὶν γενέσθαι does not mean: before he was (thus Tholuck, De Wette, Ewald), but before he came into being (compare Meyer, Hengstenberg), is beyond question, and is demanded by the contrast with εἶναι, 'to be,'—a being lying beyond the genesis of Abra-

---

[1] Irenæus, *Contra Hæreseos*, II. xxii. 5; ed. Massuet, Paris 1710, p. 148 b.
[2] Compare Luthardt, *St. John the Author of the Fourth Gospel*, Edinburgh, T. and T. Clark, 1875, p. 141, and note 91 on pp. 152, 153.

ham, a being in spite of and in the midst of the change into something else which he has entered upon. The contrast to the becoming teaches that it is an eternal being, and the ἐγώ ('I') teaches that it is a personal one. It is unnecessary to argue against Baumgarten-Crusius' explanation of an existence merely in the decree of God. And Beyschlag's explanation as to the real image of God[1] amounts finally to Baumgarten-Crusius'; since this image nevertheless exists only in the thought of God.

Lately, however, Beyschlag[2] wavers between a consciousness of Jesus—won by means of a retrospective conclusion, by which consciousness he viewed 'himself as the original image resting from the beginning in God'—and the 'mutual interaction of two different methods of thought,' the original meaning of Jesus and the change of meaning effected by the evangelist. This latter is Weizsäcker's[3] view, by which Beyschlag himself[4] confesses that he was first incited to the thought. It is not consistent with the apostolical origin of the gospel. Beyschlag's uncertainty testifies to the compelling power of the plain words. From a state of being in the presence of God—that is the way the words read—Jesus entered into the world, and is therefore the absolute mediator of salvation and of its future for all men.

Verse 59.

It is the simple self-witness of his divine Sonship, which, as an unbearable blasphemy in the eyes of the Jews, calls forth their rage so strongly that they at once make a tumultuous endeavour to execute the law upon him. It is an arbitrary assumption to say that they raised the stones more for a threat than for the actual execution of the stoning (Godet). Whether or not the stones lay in the outer court for the sake of the building of the temple (for

---

[1] Beyschlag, *Die Christologie des Neuen Testaments*, Berlin 1866, p. 86.
[2] Beyschlag, *Studien und Kritiken*, 1875, p. 440.
[3] Weizsäcker, *Jahrbücher für Deutsche Theologie*, 1857 and 1862.
[4] Beyschlag, *Die Christologie des Neuen Testaments*, Berlin 1866, p. 67.

example, Meyer, Godet), is not to be said. Josephus[1] also reports a stoning in the temple; and 2 Chron. xxiv. 21 relates the stoning of the prophet Zachariah mentioned by Christ. They took the stones just where they found them—'arma multitudinis' ('weapons of a mob'[2]).

The first ἐγώ εἰμι ('I am'), ver. 12, had only called forth the contradiction of unbelief, which based itself on a word of the law. The last ἐγώ εἰμι, with which the self-witness closes, calls forth the passionate rage of indignant unbelief, which at once sets about the actual execution of the law. This is a prefiguration of the issue. Nothing but Jesus' self-witness concerning his divine Sonship, in which the promise and the hope of Israel are fulfilled, is to bring him unto death,—a death the execution of which will adorn itself with the letter of the law, while it only has its basis in the heightened opposition of unbelief, which does not desire salvation in Jesus' person. Thus, moreover, the other event also came to pass as a type: ἐκρύβη καὶ ἐξῆλθεν ἐκ τοῦ ἱεροῦ ('he hid himself, and went out of the temple'). They, indeed, remain as victors upon the field; but Jesus has gone forth free from the judgment of Israel, and has thereby forsaken the holy place. Jerusalem and Israel are the holy place of God, from which the Christ has departed. Compare Heb. xiii. 12 f.: Ἰησοῦσ ... ἔξω τῆσ πύλησ ἔπαθεν. τοίνυν ἐξερχώμεθα πρὸσ αὐτὸν ἔξω τῆσ παρεμβολῆσ τὸν ὀνειδισμὸν αὐτοῦ φέροντεσ ('Jesus ... suffered without the gate. Let us go forth therefore unto him without the camp, bearing his reproach'). But he has found the blind on the way, and has led them to the light, while he who was τὸ φῶσ τοῦ κόσμου ('the light of the world,' viii. 12, compare Matt. xxii. 1-10) withdrew himself from those unbelievers.

But if he departs from Israel, the sanctuary, who will then be Lord in it? He had called the Israelites the children of the devil, because they stood in fellowship of the devil's kind, namely, of lying and of murderous intent. In now assuming the appearance of desiring to secure to

---

[1] Josephus, *Antiquitates*, XVII. ix. 3; *Opera*, ed. Richter, Leipzig 1826, vol. iv. p. 98.   [2] Bengel.

the law its rights against him who was the fulfilling of the promise, they show themselves thoroughly as children of the liar. And in taking up stones against him, they reveal themselves as sons of the ἀνθρωποκτόνοσ ('manslayer'). They will fall entirely into the possession of this one when Jesus has forsaken them. After that point, where Jesus the seed of Abraham is, will also be the sanctuary of God and the true Israel. The other Israel will be Satan's school; compare Rev. ii. 9, iii. 9, xi. 8.

The closing words of the received text, διελθὼν διὰ μέσου αὐτῶν καὶ παρῆγεν οὕτωσ ('going through the midst of them, and so passed by'), although supported by a large number of manuscripts, are to be struck out, with ℵ B D Itala. They are a gloss made up from the first words of the next chapter, and from Luke iv. 30 (compare Godet). It is a question how ἐκρύβη ('he hid himself') is to be understood, whether of a miraculous ἀφανισμόσ, 'growing invisible' (Bengel, Winer,[1] Baur,[2] Hilgenfeld[3]), or of a concealing himself behind the part of the crowd which favoured him (Lücke, De Wette, Meyer). The former seems to be favoured by the situation, the latter both by ἐκρύβη—in the other case it would read better : ἄφαντοσ ἐγένετο ('he became invisible')—and especially by ἐξῆλθεν ('he went out'). The directly following καὶ παράγων ('and passing') proves that ἐξῆλθεν is to be understood externally and sensibly.

Jesus withdrew himself from the Jews, and even from their gaze, surrounded and accompanied by his disciples. God then had his hand in the play. The Jews should not get possession of him; to them he had as it were disappeared. The following narrative offers a contrast to this. The Jews have been served as if they were blind. To the blind man, however, Jesus gave the gift of sight, and that he should recognise Him. The close of the ninth

---

[1] Winer, *Grammatik des neutestamentlichen Sprachidioms*, § 54. 5, 7th ed. Leipzig 1867, p. 437.

[2] Baur, *Kritische Untersuchungen über die kanonischen Evangelien*, Tübingen 1847, p. 285 f.

[3] Hilgenfeld, *Das Evangelium und die Briefe Johannis nach ihrem Lehrbegriff dargestellt*, Halle 1849, p. 244 f.

chapter points clearly to this. At the same time, the ninth chapter forms the beginning of the next circle, chap. ix. and x. Thus we perceive again how, chain-like, the rings of our gospel are fitted into each other. Every beginning of a new ring is accustomed to place itself parallel to the close of the preceding one, and yet is the start for a new progress.

Chapters IX. and X.

Jesus the salvation-bringing Light of the World; to the Jews, unto Judgment.

Baur[1] recalls justly the similarity ruling between the healing of the blind man in the ninth chapter and the healing related in the fifth chapter. That healing of the sick man is only to be taken as the concrete, pictorial view of the power of Jesus which maketh alive. And here in the same way is reflected in general the side of his divine activity, determined by the principle of light. The similarity goes still further. The evangelist is aware of it, and intends it. In that place as well as in this, the healing occurred upon a Sabbath: ix. 14, v. 9; and hence on each occasion alike called out the opposition of the Jews. In that place as well as in this, the event is followed by a discourse explaining and enlarging upon the thought which the event typified, and the discourse is followed by a dividing process. In the former passage, the discourse at Capernaum directs itself to the life which is decreed in his human nature that yet must depart unto death. And in this passage also Jesus, upon the ground of the free love with which he subjects himself to death, holds up to view in the following discourse the blessing of his death for the world. In both passages, at the close, ix. 40–42, vi. 68 f., the offence of unbelief and the confession of belief are contrasted with each other.

The miraculous act of Jesus, the following discourse, and the closing occurrence, divide themselves distinctly from

[1] Baur, *Kritische Untersuchungen über die kanonischen Evangelien*, Tübingen 1847, p. 177.

each other. Thus we obtain the three parts: ix. 1-41, x. 1-21, x. 22-42. Lampe and Olshausen, indeed, think the discourse which follows in the tenth chapter ought to begin at ix. 35. But they do not understand the characteristic difference of these words. They might have learned a better thing even from the circumstance that questions and answers cease in x. 1 ff. The very peculiarity of the following parabolic discourse is, that although in its thought it is ruled by contrast, yet it is free from the stamp of the debate, and withdraws itself more from the conflict than the discourses previously related. Jesus begins to take up a different position towards the Jews. Even the fact that he entered into debate with them,—although his words sounded so sharp and condemnatory,—yes, the fact that he told them directly the uttermost, was an act of grace, was the extreme in making deliverance possible. That now comes to an end.

He now speaks to them in parables, that they may hear and not understand. These are no longer so exciting, or so provocative of opposition as before. He points to his destiny, to the freedom of it, and to the future of his church outside of Israel, x. 16. And when he, later, comes to Jerusalem, x. 22, he gives testimony only by being silent. It says περιεπάτει ('walked'), ver. 23, without remarking that he spoke publicly, but on the contrary excluding this. The Jews also feel that he acts towards them as if indifferent to them. From the uneasiness caused by that, comes the question which clothes itself in the form of a reproach against Jesus, ver. 24. But Jesus has nothing more now to say to them. 'I have told you, but ye believe not.' That is all. What he says is only intended to remind them of previous words. On their part, they make futile the last possibility, that the uneasiness of their soul called forth by his silence should serve them unto salvation. For they show, ver. 39, that they have not learned to endure better than before his old self-witness, ver. 36, and his old claim, ver. 38. He therefore withdraws himself from them. When he shall come again, it will not be to continue his previous activity among them.

(1.) CHAPTER IX. 1–41.

This chapter divides into three sections: (*a.*) vers. 1–12; (*b.*) vers. 13–34; (*c.*) vers. 35–41.

(*a.*) VERSES 1–12.

This healing follows at once upon the departure from the temple. The circumstance that Jesus 'appears too calm, after the tumultuous uprising' (De Wette), is no reason for opposing the simple statement of the evangelist. He parted from the Jews in triumphant testification of his divine Sonship, and why then should he here preserve his composure less than at other times, and at the final issue of his life? Had he not in the temple opposed their passion with the victorious calmness of the divine consciousness? Jesus had left the Jews there as the lords of the temple, but of a temple from which the Holy One had departed.

They thought that they would also be lords over him himself, but he had rescued himself from their hand. Even though he has nothing more to do with the masters of Jerusalem, his vocation is not yet at an end. As long as he is in the world, he is the light of the world. He shows this in the case of the blind man, sitting at the side of the way from the temple. If that former event has a more general meaning, so also has this one. The blind man by the wayside is the figure for a whole class. Jesus designates himself as $\phi\hat{\omega}\sigma\ \tau o\hat{v}\ \kappa\acute{o}\sigma\mu ov$ ('light of the world'). The blind man therefore represents the world. Yet on the boundary-line lies 'Galilee of the Gentiles,' Isa. ix. 1; and this 'people which sat in darkness saw a great light; and to them which sat in the region and shadow of death, light is sprung up,' Matt. iv. 16; Isa. ix. 2.

Galilee comes into consideration, not in so far as it belongs to Israel, but in so far as it is neglected, despised; and reckoned utterly on a level with the Gentiles, and as it has many Gentile elements in itself; that is to say, it is considered from the side on which it comes in contact with the Gentiles. Jesus had come to Jerusalem from Galilee.

and he returned thither again. He therefore will address himself to the κόσμοσ ('world'), after he has in vain addressed himself to the Jews, and has forsaken them. Hence also the one whom he here heals is one who is blind from birth. Jesus turns to those who have not that light; the light which the Jews have only suffered to be a means of making them blind to the knowledge of the person of Jesus, since they nevertheless arrogate to themselves to be a φῶσ τῶν ἐν σκότει ('light of them which are in darkness').

The conduct of the Jews, as related to us in the ninth chapter, connects progressively with what preceded . it. Jesus had just before been compelled to reproach the Jews with not understanding his discourse, viii. 43, because they 'would' not receive it, v. 40, and therefore cannot, viii. 43. Here he must learn that they also will not believe that his 'works' are valid. In the fifth chapter they had let the miracle stand, and only held to the breach of the Sabbath, thinking that they had in this a reason for being able to ignore the fact itself. That very fact formed the presupposition of the disputation in the debates at the feast of tabernacles; Jesus recalls it to them, vii. 21, without their venturing to call it in any way in question as a fact. How different the case is now! They struggle to the utmost against the recognition of the publicly known fact and its most necessary consequences. This man has become so hateful to them already, that he may no longer be acknowledged in any way. They are not willing that that which is real should really be. After this vain endeavour to free themselves from history, the next step the hostile hatred can and must make is to try to rid itself of the existence of this man. It is the judgment of hardening drawing its consequences.

In order, then, to make us recognise aright this characteristic side of the conduct of the Jews, the very first section of the narrative is so constructed that the publicly known and the irrefutable character of the fact may come to light in the most decided way. In the first place, it is one born blind, and one whom many knew. In the next place, both the transaction, as it took place, and the success of it, had many witnesses. In the third place, he confessed it himself,—a confession which was so much the less possible of suspicion because Jesus was known to him only by name, and because after the healing he had not troubled himself in the least about whither He had gone. These are the three chief points of the story related in vers. 1-12.

VERSES 1-5.

The man born blind, and Jesus the light of the world, here stand at first contrasted with each other. With these two contrasts this first paragraph both begins and closes.

VERSE 1.

By the temple road sat a beggar who had been born blind. It is useless to ask how they knew that the beggar was blind from birth. He was a well-known beggar, ver. 8, and would certainly not have neglected constantly and diligently to lay stress upon this circumstance.

VERSE 2.

The disciples ask for information as to why this blindness from birth had occurred, seeing that, since all evil is only a consequence of sin in the world, it may be, and doubtless is, a punishment. This question was based on a false personal application of a correct general principle, an application familiar to the Jews. They gave the correct general principle, that evil is punishment of sin, the same false personal application as Job's unjust friends did. Compare also Luke xiii. 1 ff. The principle holds good, it is true, for the existence of evil in the world; but the individual distribution of it has its own special laws. Hence in this special case they of course are in difficulty.

Who did sin, this man or his parents, that he was born blind? **Τίσ ἥμαρτεν . . . ἵνα**, what must have occurred in order that he, etc.? Some have busied themselves greatly with the question, how the disciples could find in the sins of the very one born blind the cause of his evil, which yet passed with them as punishment. De Wette takes refuge in the Alexandrian doctrine of pre-existence. Lücke[1] replied to this, that it does not explain the doctrine of the sin and guilt of the pre-existent souls. For the latter is not so necessarily joined to the other as Brückner thinks. When Josephus[2] ascribes to the Essenes the doctrine of pre-existence, his words do not go beyond an existence in which there is no history. The case is the same with Wisdom viii. 19, 20. The other passage in Josephus[3] refers to the post-temporal life.[4] In the next place, the disciples certainly knew nothing of this, or at least did not think of it. If, as Brückner says, this belief might have been a popular one, we must have more proof of it. And finally, the disciples were far enough on in the moral knowledge not to share this belief, if it existed. Hence Lücke (Maier, Meyer) contents himself with sinfulness in the womb; or rather, following Lightfoot, he tries to prove that the Jews determined sins of deed in the womb. But the notions of rabbis are not therefore popular belief. The reference to Luke i. 41, 43 (Meyer) is utterly out of place here. The supposition that the disciples thought of an anticipation of the punishment before the later sins (Tholuck, Stier[5]), can as little be proved as refuted.

But all this seems to me to be unnecessary. Simply because they could not conceive how his own guilt could have caused his blindness, they add the other possibility. They nevertheless express the former possibility, although they cannot conceive of its reality; for if they do not find it out, perhaps the Lord will show it to them. The latter they indeed consider possible, upon the basis of Old Testament threatenings, Ex. xx. 5. Yet the former ought always to lie the nearer at hand; and hence they put it first, and put the two together. This case is a riddle for them; so they ask

---

[1] Lücke, *Commentar über das Evangelium des Johannes*, 3d ed., Bonn 1843, vol. ii. p. 372.

[2] Josephus, *De Bello Judaico*, II. viii. 11; *Opera*, ed. Bekker, Leipzig 1856, vol. v. p. 152.

[3] Josephus, *Antiquitates*, XVIII. i. 3; *Opera*, ed. Richter, Leipzig 1826. vol. iv. p. 124.

[4] Compare Lampe, *Commentarius analytico-exegeticus Evangelii secundum Joannem*, Amsterdam 1726, vol. ii. p. 528 f. note.

[5] Stier, *Reden Jesu*, 3d ed., Barmen and Elberfeld 1870, vol. iv. p. 491.

for its solution. They expect therewith a further knowledge in reference to the whole question which is here brought up.

VERSE 3.

This they receive in ver. 3, but not in the way they expect. It was God's design (hence ἵνα, 'in order that') that this man should be born blind. Jesus lets that stand, and this is also to be supplied in his answer. But the reason for this lies neither in the one thing nor in the other thing suggested. When Jesus denies the sin, it is of course merely in this relation. The reason lies in the aim. The works of God were to be made manifest in him. That this evil might have had still other reasons and as well designs in reference to the person of the blind man himself, is not considered here at all by Jesus. But it is not therefore excluded.

The point here is the emphasizing of this one thing as the essential thing: ἵνα φανερωθῇ τὰ ἔργα τοῦ θεοῦ ἐν αὐτῷ ('that the works of God should be made manifest in him'). God desired to glorify himself in him. This aim is in general the right *théodicée* ('view of God's justice') in relation to the evil in the world. We read τὰ ἔργα ('the works'), and not τὸ ἔργον ('the work'). It therefore means not merely the following healing in itself, but that healing in so far as it is a σημεῖον ('sign') of the revelation and the activity of God in Christ as the light. This whole category of action is to be designated by the plural. In the passage in which we first met the ἐργάζεσθαι ('to work'), v. 17, we found that the redeeming action of God was meant, which is mediated by the Son as the Christ. Thus also here the saving, redeeming activity of God in word and in deed is meant.[1] The word is used in that specific sense which is in general peculiar to it in John's gospel.

This activity of God is, moreover, a well-known, a general, an essential one; hence the article τὰ ἔργα, 'the works.' It is not as if it now first entered upon reality, but only that it now comes to view. It was previously in existence, and only makes itself known, becomes now for the first time visible to men (hence φανεροῦσθαι), namely, in Christ. With

---

[1] Stier, *Reden Jesu*, 3d ed., Barmen and Elberfeld 1870, vol. iv. p. 495.

this the discourse passes towards the fourth verse. This blind man therefore came into being and is present just at this time, in order that in him God in Christ should testify to himself as the light of the world. Thus that people that sat in the shade was decreed under darkness until the time that Christ's day dawned upon it, in order that in it God in Christ should glorify himself, namely, in the self-demonstration of Christ as the light of the world; compare also Rom. xi. 32. The course and the aim of God's ways are therewith designated.

Verse 4.

But the great redeeming work of God (τὰ ἔργα τοῦ θεοῦ) —by whom else is it carried out than by Him? If this blind man has the determination above given, Jesus also has a vocation in reference to him, because τὰ ἔργα τοῦ θεοῦ ('the works of God') are executed by Him. *We must work the works of him that sent us, so long as it is day.* Ἐμέ ('I'), in A C E F, Syriac, seems more suitable and easy, for the thing in question is Jesus' vocation, and hence it stands with emphasis at the beginning. But the plural ἡμᾶσ is more strongly witnessed to by the manuscripts ℵ B D L, and it is also to be preferred because it would not be a natural insertion. Then Jesus includes his disciples as the partakers of his vocation, and as an instruction for their future. If the healing on the Sabbath were to be justified (Tholuck), δεῖ ('must') would have to stand in the emphatic position. He—and his disciples have a share in this his calling—was sent into the world for this purpose; hence the works he executes are ἔργα τοῦ πέμψαντοσ αὐτόν ('works of him that sent him').

'So long as it is day.' What does this mean? Olshausen says: so long as the time of grace lasts, 'so long as that which is good prevails; the time is coming only too soon, when darkness shall gain the ascendancy, and hinder all activity (in spiritual things for a time), etc.' But that is generalizing the concrete notions, and at the same time limiting the discourse in an unjustifiable way. 'Day,' agreeably to the further use of language in John xi. 9 f., is the time of activity in one's calling. This answers at once the question: for whom it is day. Bengel says: 'Christus est lux; ea abeunte, nox venit, non lucem impediens sed terram obscurans' ('Christ is the light; when it departs night comes, not hindering the light, but obscuring the earth'). Baumgarten-Crusius, and I earlier, said it was for the world; for it closes the time of the activity of the history of salvation, and begins that of the appropriation of salvation. But if 'day' is to be explained according to xi. 9, and is to be understood of the time of one's vocation, it can only be referred to Jesus and not to the world. Hence the most (Lücke, Stier, De Wette, Meyer) have understood it of the contrast of the life and of the death of Jesus. More exactly it is to be taken of the time of activity in his calling, and of the end thereof. Godet views it in a like way, only that he understands the night of 'evening rest;' while, on the contrary, it here designates, not the beneficial rest, but the cessation of activity, not something positive, but something negative.

It is a general principle, which Jesus applies to himself. For in so far as he is in the world, and has a calling to fulfil in it, he is subject to the general law; so long as the time of his calling lasts, he has the task of his calling to fulfil. *The night cometh, when no man can work;* it comes for every one, and so also for him. If 'day' be the time of the work in his earthly vocation, 'night' is the end of it. This is also appointed for Jesus. Whether or not there be beyond it a new time of activity for him, here remains out of consideration. The thing here treated of is only his activity in his earthly calling, for which he, as much as any one else, is subject to the general law of earthly life. His calling now is to be the light of the world, and to be active as such.

VERSE 5.

When I am in the world, I am in the light of the world. 'Day' and 'night' are not to be so combined that perchance through the 'light,' which he is, it became day for the world (thus I earlier). That is an arbitrary combination. The will of God determines the day; this will appoints to each man his calling within the limits of the time set for him.

As the sun designates the bounds of the single day of work, so does this will of God as 'the light of the world,' xi. 9, determine the limits of the time of one's calling in general. When, moreover, Jesus here names himself ' the light of the world,' he designates thereby the contents of his calling as peculiarly allotted to him, and means therefore 'light,' as previously throughout in the gospel, in the saving sense. Ὅταν, 'quando,' at the time when,—designates the temporal coincidence; so that therefore the common explanation, 'so long as,' if not philologically, is yet practically justified. Only ὅταν emphasizes less the temporal than the internal material relations: if he be the light of the world when he, etc., then that is necessarily given with his being in the world. Therefore he cannot withdraw himself from the execution of this calling. And thus he prepares to point to himself as the light.

If Jesus be the life of the world, the world, as it is, is destitute of light, and stands in darkness. This contrast, according to John's gospel, does not mediate itself in the Gnostic way, that 'the light draws to itself from the darkness all elements related to itself,'[1] but thus, that the light in the dark world exerts itself and imparts itself to it. Hence, too, the 'dualism' of the 'Johannean doctrinal conception' does not mediate itself, as Köstlin declares,[2] so that the present world is annihilated, and the man, who wills not to share in this general fate of what is temporal, is removed from this place of death; but it mediates itself by the impartation of the light, which impartation then draws its consequences in the future.

VERSE 6.

The story here is a proof of this, in so far as in it the true mediation of those two contrasts is figuratively represented. For here all is meant typically. Jesus makes a paste of earth and spittle, and spreads it on the eyes of the

---

[1] Baur, *Kritische Untersuchungen über die kanonischen Evangelien,* Tübingen 1847, p. 91.

[2] Köstlin, *Der Lehrbegriff des Evangeliums und der Briefe Johannis und die verwandten neutestamentlichen Lehrbegriffe,* Berlin 1843, p. 468.

blind man. Ἐπέχρισεν αὐτοῦ τὸν πηλὸν ἐπί κ.τ.λ. ('spread the paste of it upon, etc.') is the reading of ℵ A B C L. Then αὐτοῦ (' of it') is to be referred to πτύσμα ('spittle'): the paste made from the spittle. The closing word τοῦ τυφλοῦ ('of the blind man') is omitted by ℵ B L. But that cannot be dispensed with, unless, perhaps, the reading of D is to be preferred: ἐπέχρισεν αὐτῷ τὸν πηλόν κ.τ.λ., 'He spread for him the paste on the eyes' [English: his eyes].

The evangelist connects the report of this singular transaction with the directly preceding saying concerning the light of the world by ταῦτα εἰπών ('when he had thus spoken'), and he therefore sees in it a preparation for the external representation of that saying. What does this action mean? We may mention, as an amusing curiosity, Ammon's opinion, that the blind man suffered from inflammation of the eyes, and that Jesus laid something cooling on them, which removed the inflammation. Many of the fathers held the monstrous opinion that the blind man had really no eyes, and that Jesus made them for him out of earth. The action is intended symbolically. To view the spittle as a conductor of the healing power (Tholuck, Olshausen), and therefore as necessary in this case (Meyer), contradicts other healings, and is against the possibility of miracles, as that possibility is contained in the gospel presentation of Jesus. Brückner, moreover, has proved sufficiently that the action of Jesus had no necessary reference to the belief of the blind man (Lücke), or to the possible eye-witness of bystanders, or to the breach of the Sabbath (Baur). For the former purpose the washing was enough; and the latter would not be found in this manipulation, but in the healing itself. It does not, however, follow from this that the act was utterly meaningless (Brückner), for it is too striking for that. Bengel and Hengstenberg, following Theophylact, recall the creation of man from the earth; but that is an accidental likeness, which has no place here at all.

Lampe[1] comes nearer the matter when he alleges as the meaning of the act: 'ut peccator ipse sentiat miseriam et

---

[1] Lampe, *Commentarius* . . . *Evangelii secundum Joannem*, Amsterdam 1726, vol. ii. p. 548.

convincatur de peccato' ('that the sinner himself may feel his misery, and be convinced of sin'). But he loses himself in arbitrariness by seeking a meaning for each little point. To spread on one's eyes a paste made from earth—and certainly the detailed character of the account: ἐπέχρισεν κ.τ.λ. ('he spread'), is designed, and not merely naive, as Meyer thinks—means to cover his eyes so that he certainly sees no more, if even he saw to a certain extent previously, and seems to be the very opposite of a healing the blind. It is therefore an apparently absurd means that Jesus uses. But in this very thing, namely, that he adds to the natural blindness this symbolical blindness (Godet), lies the explanation. This action is intended to say : he must become fully blind, who wishes to obtain sight. The next verse agrees with this.

VERSE 7.

Jesus sends the man thus anointed to the pool of Siloam, to wash himself there. The pool of Siloam (the upper pool) receives its water through the canal which leads from the fountain of Mary, in the valley of the Kedron at the east foot of the southern slope of Moriah, through the rock-wall into the valley of the Tyropœon.[1] The water flows from the pool gently down into the fields of the valley of the Kedron, and is lost in the lovely hollows. In all probability this is the pool we are to understand by the one mentioned here, and not the larger lower pool lying close at hand, which appears to have received its water, partly from the overflow of Siloam, and partly from the rain-water running down in the Tyropœon.[2] It is not certain whether or not the upper pool of Siloam had still another independent fountain.[3]

---

[1] Compare the investigations in Tobler, *Die Siloahquelle und der Oelberg*, St. Gallen 1852, pp. 1-58.

[This explorer of Palestine, Titus Tobler, must not be confounded with the destructive critic, J. R. Tobler (see Luthardt, *St. John the Author of the Fourth Gospel*, Edinburgh, T. and T. Clark, 1875, Appendix, p. 351). Titus Tobler died at Munich on the 21st January 1877.—C. R. G.]

[2] See Tobler, *ut supra*, p. 32.

[3] See Tobler, *ut supra*, p. 10. Compare, besides, Robinson, *Palästina*, Halle 1841, vol. ii. pp. 142-143.

The water of Siloam, 'that flows gently,' is, in contrast to the strong and destructive stream of the worldly power in Isa. viii. 6 f., an image of the unpretending promise of salvation, connected with David's house. Its fulfilling is given in Jesus Christ. In like manner, Siloam is to the evangelist an image of Jesus the Messiah. With this thought he emphasizes the meaning: ἀπεσταλμένοσ, 'sent.' שֶׁלַח is either to be taken infinitively: 'emissio,' 'sending' (Gesenius), or as a passive participle, equivalent to שָׁלוּחַ, 'emissus,' 'sent' (Hitzig).[1] The water is a thing sent, namely, from the mountain: it gushes forth between Zion and Moriah, at the foot of the height upon which God and the house of David had their seat.[2] Hence the more clearly does the evangelist see in it a type of Christ, the Son of David, the one come from God.

Meyer, it is true, following Euthymius and Bengel, declares that, according to the context, ὁ ἀπεσταλμένοσ ('the one sent') can only refer to the blind man. This is, however, refuted by the circumstance that Siloam gives the blind man his sight, and therefore is an image of Jesus. By this means also we can dispense with Meyer's other hypothesis, that Jesus ordered the washing in the pool with the design to afford the anointed spittle-paste the time necessary for its working, a time calculated by him as coinciding with the distance of Siloam. This is refuted by the other cases of healing.

One can find in that symbolizing a trifling unworthy of John (compare especially, Lücke), only on condition of altogether failing to understand the symbolical character of John's historical narrative and representation.[3] For this very reason this concession is not an endangering of the historical character of the passage (against Meyer, in spite of Strauss[4]). That would then have to be true of the entire Johannean representation. If Siloam is an image of Christ,

[1] Compare Delitzsch on Isa. viii. 6.
[2] Compare Winer, *Biblisches Realwörterbuch*, 3d ed., Leipzig 1848, vol. ii. p. 460.
[3] See vol. i. p. 77 f.
[4] Strauss, *Das Leben Jesu für das deutsche Volk bearbeitet*, Leipzig 1864, p. 432, and elsewhere.

the going to Siloam is a type of the coming to Christ, of the ἔρχεσθαι πρὸσ αὐτόν (for example, iii. 20 f.). For the subjective means of appropriating the blessing of salvation offered in Jesus is believing obedience.

VERSES 8–12.

The preceding verses have shown the mediation effected on the part of Jesus and of the man, of the contrast contained in vers. 1–5. The verses now before us show in the first instance the result.

VERSE 8.

The healed man has gone home to his parents. For the neighbours are spoken of. Whither else should he first go? Probably Jesus himself sent him thither. The change which has befallen him is so striking, that men are doubtful whether or not he be the same who previously used to sit there and beg.

VERSE 9.

This verse depicts this scene vividly: *Some said, This is he: others, He is like him: he said, I am he.*

VERSE 10.

He himself must tell how the healing came to pass. *How were thine eyes opened?*

VERSE 11.

Ὁ ἄνθρωποσ ὁ λεγόμενοσ Ἰησοῦσ ('the man that is called Jesus')—thus read ℵ B C L, while the received text omits the article, and reads 'a man,' etc. So much the less do we need to assume, with Bengel, that the blind man knew nothing at all about Jesus, which would be very unlikely. By ὁ ('the') he designates him as the well-known one. Besides, he relates the fact simply without adding a judgment. Ἀνέβλεψα could mean: I looked up, Mark xvi. 4. But vers. 15 and 18 require: I became again seeing, 'visum recipi,' 'I received sight' (Bengel, Meyer, Godet). Taken exactly, this would be impossible in the case of one born blind; but it rests upon the conception that seeing is really the natural thing, and therefore is that which is partially present.

VERSE 12.

He does not know where Jesus is. This is not strange, since after his healing he went directly home.[1] No one has a right to say that the evangelist purposely changed the story, in order to present the case as if the man born blind, even after his healing, had no definite consciousness of the person of Jesus.[2] The healed man goes through an entirely natural development. The δωρεὰ τοῦ θεοῦ ('gift of God') is the first thing: Jesus is for him only the mediator of this gift. The next point, one which offers itself to him from the inward religious self-mediation of this first certainty, is, that Jesus is a prophet. Then Jesus testifies unto him that He is the Son of God. Then, after he has assured himself of this second certainty in opposition to the Pharisees, and thereby has taken the decisive step to emancipate himself in his religious confession from the authorities of his nation, he is abundantly ripe to receive in belief the highest self-witness of Jesus.

It is the self-same way upon which the woman of Sychar went. There, too, Jesus began with the δωρεὰ τοῦ θεοῦ, and at first presented himself merely as the mediator of this. The next thing was the recognition that he was a prophet, the freeing of the woman from the bonds of her national religion. Upon this, then, follows finally his highest self-testification. This blind beggar on the wayside was, moreover, doubtless no more moved inwardly by the religious question and movement of the day, than was that Samaritan woman, although the beggar had previously heard this and that about Jesus. The fact that here a miraculous occurrence forms the point of starting, and there a promise, does not affect the case. For the healed man's feelings and thoughts were only the more filled and moved

---

[1] Compare below on ver. 37, p. 338.
[2] Baur, *Kritische Untersuchungen über die kanonischen Evangelien*, Tübingen 1847, p. 178.

in the first instance by this fact; and it was but gradually that the person of the giver lifted itself up to him out of the gift.

(b.) VERSES 13–34.

In no previous section has the not-willing of unbelief come forward so strongly as it does here. Unbelief's own dialectics strike it itself. The reasoning, that Jesus is a sinner because of the breach of the Sabbath, and therefore cannot have performed this miracle, must in view of the evidence for the fact turn its point against itself. Accordingly, also, the reasoning on the part of the healed man proceeds from the fact of the miracle.[1] The result compels this man then to place Jesus and the Sabbath over against each other, and to close with the recognition of the divine position and importance of Jesus in his calling, as raised above the Sabbath. It is, however, clearly to be seen, that the disinclination of the Jews rises to a decided not-willing, and thence to a foundationless enmity.

At the end of the first scene of the hearing, the evangelist remarks, ver. 16, that division and indecision still prevailed among them. The ἄλλοι ('others') are at a loss, and speak with hesitation as to whether Jesus really can be a sinner; this is not because they 'thought more freely' (De Wette), but because, though indeed agreeing with the rest theoretically, they found the occurrence too inconsistent with that view, and had not yet made their conscience entirely unsusceptible to such considerations. It is the beginning of the reasoning which the blind man urges against them at a later period. But since they cannot endure the logical conclusion, the beginning remains a mere beginning. It is the last motion of conscience among the spiritual authorities of Israel.

VERSES 13–16.

VERSE 13.

They led the healed man to the Pharisees. Ἄγουσιν

---

[1] Compare Baur, *Kritische Untersuchungen über die kanonischen Evangelien*, Tübingen 1847, p. 177 f.

('they lead'), namely, the ones spoken of before in ver. 8. By the Pharisees, we are not to understand directly the Sanhedrim (thus Tholuck), and as little the mere members of that party (Meyer), who would have first had to assemble, for ἄγουσιν πρὸσ τοὺσ Φαρισαίουσ ('they lead to the Pharisees') seems to require that these must have been to be found at a specified place. Moreover, we are not to think of the 'leading committee' of this 'mighty sect' (Godet), for we know nothing of such a committee. But we must think of an assembly of an official character, in which the questioners were chiefly concerned about the judgment of the representatives of orthodoxy.

If the scene were to be thought of as occurring still upon the Sabbath or feast day,[1] it would be the Sabbath assembly בְּחֵיל,[2] in the temple area at the court of the women, which of itself became a judicial process. Or it was one of the three courts of Jerusalem, which held their sittings in the neighbourhood of the temple.[3] Or the authorities designated as οἱ Φαρισαῖοι ('the Pharisees') improvised a kind of session. The design of those who led the healed man to the Pharisees was not, indeed, an accusation, but yet the requiring an official decision: what was to be thought of this singular event. The laymen in Israel had not the courage to give an opinion of their own in such questions. With this aim in view they had asked about the person of Jesus, in ver. 12. There is no need of assuming hostility, much less, like Lange, diabolical hostility; it is merely the ordinary lack of independence of judgment in religious questions.

Verse 14.

Usually the informing is said to have been based upon the question of the Sabbath. But we are in this verse to read δέ ('and') and not γάρ ('for'); so that the Sabbath only confirms the offence of the Pharisees.

---

[1] Wieseler, *Chronologische Synopse der vier Evangelien*, Hamburg 1843, p. 329.

[2] Winer, *Biblisches Realwörterbuch*, 3d ed., Leipzig 1848, vol. ii. p. 552, note.

[3] Schürer, *Lehrbuch der neutestamentlichen Zeitgeschichte*, Leipzig 1874, p. 400.

Verse 15.

Then again the Pharisees also asked him how he had received his sight. The healed man simply repeats before the court the account of the external occurrence.

Verse 16.

Instead of acknowledging the gift of God, and rejoicing at the benefit done, at least a part of the Pharisees cannot get over the supposed breach of the Sabbath. The Sabbath law forbade all work. According to the rabbinical ordinance, help was allowed on the Sabbath only in case of danger to life; and aside from this, healing was forbidden.[1] The externality of the orthodoxy showed itself in this cleaving to the outward letter. While these concluded, from the breach of the Sabbath, unfavourably towards the person of Jesus, others argued from the miraculous character of the event to its moral purity; but only timidly. They did not resolve themselves to draw the further conclusion. The certainty of the healed man contrasts characteristically with this uncertainty.

Verses 17–23.

This assurance shows itself at once in his decided answer to the question of the Pharisees. The whole judicial process is depicted in general with uncommon clearness and vividness, so as to display at the same time in a keen way both the disposition and the internal moral bearing of the parties concerned; and from the very beginning the situation is very vividly characterized in the dependence of the people together with the uncertainty of the rulers on the one side, and in the independence and certainty of judgment on the other side.

Verse 17.

He is a prophet. His confession sounds short and decided.

---

[1] Compare Winer, *Biblisches Realwörterbuch*, 3d ed., Leipzig 1848, vol. ii. p. 346; and Schürer, *Lehrbuch der neutestamentlichen Zeitgeschichte*, Leipzig 1874, p. 490.

Bengel remarks: 'Repetitis inquisitionibus agitatus hominum demum auctoritate teneri dedidicit' ('excited by the repeated questionings, he at length learned not to be held by the authority of men'). It is not possible to see why the healed man should call Jesus προφήτησ ('prophet'), merely 'taken from the theurgic side' (De Wette). The miracle is for him only the occasion for the recognition of Jesus' divine vocation in general. Hence Bengel explains it correctly: 'a deo' ('from God'), and adds: 'iucunde observari potest fides apud hunc hominem, dum pharisaei contradicunt, paulatim exoriens' ('faith in this man can be with interest observed rising by degrees, while the Pharisees are contradicting').

VERSE 18.

This second scene is characterized by the hope the Jews have, that something may be found to make it possible to represent the affair as cheating or deception. We perceive from the form of the question, ver. 17, that the Pharisees are convinced of the reality of the fact itself. For here they presuppose its reality, and show their embarrassment in regard to the judgment concerning a miracle-worker. It is only because they wish very much the thing might not have occurred, that they still hope and try to talk themselves into its non-reality. That is the way we are to understand it when the evangelist says, they believed not that he had been blind, and had received sight. To explain this he adds οὖν ('therefore'): in consequence of the decided confession, they suspect a secret understanding. Their unwillingness to believe, snatches eagerly at this possibility. Hence, in connection with this, the evangelist causes the designation Ἰουδαῖοι ('Jews') to enter, instead of Φαρισαῖοι ('Pharisees'), to characterize the developing posture of opposition.

VERSE 19.

They address themselves to the parents of the man healed: *Is this your son, who ye say was born blind? How then doth he now see?*

Verse 20.

They answer the former question in the affirmative: *We know that this is our son, and that he was born blind.*

Verse 21.

The answer to the second question they avoid, out of fear of the Jews, and refer to the healed man himself; he is old enough. But in spite of all the timidity which affects the parents of the healed man in the presence of their rulers, and in spite of all the reserve they maintain in their statement, this only serves to make the two actual cardinal points incontestable: that the man was born blind, and that he has now suddenly received his sight.

Verses 22, 23.

They are indeed as well convinced of the 'How' as their son is, but they do not attain the freedom of conduct he attains; they are afraid of being shut out from the religious society of the national life. At vii. 49, we saw the occasion, reasoning from which the chiefs of the synagogues had reached this agreement,—an agreement concerning which it was but natural that it should in an instant be spread throughout Jerusalem, because of the great sensation it must have caused as the first official step against Jesus and his followers.

Verses 24-34.

The opposition between the Pharisees and the healed man here shows itself in growing strength, until the violent solution in ver. 34. In view of the fact, their previous embarrassment turns into despair, and this into rage.

Verse 24.

Their embarrassment could not betray itself in a stronger way than by the renewed putting of questions, and by the attempt to see if they could not alter the story upon doctrinal grounds. At the very outset they give their endeavour a very weighty emphasis by the appeal, δὸς δόξαν τῷ θεῷ ('give glory to God'). This is usually taken as a form of adjuring (Bengel, Lücke, De Wette, Meyer). But though this interpretation fits Josh. vii. 19, it does not fit 1 Sam. vi. 5 or Jer. xiii. 16. Lampe[1] has hit the right view. Among other things, he urges that the Pharisees desired to impress on the one questioned, the fact that he had greatly sinned in that he had given an honouring testimony concerning Jesus, and even seemed inclined to regard Him as the Messiah; and the fact that the only impulse for their action was their zeal for God's honour: he therefore ought to join them, and thus also maintain God's honour, by declaring this man to be a sinner (similarly also Godet).

They present to him thus the strongest argument that was possible: for the sake of the honour of the God of Israel, the miracle cannot be acknowledged; for how can the holy God give his miraculous gifts to a Sabbath-breaker? Their sophistic sharpness summons everything to serve their will. In adding further: *we know*, etc., they also throw the weight of their authority into the scale.

VERSE 25.

It is highly characteristic to perceive how, in the face of this attempt of dialectics and of authority, the healed man, with the greatest calmness and simplicity, holds fast to the fact. They had said: οἴδαμεν, we know that he is a sinner. He opposes to this knowledge: οὐκ οἶδα ('I do not know'). He lets their logic alone. One thing, however, he does know: the fact. That is the point in which his logic rests, and from which it reasons.

VERSE 26.

They are embarrassed. They ask him again how it was; as if they had not already heard. *What did he to thee? How opened he thine eyes?*

VERSE 27.

The healed man sees their embarrassment, and perceives

---

[1] Lampe, *Commentarius* . . . *Evangelii secundum Joannem*, Amsterdam 1725, vol. ii. p. 574.

their disinclination to let the fact pass as true. He has already told them what they desire to hear. When, then, they act as if they had not heard it,—καὶ οὐκ ἠκούσατε, 'ye had no ears' (De Wette); it is said bitterly, as also ἤδη ('already') shows,—he observes that they are not concerned for the truth. This incites him to bitter irony: *You too do not wish to become his disciples?* 'You too,' not: as I (Bengel) —he was not so far yet,—but with reference to the other followers of Jesus, from the unlearned folk: even you scholars.

VERSE 28.

The Pharisees now, seeing that they are read through and through by the simplicity of the unlearned man, and feeling the sting of the moral reproach which lay in the words of the layman, become passionate. It is true, the healed man had thus far had in mind not himself but the people, the despised but honest ὄχλοσ μὴ γινώσκων τὸν νόμον ('multitude not knowing the law'), when he asked the Pharisees, μὴ καὶ ὑμεῖσ κ.τ.λ. ('you too do not, etc.'). And yet his relation to Jesus, as it had in the meantime inwardly developed and determined itself, was plainly enough to be recognised in these words. Hence the Pharisees, although anticipating the development, and yet even thereby helping it on, could return upon him the words touching the discipleship. Ἐκείνου ('of that one'), they say, with a contemptuous rejection of Him. Bengel observes: 'hoc vocabulo removent Jesum a sese' ('with this word they put away Jesus from themselves'). The authorities of Israel here say distinctly that they will not have anything to do with Jesus.

VERSE 29.

Moses' divine sending is certain; the authority of the person and word of Jesus is uncertain. The words are intended contemptuously (De Wette, against Lücke), when with τοῦτον δὲ οὐκ οἴδαμεν πόθεν ἐστίν ('but this man, we know not whence he is') they deny his divine commission. God spoke to Moses in plain words, as one man speaks to another; thus directly divine therefore is his vocation; in such a calling to his work lies the origin of his appearance as a prophet of God. They probably have in mind particularly Moses' call in the desert, which was the basis of all succeeding speech of God with him. But whence does Jesus date as a prophet?

Verse 30.

The healed man introduces his reply with a γάρ ('for'). It is not the γάρ which confirms a preceding sentence, and therefore perchance a sentence left out; it confirms the sentence in question, as we use 'for;' *therein*, namely, in your answer (Meyer arbitrarily: in this state of affairs), *is a marvellous thing.* Hence I must express my astonishment: for it is, etc., so that therefore γάρ serves to emphasize and make prominent the man's own answer. Ἄρα and γε are blended in γάρ: ἄρα ('then') refers to the preceding declaration of the Pharisees, γε is an assuring, like our: yes; 'therein is then, indeed, a marvellous thing.'[1] The layman finds in this (ἐν τούτῳ), namely, in their words and in this contrast, their not-knowing to be a singular thing. For whence did they know that God had spoken to Moses from the bush, and had called him, except by his miraculous legitimation? But Jesus has this to show, just as much as Moses had. Thus the healed man accepts the reasoning of the Pharisees entirely, and strikes them from their own bulwarks, behind which they had withdrawn, and had believed themselves to be secure. The step that the man makes in knowledge is no small one.

Verse 31.

This verse presents the general principle that God does not hear sinners, but those who fear God and do his will— Jesus' deed passes with the man as a hearing of prayer; for only God can work miracles;—as a consequence of the unquestionable hearing, this includes the fact: that the healing act on the Sabbath appeared to him to be not a breach

---

[1] Compare Winer, *Grammatik des neutestamentlichen Sprachidioms*, § 53. 8. b. b), 7th ed., Leipzig 1867, p. 415 f.

of the law, but a performing of the will of God, and that he therewith also freed himself from the letter of the law, in that he had learned to place the will of God, as it had appeared to him in the person of Jesus, above the letter of the Old Testament law. In such progressive emancipation from the former bonds, like the Samaritan woman, he prophesies at the same time the future relation which they, of whom he serves as type, will assume towards the letter of the law.

Verse 32.

The healed man does not, however, stop at that general truth, but emphasizes also the peculiarity of the fact in hand, the healing of one born blind. *Since the world began was it not heard that any man opened the eyes of one that was born blind.*

Verse 33.

From this follows of necessity the conclusion that Jesus is sent by God. Lücke observes with regard to the argumentation of this man, that even the most highly schooled apologetics and ethics cannot with reason object in the least to this conclusion of the proof from miracles, and that Christianity owes largely its acceptance and spread to this natural and correct method of concluding from the basis of the miraculous facts. To this Lessing has already given the answer, namely, that experience of miracles and a report of them are two different things. Yet in these single miracles was only typified that which later fulfilled itself in greater extent, and which is present to us not merely as report, but as experience.

Verse 34.

The Jews wish to beat down the irrefutable argument by insulting words and by a violent act. Does he, a man who was altogether conceived and born in sin, desire to teach them? "Ολοσ does not intend to say 'in body and soul' (thus commonly), but in all parts of his being, and therefore especially also—the point in question—in regard to his knowledge. This word has been said to rest on Ps. li. 7 (De Wette); but that touched themselves no less. 'Heightened hereditary depravity' (Hengstenberg) is not only an indistinct notion in itself, but is also unsuitable here, where the matter in hand is a retrospective conclusion from his blindness to his parents' guilt. For Bengel (also Baumgarten-Crusius and Meyer) observes correctly: 'exprobrant de caecitate pristina' ('they reproach him with his primal blindness'). For them that problem is solved. A common guilt of the parents, under which he was born, was revealed in the punishment which fell upon him. In this they strike at themselves, by involuntarily acknowledging the blindness from birth as a fact. Thus the evangelist has shown not merely how unbelief refutes itself dialectically, but much more how it condemns itself ethically. It has betrayed itself as hatred of the truth,—Bengel says: 'ipsi produnt odium veritatis, quo laborant' ('they themselves betray the hatred of the truth, under which they labour'),—and now manifests itself also in the act of violence. It agrees with the whole much better to suppose that $\dot{\epsilon}\xi\acute{\epsilon}\beta\alpha\lambda o\nu$ ('cast out') is not a designation of excommunication (Olshausen, De Wette, Tholuck), but is intended as an external act (Meyer). The evangelist lays stress upon this very point as characteristic. The exclusion from the synagogue was the natural result of that. Bengel observes: 'ciecerunt eum, tanquam christianum. Id factum magno eius bono' ('they cast him out, as a Christian. That came to pass for his great good').

(c.) VERSES 35–41.

Jesus assumes a position towards the world, concerning which position it is taught, that it mediates itself by self-impartation on the one side, and by believing reception on the other side, vers. 1-12. Occasioned by this position, a contrast has revealed itself among men, which, based in faithful sincerity on the one hand, and in obstinate insincerity on the other hand, had advanced to the most determined opposition, vers. 13–34. This contrast now completes and fixes itself, in that it receives a direct reference to Jesus' person, by which it is called forth, vers. 35–41. Jesus himself brings this about.

Verse 35.

Lücke thinks Jesus found by chance the man who had been cast out.[1] But he overlooks the fact that the order of succession of the ideas must then have been a different one. The circumstance that he found him would have had to come first, and only then the remark follow that he had heard of the casting out. As it is, the hearing and the finding are brought into connection with each other. Hence Bengel remarks: 'quaesierat igitur' ('he had therefore sought'). Meyer agrees with this, and assumes that Jesus inferred from that circumstance that the healed man confessed him as Messiah, and on that account asked him, σὺ πιστεύεισ κ.τ.λ. ('dost thou believe? etc.'). This assumption of Meyer's, however, does not conflict with the view of Chrysostom, that Jesus desired to give the man a rich indemnification. He recompensed him in the very bringing of his belief to perfection. He recompensed him by bestowing upon him His person and its fellowship, in the place of the lost fellowship with the synagogue.

In this is already given the gist of the appeal or of the comfort—according as one understands it—which the epistle to the Hebrews contains for the Jewish Christians, for whom it was written. The completion of his belief is induced by the question: σὺ πιστεύεισ εἰσ τὸν υἱὸν τοῦ θεοῦ; ('dost thou believe on the Son of God?'). This question presupposes the existence of the belief. Its form is such as to expect an affirmative answer. It seems to be an inference, which Jesus draws from the man's conduct before the court, and which he puts in the form of a question, so as to occasion a confession. In that the healed man is now induced to give a decided confession to Jesus himself, his belief is completed as a psychological fact. At the same time, moreover, it is completed in its contents, in that Jesus designates himself as ὁ υἱὸσ τοῦ θεοῦ ('the Son of God').

[1] Lücke, *Commentar über das Evangelium des Johannes*, 3d ed., Bonn 1843, vol. ii. p. 391.

It is true that ℵ B D read εἰσ τὸν υἱὸν τοῦ ἀνθρώπου ('unto the Son of Man'). But the answer of the healed man shows that Jesus must have asked with a conception that was familiar to him. That, however, was not 'Son of Man,' but probably 'Son of God.' Hence 'Son of Man' doubtless came into the text as the usual self-designation of Jesus.

In the mouth of Jesus, indeed, 'Son of God' meant more than Messiah, but to the Jews it was a familiar designation of the Messiah. Hence the man born blind understood it in the theocratic sense (thus most commentators, not in the metaphysical, Olshausen). The question of Jesus: *Thou believest on the Son of God?* expects an affirmative answer. The question is so direct that it must have surprised the one questioned, and was intended to direct his thoughts to the present. He was to observe that the matter in hand was not a theoretical doctrinal principle, but a practical conduct in the present.

VERSE 36.

The healed man before the court had confessed, and therefore probably also recognised Jesus only as a prophet of God, and not yet as the Messiah. But by the contrast with Moses, above whose ordinance he perceives that Jesus is elevated, he has already approached this latter recognition more nearly. And thus also there lies in his question: καὶ τίσ ἐστιν, κύριε; *And who is he, Lord?* the hidden suspicion that Jesus means Himself. Besides, this question as to its purpose may be compared with the like half-divining word of the Samaritan woman, iv. 25. The very connective καί ('and') shows his eagerness. For there is something hasty in this joining of his question to the question of Jesus. And that he does not ask: τί ('what'), but τίσ ('who'), is due to the fact that he is concerned, not as to theoretical information touching divine Sonship and the like, but as to the personal relation to the actual Son of God, at whom Jesus had hinted: ἵνα πιστεύσω εἰσ αὐτόν ('that I may believe on him'). For the present he does not need detailed doctrinal explanations. The lack of his knowledge will be supplied even by the personal relation of belief. The question with τί, therefore, would have been as unpsychological as unnecessary. In the personal relation of belief, ver. 38, he then possessed the whole knowledge in germ. Jesus chooses purposely as the comprehensive term for this knowledge, the designation ὁ υἰὸσ τοῦ θεοῦ ('the Son of God'), because this was the most extensive term. He testified to Himself before the teachers of Israel who owned Him as a divinely sent prophet, that He was the Son of God, iii. 13 ff., and he goes upon the same way of self-testification and of development of belief here also; compare παρὰ θεοῦ ('from God'), ver. 33.

Verse 37.

It is significant that Jesus does not merely say ἐγώ εἰμι ('I am'), but paraphrases this as we here read it. He refers the man to the circumstance that he sees and hears him. Ἐκεῖνοσ ('that one,' instead of the more common word in Greek: οὗτοσ, 'this one') is characteristic of John's gospel,[1] and lays stress upon the subject in hand, and not merely on the more distant subject. Here, as at xix. 35 (compare the comment on that verse), it means the speaker himself: *it is even he.* De Wette is certainly right in explaining καὶ . . . καί ('both . . . and') as a connection of the two thoughts in which only the second member (καὶ ὁ λαλῶν κ.τ.λ., 'and it is he that talketh, etc.') is drawn towards the other. For to take the first καί as emphasized, 'indeed thou hast seen him,' as Meyer takes it, brings too strong an accent into the discourse. But Jesus bids him recognise His person from His action and His words.

His action, which is a type of Him, His word, which expresses Him, show what are the characteristics of Him who may call himself ὁ υἰὸσ τοῦ θεοῦ ('the Son of God'). The action first, the word afterwards, are therefore the foundation and the fountain of belief, and hence also of the knowledge which is given with it and which results from it. I speak of an action by reason of ἑώρακασ ('thou hast seen'). This does not refer in the first instance to the

---

[1] See vol. i. p. 230 f., and Luthardt, *St. John the Author of the Fourth Gospel*, Edinburgh, T. and T. Clark, 1875, p. 180 f.

seeing after the healing, as he returned from Siloam,—he certainly did return thence to Jesus again (against Lücke[1] and Meyer): ἀπῆλθεν καὶ ἐνίψατο καὶ ἦλθεν βλέπων ('he went his way therefore, and washed, and came seeing'), ver. 7,—but to the present seeing, namely, that he has seen Him standing before him, while he asked after Him, καὶ τίσ ἐστιν, κύριε; Yet, nevertheless, it reminds him most emphatically and distinctly of the fact that Jesus bestowed upon him the power of seeing. It thus puts before him that action of Jesus, in which His essential meaning and his essential action were typified.

To this is added the word that Jesus speaks to him. That is the word of the Son of God and of belief on him. In that action the word of Jesus intends to teach him to recognise the Son of God. Hence, then, it is the word of Jesus' self-witness, which bestows upon his belief its specific contents and its specific religious form, and thereby completes it.

Verse 38.

The belief demanded is as a natural consequence followed by its proof in the προσκυνεῖν ('worshipping'), which was not demanded. Bengel says: 'Agnitionem sponte sequitur adoratio' ('adoration follows of its own accord recognition'). That which involuntarily displays itself in this act is no longer the conclusion from the miracle to the divine mission, but the inward, direct certainty of belief, a certainty wrought by the word. The contents of ὁ υἱὸσ τοῦ θεοῦ ('the Son of God') have not yet come to consciousness in him in an explicit manner, nor has the meaning of the προσκυνεῖν. But as the former is the essential confession of belief in Jesus, so is the latter the essential religious testification of belief exercised towards Him. That direct certainty of belief is shown to us as complete in Thomas; and in like manner this testification of belief is displayed to us in his words of worshipping reverence: ὁ κύριόσ μου καὶ ὁ θεόσ μου ('my Lord and my God'). Thus also here κύριε ('Lord') is

---

[1] Lücke, *Commentar über das Evangelium des Johannes*, 3d ed., Bonn 1843, vol. ii. p. 392. See also above, p. 324.

said with special emphasis: 'iam augustiore sensu ita dicit, quam dixerat ver. 36' ('he now speaks thus in a sense more reverential than that in which he had spoken in ver. 36').

VERSES 39–41.

We have above seen, in the relation and conduct of the healed man towards Jesus, the one side of the contrast—called forth in the world by the direct relation given to it to the person of Jesus as the Son of God—come to a preliminary completion. In the verses now before us, vers. 39–41, the other side of the contrast is placed over against the former. Jesus turns from the healed man to the circle standing around, with a general characterizing of the result of His mission. His opponents come specially forward out of the crowd, and lend to these words a particular application to themselves.

VERSE 39.

This whole section proceeded from the contrast between φῶσ ('light') and κόσμοσ ('world'). Hence the words εἰσ τὸν κόσμον τοῦτον ('into this world'). For the κόσμοσ was designated from the very outset as standing in contrast with the φῶσ, and as needing it. *For judgment I am come into this world.* At iii. 17, we saw that the process of judgment as a task of the Son was denied at his first coming. Here, the self-judgment of the world is taught as a conclusion of his revelation in the world. The apparent contradiction solves itself in this difference. The same thing is confirmed by the language.

It reads εἰσ κρῖμα ('unto judgment as completed') and not εἰσ κρίσιν ('unto judgment as being passed'), and therefore says, not that he executes a judgment as an act, but that a righteous judgment issues as a result. This judgment consists in the circumstance 'that those who see not receive sight, and that those who see become blind.' Want is designated by Jesus as the presupposition for the gift, substantially, indeed, here in the same way as elsewhere, for example, Matt. ix. 12, but from another side. The reason for this is not merely the actual occasion, which here is a healing of the blind, there, a healing of the sick. Nor is the reason simply to be found in John's choice of discourses in general,[1] as indeed the well-known Johannizing passage, Matt. xi. 25, has a strong resemblance to the one before us. The reason is, in especial, that we have before us that part of the self-witness, the fundamental notion of which is the light. This phrase could hardly have found a place before the seventh chapter.

Who are, however, these μὴ βλέποντεσ, 'that do not see,' except ὁ ὄχλοσ ὁ μὴ γινώσκων τὸν νόμον ('the people who knoweth not the law'), vii. 49? But then οἱ βλέποντεσ, 'they that see,' are those who say ἡμεῖσ οἴδαμεν, 'we know,' ix. 29, because they have the knowledge of the law, and therewith τὴν μόρφωσιν τῆσ γνώσεωσ καὶ τῆσ ἀληθείασ ἐν τῷ νόμῳ ('the form of knowledge and of the truth in the law'), Rom. ii. 20. And that is indeed a knowledge and a 'seeing in the exact sense' (against Stier[2]). We saw above that the very knowledge of the letter of the law, in which they so prided themselves (compare Rom. ii. 18, 19), became to the Pharisees a hindrance to seeing in Jesus the fulfilment of the promise. They have therefore become blind to the essential contents of the Old Testament. Those who lacked this knowledge, but instead were possessed of a longing both for the fulfilment of the promise and for the supply of their own need, received sight from Jesus, that is, found in him the truth of the Old Testament, of the revelation of God, and of the communion with God. The others, on the contrary, became blind through Jesus. For, by reason of the contradiction in which the truth of the Old Testament, etc., in Jesus seemed to stand with the letter of the law, they became incapable of acknowledging that truth.

VERSE 40.

The Pharisees—who were present to make their observations—at this ask Jesus whether they, perchance, are also blind. This cannot possibly be meant in the sense of τυφλὸν γενέσθαι ('becoming blind'), but must be intended in the

---

[1] Stier, *Reden Jesu*, 3d ed., Barmen and Elberfeld 1870, vol. iv. p. 513.
[2] Stier, *ut supra*, p. 514.

sense of μὴ βλέπειν ('not seeing'), Meyer. Τυφλὸν γενέσθαι is a result which still has to show itself; besides, in that case γενέσθαι, and not εἶναι, must have been used in the question. On the contrary, it is said pointedly and sarcastically: *We too are surely not blind?* The offensive or the ridiculous thing is not that there are blind people, or that the blind should receive sight, but that this reversal of affairs should be brought about by Jesus. Their question therefore is this: Shall we, indeed, hence also be said to belong, like the ignorant people, to the blind, who must be by thee made to see?

Verse 41.

If they belonged to those, it would be well for them, in so far as the sin would not remain for them; which, since they do not belong to those, but think that in their legal knowledge they have a true knowledge, still remains. Thus is ver. 41 to be understood. The contrast for οὐκ ἂν εἴχετε ἁμαρτίαν ('ye should have no sin') is found in ἡ ἁμαρτία ὑμῶν μένει ('your sin remaineth'), and the meaning therefore is, that their sin would in that case have been taken away, and that they in consequence would have had no more. But the sin, which would have fallen away from them if they had had a curable blindness, and therewith the possibility and receptibility for illumination, on the contrary remains upon them, because in their fancied knowledge they blind themselves towards the light. Their sin is by this connection of thought necessarily shown to be the sin of this reserve, shown clearly enough to be the sin of this hardened self-blinding itself.

Hence Olshausen was wrong in understanding by ἡ ἁμαρτία, the 'sinful understanding in general;' and much more were De Wette and Lücke at fault in explaining the words εἰ τυφλοὶ ἦτε κ.τ.λ. ('if ye were blind, etc.') of the imputation and guilt as decreased by ignorance; De Wette thereupon cites the corresponding paragraphs of his handbook on morals. For the same reason we must reject Meyer's view: that their unbelief towards Christ would not then be sinful, because it would not be an opposition to the divine truth, but only an irresponsible lack of attaining unto it.

Similarly Godet. Contrariwise there would then be no question as to unbelief in their case, since they would even come to belief. Bengel observes : ' Si diceretis, cæci sumus, visum peteretis et peccatum vestrum iam desiisset ' (' if ye should say, we are blind, ye would seek sight, and ye would already have left off your sin '). Now, however, their sin remains ; because, by their supposed knowledge, they allow themselves to be prevented from coming to belief, and thus shut themselves up towards the revelation of Christ.

In this manner, then, the other side also of the contrast has definitely fixed itself. By Jesus' self-testification it has come to pass that those who will not believe because they see, have thereby become completely subject to the darkness, and hence their sin of self-blinding remains an unremoved one. Considering both sides, Jesus in what follows now tells what is appointed to each of the two : a blessing to the ones who confess him—x. 1–21, or rather to 18 ; and to the others, who refuse to own him, an unbearable offence— x. 22–42, or rather to 39. Accordingly the two next following sections are based upon the contrast represented and developed in the ninth chapter. These sections carry on the mutual relation of Christ and of men, and in especial portray it from such a point of view, as to show what Christ is to men in consideration of their posture towards him.

X. 1–21.

Jesus here depicts himself as a blessing to those who confess him, and that in the first place in the closest connection with what precedes. For he there had addressed himself in the first place to those who ' knew.' Upon the basis of their knowing, of their knowledge, they think they ὁδηγὸν εἶναι τυφλῶν, φῶσ τῶν ἐν σκότει, παιδευτὴν ἀφρόνων, διδάσκαλον νηπίων (' are a guide of the blind, a light of them which are in darkness, an instructor of the foolish,' Rom. ii. 19 f.). Such is the thought Jesus has in view when he contrasts himself to such supposed leaders (De Wette, Lücke, Baumgarten-Crusius, Bengel). The ὑμεῖσ (' ye ') with which he closed is met by his ἐγώ (' I '). Although, however, this section rests entirely upon the contrast, nevertheless the contrast forms only the basis and the background for his self-proclamation, which in the first instance is intended for his own followers. For in the whole parabolic discourse there is no further address to his opponents. In his internal bearing and mood, Jesus recedes more, and stands at a greater distance from the previous direct opposition to the Jews. This, however, is only because he begins in general to maintain a greater distance from the Jews.

This whole discourse is pervaded by a great calmness, which, nevertheless, has as its foundation the vivid consciousness of the contrast, a spirit of the most loving self-devotion, from which, at the same time, the proud consciousness of free self-possession expresses itself. After the restless motion of the preceding chapters, this discourse is like a place of rest, in which Jesus' feelings at the same time desire to satisfy themselves, and to let the conflict die away in almost melancholy words. Hence flows also the full development of the thoughts (Baumgarten-Crusius). The great thing that speaks for the genuineness of this discourse is above all the psychological truth, which lies in the fact that just such a discourse should now follow upon the previous events.[1] A certain warmth of feeling, in which a love of irresistible power reveals itself, has here bestowed a peculiar stamp, and at the same time a comprehensive meaning, upon the figure of the light which lies at the foundation of the preceding sections. And in that the point of its blessing-bestowing power is particularly emphasized, it comes to pass that the figure of the light in the progress of the discourse passes into the idea of the life as the essential blessing of salvation.

In the comprehensive character of this discourse, and in the prominence of the soul, of the personality of Jesus, lies a certain similarity to the seventeenth chapter, although only the likeness of a lower stage to a higher one. Here also we feel the heart of Jesus beating. And therefore this discourse and its figure have made a deep and lasting impression on the church. This figure—especially, indeed, in

[1] Compare Luthardt, *St. John the Author of the Fourth Gospel*, Edinburgh, T. and T. Clark, 1875, p. 229.

connection with Luke xv.—is one of the first and most frequent symbols of Christian and churchly art-representation, and a favourite figure of Christian conception. Baur, on the contrary, puts the importance of this chapter at a low figure, and concedes to it [1] 'no particular weight for the pursuit of the chief thought of the gospel.' The reason for this is, that Baur sees in the gospel only the development and unfolding of an idea, and hence only knows of points of the conception or of the idea, while the chief weight and the importance of this section lie in the personal element which is peculiar to it. The evangelist is not busied in the first place with an idea; and perchance in the second place, and only for the sake of its aid as proof, with the person of Jesus. The latter is the first thing for him; and he presents the former only because and in so far as it is given in and represents itself in the latter.

This parable consists of three parts: (*a*) vers. 1–5; (*b*) vers. 6–10; and (*c*) vers. 11–18.

(*a*.) Verses 1–5.

Jesus here draws the picture of the true shepherd and his relation to the flock, in the first place purely for itself and without application. But since it rests on the opposition to the Pharisees, who desire to be shepherds, so that they reject Him, and who are shepherds in an entirely different disposition towards Israel from his disposition,— since this is the case, the twofold application is already prepared for, namely, that he himself is both the true mediation of all pastoral vocation in Israel, in the church of God, and also the real and true shepherd.

Verse 1.

With emphatic stress upon what he is about to say to them,—ἀμὴν, ἀμὴν κ.τ.λ. ('verily, verily, etc.'),—Jesus addresses himself to those about him, and, as ὑμῖν ('to you'), pointing back to the close of the ninth chapter, shows, especially to his opponents, in order to show them

[1] Baur, *Kritische Untersuchungen über die kanonischen Evangelien*, Tübingen 1847, p. 180.

who is a true shepherd, — that one, namely, who comes to the church in the way appointed by God. For: *He that entereth not by the door into the sheepfold, but climbeth up some other way,*—over the wall,—*the same is a thief and a robber.* What led Jesus to use this figure of a shepherd, whether the sight of a flock in the fields (Neander) or the like, is a very superfluous question. The comparison is brought close to hand both by the Scriptures in general and by the special connection here, namely, the contrast to the evil leaders of the people.

The various features of the picture are drawn from the then existing circumstances. The shepherds spent the night in the wall-enclosed fold ($αὐλή$), at the door of which an under-shepherd (ὁ θυρωρόσ, ver. 3) kept watch during the night (Meyer). The right way leads through the door. He who 'climbs up,' ἀλλαχόθεν = ἄλλοθεν ('some other way'), upon the wall, in order to get over it into the fold, goes a wrong way, not the appointed way. The fold is the church, which God has gathered for himself upon earth; the door is the way which he has appointed (thus most exegetes, Tholuck, Hengstenberg, Godet). Which way this is, is not yet said. It is enough for the present to know that God's ordering and calling here has sway, and not human despotism. Whether Christ is to be understood as the shepherd or as the door (for example, Meyer), is a misplaced and anticipating question, since the first thing in this place is only the portraying the requirements of the true shepherd as he ought to be.

Verse 2.

To this must be added the circumstance that he enters by the door, as the 'legitimus aditus' ('lawful approach'), Bengel. *He that entereth in by the door is the shepherd of the sheep.*

Verse 3.

Vers. 3–5 now depict the relation of fellowship in which the true shepherd stands towards the flock. The first thing is, in this third verse, that he, in that he comes to the flock by the divinely-appointed way, approaches it also with God's permission. This is what is intended as the meaning of the porter and his opening the door. Some have understood by this, God (Calvin, Bengel, Tholuck, Hengstenberg), or Christ (Cyril, Augustine), or the Holy Ghost (for example, Stier[1]), or Moses (Chrysostom, Theodore of Mopsuestia), or John the Baptist (Godet). All this is arbitrary. The question is not the things or the persons, but the relations and transactions. The fact that the porter openeth, indicates that God secures approach to the flock. A true shepherd will therefore in the first place succeed in obtaining approach, and in the next place, in finding entrance into the church of God. For the two know each other, and belong to each other, the true shepherd and his flock.

The sheep hear his voice, and he calleth his own sheep by name, and leadeth them out. In that they hear his voice, they show that they belong to him. The propriety meant is one mediated morally. Hence also in this sense it is said, emphasizing the propriety or property of the shepherd in them, τὰ ἴδια πρόβατα ('his own sheep'). It is not as if these were hereby in general designated as a part of the sheep contained in the fold (Lücke, Baumgarten-Crusius, Meyer); for that not only would have had to appear more distinctly, but also is refuted by the fact that τὰ πρόβατα ('the sheep'), which hear (ἀκούει),—words which, linguistically, can only be understood of all the sheep in the fold, —from internal reasons must necessarily be the same as those which are afterwards designated as τὰ ἴδια ('his own'), and by the fact that at the end again these are spoken of in such a way, καὶ τὰ πρόβατα ... ἀκολουθεῖ ('and the sheep follow, etc.'), that all are evidently to be understood. "Ἴδια ('own') does not denote separation, but the inward mutual propriety of shepherd and flock in each other, and characterizes the sheep from this point of view; thus also Bengel and Hengstenberg, against Meyer.

'He calleth them (φωνεῖ, with ℵ A B D L, against καλεῖ) by name,'—each by his own name: 'etiam oves ab antiquis nominibus distinguebantur' ('even sheep were distinguished

---

[1] Stier, *Reden Jesu*, 3d ed., Barmen and Elberfeld 1870, vol. iv. p. 521.

by their names by the ancients'), Bengel;[1] they are all singly known to him, and lie upon his heart—'and leadeth them out,' not out of the Old Testament theocracy, so that they break with it (thus Godet, arbitrarily), but out into the pasture.

VERSE 4.

What follows is based upon this relation, that they are ἴδια ('his own'). They belong to him because he has a vocation unto them; hence he knows them, and hence they follow him. He belongs to them: hence he goes before them, and hence they know his voice and hearken unto it. *And when he putteth forth all*—for πάντα is to be read with B D L, against ℵ, which omits it—*his own*. This ἐκβάλῃ ('putteth forth') depicts the method of the ἐξάγειν ('leading out'): he putteth them forth, in that he lays hold upon them, and so on. It is a feature taken from real life, which lets us see the care the shepherd bestows on each separate one. The sheep which are divinely kept in the secure fold are not the outward Israel, but the church of God. Therefore they belong together, and they know each other, this church and the shepherds who come to it with a vocation from God. On this account also the conduct of the sheep is portrayed as a unanimous, and not as a discordant one.

VERSE 5.

By this now also it may be perceived which is and which is not a true shepherd, whether the church of God knows his voice and hearkens unto it or not. *A stranger will they certainly not follow* (ℵ and the common text, ἀκολουθήσωσιν, the subjunctive, according to the common construction; A B D, etc., ἀκολουθήσουσιν, future, less common[2]), *but will flee from him, because they know not the*

---

[1] [Travellers in Palestine tell of the same custom of naming sheep as prevailing to-day. See, for instance, Smith, *Dictionary of the Bible*, under the word 'Sheep,' with the citation from Hartley.—C. R. G.]

[2] Compare Winer, *Grammatik des neutestamentlichen Sprachidioms*, § 56. 3, 7th ed., Leipzig 1867, p. 472.

voice of strangers. For the word which the stranger brings is not the old well-known word, which has ever called them and led them to the green pasture. They have in themselves a sensorium for the latter; the former sounds strange to them.

Lampe called attention to the future: 'Non sine emphasi est futurum. Id enim monet, verba nostra consideranda esse ut prophetiam, describentem totalem illam oeconomarium immutationem, quae ante fores erat, quando cathedra Mosis plane deserenda' ('The future is not without its emphasis. It tells us that the words before us are to be regarded as a prophecy, describing that total change of economies which was at hand, when Moses' seat was to be altogether deserted').[1] The Old Testament church of God will separate itself from the spiritual authorities of Israel, because the latter will, by their own fault, lack the divine vocation unto the former. That separation will be like a flight, as one flies from a danger (compare ver. 1: κλέπτησ ἐστὶν καὶ λῃστήσ, 'is a thief and a robber'), as one escapes from destruction. Lampe recalled Israel's departure from Egypt, and Lot's flight from Sodom. In that case this would offer the foundation for the designation of the external Israel, deserted by God and God's church, in the book of Revelation: ἥτισ καλεῖται πνευματικῶσ Σόδομα καὶ Αἴγυπτοσ ('which spiritually is called Sodom and Egypt'), Rev. xi. 8.

The true shepherd was at first only generally characterized, yet in such a way that the counterpart, standing before men's eyes in the Pharisees, formed the background of the thought. Now, in that the thought, upon coming to the statement of the contrast, receives the form of a historical statement, and thereby takes a personal turn, Jesus is led to give a direct personal turn also to the positive side. The personal designation, in consequence, must take the place of the general characterizing. Two things were emphasized in the foregoing: the divinely-ordered way of vocation, and the relation of fellowship which accorded

---

[1] Lampe, *Commentarius . . . Evangelii secundum Joannem*, Amsterdam 1726, vol. ii. p. 632.

with the vocation. Both these will now come to expression
in personal designation. Jesus had given the Pharisees to
understand at first that they were no true shepherds of the
church of God, because they had not become shepherds
upon the God-appointed way, so that they in consequence
also did not stand in the true fellowship of love with the
church of God. He will therefore at first make prominent
(against Lücke) the circumstance that the true mediation
is given in him, and in the next place, that the true relation
of a shepherd has appeared personally in him.

(b.) VERSES 6–10.

These verses develop the first thought: Jesus is personally the true mediation; he is the mediator.

VERSE 6.

What Jesus said allegorically in vers. 1–5 in the form
of a παροιμία ('parable'), that is, of a discourse departing
from (παρά, 'praeter') the usual way (οἶμοσ), had reference
to the Pharisees. Hence αὐτοῖσ ('to them') is said purposely twice. It was addressed to them and meant for
them, for certainly the same persons are intended by ἐκεῖνοι
and αὐτοῖσ (against Baumgarten-Crusius). They might
well understand that he had them in mind, but what he
really meant by this escaped them. In this we are to
think not merely of the anticipatory historical statement
in the fifth verse, which the proud feeling of secure domination prevented them from understanding, but also of the
preceding characterization, and perhaps especially of the
'going in by the door,' which the proud consciousness of
their studies may have kept them from understanding.
Therefore, that which he really intended (τίνα ἦν ἅ κ.τ.λ.,
'what things they were which, etc.'), which he spake unto
them, remained concealed from them. Hence Jesus tells
them so. But although he speaks distinctly and strongly,
yet he avoids the direct address and designation, and rests
by preference upon the development of the blessing which
he bestows. We see by this that in his mood, and hence
also in the bearing of his words, he draws back more and

more from the contrast, although this remains the background of his self-witness.[1]

Verse 7.

Jesus had spoken at first of the divine vocation unto the sheep. If he turns this to himself, he must say that in him alone it is given and mediated. He begins afresh with great emphasis ($ἀμήν$ κ.τ.λ., 'verily, etc.'), and calls himself *the door*. This figure finds a rich echo in the literature of the early church, but with various applications. In Ignatius,[2] Jesus is called the θύρα τοῦ πατρόσ ('door of the Father'). In Hermas,[3] Jesus is called the πύλη ('gate'). Clement says:[4] πολλῶν οὖν πυλῶν ἀνεῳγυιῶν, ἡ ἐν δικαιοσύνῃ αὕτη ἐστὶν ἡ ἐν Χριστῷ ('therefore of many gates that have been opened, the one in righteousness, this is the one in Christ'). Hegesippus[5] relates that the Jews asked James, τίσ ἡ θύρα τοῦ Ἰησοῦ; ('what is the door of Jesus?'); and again,[6] ἀπάγγελον ἡμῖν, τίσ ἡ θύρα τοῦ Ἰησοῦ τοῦ σταυρωθέντοσ; ('tell us, what is the door of Jesus the crucified?'). Clement[7] writes: διὰ τοῦτο αὐτὸσ ἀληθὴσ ὢν προφήτησ ἔλεγεν· ἐγώ εἰμι ἡ πύλη τῆσ ζωῆσ ('on this account he himself, being a true prophet, said: I am the gate of life'). And in Hippolytus[8] we read: διὰ τοῦτο φησί (sc. Naassenus quidam), λέγει ὁ Ἰησοῦσ· ἐγώ εἰμι ἡ πύλη ἡ ἀληθινή ('hence he [a certain Naassenus] says, Jesus saith: I am the true gate'). Thus also the use of this figure continues with different variations among later writers. We therefore see that

---

[1] See above, p. 343.

[2] Ignatius, *Ad Philadelphenos*, ix. 1; *Patrum Apostolicorum Opera*, ed. Gebhardt, Harnack, Zahn, Leipzig 1876, fasciculus ii. p. 78.

[3] Hermas, *Pastor*, similitudo ix. 12; *ibid.* 1877, fasciculus iii. pp. 220, 222.

[4] Clement, *Ad Corinthios*, I. xlviii. 4; *ibid.* 1876, fascic. i. part i., 2d ed., p. 80.

[5] Hegesippus in Eusebius, *Historia Ecclesiastica*, II. xxiii. 8; *Opera*, ed. Dindorf, Leipzig 1871, vol. iv. p. 77.

[6] *Ibid.* II. xxiii. 12; *ibid.* p. 78.

[7] Clementina, *Hom.* iii. 52, ed. Lagarde, Leipzig 1865, p. 50, ll. 29, 30.

[8] Hippolytus, *Refutatio Omnium Hæresium*, v. 8, Göttingen 1859, p. 156, line 47 f.

such a saying as we read here, and as we find reported no where else in the gospels, must have been at hand in the early Christian tradition. In the context now and here the subject is the mediation of the pastoral vocation to the church by Jesus.

Accordingly, ἡ θύρα τῶν προβάτων ('the door of the sheep') must in the first place mean: door to the sheep (Bengel, Meyer). It is true that also 'for the sheep' (Chrysostom, Lampe, Hengstenberg, Godet) follows materially from this, but it is still to be kept at a distance here. How can Jesus oppose this now to the Pharisees as a claim? It is the promise of the future salvation, the belief and confession of which established a divine pastoral right in Israel. Therefore he who appeared duly authorized as a shepherd in Israel, appeared upon the basis of Christ, the one to come. This, however, was the peculiarity of the Pharisees, that for the sake of the letter of the law they believed they might venture to reject the fulfilling of the promise given in Jesus. Thus, then, Christ had not served as an entrance to the church of God for them, who boasted that they were Moses' disciples. This occasions the next statement.

VERSE 8.

All that came before me, that have appeared, *are thieves and robbers.* But these words, by the unconditionality and sharpness of their expression, offer difficulties in the exposition. All previous teachers of Israel appear to be rejected by them. This doubtless caused the omission of πρὸ ἐμοῦ ('before me') in ℵ: so that the prophets of the Old Testament should not seem to be struck by the words, but that they should seem exclusively intended for the Pharisaic teachers of the present. That, however, is too evidently a correction. Πρό ('before') is, moreover, to be left in its temporal sense, and is therefore not to be taken locally, as especially Stier[1] takes it. Stier regards it as contrasted with δι' ἐμοῦ ('by me'), namely, τῆσ θύρασ ('the door'), and therefore to mean πρὸ τῆσ θύρασ ('before the door').

[1] Stier, *Reden Jesu,* 3d ed., Barmen and Elberfeld 1870, vol. iv. p. 528 ff.

That, however, would have had to be more clearly expressed. Hence it is not to be found in the words. Still less is πρό to be exchanged with ὑπέρ ('instead of') or the like, or to be made to mean χωρίσ ('without'), all of which would be arbitrary.

Or should we have a right to supply in thought a χωρίσ ἐμοῦ ('without me')? Olshausen. And yet, again, we shall not endeavour, with De Wette, to censure the words of Jesus, or of the evangelist, and say: they do not correspond to the wisdom and mildness of Jesus. Hilgenfeld stopped half way when he made use of this passage as a proof of the anti-Jewish character of the fourth evangelist, in that he 'referred' it 'partly also to the Jewish religion.'[1] What gave him a right to except a 'part' of the 'Jewish religion,' and extend the condemnation perhaps only to the law, since 'the statement is nevertheless kept general'? Either he must find that in the early Gnostic manner the Old Testament prophets are also rejected here, or he must refrain altogether from making this application of the statement. And of late Hilgenfeld[2] does also give it that extension to the whole Old Testament past. In the next place, the thing in hand is not a theft, which 'every revelation of the divine, which places itself independently over against the Logos,' commits upon the 'Logos.' For κλέπτησ and λῃστήσ ('thief and robber') have for their object, not Jesus and his truth, but the sheep, as the preceding and succeeding context (compare, for example, the tenth verse) irrefutably shows. We must not dispose of the words thus arbitrarily in order to draw Gnostic references from them.

Or they have sought the solution of the exegetical riddle in ἦλθον ('came'). But in itself ἦλθον has no evil side notion, such as: of one's own motion without divine vocation (for example, Augustine), or the like. Nor is the

---

[1] Hilgenfeld, *Das Evangelium und die Briefe Johannis nach ihrem Lehrbegriff dargestellt*, Leipzig 1849, p. 266, note.

[2] Hilgenfeld, *Zeitschrift für wissenschaftliche Theologie*, 1870, p. 266, and *Historisch-kritische Einleitung in das Neue Testament*, Leipzig 1875, p. 723. Against him, see Weiss, *Der johanneische Lehrbegriff*, Berlin 1862, p. 106; and Beyschlag, *Studien und Kritiken*, 1875, p. 245, appealing to v. 45 and xii. 38.

position of ἦλθον at the front to be so pressed, as that the emphasizing of his own person would be thereby indicated (thus I earlier, against which Meyer, rightly). That would be putting too much into the text. Nor does it do any good to urge εἰσίν ('are'), in the sense that ἦλθον also must refer to the time of Christ (Bengel, Lücke, Baumgarten-Crusius). A thing can perfectly well be said of historical persons in the present tense, if something is to be said about them which is true of them once for all. If any one desires to say that it refers to false Messiahs (Chrysostom, Cyril, Weizsäcker [1]), it is only to be said that there is no justification for such an anachronism.

The difficulty lies in the generality of the expression. But this generality is limited by the context and by the situation. Jesus speaks, although in a general form, to his opponents and about his opponents. They all have come forward without receiving their title from the Messiah,—historically, therefore, from Jesus Christ, as for instance the Baptist, compare i. 23,—but sought their title, in view of the church of God, in their own person, in their knowledge of the law, orthodoxy, legal righteousness, and so forth. And yet they appeared with the claim that they were the necessary leaders of the nation unto salvation. This does not lie in the ἦλθον, but is a matter of necessity from the whole historical connection.

Concerning all these Jesus expresses the condemning judgment that they are thieves and robbers; thieves, who only seek their own advantage—'lucro suo, clam' ('their own gain, secretly'), Bengel,—robbers, who seek it so openly as to injure the flock—'ovium damno, aperte' ('with harm to the flock, openly'), Bengel. When, moreover, he now adds: πρὸ ἐμοῦ ('before me'), we are not to think of Moses and the prophets,—they are utterly out of the question,—but of the predecessors of the party hostile to Jesus. He pursues his soul-destroying opponents back historically to the earlier time, into the beginnings of this corruption in Israel; similarly Meyer. But a division has begun to take

---

[1] Weizsäcker, *Untersuchungen über die evangelische Geschichte, ihre Quellen und den Gang ihrer Entwicklung*, Gotha 1864, p. 526.

effect. *The sheep did not hear them.* Jesus takes the beginning for the whole. The true sheep have begun to listen to Jesus' voice and to leave the other teachers. This is designated as already consummated, as for example in iii. 19.

VERSE 9.

Jesus said previously, that in him and only in him was mediated duly the entrance of the shepherd to the flock. Now he adds, that through him alone — δι' ἐμοῦ ('by me') is put first, in this exclusive sense—also all blessed pastoral activity is mediated. Lücke and Meyer, against most commentators (for example, Chrysostom, Bengel, De Wette, Baumgarten-Crusius, Hengstenberg, Godet), are certainly right in declaring that the subject is not now of a sudden the sheep, but, as before, the shepherd. How could it then read: δι' ἐμοῦ ἐάν τισ εἰσέλθῃ, instead of ἐξέλθῃ ('by me if any man enter in,' instead of 'go out')? For we have thus far only heard that the shepherd goes in to the sheep by him. If the discourse were to pass over to these, we should have to read, in the first place, that these also only by going out through him find the true pasture.

As, then, Paul, 1 Tim. iv. 16, writes to his Timothy: τοῦτο ποιῶν καὶ σεαυτὸν σώσεισ καὶ τοὺσ ἀκούοντάσ σου ('for in doing this thou shalt both save thyself and them that hear thee'), so does Jesus here speak concerning the true shepherd in general. For although the σώζεσθαι ('saving') in the figure denotes first the sheltering and delivering from danger without, before the fold (Meyer), yet that finds its truth in the Messianic σωτηρία ('salvation'). It is not as if the σωτηρία consisted in that which follows as a second thing; but this concerns first itself, the other point concerns the flock. The true shepherd wins for himself that σωτηρία, and for his flock, free and secure exit and entrance and rich pasture.

VERSE 10.

If in the above lies the thought, how full of blessing the

activity of the true shepherd in his calling is, the verse now before us offers the contrast to that, as the eighth verse offered the contrast to the seventh. Hence it does not seem to me to be right to begin a new section with ver. 10. Moreover, the thought, how ruinous the action of the false shepherd is, calls forth the contrasted thought, how rich in blessing, on the contrary, His action is; and this of itself leads to the new turn given to the figure in the next verse, ver. 11 (thus also Meyer). In this way ver. 10 forms the middle member. The thief comes to steal; He, to give; the former, to satisfy himself upon the others (Ps. xiv. 4; Ezek. xxxiv. 2, 3); He, to bestow the blessing of life; the former, to lead into ruin of body and soul (against Lampe); He, to give the fulness of the blessing.

(*c.*) VERSES 11–18.

All saving vocation in the kingdom of God is based in him, mediated by him. This comprehensive declaration is expressed by the figure of the door. He imparts all the fulness of the blessing of salvation: the discourse at the close had passed over to this comprehensive promise. He gives himself up for the salvation of his own, who are to be gathered in every place: this is the comprehensive glance at the strength of his loving disposition, at the warmth of his loving fellowship, at the future of his loving activity, which is displayed in the now succeeding section.

There, he placed himself at the end of Israel, as the aim which lay at the base of and mediated all saving vocation in Israel, and therefore as the end and aim of the old time. Here, he places himself at the beginning of the new time, as Lord, shepherd, founder of the new church of God, which is to be gathered in all places of the earth. That can only be true of one who is at once the Son of Man and of God. The disposition, moreover, and the deed, with which he takes up the leadership of the time beginning with him, is the self-sacrificing devotion of love. This, therefore, will be the characteristic of the new time and church of Christ. Hence the whole demeanour of God in Christ is comprehended in one, when it is designated as love. The demeanour, moreover, of the flock to the shepherd is one of a confident devotion. In consequence, the right behaviour of man towards God and Christ consists first in this, and therefore in belief.

We find accordingly the same thoughts, that hitherto as witness and as claim have lain at the basis of all Jesus' action and speech, and of the whole gospel, here repeated with such modification of form as was occasioned by the different character of the self-proclamation, which here has become the warmest utterance of the soul. That which previously was to be learned by way of thought, is now mediated by the feelings, to stamp itself upon the receptive soul. Yet, although everything here seems to issue in loving disposition and conduct, the word itself is avoided. Jesus has not yet so far left the realm of the contrast and addressed himself so exclusively to his relation to his own, that the point of love should come to its pure, full, and decided expression.

It is well known how thoroughly the figure and the material view, which lies at the base of Jesus' whole discourse, is rooted in and taken from the Old Testament; compare for example, Ps. xxiii.; Isa. xl. 11 ; Jer. xxiii.; Ezek. xxxiv. 23, xxxvii. 24; Zech. xi. When the thought desires to choose the most fervent expression for the present relation of grace, or for that which is to be expected in the Messianic period, it chooses this figure. Not a single side, but the entire relation of Jehovah and of his people is summarized in it. Hence, therefore, Jesus declares that the most ardent communion of love between Israel and its God, as partly temporarily present in the Old Testament, and partly promised in it as complete, is given and fulfilled in him. This figure rests upon the historical leading of Israel from the beginning onwards. He desires it therefore to be understood that he is the goal of the entire history of Israel. In the first instance, the figure only serves to designate the peculiar pre-eminence of Israel over the other nations, in its relation to God. Here, however, starting from the ground of Israel, it gains an importance also for the other nations. Jesus in this way shows that with him as the goal of Israel, the universalism decreed in the particularism of the Old Testament, often enough witnessed to by the Old Testament, is dawning and enters upon history.

Verse 11.

I am the good shepherd. There was no Israelite, who, if he knew his Old Testament but to a certain degree, must not at this self-proclamation of Jesus: ἐγώ εἰμι ὁ ποιμὴν ὁ καλόσ ('I am the good shepherd'), be reminded of the similar announcements of the Messianic time. Although the article is not meant (against Bengel) as such a recalling, but is intended to emphasize the speaker strongly as the good shepherd, still that retrospective glance lay in the thing itself. This reference also explains the καλόσ ('good') which takes the place of the ἀληθινόσ ('true') common to John. The weight of the καλόσ lies in the article: 'the' good shepherd absolutely, the realization of the ideal as contained in the Old Testament. Because there, as for example in Ezek. xxxiv., 'shepherds' are spoken of who attended ill upon their calling, Jesus here designates himself as the shepherd who fulfils his calling well.

At first now he speaks generally of such a shepherd, before he then, in ver. 14, applies it to himself. He describes the shepherd in contrast with the hireling—a figure offered of itself by the progress of the thought, and to be taken in the ethical sense. In the one he has the Pharisees in view, as in the other himself; but he no more names them than he does himself. He leaves it to their own conscience to make the application, which became so much the easier for them when he afterwards explained the positive side of the figure as referring to himself. The very fact that he explains only this and not the negative side of the picture, shows that also in vers. 11-13 he was in the first instance concerned only with the former. He could not do otherwise in the mood which, as we have seen, expresses itself in the entire discourse, and above all in this third section.

In order to characterize the good shepherd, Jesus names at once the highest expression of a shepherd's love, one which contains it all. Ψυχὴν τιθέναι ('to give one's life') (Matt. xx. 28, δοῦναι τὴν ψυχήν) is a characteristic Johannean expression; compare xiii. 37 f., xv. 13; 1 John iii. 16; not used elsewhere either in profane Greek or in the Septuagint; here five times, 'summa vi; hoc summo omnia reliqua beneficia pastoralia praesupponuntur, includuntur, referuntur' ('with the utmost force; in this highest benefit the remaining pastoral benefits are presupposed, included, told'), Bengel.

It is well known (see, for example, Baumgarten-Crusius) that this does not mean to venture his life, but really to give it up. The word itself is explained by its being used for paying, τιθέναι = 'impendere,' and not as Godet, for example, says, in the sense of putting off, compare xiii. 4, ἱμάτια τιθέναι ('to lay aside garments'), to give up his life voluntarily. Why, then, is not διδόναι ('to give') used? Besides, this would be spoken too indifferently concerning life, and too irrelevantly for the purpose of a devotion of life. The life is looked at as a ransom (Meyer), in the sense that the shepherd dies to keep the others from dying. The point of the deliverance by self-sacrifice is first given by the context. When there is no further alternative, the shepherd lays down his own life as a payment, to redeem the sheep from the approaching enemy who threatens to destroy the flock. Thus τιθέναι contains both the devotion and the freedom of this act. In the figure, the redeeming can indeed only thus take place, that, namely, the sheep gain time for deliverance by the self-sacrifice of the shepherd. But this trait is not applied here; the thing in question is only the fact that the free devotion of the life of the shepherd is the redemption of the life of the sheep.

In this sense then is ὑπέρ said, not: instead of, but: for the good of, for the advantage of, 'in order by his own sacrifice to turn away the destruction from them' (Meyer). This does not deny that Jesus died also for other men; the limitation to the sheep is caused by the picture.

VERSE 12.

In contrast with this, the hireling gives up the herd

under his care to the enemy, in order thereby to secure his own life. It is true the wolf here in the figure is in the first instance every enemy of the church of God in general (De Wette, against Olshausen and Stier[1]), and that Jesus did not intend by the word to designate the devil in particular. But since all hostility towards the church of God has its basis in the devil, the wolf is indeed substantially the devil, especially if from this negative portion of the picture we supply the positive portion, and conceive to ourselves the wolf as the one to whom Jesus as the good shepherd τὴν ψυχὴν αὐτοῦ ἔθηκεν ('gave his life'). This completion of the thought is as properly allowed as the other, namely, to take from ἁρπάζει καὶ σκορπίζει ('catcheth and scattereth'), in ver. 12, the contents of the ὑπέρ in ver. 11.

Verse 13.

Deliverance of life, and gathering together, are what the life-sacrifice of the good shepherd unto the enemy of the flock is to gain for it, and this because the sheep lie on his heart. This, however, is not the case with the hireling.

Verses 14–16.

Jesus now says definitely that he desires what he has said of the good shepherd to be understood of himself. He here resumes also the thought which was so weighty in the first section of the parable: namely, that of the relation of fellowship which exists between the shepherd and the flock, ver. 3 f.; and he unites to this the chief thought from the beginning of the third section, vers. 11–18: that of the devotion of his life, ver. 11. The presupposition that the sheep even before the life-sacrifice of Jesus are his property, does not appear for the first time as the basis of these verses, vers. 12, 13; it is clearly contained even in vers. 3–5. There, we saw that it is the word of God by which and in which the shepherd and sheep recognise and belong to one another. Here, the shepherd is spoken of, and therefore here also it is the word by the reception of which, because it treats of Him and is His, they have

---

[1] Stier, *Reden Jesu*, 3d ed., Barmen and Elberfeld 1870, vol. iv. p. 538.

become the sheep of the shepherd,—the word, by the final revelation and appearance of which the sheep recognise the shepherd as their old shepherd, as the one who was ever their shepherd.

By the reception of the Old Testament word of God they have become the subjects of him who was to appear in the fulness of the time as 'the' word of God to men. By the reception of that word, for the sake of which they also accept him as the word, he recognises them as his own. And because he shows himself to be the fulfilment of that word, as the word, they recognise him as the one to whom they have belonged from the beginning, and who has given himself to them as their own, and promised himself as their shepherd. When, therefore, in ver. 16, Jesus passes beyond the sphere of Israel and here too speaks of sheep, it is meant proleptically, in so far as they shall be added to the flock. Bengel says: 'iam oves dicuntur, quia prævisæ' ('they are now called sheep, because foreseen'); and Lampe: 'denominatio a futuro eventu petitur' ('the designation is drawn from the future event').

Verse 14.

The relation of fellowship which rules between him and his own—for that γινώσκω is a 'knowledge' resting upon communion, is well known from the constant method of conception and of speech in the Scriptures[1]—proceeds from him. Καί ... καί ('and ... and'): Bengel observes: 'semper initium boni fit a Deo et Christo' ('the beginning of good always is from God and Christ'). The two sentences are apparently but externally placed side by side: *and I know mine, and mine know me* (ἐμά, sc. πρόβατα, 'mine,' namely, 'sheep'), according to John's method of adding sentence to sentence,[2] while, nevertheless, there is an internal relation of confirmation.

His loving recognition is the first; only after that follows the recognition on the part of men. If it be true of his,

---

[1] See Hofmann, *Der Schriftbeweis*, 2d ed., Nördlingen 1857, vol. i. pp. 258-262.

[2] Compare vol. i. p. 38 f.

that they have known him, much more is that other and fundamental fact true, that he has known them; Gal. iv. 9, νῦν δὲ γνόντεσ θεόν, μᾶλλον δὲ γνωσθέντεσ ὑπὸ θεοῦ ('but now, that ye have known God, or rather are known of God'); 2 Tim. ii. 19. The former is a proof that the latter is there; 1 Cor. viii. 3, εἰ δέ τισ ἀγαπᾷ τὸν θεόν, οὗτοσ ἔγνωσται ὑπ' αὐτοῦ ('but if any man love God, the same is known of him').

VERSE 15.

In this relation of fellowship is mirrored that existing between the Father and the Son. From this fact we may learn how intimate and full this former is. This comparison corresponds to the Johannean method of thought, the conceiving of the lower stages as analogous copies and repetitions of the higher. It is the spirit of analogy which pervades the thought and speech of the evangelist.[1] 'Sæpe habitus fidelium ad Christum deducitur ex habitu Christi proprio ad Patrem' ('the posture of believers towards Christ is often deduced from Christ's own posture towards the Father'), xiv. 20, xv. 10, xvii. 8, 21; Bengel. As in the former the communion proceeds from Christ, so also in an analogous manner this, that the Father knows him, is put first; that he knows the Father, is said in the second place. He knows that his eternal communion of love with the Father was established by the Father.

Since in the whole context only saving relations are spoken of, we are at once referred to these for the understanding of these words also. That is, we are referred to the eternal relation of the Son to the Father only in the sense in which it stands in connection with the eternal decree of love, and is determined by the same. Yet we must not forget that the historical relations into which God enters have their basis in the essential relations of God himself. In other words, the law of analogy, as it comes to view in our gospel as a divine law, justifies us in seeking the basis of this historical and gracious relation of Father and Son in their inner-divine, essential relation, as

[1] As to this spirit of analogy, see vol. i. p. 39.

in its higher analogy. The Father knows him, means accordingly here, in the first place: He stands in communion with him as Christ, that is, as the personal loving and saving thought of God. And (καί) thus also Christ knows him as his own basis, in so far as he is the appearance of the real loving and saving thought of God among men.

The contents of this divine thought of love was, however, that the Son should give up his life for his own. For this reason the words: καὶ τὴν ψυχήν μου τίθημι ὑπὲρ τῶν προβάτων ('and I lay down my life for the sheep'), join themselves directly to the other words: γινώσκω τὸν πατέρα ('I know the Father'). Jesus speaks of this devotion of his life in the present (τίθημι, 'I lay down'): for him it is already present. His death even is only the end of the way which he began with his entrance upon the world in general: 'tota illa vita Christi erat itio in mortem' ('that whole life of Christ was a going unto death'), Bengel. His death is the acme in the execution of the divine will of love, and therefore also of his historical and saving relation of communion with the Father. And yet his death seemed to be his ruin, and the denial of that divine fellowship. In the very union of these two sides lies the world-conquering and Godward-leading power of his death, and thus the discourse passes on to the Gentiles.

Verse 16.

It is beyond question that by ἄλλα πρόβατα ('other sheep') are meant the sheep of the Gentile world. And the comparison with xi. 52 shows that the love revealed in his death is the power which brings them together. Here, indeed, the 'idea of complete equality of birth' (Baumgarten-Crusius, Lücke) is not expressed; but neither must exegetes speak of 'the Johannean idea of the Gentiles' as τέκνα τοῦ θεοῦ ('children of God,' Brückner), since at least in expression this is a thought that cannot be accepted. Those who do not belong to the αὐλή ('fold') of Israel, are those who live outside of the hedge of the law, form no flock (against De Wette; for the accent lies, not on ταύτησ, 'this,' but on αὐλή; Bengel says: 'alias oves dicit, non aliud ovile; erant enim dispersæ in mundo,' 'he says other sheep, not another fold; for they were scattered in the world'), and hence are devoid of leading.

In spite of that they are called πρόβατα ('sheep'). This is not because they for the present already belonged to Christ by their conscientious obedience. I held this view earlier; and Weiss[1] says: 'a moral condition of likeness to God, by which they have become ready to receive the revelation in Christ, who therefore makes them his sheep, even before they know him.' Nevertheless, this view is to be rejected, as against the constant Scripture view of the children of God. For the Scriptures know nothing of a temporary relation of children of God to him.[2] On the contrary, the thing here spoken of is, as in xi. 52, that which did not indeed exist as yet, but which should come into being. They are not yet πρόβατα, because they do not yet belong to the flock, that is, to the people of God, but they are to become sheep. Because this is beyond question, the present is used: ἔχω, 'I have.' Bengel remarks: 'hoc verbum habet magnam potestatem' ('this word has great force'). Jesus does not merely know them, but he has them, they belong to him, he is their owner. For them too must he become shepherd.

Ἐκεῖνα ('those'), not ταῦτα ('these'), since they still lie without the narrowest sphere of sight. But it is God's will (δεῖ, 'must') that he become their shepherd. Thus is ἀγαγεῖν in fact to be understood. It is not: 'to lead hither' (Tholuck, Hengstenberg, Godet, I too earlier), but according to the word: lead, precede them as shepherd, so that they follow (Meyer). 'Non dicit: educere, uti v. 3, neque introducere in hoc ovile, sed simpliciter, ducere. Non opus est illis solum mutare' ('he does not say: to lead out, as ver. 3, or to lead into this fold, but simply, to lead. They do not need to change ground'), Bengel. The exalted one is their shepherd. The ἀκούειν ('hearing') on their part corresponds to the 'leading.'

And there shall be one flock and one shepherd: a flock made

[1] Weiss, *Der Johanneische Lehrbegriff*, Berlin 1862, p. 124.
[2] Compare Luthardt, *Die Lehre vom freien Willen*, Leipzig 1863, p. 421.

up of the two parts, Israel and the Gentile world, united to the one church of God under the one shepherd Jesus Christ. This saying therefore removes for the church of Christ the dividing importance of national and in general of natural distinctions, which from the pre-Christian standpoint formed the dividing boundaries both for the religious and for the general human life. It still has its application to-day, against a false emphasizing of nationality in the sphere of the church, which would be a renewing of the pre-Christian standpoint. Yet, on the other hand, as necessarily follows, it is not to be used—as often happens—in a sentimental way, or in the interest of doctrinal indefiniteness, against the right of separate churches and of the creed and the like.

It serves, indeed, as an expression of the longing which lives in all Christian hearts, that all distinctions may ever yield more and more to the full unity of belief, of love, and so forth. For it found its earliest fulfilment in the summoning and gathering the heathen into the church of Christ. But in the course of history it finds its progressive realization up to the final goal of complete unity, when $\tau\grave{o}\ \pi\lambda\acute{\eta}\rho\omega\mu\alpha\ \tau\hat{\omega}\nu\ \grave{\epsilon}\theta\nu\hat{\omega}\nu$ ('the fulness of the Gentiles') shall have come in, and then also Israel shall own its Messiah, Rom. xi. 25 ff. 'Hæc unitas gregis, hæc unitas pastoris cœpit, postquam bonus pastor animam suam posuit, xi. 52; et suo tempore, sufflamine omni sublato, consummabitur. De jure Jesus semper unicus *est* pastor; de jure et facto igitur unus *fiet*' ('This oneness of the flock, this oneness of the shepherd, begins after the good shepherd hath laid down his life, xi. 52; and in its own time, every hindrance being removed, it will be consummated. By right, Jesus always is the one only shepherd; by right and in fact, therefore, he will become the one'), Bengel. This saying concerning the one flock and the one shepherd combines the corresponding Old Testament prophecies of the Messianic future, which will gather all nations about Zion, and in which Jehovah 'will be king over all lands,' Zech. xiv. 9.[1]

---

[1] See Oehler, *Theologie des alten Testamentes*, Tübingen 1874, vol. ii. p. 247 ff.

This summary of Old Testament prophecy has become, then, the basis of the apostolic, and especially of the Pauline, knowledge and doctrine. Following Lampe's example,[1] Lücke and Olshausen recall the chief passage, Eph. ii. 14 ff., in which the μεσότοιχον ('middle wall') between Israel and the Gentile world is spoken of, the wall which was removed by the death of Christ. One shepherd then assumed the leadership of both, in so far as the heathen, before χωρὶσ Χριστοῦ (' without Christ '), now are ἐν Χριστῷ Ἰησοῦ ('in Christ Jesus'), Eph. ii. 12, 13. Hence that which Paul calls the μυστήριον ('mystery') which was revealed to him, and by the preaching of which they could recognise his insight into the secret of Christ, Eph. iii. 3 ff., rests, as do all apostolic knowledge, doctrine, and preaching, upon words of Christ's.

Paul, however, would not be satisfied with gathering the Gentiles into the church of God as it formed itself in Israel. He busied himself, as for instance in gathering the love-gifts of the Gentile Christians, in making more intimate, and in confirming the unity of the two parts. Nor did he look upon this as a thing he could let alone if he liked. He regarded it as a necessary action which was included in his special vocation. He also speaks of a unity of belief and of knowledge, which is a thing of the future, towards which the church is ripening, Eph. iv. 13. All this justifies us, not in limiting the unity of which Christ speaks to the unity of the objective blessings of salvation, but in extending it to the unity of the subjective possession of salvation and of the uniting fellowship of love.

Jesus first said, vers. 11-13, of what description the true shepherd was. Then, vers. 14-16, he added, that this applied to him, since he, in which indeed the characteristic mark of the true shepherd consisted, would give his life for the sheep. Now, in vers. 17, 18, he says that he does this with the most entire freedom, and for this reason in each of the two verses an ἐγώ (' I ') is added to the previous τίθημι τὴν ψυχήν μου (' I lay down my life ').

---

[1] Lampe, *Commentarius* . . . *Evangelii secundum Joannem*, Amsterdam 1726, vol. ii. p. 669.

Verse 17.

It is not proper to make ὁ πατὴρ ἀγαπᾷ με ('the Father loveth me') in this verse the chief thought (Baumgarten-Crusius, Meyer), or to put it on a level with the thought of the freedom of his action (De Wette, Lücke), since it is, on the contrary, subordinate to this latter thought. Διὰ τοῦτό με ὁ πατὴρ ἀγαπᾷ ('therefore doth my Father love me'), moreover, forms the connecting thought for what is said in ver. 17, for the sake of the point of view under which Jesus had previously placed his devotion of his life. Διὰ τοῦτο ('therefore') points to the following ὅτι ('because'); his Father loves him because he gives up his life for his sheep. Ὅτι gives us the ground of the Father's love from this point of view. The eternal relation of love between him and the Father completes itself historically. If, now, there be a loving posture of the Father towards him in so far as and because he is the loving thought of God which has entered into extra-divine history, so much the more will there be a loving posture of God towards him in so far as and because he gives himself freely unto death; compare Eph. v. 2: 'an offering and a sacrifice to God for a sweet-smelling savour' (Godet). The peculiarly emphatic point of the progress in thought in this passage is the freedom of Jesus' action.

Because Jesus, in announcing His death, lays especial stress on this point, the evangelist does the same in his historical account. It appears in no other to the extent it does in the case of the fourth evangelist. It is connected with the entire task which he has set before himself. The proof of the freedom with which Jesus goes into death is intended to aid in proving his divine sonship. Such, therefore, is the character of the announcement of His death, which the evangelist has interwoven with his history of Jesus' self-testification. It is distinguished from the synoptic announcements of His death, much as the twofold reports of the death are distinguished from each other. Our evangelist will teach us how to judge rightly concerning Jesus' death, for he is throughout busy with the essence and substance of the history.

If, however, Jesus gives up his life unto death, he does it only in order to take it again. He has this intention therein. Hence we read: ἵνα πάλιν λάβω αὐτήν ('that I might take it again'). For this does not belong with ἀγαπᾷ ('loveth'), but with τίθημι ('I lay down'), and designates not merely the result or the condition (De Wette), but the design of Jesus' devotion unto death. This design, moreover, is not the design of God, since, indeed, ἵνα ('that') belongs to the confirming God's love, but the design of Jesus. He will take his life again, in order as the glorified one to exercise his office as shepherd, and particularly to gather the heathen (Eph. ii. 17 : καὶ ἐλθὼν εὐηγγελίσατο εἰρήνην ὑμῖν τοῖσ μακράν, 'and came—in the spirit as the glorified one — and preached peace to you which were far off').

Verse 18.

These words explain the freedom of his action; as he has power to give up his life, so also hath he power again to resume possession of it. Such commission hath he received from his Father, namely, that he give up his life in order to take it again. *No man taketh it from me, but I* (ἐγώ, emphatically) *lay it down of myself.* Ἀπ' ἐμαυτοῦ, 'mea ipsius sponte,' 'of my own accord.' Bengel says : 'Sua sponte Jesus se hostibus capiendum permisit; et in ipsa cruce, non debilitate ulla, sed cum clamore spiritum emisit' ('Jesus let himself be taken by his enemies of his own accord; and on the very cross he sent forth his spirit, not in any weakness, but with a shout'). God's will gave him authority (ἐξουσία) to do this; for, for this purpose (ταύτην), namely, to give up his life and to take it again, did God commission him (ἐντολήν) when he entered into the subjection to the Father contained in his saving vocation. Ἐντολή ('commandment') designates the calling transferred to him by the Father, which includes both his resurrection and his death.

The Scriptures elsewhere teach constantly that the Father raised up the Son, and this text does not rebut that statement. Jesus' former words do not mean that he will kill himself; and as little do the others mean that he will call himself back again, or raise himself up again into life. Men brought him into death; but what they did came to pass at the same time according to his will, so that it would not have come to pass without that. The Father has called him back again into life; yet this also with his will, and so that it would not have come to pass without that. Slaying and raising have been experienced by him; yet he did not merely submit to both, but he himself also wished both, and helped to bring them about. In consequence, λαβεῖν ('to take') does not mean a taking which might stand in contrast with receiving (De Wette against Meyer), and not merely a receiving or accepting of something given, but a reception of life by the Son which comes to meet the resurrection on the part of the Father, and which joins itself to that resurrection. In this reception of life he made himself free from the bonds of Hades. Hence an action on the part of the Son met in each case; in the former, the action of men; in the latter, the action of the Father.

Jesus now must say this, in order that they may then also recognise it in the events. But after he said it, it is also possible to perceive it. The recognition of this double power, which he has proved in his death and in his resurrection, serves also to promote the recognition of his divine Sonship. For he has therein shown himself to be one who is not subject to the necessary law of death, and as one who is in essential possession of life. In consequence, therefore, his being must be based beyond a world and a life both of which are fallen under the dominion of death. He springs from the world of life, and is only come into this world of death. He bears life essentially in himself, and only goes into the suffering of death. How else could the power be his in death to take his human life again unto himself? And further, he must have been before he became man, and he only entered into human form: how else could he have such a power over his human life as not merely to let death take it, but to give it to death, so that in the very removal of his self-activity as man He is himself most peculiarly active? Accordingly, it is Christ as the Son of God, in the sense in which we have understood this word from the first, who desires to be recognised in this. Such display of his ἐξουσία ('authority') now forms, it is true, the contents of the ἐντολὴ τοῦ πατρόσ ('commandment of the Father'); but we may not therefore say that it is merely 'transferred power,' in contradistinction to that which is really his own (De Wette, against Olshausen), since it rather is necessarily given and contained with and in his divine Sonship.

The prophecy of the resurrection here has been found to be indefinite (De Wette). It is as definite as the prophecy of his death. Indeed, this πάλιν λαβεῖν ('to take again') stands in direct contrast with τιθέναι ('to lay down'). Moreover, the fact is not to be named here as such, from its historical side, but is to be taught in its importance. The evangelist has this constantly in view in his reporting. Compare what was said concerning Jesus' death.[1] Jesus at the beginning witnessed to himself as light in the figure of the shepherd, but as τὸ φῶσ τῆσ ζωῆσ ('the light of life'). He proclaims the saving blessing of ζωή ('life') to the degree, that his discourse withdraws itself from the sphere of the contrast. And he shows this saving blessing unfolded for all the world in that event in which he will display himself as the life itself.

These words had nothing else to which they could appeal than Jesus' person. For they went far beyond the realm of the miraculous deed on which they followed. The hearers therefore must needs credit Jesus' person with such power for its own sake; they must believe. He who, by reason of the impression which Jesus' person had made on him, could persuade himself of this, must have received from these words a great strengthening and securing of his belief. For it taught him to understand those events, and made him recognise in them a proof of the Son of God, above all, the fact of the death, which more than any other was a trial of belief. He who could not agree to this, could only perceive in these words an expression of insane presumption. This fact showed itself in the result of Jesus' words.

[1] See above, p. 366 f.

Verse 19.

There was a division again, as at ix. 16, *among the Jews* —thus, in John's method, the Pharisaic opponents of Jesus, ix. 40, are designated, in order to characterize them in their posture of opposition to Jesus—*because of these words.* For the majority, Jesus' words were in vain, and were only the occasion of violent contradiction.

Verse 20.

Πολλοί, *many*, therefore the majority, *said, He hath a devil, and is mad.* They cleave to their former decision. *Why hear ye him?* They seem to be ashamed that they have allowed Jesus' words to fetter them so long. It is not: what is the use of listening to his discourses (Meyer); but: we must not hear him at all. They withdraw themselves purposely from all influence. 'Plena periculi res, ubi vel auditui renunciatur' ('the thing is full of danger, when even hearing is given up'), Bengel.

Verse 21.

Others had not been able to withstand altogether the impression which the miracle had made upon them. The miracle of healing the blind man seemed to them too great for a demon to have been able to bring it about. For narrow limits are appointed to the demons. They may have thought of the limits of the miraculous power of the Egyptian sorcerers in contrast to Moses. They are even less prejudiced and more accessible; compare ix. 16. But because it was not the person of Jesus, but only the miracle as such, they did not advance beyond the merely negative result; we cannot judge of him in the way that those men judge. But what his importance was, what was to be thought of him and of his word: for this they knew no answer.

(3.) Verses 22–42.

The following section brings us into the same situation. After that Jesus' first miracle in Jerusalem had gained him a certain applause, which, however, was of no moral value, the healings on the Sabbath served to bring the relation to decision. The evangelist causes us to perceive the progress of this, on the thread of three miraculous deeds. The first, in the fifth chapter, had brought the disposition against him to a preliminary decision, vers. 16, 18; the memory of this, vii. 21, served to give Jesus' words, in the eighth chapter, only a so much the more incisive and soul-revealing power. The enmity now made known, which believed that it found its justification both in the word and history of the Old Testament and in the vocation of Israel, is met by the new event of the healing the blind man, with such evidence and urgency that no one could easily withdraw himself from its influence. The uncertainty of bearing brought about by this, was led to new decision by Jesus' clear self-testification as God's Son, which was unbearable for unbelief. And then the third miraculous deed, the raising of Lazarus, gave occasion to the decisive act of the judicial decree.

Externally viewed, indeed, x. 39 forms no climax to viii. 59, but substantially it does. For while the words of Jesus in the eighth chapter are much more sharp and provoking, in this chapter they have a much more thetical stamp, and are much less of a challenging nature, so that therefore the new outbreak of hostility causes us to infer a further progress in the mood of hostility. Besides, the opposition had been in the meanwhile shaken by the new healing which had interposed, and had occasioned a greater favourableness of disposition. Hence the renewal of the hostile conduct was the more reprehensible.

From the method of the narrative we cannot infer that, in the two months between tabernacles and the feast of the dedication of the temple, Jesus stayed in Jerusalem and its neighbourhood (Bengel, Tholuck, Olshausen, Meyer, Stier, Lücke, Wieseler [1]). We have no right to say, that if he had gone to Galilee or Perea, the evangelist would have expressed this (Lücke), since he was here concerned solely

[1] Wieseler, *Chronologische Synopse der vier Evangelien*, Hamburg 1843, p. 318, note.

about the internal connection. What lay between was of no importance for him. He gives only so much of the external circumstances, ver. 22 f., as belongs to the most necessary historical frame, and as has for him at the same time a value for the matter itself. At the close of the fifth chapter, the return of Jesus to Galilee is not mentioned, and yet is unquestionable, and as little did a like return need to be mentioned here (see Godet).

Jesus did not indeed go from Galilee to Jerusalem expressly on account of this feast, but, aside from it, he had already moved into the neighbourhood of the capital. The time of his Galilean activity was at an end. From the synoptists, if in the incompleteness of the Johannean historical narrative we may call them in to supply the gap, we perceive that Jesus in the late autumn had left Galilee for ever, and had gone over to Perea, Matt. xix. 1, where he spent the winter continuing the activity he had exercised in Galilee, passing from place to place along the Jordan, and thus coming into the neighbourhood of Jerusalem.[1] This led him then to visit the feast of the dedication of the temple at Jerusalem. And indeed he did not come to satisfy his duty as a Jew, but for the sake of the many people whom he here found gathered together.

VERSE 22.

The feast of the dedication of the temple, חֲנֻכָּה, ἐγκαίνια, feast of renewing, was appointed (1 Macc. iv. 56 ff., 2 Macc. x. 6 ff.) by Judas Maccabeus for the celebration of the purification and dedication of the temple, which had been desecrated by Antiochus Epiphanes (consecration of the new-built altar of burnt-offering, 1 Macc. iv. 59). It was celebrated on the 25th of Kislev (December) for eight days by brilliant illumination of the houses in Jerusalem and in every place.[2] There was no obligation to visit Jerusalem; the feast was celebrated all over the land. The addition of ἐν Ἱεροσο-

---

[1] Lichtenstein, *Lebensgeschichte des Herrn Jesu Christi in chronologischer Uebersicht*, Erlangen 1856, pp. 28 f., 320 f.

[2] See Keil, *Handbuch der biblischen Archäologie*, Frankfort-on-the-Main and Erlangen 1858, vol. i. p. 420.

λύμοισ ('at Jerusalem') is not made because Jesus was still in Jerusalem (Meyer), but because he went thither. This he did, as we have seen, not for the fulfilment of a religious duty, but in the service of his calling. Hence also a ἑορτή, 'feast,' is not mentioned here as it is elsewhere; ii. 23, v. 1, vi. 4, vii. 2. To this, too, refers the observation: χειμὼν ἦν, *it was winter;* not: it was stormy weather (Lampe, after Matt. xvi. 3), which would have had no bearing on the context. Nor is this a merely external note. It is occasioned by, or has its reason in, the context. It is not merely added to explain for the Gentile-Christian readers the subsequently-mentioned walking in Solomon's porch (Meyer); why should John mention that? and could not Jesus, moreover, tarry in this porch as well as the early Christians? This phrase serves the thought of the evangelist in general: neither by the lately-experienced hostility of the Jews, nor by the wintry season of the year, did Jesus let himself be kept from making still another attempt.[1]

VERSE 23.

Solomon's porch was a colonnade on the east side of the temple; hence called by Josephus[2] ἡ ἀνατολική ('the eastern'). According to Josephus, it took its name from the circumstance that it was said to come from Solomon's temple, to have been left standing when Nebuchadnezzar destroyed that temple. Meyer says that this note indicates an eye-witness. But why should this note be given at all? It is only in order 'to call the attention of readers ignorant of the Jewish festal-calendar to the fact that the bad season of the year compelled Jesus to withdraw from the open air to the covered walk of the temple.' (Thus Lücke and most commentators.) Why, then, is not the temple in general named? There is a reason for naming the place expressly. We know from the book of Acts that the apostles and early Christians as well, liked to stay in Solomon's porch; see Acts

---

[1] Compare vol. i. p. 72 f., and Lichtenstein, *Lebensgeschichte des Herrn Jesu Christi in chronologischer Uebersicht,* Erlangen 1856, p. 321.

[2] Josephus, *Antiquitates,* XX. ix. 7; *Opera,* ed. Bekker, Leipzig 1856, vol. iv. p. 279.

iii. 11. The evangelist names the place for the sake of this its historical importance, which was known to the readers of the gospel. And the readers of the gospel knew the place from the same source from which we draw our knowledge of it, namely, from the Acts. If, however, the author of our gospel be the apostle John, the naming becomes still more easy of explanation. What a rich store of recollections were knit to this place for him! Why, however, Jesus chose just this place, and whether he did it in order 'to express in a sensible figure the unity of the old and of the new covenant,' as Thiersch[1] thinks, we shall have to leave undecided.

Verse 24.

Here he walked up and down, silently; for he had nothing more that was new to say to the Jews. What was necessary for them to know in order to believe on him as the Christ, or to own him as such, this he had said to them, and they knew it or might know it. But the blame, it is alleged, belongs not to them, but to Jesus; he does not declare himself freely and openly, and hence they do not know how to judge of him. *They surrounded him*—'quam gratum id fuisset salvatori, si fecissent in fide!' ('how pleasing would that have been to the Saviour, had they done it in faith!'), Bengel—urgently, and forcing their words upon him: καὶ ἔλεγον ('and said'), 'importuno frementis naturæ impetu' ('with the importunate impetus of a raging nature'), Bengel. It is not with an earnest purpose, perhaps half inclined to belief (against Hengstenberg), but in a positive way, and in the sense of a reproach against Jesus. They complain of Jesus for the circumstance that they do not do what he demands. Not merely is his claim said to be unjustified, but also his conduct is said to be wrong, because by it he keeps their soul in constant tension and uncertainty concerning that which yet is for an Israelite the highest and most important thing.

How long dost thou hold our soul in suspense? Αἴρειν

---

[1] Thiersch, *Die Kirche im apostolischen Zeitalter*, Frankfort-on-the-Main and Erlangen 1852, p. 73.

here, as throughout : to lift up, and thus to put in suspense, tension, 'suspensam tenes' ('thou holdest suspended'), Bengel. *If thou be the Messiah, tell us plainly.* 'Quasi vero nunquam dixerit et ostenderit.... Sæpe cogitamus : si hoc illove modo expressum audirem aut legerem, credere possem. Sed Deus solus scit, quomodo nobiscum loqui deceat ad fidem nostram alendam et exercendam' ('As if, indeed, he never has told and shown it.... We often think : If I could hear or read it expressed in this or that way, I could believe. But God alone knows how it is fitting to speak to us in order to cherish and exercise our faith'), Bengel. It is true that Jesus had not said it, and he never testified to himself in Jerusalem so plainly and roundly as, for instance, to the Samaritan woman at Jacob's well. Yet he had told it clearly enough for them to be able to know that it was he, for him to be able to say he had told it, and for it to be possible for them themselves to confess : σὺ εἶ ὁ Χριστόσ, ὁ υἱὸσ τοῦ θεοῦ ('thou art the Christ, the Son of God'), Matt. xvi. 16. If they could never have done it before, they could do it now.

VERSE 25.

For when Jesus says, εἶπον ὑμῖν ('I told you'), the words contain the answer to their question, and that an affirmative answer. Hence also he can follow this with the claim for belief, or rather with the reproach against their unbelief. If his word be not sufficient, he reminds them of the legitimation from his Father in the ἔργοισ ('works'). He recalls these to them ; for the healing of the blind man was still in fresh memory. They need only to draw from his works the necessary conclusion as to his vocation and his person.[1] But τοσαῦτα αὐτοῦ σημεῖα πεποιηκότοσ ἔμπροσθεν αὐτῶν οὐκ ἐπίστευον εἰσ αὐτόν ('though he had done so many miracles before them, they believed not on him'), xii. 37. And thus it appears that the blame does not lie on his, but on their side.

---

[1] Weiss, *Der Johanneische Lehrbegriff in seinen Grundzügen untersucht*, Berlin 1862, pp. 197 ff., 202.

Verse 26.

Hence in this verse ὑμεῖσ ('ye') is added emphatically to οὐ πιστεύετε ('believe not'); compare on the other hand, v. 40. But, in return, the reason for their not-believing is from a point still farther back, namely, the fact that they do not belong to his πρόβατα ('sheep'), that is, to the true people of God. Of course, this is not said in the anti-Judaistic or in the dualistic sense (against Hilgenfeld[1]). Were they sheep of his, believing obedience, the relation of fellowship, and following of him would be there. The discourse moves in the same figure as in the preceding section, although καθὼσ εἶπον ὑμῖν ('as I said unto you') at the close of ver. 26—which would refer not merely to the figure, but also to the negative statement itself (Meyer) —is to be struck out, according to the testimony of the manuscripts; it is omitted in ℵ B K L, and found in A D E F G H. It was very easy to insert these words in recollection of the preceding discourse of Jesus (against Meyer). Least of all are the words to be taken as an introduction to what follows (against Tholuck, Godet). It is not Jesus' habit to bring in long quotations of his own earlier discourses (Meyer).

It has been said that only the evangelist, and not Jesus, could have the words previously spoken so directly present (for example, Baur[2]). Why should it not have been possible that these were the same Jews who had heard the discourse spoken at the feast of tabernacles, and whom Jesus desires to remind of the words then spoken? But this supposition is not at all necessary, for the figure of the shepherd is sufficiently familiar, especially from the Old Testament, for Jesus to have been able to use it more than once; see Ebrard.[3] Hence we shall not be forced to transfer 'the first shepherd-discourse' to the middle time between

---

[1] Hilgenfeld, for example, in the *Zeitschrift für wissenschaftliche Theologie*, 1870, p. 270.

[2] Baur, *Kritische Untersuchungen über die kanonischen Evangelien*, Tübingen 1847, p. 181.

[3] Ebrard, *Wissenschaftliche Kritik der evangelischen Geschichte*, 3d ed., Frankfort-on-the-Main 1868, p. 544.

the two feasts (Stier,[1] following Bengel). For if the second discourse is to be supposed to refer to the first, that is quite possible if Jesus after the first discourse withdrew from Jerusalem and now visited it again for the first time, because that would make the discourse stand out more strongly in memory. But it would not be possible if Jesus remained in Jerusalem in unceasing activity, and therefore also giving doctrinal instruction, because then other discourses would have followed that one.

VERSES 27, 28.

The description of the relation of the sheep to the shepherd shows plainly that the Jews did not belong to the sheep. *My sheep hear my voice, and I know them, and they follow me: and I give unto them eternal life; and they shall never perish, neither shall any man pluck them out of my hand.* Bengel found here: 'tria sententiarum paria, quorum singula et ovium fidem et pastoris bonitatem exprimunt per correlata' ('three pairs of sentences, each of which expresses in correlated terms both the faith of the sheep and the goodness of the shepherd'); but this is hardly correct. There are rather two triplets than three pairs.

Ἀκούειν ('to hear') is the first point; it is believing obedience to Jesus' word. Κἀγὼ γινώσκω αὐτά ('and I know them'), that is a loving recognition; the experience of his loving fellowship is the next point. The following him, the exercise of the believing fellowship of love in life, springs from the former two.

Corresponding to this, the next triad names the blessing of salvation, the blessing which is imparted to those who stand in such loving communion,—a communion resting on believing obedience, and exercising itself in life. The ζωὴ αἰώνιοσ ('eternal life') is the most immediate fruit of belief, and at heart is already the entire blessing of salvation, as also belief at heart names the entire relation and posture of salvation. It corresponds to the ἀκούειν, just as οὐ μὴ ἀπόλωνται εἰσ τὸν αἰῶνα ('shall never perish') corresponds to the γινώσκω ('I know'). For the certain existence of salvation rests in the

[1] Stier, *Reden Jesu*, 3d ed., Barmen and Elberfeld 1870, vol. iv. p. 546 f.

fact that Christ knows us, that he has made us his own in love. The assurance that no hostile power shall snatch us from him, corresponds to the dangers which attend upon following him. Οὐχ ἁρπάσει τισ κ.τ.λ. ('no one shall pluck, etc.') points to the hostile powers who in manifold forms endanger the band of disciples, and corresponds to the ἀκολουθεῖν; compare, for example, Rom. viii. 31–38. The possibility of one's own apostasy is, of course, not excluded by this (against the doctrine of predestination).[1]

The twenty-fifth and twenty-sixth verses had served as a punishing reply, and the twenty-seventh and twenty-eighth have laid stress upon the true saving relation and conduct, and upon its blessing and its secure stability. The twenty-ninth and thirtieth verses now give the reason for this, in such a way that the twenty-ninth verse forms the major premiss and the thirtieth verse the minor premiss for the conclusion already expressed in the twenty-eighth verse.

VERSE 29.

The common text reads: 'my Father, which gave them me, is greater than all.' ℵ B L, Itala, Vulgate read: ὁ δέδωκεν (D: ὁ δεδωκώσ), and A B, Itala, Vulgate: μεῖζον (ℵ: μείζων). According to the reading of the Vatican manuscript it would stand: what the Father hath given me is greater than all or everything. But that is no endurable thought. The difference of the readings shows that an uncertainty came into the text at an early date. The masculine in the singular μείζων is hardly a correction (Meyer), but a remnant of the original text. The neuter ὅ is certainly an ancient error. Perhaps the ὁ δεδωκώσ of D, doubtless a stylistic change, shows us the way in which the ὅ arose.

The connection of thought requires, in spite of the authority of the best manuscripts, that we hold fast to the

---

[1] [That is to say: The devil and nobody else can take the believer from Christ, but the believer can cease to believe. It is pertinent to ask whether the believer will cease to believe if the devil does not tempt him. If this be answered affirmatively, the answerer is permitted to afford an instance in which the devil has been so far off his guard as to forget to tempt any Christian. If it be answered negatively, what is the sense of the text? The devil tries for the man and gets him.—C. R. G.]

received text. The Father gave them to him. For they were the Father's; compare v. 42, viii. 42, 47, iii. 21, xi. 52, xviii. 37, xvii. 6, 9, 12. The Father's power is exalted above all extra-divine power. This is the immediate meaning of πάντων μείζων ἐστίν ('is greater than all'). But it is designedly expressed more generally, to hint at the fact that the special relation, which the context lends to these words, is determined and established in the general circumstance that the Father is greater than all else, or than all others (for πάντων, 'all,' is doubtless masculine). Bengel adds: 'maior etiam me' ('greater also than I'), xiv. 28; but that does not belong here, since the Father and Son in this passage are not contrasted with each other. Moreover, it means, not merely greater than all hostile powers (Lücke), but greater than all, which are not God and which could exercise an utterance of power in reference to the πρόβατα ('sheep'). How far this remaining in the hand of the Father is also on the part of this hand established or conditioned, finds no consideration here, since the divine certainty of salvation and of the condition of salvation were to be emphasized.

VERSE 30.

If that be true of the Father, it is also true of him who speaks, of the Son: for the Father's power is also proper to him, because he and the Father are one or are together, that is, they form a unity. Nothing is said here of unity of will (thus the Arian and Socinian exposition), but of unity of the power which is proper to the Father and which is proper to the historical person Jesus Christ. We are compelled to think at once of the power, by the confirmation of οὐδεὶσ. δύναται ἁρπάζειν κ.τ.λ. ('no one is able to pluck, etc.'). Moreover, the same thing is true here as above, that to designate this special reference a general expression is purposely chosen, in order at the same time to express thereby the deeper-lying confirmation of this special fact.

But when Stier,[1] at once, without middle clauses, calls this saying 'an unshakable "dictum probans" ("proof text")

[1] Stier, *Reden Jesu*, 3d ed., Barmen and Elberfeld 1870, vol. iv. p. 554.

for the doctrine of the Trinity,' he draws a too hasty conclusion; as also does Hengstenberg, who explains the words simply as trinitarian. It is true that not merely a 'similitudo' ('likeness,' Fritzsche) is expressed, but a ἑνότησ, 'unity,' of power (Lücke[1]). Nor does it say that Jesus 'works' what God 'wills' (Baumgarten-Crusius), but declares the coincidence of the two powers. Yet for this very reason Bengel passes beyond exact exposition and enters the sphere of dogmatical conclusion, when, following Augustine (as Stier also does), he observes: 'per "sumus" refutatur Sabellius, per "unum" Arius' (' "we are" refutes Sabellius, "one" refutes Arius'). For the former (ἐσμέν, 'we are') at first points to the difference between God the Father and the man Jesus, and the latter (ἕν, 'one') does not immediately refer to essence.

Beyschlag is right[2] when he denies that 'a metaphysical unity' is in question. When, however, the two, God the Father and the man Jesus Christ, are put on a level and taken together in view of their power, that leads further. He the man has as his own the same power as God his Father, not as if it were not the power of two, but because where the one is there also is the other. This, moreover, could not be the case in reference to their power, were it not true of the persons that where the one is there also is the other, so that Beyschlag[3] speaks also of a 'real fellowship of life' which for him is only ethically conditioned. Jesus too, later, himself explains ἕν ἐσμεν ('we are one') by ἐν ἐμοὶ ὁ πατὴρ κἀγὼ ἐν τῷ πατρί ('the Father in me and I in the Father'), ver. 38,—words which essentially say the same as ver. 30,[4] only that in ver. 30 the expression is determined from the point of view of equality, and in ver. 38 from the point of view of a living the one in the other. Yet the expression in ver. 30 is more indefinite than in ver. 38. And as ver. 38 is not to be weakened to: the

---

[1] Lücke, *Commentar über das Evangelium des Johannes*, 3d ed., Bonn 1843, vol. ii. p. 435.

[2] Beyschlag, *Die Christologie des Neuen Testaments*, Berlin 1866, p. 78.

[3] *Ibid.*

[4] Hofmann, *Weissagung und Erfüllung im Alten und im Neuen Testamente*, Nördlingen 1844, vol. ii. p. 21.

Father works, appears in me; it is one work, one cause (Baumgarten-Crusius),—but is to be understood of the persons, and to be taken exactly, so also here. Jesus used a word of such a general character, because he desired to designate at the same time the relation of the persons, his and the Father's, and that in its fundamental generality.

It is, indeed, in the first instance the relation of the one who has become man to God in heaven, as Jesus usually throughout speaks of himself in historical reality. But Beyschlag is not right when, in his 'Christology,' he urges this against the traditional exposition of this passage in the church. For that which became historical in the human personality of Jesus Christ, is only the historical appearance of an eternal person lying at the foundation. As, then, he who became man would not have stood in the divine fellowship, as it existed historically, if this fellowship had not been essentially his own in so far as he was before he became man; so also here he would not have been able to say this of himself, the incarnate one, if it were not true of him essentially. These words express the relation of the being one, or equal and together, between him who is God and him who is man,—and who in so far is not God,—in an absolute generality, which could not occur in the case between God and that which at foundation is not God. Hence Meyer well observes on this passage, that in the fellowship designated by ἕν ἐσμεν ('we are one') the homoousia is to be presupposed. Weiss[1] refers to the herein expressed 'mutual fellowship' of the 'being' on each side, 'at which therefore the apology of Christ in ver. 38 aims.'

Verse 31.

This word was unendurable for the Jews. They brought stones, πάλιν ('again'), as in viii. 59, to execute upon Jesus the punishment of blasphemy. When he reproached them, ver. 26, when he spoke of his gift and spoke loftily of himself, ver. 27 f., they remained calm. But these words

[1] Weiss, *Der Johanneische Lehrbegriff in seinen Grundzügen untersucht*, Berlin 1862, p. 206.

seemed to them to go entirely too far beyond the measure allowable for a man. At the same time, it is one of those short, sharp 'dicta' ('sayings') which at the close of a discourse involuntarily turn their point against the opponents and excite their anger.[1] With this begins the second circle of this section. Brückner blamed Olshausen for speaking of a right understanding on the part of the Jews, against 'the pervading analogy of the gospel.' We have, however, seen that the cases of misunderstanding are much fewer than is commonly believed.[2] Should we suppose that Jesus spoke so very unintelligibly as it is the custom, since Baur, to reproach the fourth gospel with speaking?

Stier[3] finds a progress in $\dot{\epsilon}\beta\acute{a}\sigma\tau a\sigma a\nu$, in the 'bringing' stones, in comparison with $\ddot{\eta}\rho a\nu$, the mere picking them up, at viii. 59, which is recalled by $\pi\acute{a}\lambda\iota\nu$. But $\beta a\sigma\tau\acute{a}\zeta\epsilon\iota\nu$ can also mean 'to take up' (thus Meyer, because of $\pi\acute{a}\lambda\iota\nu$). And if it is to be understood in the further meaning, 'to carry to' a place, we should have to reply: there were no stones lying in Solomon's porch, and so they had to carry them in; Godet perceives in this the eye-witness. Weisse questioned the historical possibility of the continuation of the conversation. Ebrard[4] defends it, by appealing to the evil conscience of the opponents of Jesus. The scene is not so tumultuous as at viii. 59, but the disposition of the opponents is not therefore less determined. Their decision shows itself in the fact that they do not let themselves be drawn off by Jesus' defence, but as soon as he has done speaking, prepare to set about the work in which they had been interrupted. The circumstance that ver. 39 speaks not of stoning but of seizing, is explained when we remember that they must first have led him out of the porch.

Verse 32.

When Jesus calls his works $\check{\epsilon}\rho\gamma a\ \kappa a\lambda\acute{a}$, he does not intend to designate them as beneficent (Baumgarten-

---

[1] See vol. i. p. 35 f.   [2] See vol. i. p. 121 ff.
[3] Stier, *Reden Jesu*, 3d ed., Barmen and Elberfeld 1870, vol. iv. p. 555.
[4] Ebrard, *Wissenschaftliche Kritik der evangelischen Geschichte*, 3d ed., Frankfort-on-the-Main 1868, p. 543.

Crusius) or as glorious (De Wette), but as good, as those which cannot be reproached. Judging from his works, he cannot be blamed in anything: that is the negative side. On the contrary, since he did them ἐκ τοῦ πατρόσ ('from the Father'), they prove the relation to his Father which he has stated: that is the positive side. For ἐκ τοῦ πατρόσ does not mean simply: in his power (Brückner, Stier), but is purposely said just thus in order to point to the circumstance that his action itself all takes its internal departure from the Father, and that he therefore, in all his actions, exercises his internal fellowship with the Father. With this point Jesus returns, at the close of the debating discourses, to the beginning of them, v. 17, 18. This constant doctrinal representation of Jesus is indeed a testimony to his dependence upon the Father,[1] but at the same time to his fellowship with him. When he now asks which (ποῖον) of these works is of such a description that it deserves stoning, why must it necessarily be irony (De Wette, Lücke, Stier), even 'the irony of deep indignation' (Meyer, Godet)? Does Jesus affect not to observe that they desire to stone him, not because of a work, but because of his words? But we saw at v. 18 that his words seemed to them unendurable, just because of the healing on the Sabbath. Had they not taken offence at his actions from the very outset, his words would not have been so offensive. On this account Jesus wishes first to bring out plainly the offence at his actions as the causal reason, before he speaks of the offence at his words. But he makes the struggle a hard one for them by the anticipatory word directed to their conscience: ἔργα καλά, works with which no fault can be found. Hence the Jews move to the attack at this.

Verse 33.

Yet they do not say περὶ τῶν καλῶν ἔργων ('for good works'), but περὶ καλοῦ ἔργου ('for a good work'). Therefore, in not entering on this question, they leave this whole matter undecided (Baumgarten-Crusius). But the λιθάζομεν

[1] Beyschlag, *Die Christologie des Neuen Testaments*, Berlin 1866, p. 71.

('stoning') they acknowledge: they are on the very point of doing it, and that because of his alleged blasphemy. For even if they were willing to turn aside from his works, they must nevertheless stone him for his blasphemous words.

The Jews understood Jesus, that he, though a man, made himself God, ver. 33. It is said that this is at least an exaggeration (Brückner), which then Jesus also beyond the possibility of misunderstanding denies (Beyschlag[1]). But, as we have seen, Jesus has so combined himself with God, that what is true of the one must be true of the other. He has placed himself at the side of and in God, and therefore on the same basis as God, and has made himself ἴσον τῷ θεῷ ('equal to God'), v. 18. In speaking of himself thus, he does not indeed make himself ὁ θεός, but equal to τῷ θεῷ, and therefore θεός.

But now ἄνθρωπος ('man') and θεός ('God') are a contrast, and one seems necessarily to exclude the other. How is this contrast mediated? In hardly any other way than this, that he who could speak thus of himself must have been God, and therefore also in an inner divine communion with ὁ θεός before he became ἄνθρωπος, so that essential divine fellowship is peculiar to him, even in so far as he now has become man; it is, however, in a historical temporal form, but resting on that eternal basis. Hence Jesus intends to justify his words by designating himself as the man who has become man, as having proceeded from God, that is, as υἱὸς τοῦ θεοῦ ('Son of God'). For in that he said what precedes, he has said nothing but this. And in consequence he has justified the former when he names the fact by reason of which he may attribute to himself this name. He bases this justification, which is contained in vers. 34–36, on the word of the Old Testament Scriptures.

Verse 34.

Ἐν τῷ νόμῳ ὑμῶν ('in your law') designates the Old Testament Scriptures in general. The name for the first

[1] Beyschlag, *Die Christologie des Neuen Testaments*, Berlin 1866, p. 63 f.

of the three parts of the Old Testament canon serves to designate the whole, because it is the chief part and the foundation of all that follows: the ὁ νόμοσ ('the law') is as much as ἡ γραφή ('the Scriptures'); compare xii. 34, xv. 25. Jesus says ὑμῶν ('your'), as in viii. 17.[1] The Jews appeal to and support themselves upon the Old Testament Scriptures against him. For this very reason Jesus now urges it for himself. The eighty-second Psalm describes God as holding judgment among the 'elohim' of the earth. 'I have said: ye are elohim (" gods "), and all of you are children of the Most High. But ye shall die like men, and fall like one of the princes,' Ps. lxxxii. 6, 7.

The psalm is not addressed to angels (Bleek and Hupfeld)—how should these be condemned for unjust judgment? —but to the bearers of authority. They are called elohim, אֱלֹהִים, as the representatives of God, who has transferred to them his right of majesty over life and death.[2] We are not to think of heathen princes (De Wette, Hitzig), but of the authorities of the theocratic nation (Meyer).

'By referring to this psalm, Jesus proves to the Jews, by an "argumentatio a minori ad maius" (a "reasoning from the less to the greater"), that he does not blaspheme God in calling himself God's Son. If the law— thus he reasons—names even those as gods who received this name officially by an utterance of the divine will made in time (and the Scriptures, as in general, so also here, are not to be broken), then it can be no blasphemy if he names himself God's Son. For it was not merely a temporal word of God which called to this or that earthly office after the image of God, but with his whole life he carries out a work to which the Father hád consecrated him before he entered into the world.'[3]

---

[1] See vol. i. p. 125 f.
[2] See Delitzsch, *Biblischer Commentar über die Psalmen*, 3d ed., Leipzig 1874, vol. ii. p. 66 f.
[3] See Delitzsch, *ut supra*, p. 66 f.

Verse 35.

If it—namely, ὁ νόμοσ ('the law'), not ὁ θεόσ ('God;' thus Hengstenberg), as results from the following γραφή (Meyer)—*called those*, of whom the psalm treats,—Jesus can presuppose it as well known,—*gods unto whom the word of God came*: this does not mean the word of the psalm itself, 'the address contained in the psalm' (De Wette; Lücke: 'a punishing word of God's'); for in the psalm it is said אֲנִי אָמַרְתִּי ('I have spoken'), which is a reference to an earlier word; and this earlier word is not revelations from God which they have received (Olshausen), but the word with which God called them and appointed them to their office (Hofmann,[1] Meyer).

It is true that πρὸσ οὕσ ('unto whom') is not intended by way of confirmation (thus Bengel, and I earlier), but stands in contrast to the following ὃν ὁ πατήρ ('whom the Father'), Hofmann. Yet substantially the phrase contains the statement of a reason : because God appointed them by his word, and thus designates them as gods and sons of God, so also the Scriptures of the Old Testament name them, just as the psalmist has already named them, אֱלֹהִים ('elohim, gods'), and therefore before the sixth verse. For the subject of εἶπεν ('called') is, as we have seen, ὁ νόμοσ, that is, ἡ γραφή ('the Scriptures'), which designation at once comes forward.

And the Scripture cannot be broken. It makes no difference whether we let this sentence depend on εἰ ('if') (Meyer, Hengstenberg, Godet), or whether we take it as a note thrown in parenthetically (thus commonly). Perhaps the second construction is more agreeable to the looser periodology of John's style. The clause is, in either case, an aiding thought (Meyer), but of great weight. For it contains the two truths of the unity and of the normative authority of the Scriptures. Compare on λύειν, dissolve, break, that is, to put out of currency, Matt. v. 19 ; John ii. 18, vii. 23. This is said of the Scriptures as a whole. Hence the Scriptures must be owned in each

[1] Hofmann, *Der Schriftbeweis*, 2d ed., Nördlingen 1857, vol. i. p. 126.

one of their parts as an authority. Bengel says: 'Non potest dissolvi scriptura, ne minima quidem ex parte. Firmissimum axioma' ('the scripture cannot be broken, not even in the least part. A most certain axiom'). Thus, here, if the Jews now, Lev. xxiv. 16, executed the stoning upon Jesus for alleged blasphemy, the eighty-second Psalm would be robbed of its validity.

On the contrary, the Scriptures are to be acknowledged in each of their parts. And the separate words of Scripture are of authority for this reason, namely, that they are the words of Scripture, that is, parts of the whole. Therefore the authority attaches in the first place to the Scriptures as a whole, and then in the second place attaches to the various words or sayings. The detached saying is a word of God, and is normative, because it is a constituent part of the whole. Accordingly, the divine influence in virtue of which the Scriptures are valid as God's word, and hence as a normative authority, is asserted in the first place of the whole, and only in the connection with this, of the separate parts of the whole. Hence, in the religious and dogmatic valuation of the Scriptures, we must proceed from the whole Scriptures as the united word of God, and after that determine the importance of the various sayings of Scripture, according as each assumes a place in that whole.

Verse 36.

Thus Jesus, on the basis of the one and irrefutable Scripture, proves that—if those are called gods and sons of God who only stood in a relation of vocation to God— He much more deserves this name who stands in a personal relation to him. In drawing the conclusion here, he calls himself υἱὸσ τοῦ θεοῦ ('Son of God'), and not θεόσ ('God'). This he does partly because υἱὸσ τοῦ θεοῦ was suggested by the progress of thought, partly because it was a more appropriate statement for him who became man, and partly, in connection with the last point, because he desired what he intended to say of himself to be stated and understood in the exact sense, whereas he could not claim recognition as θεόσ in the exact sense so long as he lived in the flesh, but only after he, with the glorification, had again gone back into the divine state, where also that recognition then at once took place, xx. 28.

It is therefore singular when Beyschlag[1] claims that in the traditional orthodox conception of Jesus' divine Sonship the answer ought necessarily to have read: I am God, instead of: I am God's Son. Jesus only desires to prove his divine Sonship. If the designation sons of God—which alternates with 'gods' in the eighty-second Psalm—is valid for those who yet, because of their unholy nature, had to be reproached in that psalm,—for Jesus could well presuppose that the context of that statement was in the memory of those to whom he spoke,—how much more was it valid for him ὃν ὁ πατὴρ ἡγίασεν (' whom the Father sanctified')! It is a conclusion 'a minori ad maius' ('from the less to the greater'), which, indeed, does presuppose the historical dependence of Jesus on the Father. Jesus says ὁ πατήρ ('the Father') designedly, because he wishes to confirm his special relation as Son to the Father.[2] For him God is not merely, as for them, ὁ θεόσ, but ὁ πατήρ. By this he is elevated above the mere relation of vocation to God.

Ἁγιάζειν ('to sanctify') is not simply equivalent to ἀφορίζειν ('to separate,' Baumgarten-Crusius), or 'to set apart,' as God intends it in the prophet Jeremiah: 'before thou camest forth out of the womb, I sanctified thee,' Jer. i. 5, which is related to ἀφορίζειν, Gal. i. 15.[3] Were it so, why do we not read ἀφώρισεν ('separated') or ἐξελέξατο ('chose')? But the peculiarity of Jesus' person and of his relation to God causes the word to be intended here more fully than in Jeremiah. We saw before, at vi. 69,[4] that it was meant to say that Jesus also as to his nature was removed from the fellowship of the ordinary, and thereby also of the sinful, life of the world. There is no need to prove that it refers to the sending into the world, and not to the consecration at the baptism.

---

[1] Beyschlag, *Die Christologie des Neuen Testaments*, Berlin 1866, p. 68 f.
[2] See Weiss, *Der Johanneische Lehrbegriff*, Berlin 1862, p. 196.
[3] Hofmann, *Der Schriftbeweis*, 2d ed., Nördlingen 1857, vol. i. p. 85 f.
[4] See above, p. 195.

Beyschlag[1] thinks that this statement stands in irreconcilable contradiction with the church doctrine of the Trinity. But such is by no means the case. There is nothing said here of the internal divine relations as they are in themselves, but only of the historical form they have assumed, in that he who was eternally with the Father set himself to become man. In that Jesus, proceeding from the Father, entered into the world's fellowship, the Father hath at once freed him—in so far as he was to become the son of man—from that fellowship, and sent him into the world as one not inwoven in its nature. What God sanctifies, he takes from the world and appropriates to himself. If the Father sanctifies (for ἡγίασεν precedes the ἀπέστειλεν, 'sent;' compare Bengel) him who was to come into the world, then Jesus is not merely, in so far as he comes forth from God, in God's fellowship and the Son of God, but even as man he is from the outset appropriated unto God. How else is this to be thought of, than that God had before received into his will of love the one who was to become the son of Man, and had afterwards begotten him holy, and thus thereby made him his Son also as the son of man? As one thus made holy, he then sent him into the world. How *say ye* then—ὑμεῖσ ('ye'), emphatically: ye people! (Meyer) — *thou blasphemest?* The beginning with ὅν ('whom') would lead us to expect the third person, because in the 'oratio obliqua' ('indirect discourse'); but the vividness of the discourse passes into the direct form, and thus to the second person.

Verse 37.

He proves by his ἔργα ('works') this divine Sonship which is true of him. The words are challénging in sound: *if I do not do* them! He designates them at once as *works of the Father's*, that is, which the Father works through him. In this he assumes as proved what he is in the act of proving. But the proof lay in the works themselves. They prove his divine fellowship.

[1] Beyschlag, *Die Christologie des Neuen Testaments*, Berlin 1866, p. 69.

Verse 38.

Therefore, if they will not believe him, that is, his word, his self-witness,[1] they should at least believe the works, that is, the testimony concerning him contained therein. The aim, however, of this his demand is, that they may then recognise his and the Father's living mutual being in each other. "Ἵνα γνῶτε καὶ γινώσκητε, saith Jesus,—for so it is to be read with B L, against ℵ, which has ἵνα γνῶτε καὶ πιστεύητε, an evident change to avoid the striking repetition of γινώσκειν,—that is, that ye may attain the knowledge and know (lastingly). The act and state are distinguished (Meyer). *That the Father is in me, and I in the Father;* compare upon ver. 30. 'Hæ duæ sententiæ: ego et Pater unum sumus, et: Pater in me et ego in Patre, se mutuo exponunt' ('These two sentences: I and the Father are one, and: the Father in me and I in the Father, mutually explain each other'), Bengel, Weiss.[2] This statement proceeds from the ground of the dynamical fellowship (Meyer) by means of which Jesus is the organ for the activity of the Father, and it reaches out beyond this ground (against Lücke, De Wette). It does not, indeed, designate the internal divine fellowship of essence, the 'περιχώρησισ, essentialis patris in filio et filii in patre' ('the essential abiding of the Father in the Son, and of the Son in the Father'), Calov. But it denotes the personal fellowship between the Father and Son, which finds its eternal presupposition in the fellowship just named. Such, then, is the importance of the σημεῖα ('signs') of Jesus, that they may cause the relation to be recognised.

Verse 39.

Just as in ver. 30 above, the decisive words only called forth the greater bitterness on the part of the opponents, so also in the case of these words, neither the preceding justification and the refutation of the reproach, nor the less provoking form of the expression itself, could remove the

---

[1] Compare Weiss, *Der Johanneische Lehrbegriff*, Berlin 1862, p. 203.
[2] Weiss, *Der Johanneische Lehrbegriff*, Berlin 1862, p. 205.

exasperation of his opponents. For it can hardly be said that by Jesus' defence their bitterness was softened, and that they were led to give up the stoning (thus Meyer). They did not give up the stoning when they made the attempt and preparations to seize him, but doubtless only intended to lead him out of the temple for that very purpose (Calvin, Hengstenberg). By πάλιν ('again') we are reminded of previous similar attempts. But, as before, he withdraws himself from their hands, whether or not miraculously, as at viii. 59 (Baumgarten-Crusius, I earlier), must be left undecided, as the evangelist does not remark upon it. However it took place, it served the Jews as a testimony that they, without his will and before the time, had no power to get him under their control. It is unnecessary to bring in the Basilidian gnosticism for this purpose, as Keim[1] does, referring to Irenæus:[2] 'quum teneri non posset, et invisibilis esset omnibus' ('since he could not be held, and was invisible to all').

VERSES 40–42. *Jesus in Perea.*

Jesus returns to Perea, not in order to secure himself from the wiles of the church authorities (Maier, Meyer), but because he now has no more to do among the Jews until he gives himself up to them unto death.

VERSE 40.

'Ἀπῆλθεν πάλιν πέραν τοῦ Ἰορδάνου ('he went away again beyond Jordan'), says the evangelist. One might be inclined to find in this a hint that it was also from that place that he had come to the feast of the dedication of the temple, so that we should have here a contribution to filling out the time falling between the twenty-first and twenty-second verses. It is, however, improbable that the evangelist intends to refer to a fact which he did not mention. Hence the usually accepted reference to i. 28 remains the more likely one. At any rate, this is more correct than Baumgarten-Crusius' reference to iii. 22. It will be but

---

[1] Keim, *Jesu von Nazara*, Zürich 1872, vol. iii. p. 64.
[2] Irenæus, *Contra Hæreses*, I. xxiv. 4; ed. Venice 1734, vol. i. p. 101.

the more necessary if πάλιν ('again') should avail, not merely for πέραν τοῦ Ἰορδάνου (' beyond Jordan'), but also for εἰσ τὸν τόπον κ.τ.λ. ('into the place, etc.'). Jesus' public work has reached its end. And this returns to the beginning. On the same scene on which John, first baptizing,—(τὸ πρῶτον, ' the first,' in contrast to the change of his scene of work, iii. 23),—had testified to Jesus, the latter now testifies to himself, so that he by this display of himself confirms John the Baptist's testimony to him.

Verse 41.

Hence the testimony of the Baptist appears as true, although not accompanied by miraculous signs. This is indeed the closest connection of thought, in which it is said of the Baptist: Ἰωάννησ μὲν σημεῖον ἐποίησεν οὐδέν ('John did no miracle'). In so far Brückner was right in rejecting Baur's[1] opinion. Baur thought that this was intended to name the characteristic difference between the Baptist and Jesus, and to give a comprehensive retrospect of the whole previous representation of the life and work of Jesus from the point of view of the σημεῖα ('signs'). And yet by this remark we are involuntarily reminded of the σημεῖα which Jesus did, in distinction from the Baptist, and the evangelist certainly intended to remind us of them. Only it is in a different sense from the one Baur urges.

It is a question, with what design in general does the evangelist bring these verses in here, and mention that Jesus stayed for a time beyond Jordan and found belief. He does not introduce the note for its own sake; for in that case it would be more detailed and more definite. He does not even say whether or not, and how, Jesus was active in Perea. He uses only the indefinite word ἔμεινεν ('abode'), ver. 40. ' And we can only conclude that Jesus was active in doctrinal instruction from the circumstance that ' many resorted unto him,' and found in him the promised one, ver. 41. Thus little, therefore, the evangelist troubled himself to tell about that residence in Perea.

---

[1] Baur, *Kritische Untersuchungen über die kanonischen Evangelien*, Tübingen 1847, p. 182 f.

From this we perceive that he introduces this note only for the sake of what precedes. A contrast is intended between the Jews in Jerusalem and these people in Perea. How much more was offered to the former than to the latter, and yet how utterly opposite the result was; this is what the evangelist wishes to direct our attention to. Besides, Jesus was only a short time in Perea, for we find him later in Ephraim, xi. 54. In this connection we are reminded that those in Perea must have let themselves be satisfied by testimony of the Baptist, unsupported by miracles, while in Jerusalem from the very beginning σημεῖα (signs ') had occurred in great numbers, and with incontrovertible evidence.

VERSE 42.

And yet the former, those in Perea, permitted the mere word of the Baptist to serve (Bengel says: 'fructus postumus officii Johannis,' 'posthumous fruit of John's activity') to win them to belief in the word of Jesus' self-witness; while in the case of the latter, even the σημεῖα could not attain such success. In this connection it is emphasized that the Baptist σημεῖον (μὲν) ἐποίησεν οὐδέν ('did no miracles'). The Jews therefore cannot excuse their unbelief in the face of such people. For these prove how very possible it was, and what a duty it was, to obtain belief. These verses belong to the great indictment which this whole gospel forms against the Jews as the historical representatives of unbelief.

CHAPTERS XI. AND XII.

Jesus, given up unto death, is the Life and the Judgment.

The section to which we now have to pass brings to a decision the conduct of the Jews towards Jesus, and thereby the relation of both. After the preceding events have shown us how the mood and the determination of the Jews decided themselves, it is only necessary that this become a decree, by which the relation of Israel to its Saviour is fixed even for the future. The raising of Lazarus served as the occasion for this. Baur justly calls attention to the fact that this σημεῖον ('sign') of the resurrection is essentially different from the preceding signs: it is not the subject of a discussion with the Jews; no long discourse is attached to it; in short, it belongs no more to the public doctrinal activity of Jesus. It is in this respect like the first miracle at Cana. This as well as that could be left out if an evangelist desired to limit himself to the sphere of the public teachings of Jesus. This is as true for Mark as it is for Matthew (against Brückner); compare also Meyer.

Hence, in order to explain this omission in the synoptists, we shall have no need to recur to a respect they thought they must pay to the still living Lazarus on account of the hostile Jews (Olshausen, Lange [1]),—a respect which, at the time in which the gospels were written, would have been entirely unnecessary and purposeless. Nor need we think of a respect paid to the personal character of the relation in which Jesus stood towards the sisters and the brother, and which demanded that the sacred privacy should not be exposed to the multitude so long as the persons in question lived (Godet),—a fiction which is destroyed even by Matt. xxvi. 13. Nor need we assume that the synoptists were not acquainted with this incident (De Wette, Lücke),—a lack of knowledge which must, indeed, have made the credibility of the synoptists very questionable. As arbitrary is the assumption that this story, because of its profound character, was destined for the gospel of John (Hengstenberg, and also Philippi[2]). For this does not depend merely upon the story itself, but rather upon the conception and application of it.

The importance of this miracle for the historical catastrophe of the life of Jesus has been exaggerated. It is said to be the greatest miracle; should the synoptists 'have slept through' (Keim[3]) this very one? Since in John the death

---

[1] Lange, *Das Leben Jesu*, Heidelberg 1845, vol. ii. part ii. p. 1133 f.

[2] Philippi, *Der Eingang des Johanneischen Evangeliums*, Stuttgart 1866, p. 11 f.

[3] Keim, *Geschichte Jesu von Nazara*, Zürich 1867, vol. i. p. 132.

of Jesus hangs on this, and the synoptists know nothing of this, therefore 'it hangs altogether in the air' (Keim[1]). But the death decree of the Sanhedrim is not based upon this, but upon the 'many signs' that Jesus did, xi. 47. If, then, this event was also the occasion for this last step, it was not the reason.[2] It is an exaggeration when Gess[3] explains the raising of Lazarus as the 'key without which the synoptic narrative becomes a riddle,' or when Pressensé[4] finds that without this, both the enthusiasm of the people and the outbreak of hatred on the part of the authorities are inexplicable. The history of Jesus would have proceeded, as it did proceed, even without this event. The synoptists, therefore, have no need of this miracle to explain the issue of Jesus' life.

Thus they pass over this miracle as they in general are silent concerning Bethany, or mention it only in passing. They arrange their narration upon the chief points, Galilee, Perea, Jerusalem. Before the prominence given to these three great stations, everything else retires from view.[5] John, moreover, mentions it in the first place, because to him it is an essential point in the history of the rising conflict, which he has made it his task to portray; and in the second place, because for him it presents figuratively the thought which, in the progress of his doctrinal development, he desires to express at this very place. If it be certain (in so far Baur[6] is right) that the words ἐγώ εἰμι ἡ ἀνάστασισ καὶ ἡ ζωή ('I am the resurrection and the life'), xi. 25, are the theme and centre of this story, then also the story itself is essentially to be understood from that point of view. Insomuch as it teaches us something about Jesus, the evangelist reports it in detail. But Baur is utterly

---

[1] Keim, *Geschichte Jesu von Nazara,* Zürich 1867, vol. i. p. 131.

[2] Compare the previous remarks, vol. i. p. 132 f.

[3] Gess, *Christi Zeugniss von seiner Person und seinem Werk* [*Christi Person und Werk nach Christi Selbstzeugniss,* vol. i.], Basel 1870, p. 120.

[4] Pressensé, *Jésus Christ,* German edition, Halle 1866, p. 400, note.

[5] Compare vol. i. p. 132 f., and Luthardt, *St. John the Author of the Fourth Gospel,* Edinburgh, T. and T. Clark, 1875, p. 212 f.

[6] Baur, *Kritische Untersuchungen über die synoptischen Evangelien,* Tübingen 1847, p. 192.

unjustified in using this truth in the service of his view, so as to conclude from it the unhistorical character of the narrative.

The Johannean narrative of the raising of Lazarus is the most essential point of support for the newer criticism in its critical operations. This criticism thinks it can here most distinctly look in at the mental workshop of the fourth evangelist, and disclose most convincingly his manipulations. It stands sure from the outset, for this view, that the story, although 'touching and grand,'[1] is nevertheless unhistorical, so that there 'remains no doubt at all'[2] of its spuriousness. The religious treatment and application of it has always admired its tenderness, and 'emphasized the fulness of the comfort which lies in it.'[3] The criticism named finds, however, in it 'a series of features,' unnaturalness, heartlessness, and the like, which must 'most unpleasantly surprise' every one.[4] And while others find that each thing here knits itself into the other points, and all mutually explain each other,[5] this criticism discovers 'an artificial, stilted story, and an unnaturally complicated Christology which confuses man and God.'[6]

If, however, the narrative be unhistorical, criticism has no doubt whence it arose. The synoptic fragments concerning the poor Lazarus, concerning the sinful woman who anoints Jesus' feet, and concerning the two sisters with whom Jesus stays,—these form the materials out of which this revelation of the glory of the Logos is woven. It was already a web of arbitrary notions when Hengstenberg upon twenty-six pages[7] spun out an entire romance, according to which Mary of Bethany, Mary Magdalene, and the sinful woman in Luke vii. were identical (as this, it is true in

---

[1] Keim, *Geschichte Jesu von Nazara*, Zürich 1872, vol. iii. p. 68.

[2] *Ibid.* vol. iii. p. 71.

[3] See, for example, the fine work by K. W. Eug. Fries, *Christus die Auferstehung und das Leben*, Erlangen 1863.

[4] Keim, *ut supra*, vol. iii. p. 70.

[5] Compare the thorough treatise by Gumlich, 'Die Räthsel der Erweckung Lazari,' *Studien und Kritiken*, 1862, pp. 65-110, 248-336.

[6] Keim, *ut supra*, vol. iii. p. 71.

[7] Hengstenberg, *Das Evangelium des heiligen Johannes erläutert*, Berlin 1862, vol. ii. pp. 198-224.

distinction from the Greek conception, is the tradition fixed in the West, especially by Gregory the Great); Lazarus was identical with the poor Lazarus; and Martha had married the rich Pharisee Simon, living in Bethany, and received her poverty-stricken brother Lazarus into her house, where he lived on her mercy. But this combination becomes absurd in the newer criticism, which further joins to it both the other cases of raising the dead, in order by their help to prove that the story was a mere product of literary fiction. Appealing to the comparison in Irenæus,[1] the critics behold in the raising of Lazarus only a higher development of those other cases of raising the dead: that of the daughter of Jairus, in Matthew, occurs upon the bed of death; that of the youth at Nain, in Luke, on the way to the grave; that of Lazarus, in John, occurs after four days, and from the grave itself,—the first is to be designated as the positive, the second as the comparative, and the third as the superlative. They then add the parable from Luke about the poor Lazarus.[2] Zeller, Baur, and Strauss urge this view. Holtzmann[3] presses it with particular emphasis, and with special consideration of the points of contact even in the expressions.

But it is purely arbitrary to conclude from the climax want of historical character. Why should there be exactly four days—why not three, or two, or one? The four evidently do not belong to the climax, but stand in an accidental relation towards it. The story, therefore, does not permit of entire dissolution into the thought, but contains things indifferent for it, and thus doubtless historical points. As for those combinations, the points of contact cited are rather so many points of difference. Saying

[1] Irenæus, *Adversus Hæreses*, V. xiii. 1; ed. Stieren, Leipzig 1853, vol. i. p. 750 f.

[2] Thus even Zeller, *Theologische Jahrbücher*, Tübingen 1843, p. 89; Baur, *Theologische Jahrbücher*, Tübingen 1844, p. 408; *Kritische Untersuchungen über die kanonischen Evangelien*, Tübingen 1847, pp. 191 f., 249; Strauss, *Leben Jesu*, 1st ed., Tübingen 1836, vol. ii. p. 153, and *Das Leben Jesu für das deutsche Volk bearbeitet*, Leipzig 1864, p. 470.

[3] Holtzmann, *Zeitschrift für wissenschaftliche Theologie*, 1869, p. 450. See also Keim, *Geschichte Jesu von Nazara*, Zürich 1867, vol. i. p. 132; 1871, vol. ii. p. 133; 1872, vol. iii. pp. 66 f., 72 f., 229.

nothing of the difference between the sinful woman and the Mary of Bethany, in whom nothing causes us to see a 'sinner,' let us limit ourselves to Lazarus. Holtzmann places together πτωχόσ ('poor'), Luke xvi. 20, and ἀσθενῶν ('sick'), John xi. 1; but to be poor and to be sick are two very different things, and in themselves have nothing at all in common with each other. The poor Lazarus has sores, and lies at the door of the rich man; this one is dead. Holtzmann mediates this point of comparison by saying, that 'leprosy excluded from the society of the living,' whereas there is nothing to be read of a leprosy in the case of the poor Lazarus, and he is not excluded from the society of the living, since otherwise he would not have lain at the door of the rich man, and therefore in the city. And were it so, to be leprous and to be dead are not the same thing. There, in the parable, the return of the poor Lazarus is prayed for; here, a return occurs—only with the difference that in the former the return is denied. There, it says: even if the return took place, they would not believe; here, on the contrary, xi. 45, 'they believed on him.' And finally, 'the sore-covered Lazarus of Luke' changes[1] into Simon the Leper, Matt. xxvi. 6, though the two have not the least in the world to do with each other. That, however, is enough of the single points. If one mingles the materials of history thus arbitrarily, he can finally reach all possible fancies.

Let us turn to the story itself. The first thing is to settle its point of view.

At x. 18 the evangelist purposely reported the words of Jesus: ἐξουσίαν ἔχω θεῖναι αὐτήν (τὴν ψυχήν μου), καὶ ἐξουσίαν ἔχω πάλιν λαβεῖν αὐτήν ('I have power to lay it [my life] down, and I have power to take it again'). Hence, when he now proceeds to the account of the historical fulfilment of these words, he has not himself forgotten them, and therefore will not fail to lay stress upon the point of view therein stated, in order to teach us how to understand from it the history of the issue of Jesus' life. Hence the whole narrative is evidently so ordered as to make us per-

[1] Keim, *Geschichte Jesu von Nazara*, Zürich 1873, vol. iii. p. 73.

ceive how freely Jesus went into death; and that because
salvation should unfold itself even in his death. Now the
blessing of salvation is: Life; the impartation of life to the
world is the purpose of his devotion of himself, and at the
same time its result is the judgment of those who exclude
themselves from this impartation of life. In consequence,
this future must unfold itself from this free death. All
that is told in the eleventh and twelfth chapters is gazing
into the future. The eleventh chapter first emphasizes the
fact that Jesus in death is life for his own. This is followed by the second point, that his death becomes a judgment for the others. Jesus' δόξα ('glory') appears in the
former as well as in the latter. And the raising of Lazarus at
once serves to help us to perceive this. He promised Martha,
on condition of belief, ver. 40, that she should behold the
δόξα τοῦ θεοῦ ('glory of God') as peculiar to him, and this
by the fact that in the resurrection of Lazarus he revealed
himself as life in death.

The contents of the eleventh chapter form a consistent
whole. Upon it follow in the twelfth chapter three events
which clearly are by design placed side by side. And these
are followed by a closing word, both of the evangelist's and
of Jesus'.

XI. 1–57.

The Raising.

That which happens to Lazarus is a prophecy in reference to Christ himself. Both historically and logically this
chapter is composed of three parts—(1) The preparation,
vers. 1–16; (2) The event itself, vers. 17–44; (3) Its
effect, vers. 45–57. The thought of death rules in the
first, the thought of life out of death rules in the second,
and the thought of salvation, which therefore is given to
the world with this death, rules the third.

(1.) VERSES 1-16.

The Preparation.

The evangelist places us in a well-known neighbourhood.

Verse 1.

Mary and Martha are mentioned as well-known persons; Bethany is mentioned as 'their' place, as a thing known from previous occurrences (compare Luke x. 38); and the anointing, which nevertheless does not come till afterwards in the twelfth chapter, is presupposed as already known.[1]

Verse 2.

Martha seems to have been the elder; observe her precedence, vers. 5, 19, 20, and Luke x. 38; here, however, Mary is put first as the better known. Lazarus (exactly, 'Ελεάζαροσ, אֶלְעָזָר, Eleazar[us], shortened in the Talmud to לְעָזָר, Lazar) appears to have been younger than his sisters. According to an ancient tradition in Epiphanius,[2] he was then thirty years old, and lived that much longer. Later, in 890 A.D., they said they had found his remains on the island of Cyprus. According to a western legend, he and Martha went with others to Gaul, to Provence, and preached the gospel in Massilia.[3] The name Lazarus means: 'God help,' or exactly: whom God helps. Keim[4] uses this meaning as a support for his explanation of the poor Lazarus as 'Judaism maltreated by the earthly powers, by the Herodians and the Romans.' It is enough to observe that the poor Lazarus in Luke is not maltreated by the rich man, but only ignored; and in John is, on the contrary, loved. These are specimens of trifling. Names in Israel had meanings, and indeed the same meaning in the case of different bearers of them.

Bethany lay on an eastern outlying hill of the mount of Olives, fifteen stadia, or forty minutes, south-east from Jerusalem. At the present day they show the alleged houses

---

[1] Compare Luthardt, *St. John the Author of the Fourth Gospel*, Edinburgh, T. and T. Clark, 1875, p. 197 f. And for a characterization of the two sisters, see vol. i. p. 100 ff.

[2] Epiphanius, *Contra Hæreses*, lxvi. 34; *Panaria* [corp. Hæreseol., ed. Oehler, tom. ii.], Berlin 1860, vol. i. part ii. p. 464 [652 b, c].

[3] See Winer, *Biblisches Realwörterbuch*, 3d ed., Leipzig 1848, vol. ii. p. 10. [Smith, *Dictionary of the Bible*, sub voce 'Lazarus.'—C. R. G.]

[4] Keim, *Geschichte Jesu von Nazara*, Zürich 1872, vol. iii. p. 72.

of Simon the leper, of Lazarus, etc., and the rock-hewn tomb of the latter, up to which a flight of twenty-six steps leads; the grave is mentioned about 333 A.D. in the *Itinerarium Hierosolymitanum* (*Guide-book to Jerusalem*); and Jerome alludes to a church built over the vault. There is now a Turkish mosque by the grave.[1] Travellers praise the loveliness of the valley, which is adorned with fig, almond, and olive trees, and in which on the ascent lies Bethany nestling amid grain-fields and trees.[2] Since it owes its note in Christian circles to the sisters and their brother, and to the friendship of the family with the Lord, the evangelist names it after them, the village of Mary and of Martha her sister. Keim[3] explains the name as 'house of mourning,' בֵּית עֲנִיָּה; but עֲנִיָּה is the feminine of the adjective, and means: poor, wretched, but not: lamentation or sad. It is explained either as 'locus depressionis' ('place of depression'), owing to the lowness of the ground on which it lies,—hardly probable,—or better: בֵּית הִינִי, 'locus dactylorum' ('place of dates'), more exactly: place where there are dates which do not come to full ripeness (this occurs as a name of a place in the Talmud), or even according to the first meaning: house of the poor. To-day the name El Azarijeh, from El Azir = Lazarus, has entirely supplanted the old name. Keim[4] sees in the two Bethanys (x. 40, the one on the Jordan) 'a speaking playfulness.' But in this case the one on the Jordan must at least have been named!

Verse 3.

The sisters do not venture to ask Jesus directly. Their request lies in the message and in the phrase: *whom thou lovest*,—it is equally modest and confident. Ὅν φιλεῖσ, 'hoc modestius quam si dicerent: qui te amat, vel: amicus tuus' ('whom thou lovest; this is more modest than to say: who loves thee, or: thy friend'), Bengel. Jesus takes up this

---

[1] See Raumer, *Palästina*, 3d ed., Leipzig 1850, p. 274; and Robinson, *Palästina*, Halle 1841, vol. ii. p. 310 ff.

[2] See, for example, Furrer, *Wanderungen durch Palästina*, Zürich 1865, p. 147.

[3] Keim, *Geschichte Jesu von Nazara*, Zürich 1872, vol. iii. p. 67.

[4] Keim, *ut supra*, vol. iii. p. 70.

phrase in ver. 11: Λάζαροσ ὁ φίλοσ ἡμῶν ('Lazarus our friend'). It is therefore important to him. There lies in it for him a moral demand and a sign of the Father's will, at the service of which he readily places himself. His friend's death compels his love to the errand which brought Him himself unto death.

Verse 4.

Jesus speaks these words, which show his secure consciousness concerning God's will, in the first place to the disciples, who were frightened at the news, and yet also before the ears of the messenger, who on his return to the sisters could give them this statement for their comfort. He names as God's will, not that death is not the final, determined aim of this sickness (πρόσ, 'unto,' expression of destination), but that God shall be glorified in the resurrection (ὑπέρ, for, to the advantage of, it serves to further the δόξα, 'glory,' of God), in that God's Son will be glorified. Hence we read ἵνα δοξασθῇ κ.τ.λ. ('that ... might be glorified, etc.') as an explanatory nearer definition of the preceding ὑπέρ τῆσ δόξησ τοῦ θεοῦ ('for the glory of God'). 'Gloria Dei et gloria Filii Dei, una gloria' ('the glory of God and the glory of the Son of God are one glory'), Bengel.

It does not say that he intends to glorify himself, but that he will be glorified. Therefore it is not he, but the Father, who so orders it that the sickness reaches this issue. Hence we cannot say, with Baur,[1] that 'he purposely first let Lazarus die, in order to be able to raise him;' so that we may then take offence at this, and be able to prove in this way the unhistorical character of the account (similarly Keim[2]). For we have not come to know Jesus in the fourth gospel to be so heartless as, according to Baur and Keim,[3] he is said to appear to be.[4] He does not 'in cold blood sacrifice the interests of his friends to his own

---

[1] Baur, *Kritische Untersuchungen über die kanonischen Evangelien*, Tübingen 1847, p. 193.

[2] Keim, *Geschichte Jesu von Nazara*, Zürich 1867, vol. i. p. 132.

[3] Keim, *ut supra*, 1872, vol. iii. p. 70.   [4] See vol. i. p. 83.

interests,' but he makes this suffering also serve that highest aim which all suffering is meant to serve. That the words ἵνα δοξασθῇ κ.τ.λ. ('that ... might be glorified, etc.') are intended as a designation of the will of God (Brückner, against Baur), is taught by vers. 9 and 10, with which the second circle closes, the circle we now pass over to.

VERSE 5.

The evangelist begins again with a remark, which some have thought they must regard as a supplementary explanation of the third verse (De Wette). But that is certainly wrong, for with ver. 5 the narrative begins to take a further step. Ver. 5 leads towards the point, that Jesus after two days sets out upon the journey. For the contradiction in which ver. 5 stands with his remaining still two days beyond Jordan, solves itself in the contrary. It was not lack of love, but love itself, that Jesus showed, and that for all the members of the family (καί ... καί, 'felix familia' —'and ... and, happy family,' Bengel)—the evangelist here uses ἀγαπᾶν purposely, and not the more pathetic φιλεῖν used in ver. 3. In that he was to, and intended to, glorify himself in Lazarus, he prepared for the sisters and for him a joy which far outweighed the pain of the death. The two aims are inseparably combined in all God's self-testification, love toward men and God's honour. Hence he was not detained (see Meyer) by the purpose of exercising the sisters in belief (Olshausen), nor by the weighty matters of his activity in Perea (Lücke, Tholuck), of which the text contains nothing. The evangelist did not need to mention particularly that Jesus in all this fulfilled the will of God. He has already taught sufficiently the fact that all motion of will on the part of Jesus had its inner incitement from that of the Father's will.

VERSE 6.

But in another feature he causes us to look at the internal intercourse of the Son with the Father. In this sixth verse he intentionally emphasizes—in the words ὡσ οὖν (taking up again ἀκούσασ, ver. 4) ἤκουσεν ὅτι ἀσθενεῖ ('when he had heard therefore that he was sick')—the circumstance that Jesus had learned only this and nothing further, when he afterwards says κεκοίμηται ('sleepeth'), ver. 11, and ἀπέθανεν ('is dead'), ver. 14. Τότε μέν, tum quidem, 'then indeed,' in contrast to the start afterwards. 'Τότε tunc, quamvis aliis videri possit maxima esse properandi causa' ('then, although to others it might seem as if there were the greatest reason for hastening'), Bengel.

Thus therefore the two lines stand side by side: the knowledge and the determination of will (to help Lazarus at once) which came to him from the human side, and the knowledge and the determination of will which were imparted to him from his internal intercourse with God. He did what he did, divinely certain and conscious. When, however, he now, in appearance, withdraws himself from his activity in his calling to help his friends, we must remember that it is an errand which is to introduce the decision of his fate. This stands in the foreground.

VERSE 7.

Jesus expresses his consciousness of this, in that he ἔπειτα μετὰ τοῦτο ('then after that,' heaped up as in the classics to make very emphatic that which is temporally later), turning to his disciples, does not speak of Bethany and Lazarus, but says: ἄγωμεν εἰσ τὴν 'Ιουδαίαν πάλιν ('let us go into Judea again'). These words are not to be understood as if he had intended to renew an activity there, which was to begin with this miracle, and which was frustrated only by the decree of the Sanhedrim, so that in consequence of the decree he had to give up the plan, ver. 54. We saw by the closing section of the tenth chapter that Jesus' activity among the Jews in the preceding sense was at an end. But he wills to go into the land of unbelief and of hostility, that is, to meet death (similarly Godet also, against Meyer).

VERSE 8.

The disciples also understand what it means when he says he wishes to go into Judea again. In memory of the disposition which characterizes this land, they mention its latest outbreak; *νῦν*, just now, but a very short time ago. *And dost thou intend to go thither again?* Πάλιν ('again') is placed in front emphatically. Baumgarten-Crusius suggests that the danger of which they spoke threatened not at Bethany, but only at Jerusalem; but in the first place Bethany lies quite close enough to Jerusalem, and in the next place he misunderstands both Jesus' meaning in the word 'Ιουδαία ('Judea'), and the disciples' meaning in their recalling the fact stated. The thing in question is the disposition of 'the Jews' in general, which found only one expression in that single occurrence. But even by this we are reminded that Jesus now goes to meet death when he goes into this land.

VERSE 9.

If this be correct, then Jesus' answer cannot be directed against the fear of the disciples in the sense that he called their attention to the fact that he had nothing to fear so long as his time lasted (Baumgarten-Crusius, Maier, Meyer), and that this time was not yet up; because, though it were indeed 'jam multa hora, sed tamen adhuc dies' ('already late, yet it was still day'), Bengel. Meyer says: 'The time appointed me by God for working is not yet consumed. So long as it still lasts, no one can injure me. But when it is ended, I shall fall into the hands of my enemies, like one walking at night, who strikes things (stumbles) because he is without light.' It is true that the *twelve hours in the day* designate the temporal limitation of the work in one's vocation. The day is intended for the work in one's vocation.

If any man walk in the day, he offendeth not, that is, not: no misfortune happens to him (thus Meyer and commonly), for in that case the thing spoken of would be passive and not active,—what he experiences, and not what he does. Besides, προσκόπτειν means to strike against something, Matt. iv. 6, in that one makes a false step; and hence we find in the New Testament use of language προσκόπτειν and πρόσκομμα used for 'offending' and 'offence' in the moral sense. That it is here intended of false steps that one makes, is proved by the reason given: *because he seeth the light of this world.* It is arbitrary to see in this only an ornament which has no relation to the thought (Meyer). 'The light of this world' is in the first place the sunlight, but as the revelation of the will of God, which will directs us to our work. 'In the light everything must be active and address itself to its work.' Hence this does not mean the 'providentia patris respectu Jesu, et providentia Christi respectu fidelium' ('providence of the Father in respect to Jesus, and the providence of Christ in respect to believers,' Bengel), but the 'voluntas Dei' ('will of God'). If this will gives us light, we shall make no false steps. Thus the disciples are to be assured that Jesus acts rightly in going to Bethany; for he follows the will of the Father who appoints him his calling; the time of his vocation is not yet at an end.

Verse 10.

But if a man walk in the night,—which is not given for working but for resting, and which will come even for Jesus when the time of his work in his earthly vocation is at an end, compare ix. 4,—*he offendeth*, he makes false steps, *for the light is not in him,*—it is not merely dark outside of him, nor is it merely lightless and gloomy in his conception of his surroundings (Meyer), but 'in him,' that is, God's will does not illuminate and direct him internally. It does not say 'coram' ('before'), or 'in oculis' ('in his eyes'), as Grotius and Lücke think, but 'in him;' still less does Jesus speak perchance of the purity of his designs and of his action and the like (De Wette). That would be much too general if expressed thus, and also would be against the analogy of the other explanations which Jesus elsewhere gives his disciples concerning his action. But he speaks here, as elsewhere, of the fact that he does the will of his Father, and walks upon the path of the calling to which the Father hath directed him. Hence these words are not intended to serve the purpose of calming the disciples in view of the possible dangers, and of dispelling their apprehensions (thus commonly), but rather to justify Jesus' action, and thus to make the disciples joyful and comforted.

Verse 11.

This verse opens a new circle, in which the thoughts of death and life come to definite expression. *He said this, and after that he saith unto them*—with these words the evangelist separates what follows from what precedes, and causes us to think of a pause between the two: *Lazarus our friend hath gone to sleep; but I go that I may wake him;* 'our friend'—'quanta humanitate' ('what friendliness'), Bengel. Jesus' knowledge concerning Lazarus is a direct one. Jesus names death a sleep, as also antiquity did. But each in a different sense: antiquity, to conceal the essence of death; Jesus, to reveal it. Antiquity covers the horror of death with a euphemism:

> 'Das sie am Schmerz, den sie zu trösten
> Nicht wusste, mild vorüberführt:
> Erkenn' ich als der Zauber grössten,
> Womit uns die Antike rührt.'

('I recognise as the greatest of the spells by which antiquity touches us, the fact that it passes gently by the grief it knew not how to comfort.'[1])

When Jesus, on the other hand, designates death as sleep —'cœlesti lingua' ('in heavenly language,' Bengel), he does it because the sleeping in death is followed by a waking, with which even the psalmist comforted himself, Ps. xvii. 15, but the joyous future of which was to be much more definitely perceived from Christ's resurrection than was previously possible. On this occasion Jesus speaks thus because of the typical awakening which was decreed for Lazarus. The disciples, however, understand the word of

---

[1] Lenau, *Savonarola*, 3d ed., Stuttgart and Tübingen 1849, p. 100. [See on this point, Münter, *Symbolæ ad interpretationem evangelii Johannis ex marmoribus et numis, maxime græcis*, Copenhagen 1826, pp. 18–23. In discussing the idea of rest in death, see ver. 13, Münter cites several Jewish epitaphs, for example: מנוחתו תהא בגן עדן, 'May his rest be in the garden of Eden (paradise);' יבוא שלום וינוח על מנוחתו, 'May peace come and rest upon his repose.'—C. R. G.]

ordinary sleep. This misunderstanding is not so inexplicable as Strauss finds it to be. It has its natural foundation in the fact that—considering not only Jesus' perfectly definite words in the fourth verse (see also Ebrard,[1] against Strauss), and his delay, but also the approaching future of the kingdom which they expected for themselves as well as for the other friends of Jesus—they could not think of a death at all. It does not occur to them, that in case of a real sleep there could, precisely speaking, be no mention of going to him to wake him up. The fact that Jesus knows of this condition of his friend, does not in any way strike them as singular. Bengel remarks that the disciples seem to have regarded this sleep as a work of Jesus' assisting love — 'somnum ab Jesu immissum esse Lazaro, ut eveniret quod prædixerat ipse, ver. 4' ('the sleep had been sent to Lazarus by Jesus, so that what He himself had predicted in ver. 4 should come to pass'). This is very likely, and perhaps also has a certain exegetical support in the first person, $\pi o \rho \epsilon \acute{u} o \mu a \iota$, 'I go,' whereas before, in ver. 7, it says $\mathring{a} \gamma \omega \mu \epsilon \nu$, 'let us go.' If He goes now to do the one thing, He doubtless also had done the other. These words contain an emphasizing of his action, and not the goad of a shaming question as to whether they are unwilling to accompany him (Stier).

VERSE 12.

Lord, if he has gone to sleep, he will be delivered. These words of the disciples are commonly taken as a dissuading from the journey, as not necessary under such circumstances (Calvin: 'libenter hanc fugiendi periculi occasionem arripiunt,' 'they eagerly seize this chance for escaping the danger;' Grotius: 'discipuli omni modo quærunt dominum ab isto itinere avocare,' 'the disciples seek in every way to dissuade the Lord from that journey;' Maier, Olshausen, Baumgarten-Crusius, Brückner, Meyer, Hengstenberg). This is hardly correct. The disciples had received reply enough to their hesitation, in the ninth and tenth verses. As little

---

[1] Ebrard, *Wissenschaftliche Kritik der evangelischen Geschichte,* 3d ed., Frankfort-on-the-Main 1868, p. 549.

will they have thought that Jesus 'intended to interrupt this physically beneficial condition' of their friend (Ebrard).[1] Still less did they conceive of it as a jesting word, that He wished to see Lazarus wake up and find himself so well (Stier)! They doubtless understood the words as to waking, of the completion of the healing begun by Jesus,—with the sleep,—of the return to full active life, and they rejoiced at this. So much the more must Jesus' words concerning the death surprise and astound them, so that in view of this thought they are not in a position to think at once of the comforting promise which lay in the former words of Jesus, and still less to comprehend the joy of Jesus in ver. 15.

Verse 13.

Jesus had intended his words to refer to death: *Jesus spake of his death, but they thought that he had spoken of taking rest in sleep.*

Verse 14.

He now tells them that plainly: *Lazarus is dead.*—The words are sharp and short, and for that very reason make the hearers tremble.

Verse 15.

And I am glad for your sakes that I was not there, to the intent ye may believe. "Ὅτι οὐκ κ.τ.λ. ('that . . . not, etc.') of course depends on χαίρω ('I am glad'), and the clause of purpose is thrust in, in order to explain the δι' ὑμᾶσ ('for your sakes'). 'To the intent ye may believe:' they did believe already; but every progress of belief is a higher entrance on belief; compare ii. 11 (Meyer). Jesus is glad that he was not in Bethany, and that therefore things have gone as they have gone. This does indeed imply that if Jesus had been in Bethany, Lazarus would not have died. But this would have been less because he could not have resisted the prayers of the sisters (Maier), than because death could not have touched his friend in the presence of

---

[1] Ebrard, *Wissenschaftliche Kritik der evangelischen Geschichte*, 3d ed., Frankfort-on-the-Main 1868, p. 547.

Him the personal life. Bengel says: 'cum decoro divino pulchre congruit, quod præsente vitæ duce nemo unquam legitur mortuus' ('it fits beautifully with divine propriety, that we never read of any one's dying in the presence of the leader of life').

It is not only a higher display of Jesus' power (Maier, Meyer) when he delivers out of death than when he keeps from death, but much more a display of power better suited to, and more necessary for, the needs of the disciples, the securing of their belief for the time towards which he and they are moving. He therefore is glad, not at the circumstance that Lazarus died not in his presence but in his absence (Paulus), but that it was not given to Him by the Father to keep him from death, but to raise him from death. For in this way the disciples can gain belief on Him as the absolute life, even though He himself shall now be given up unto death. This is indeed awaiting him. He will, however, now address himself to his manifestation of himself as the life: *nevertheless, let us go to him.* 'Eo ubi iacet mortuus' ('thither where the dead man lies,' Bengel), says his summons, short, swift, decided.

VERSE 16.

The disciples now hear the death and do not notice the promise of life, and the words ἄγωμεν πρὸσ αὐτόν ('let us go to him') sound to them as if they pointed to Hades (thus also Bengel). For with Lazarus it seems to them as if all their hopes of the new day which was to dawn upon Israel, were buried in Hades. Jesus seems to intend or to be about to follow Lazarus: then they will go with Jesus (this is what the καὶ ἡμεῖσ, 'we also,' refers to, Lücke; and of course μετ' αὐτοῦ points, as the repetition of ἄγωμεν, 'let us go,' shows, to Jesus and not to Lazarus) unto death. Thus Thomas calls upon the rest to come, not to die by disease after Lazarus, which would be a singular demand (Lücke), but with Jesus to despair of this life in the mood of awaiting death. The evangelist has purposely preserved these words of Thomas.

They belong to the history of the disciples' development

in belief. They form a contrast to the confession of Thomas at the close of the gospel. Thomas, Θωμᾶσ, תְּאֹמָא, is from תאם, to be double, whence תֹּאֵם, 'twin,' and in consequence in Greek, Δίδυμοσ, Didymus. Here, as at xx. 24, xxi. 2, the evangelist adds the latter name to explain the Hebrew name, just as, for example, he interprets Messiah, iv. 25, by ὁ Χριστόσ, 'the Christ,' 'the anointed,' for the sake of the readers of the gospel. It does not follow from this that the name Thomas was first given to the apostle by Jesus (Hengstenberg). Were that the case, the evangelist would at some point or other have named his original name, as in the case of Simon Peter. Yet certainly the thrice repeated interpretation is somewhat striking. Luke vi. 15, and the traditional name of this apostle in the church, refute the conjecture that the apostle was only known to the heathen-Christian readers by the name of Didymus, or was so named by the heathen-Christians (Meyer). Therefore the name carried an important thought for the evangelist. The Greek readers did not understand the meaning of the name Thomas, but they did understand the meaning of Didymus. As the evangelist elsewhere calls attention to the meaning play of apparent chance in names,[1] so does he here. Thomas is a double person; none of the disciples is like him: in the deepest 'little faith' at the first, and afterwards at the highest stage of belief; see the characterization of Thomas.[2]

These words of Thomas stand at the conclusion of this section, without being followed by a correcting or some such statement on the part of Jesus, just as the other words of Thomas, xx. 28, stand at the close of the gospel. The book and its issue desire to transfer us into the worshipping mood of belief; the present section puts us involuntarily into an elegaic mood: It is right that it should; the thought of death predominates in it.

But in contrast with this, Jesus soon places at its side the other thought, which has found its most precise expression in ἐγώ εἰμι ἡ ἀνάστασισ καὶ ἡ ζωή ('I am the resurrection and the life'), ver. 25, and its explanation and pre-representation in the following story.

[1] Compare ix. 7.   [2] See vol. i. pp. 84-86.

(2.) Verses 17–44.

The Event itself.

The first scene of the transaction, vers. 17–27, depicts for us Jesus' meeting with Martha; the second, vers. 28–38, his meeting with Mary; and the third, vers. 39–44, shows us Jesus at the grave, and places him thereby in direct actual relation to death itself.

The first paragraph, vers. 17–20, draws the general frame for the historical occurrence which is to be reported. Yet it is not without its importance for the thing itself, which is in question, that the single points are placed together.

Verse 17.

Jesus found that Lazarus had already lain in the grave four days. When did he die? According to Jewish custom, the dead were buried on the very day of their death; but Jesus remained in Perea for two days after the message came from the sisters. The question arises, how far distant Jesus was from Jerusalem or Bethany. Furrer[1] reckons from Jerusalem to Jericho, six hours and a half, and from Jericho to the Jordan, one hour and forty minutes. Hence the distance from the in any case not very distant Jordanic to the Jerusalemitic Bethany, could with difficulty have amounted to more than nine or ten hours. Even if we may reckon a day perhaps for the messenger's journey, Jesus nevertheless will only have arrived at Bethany on the day following his departure from Perea.

Hence the death of Lazarus occurred soon after the departure of the messenger and his arrival in the presence of Jesus. It is not certain whether or not it happened on the very day of the arrival of the messenger himself at the place where Jesus was (thus I earlier, Ebrard, Gumlich, Hengstenberg, Godet). In any case, Jesus did not begin his journey on the day of the death, and thus spend four days, even if not full days, upon the journey, for the distance under no circumstances is so great as that (against Meyer).

[1] Furrer, *Wanderungen durch Palästina*, Zürich 1865, p. 412.

It was quite natural that the sisters should delay sending the messenger till the danger increased. If Lazarus be already for the fourth day in the grave, the hope of the sisters has the more completely disappeared, and the raising of the dead is the more unexpected and striking. Therefore, where there seemed to be no more hope, Jesus manifested himself as Lord of life over death. We are involuntarily reminded of the mournful words of the two disciples going to Emmaus, Luke xxiv. 21: ἡμεῖσ ἠλπίζομεν, ὅτι αὐτόσ ἐστιν ὁ μέλλων λυτροῦσθαι τὸν Ἰσραήλ· ἀλλά γε καὶ σὺν πᾶσιν τούτοισ τρίτην ταύτην ἡμέραν ἄγει σήμερον ἀφ' οὗ ταῦτα ἐγένετο ('we trusted that it had been he which should have redeemed Israel. And besides all this, to-day is the third day since these things were done'), hence all hope is gone. But so it was to be, in order the more incontestably to prove Him to be the one who He was.

Verse 18.

The next remark as to the nearness of Bethany to Jerusalem—ἀπὸ σταδίων δεκαπέντε reckons from a reversed view, at the end of a space of fifteen stadia[1]—is intended to show how easy it was for this occurrence to excite attention.

Verse 19.

Then follows the third remark, that accordingly many Jews had gathered together, who could serve as heralds of the deed.

Πρὸσ τὰσ περὶ Μάρθαν καὶ Μαριάμ have those Jews come, that is, to Martha and Mary and their surroundings. This is not a mere paraphrase of later Greek for Martha and Mary (Tholuck, Lücke); compare against that, Acts xiii. 13. It hardly means the mourning women,[2] but rather the female servants of the sisters. These servants are especially mentioned because it was a male visitor whom they received

---

[1] See Winer, *Grammatik des neutestamentlichen Sprachidioms*, § 61. 5, 7th ed., Leipzig 1867, p. 518 f.

[2] See Winer, *Biblisches Realwörterbuch*, 3d ed., Leipzig 1848, vol. ii. p. 631 ; *sub voce* 'Trauer.'

(Meyer). It is probably also correct to find in this mention of the servants a sign of the comfortable circumstances of the family. Those friends had come to testify to their grief in a Jewish way.

Being expressly designated as ἐκ τῶν Ἰουδαίων ('of the Jews'), we shall have no right, with Baumgarten-Crusius, to find that utterly meaningless, particularly in consideration of utterances like ver. 37. They belonged to the opposition (Brückner, Gumlich, Godet, Meyer). But it does not follow from that, that they intended to use the opportunity to lead this family back to the path of the ancient orthodox Judaism (thus Lampe and Lange). They only fulfil the ordinary duty of condoling with the sisters. Usually this condoling lasted for seven days, and was connected with all kinds of formalities; compare, for example, Sir. xxii. 12.[1] The speech which accompanied this is called παραμυθεῖσθαι, 'alloqui,' then 'consolari,' 'to address,' then 'to console.' Evidently the comfort which these Jews had to offer, who would know nothing of Jesus, is contrasted with that which Jesus was able to offer.

Verse 20.

Martha, 'now, too, the hostess' (Meyer), had busied herself in and out of the house. The news of Jesus' approach comes to her, probably by means of a passing Jew who had overtaken Jesus. Mary remains in the house,—ἐκαθέζετο, 'sat:' it was the custom to sit while receiving the visits of condolence,—hence she knows nothing of this, and Martha is too much excited by the news to think of first sending word of it to her sister.

Verse 21.

Lord, if thou hadst been here (ἦσ, the imperfect, here also not instead of the pluperfect, but to express the conception of contemporaneity), *my brother had not died* (οὐκ ἂν ἀπέθανεν, according to the manuscripts, not ἐτεθνήκει): she receives Jesus with these words. And so does her sister

---

[1] Keil, *Handbuch der biblischen Archäologie*, 2d ed., Frankfort-on-the-Main 1875, p. 573.

afterwards, ver. 32. We see from this that this thought had occupied them much, both during the illness and during the days since the death of their brother ('ex quo colligi potest, hunc earum fuisse sermonem ante fratris obitum: utinam adesset Dominus Jesus,' 'whence we may gather that this was their speech before the brother's death: Oh that the Lord Jesus were here!' Bengel). Therefore it at once presses forward. The words are not intended as a reproach (against Lücke and Baumgarten-Crusius), but only as a complaint, resting upon the certainty of belief.

Verse 22.

And this belief then also breaks forth: *I know* (without ἀλλά, ' but,' at the beginning, according to the manuscripts), *even now, that whatsoever thou wilt ask of God, God will give it thee.* The sudden presence of Jesus awakens in her the hasty belief that Jesus even now can still bring miraculous aid. The fact that she thinks of something extraordinary (Lücke) is, aside from the whole situation, clearly to be seen in the very repetition of ὁ θεόσ ('God'). 'Quanquam mortuus sit, tamen non dubito quin excitare possis' ('though he be dead, yet I do not doubt that thou canst raise him'), Melanchthon.[1] The thought is connected with Jesus' reply in ver. 4, but it only comes to her now, and ventures to shape itself into a wish. Yet the wish is too strong for her to dare to express it directly, so she clothes it in this more general form, that God hears the prayers of Jesus.

Bengel found the word αἰτεῖσθαι ('to ask'), 'minus dignum,' 'less worthy.' That is too critical a judgment. It is true Jesus uses only δέομαι, ἐρωτῶ, and θέλω of his own requests which he directs to the Father; and αἰτεῖσθαι, to beg something for oneself, is elsewhere in John only an expression of human neediness and childlike expectation towards God (compare John xiv. 13, xv. 7, 16, xvi. 24; 1 John v. 14, 15); yet it fits the situation here, and is quite natural in Martha's mouth. Jesus also addresses himself, as we see later, ver. 41 f., praying in spirit unto the Father, not indeed as elsewhere men do in the αἰτεῖσθαι,

---
[1] Melanchthon, *Opera*, ed. Halle 1847, vol. xiv. col. 1142.

for the supply of a need, but yet for the grant of the revelation of the power that the Father hath given him. For as in other things, so also in his working, he is conditioned on the Father.[1] Meyer observes that Martha's Messianic view of Jesus does not seem yet to comprise in itself the belief in his divinity; at least she has no clear conception of it, or she would have used πατήρ ('Father') instead of θεόσ ('God'). To this we must reply, that even Jesus' disciples had and could have no clear conception of his divinity so long as Jesus was not yet perfected. Only by the resurrection, the ascension to God, and the pouring out of the Spirit, did the higher knowledge dawn upon them. And yet, therefore, the whole was also contained in the previous general and indefinite impression. How else could Martha be impelled to so bold a hope?

VERSE 23.

That this hope, however, vanishes so speedily again, is due to the form of Jesus' reply: ἀναστήσεται ὁ ἀδελφόσ σου ('thy brother shall rise again'). For he speaks of a future event without putting it into direct relation to himself. The point that tried their belief, was not merely that Jesus did not add the time (Bengel), but rather that he did not speak in the first person. The brevity of the answer contains the affirmation. Jesus does not speak of the future resurrection at the last day, nor even 'especially' of it (Hengstenberg), but of the one at hand, which he has in mind. Yet for pedagogical reasons touching their belief, he speaks of this designedly in such a form of expression that Martha could understand the words in another way, namely, only as a comforting allusion to the future (compare Meyer). Nor does Martha find in Jesus' words a granting of her hope. Instead of the 'yes,' she hears a 'no.'

VERSE 24.

Hence her reply is not intended inquiringly (De Wette), but mournfully, in the fullest sense. She knows that quite well; but how does that help her now? This passage has

[1] Beyschlag, *Die Christologie des Neuen Testaments*, Berlin 1866, p. 71 f.

been called a classical one 'for the existence of such a popular conception of the resurrection at the last day' (Baumgarten-Crusius). But this conception is attested even by Dan. xii. 2 and 2 Macc. vii. 9, 14, 23, 36, xii. 43, 44, and formed an essential constituent of the Pharisaic belief, and therefore also of the ruling view of the people; compare Schürer[1] on this point, and the literature he cites. But from the very beginning this belief was included in the belief in Jehovah, who is indeed a God of the future, and therefore also of his own, who have entered into communion with him; compare Matt. xxii. 31 f.[2] From that point arose the belief, the more certainly as time advanced, that the dawn of the day of Jehovah will also break upon those who dwell in the shadows of Sheol. When Jesus, in what follows, names himself the resurrection and the life, the future hope is indeed for Martha's belief knit to Jesus; but no more. To her Lazarus still remained withdrawn beyond Jesus, for she knew of the latter as in life, of the former as in death. Hence Jesus must show to her that Lazarus is not lost to Him, that communion with Him is not destroyed by death, and that even in this sense also he is the life in death. Hence Bengel observes justly upon ver. 25: 'non adstrictus ad futurum' ('not bound to the future').

Verses 25, 26.

I am the resurrection and the life: he that believeth in me shall live, even though he were dead: and whosoever liveth and believeth in me, shall certainly never die. Jesus is what he calls himself and what his own believe him to be, absolutely, so that this is not altered by external temporal changes. Jesus desires to lift Martha's thoughts from the momentary and the individual to the higher general, constantly existing, essential part of believing certainty (ἀνάγει

---

[1] Schürer, *Lehrbuch der neutestamentlichen Zeitgeschichte*, Leipzig 1874, p. 594 f.

[2] See also Delitzsch, *Biblischer Commentar über die Psalmen*, Leipzig 1873, vol. i. pp. 55-58.

τὸν νοῦν αὐτῆσ, 'he leads her mind upward'[1]), in that he guides her from her own interests to his person. 'I'— this is emphatic (De Wette, Lücke, Meyer, Godet). All depends upon him and is determined in him. It is the great 'I am' of the gospel of John, and at heart also of the other gospels.[2] The present εἰμί ('I am') expresses that which is true of him essentially, and therefore at all times, now as well as in the future: the resurrection and the life.

As a rule, both statements, ἀνάστασισ and ζωή ('resurrection' and 'life') are supposed to be developed in the two following sentences (Bengel). But only the ζωή ('life') is developed. For the life which he attributes to the believer even in death is not the future resurrection, but simply the life in death. Therefore, with ἐγώ εἰμι ἡ ἀνάστασισ ('I am the resurrection') Jesus points back, ver. 24, to that final ἀνάστασισ ('resurrection') of which Martha knew. That fact of the future is decreed in his present person, according to its ability and vocation; and this because life essentially dwells in him. Hence ζωή ('life') does not name the consequence of the resurrection (Lücke, Meyer, Gumlich[3]), but the confirmation of the future event, a confirmation lying in Jesus' person. Because the life, the essential life, the ζωὴ αἰώνιοσ ('eternal life'), in the change of times is decreed in him, therefore is the future resurrection also connected with him.

Martha now is to hold fast to this essential point, that he who by πίστισ ('belief') has entered into communion with Him, has in consequence also entered into communion with life itself, so that therefore the believer, κἂν ἀποθάνῃ, even though dead, has not fallen from life. And, in ver. 26, now still rising: πᾶσ (Bengel: 'hoc, versu 25 non adhibitum, ad maiora sermonem profert,' 'this, not used in ver. 25, directs the discourse to greater things'), every one, among the living, who believes, need not fear falling into

---

[1] Euthymius Zigabenus, *Commentarius in quatuor Evangelia græce et latine*, ed. Matthœi, Leipzig 1792, vol. iii. p. 405.

[2] Compare Luthardt, *St. John the Author of the Fourth Gospel*, Edinburgh, T. and T. Clark, 1875, p. 237 ff.; and see vol. i. p. 237.

[3] Gumlich, *Studien und Kritiken*, 1862, p. 165.

the power of death: οὐ μὴ ἀποθάνῃ ('shall not die '),—the double negative strengthening the denial of death,—and that εἰσ τὸν αἰῶνα, 'for all eternity.' As a matter of course, in ζήσεται ('shall live '), ver. 25, Jesus speaks at first of the internal spiritual life of the person, not of the bodily life. Bengel's supplying 'etiam corpore,' 'even in the body,' is arbitrary. It is true that ἀναστήσεται ('shall rise') is the consequence of this, but it is only the consequence. On the other hand, the following ζῶν ('that liveth'), ver. 26, is just as unquestionably to be understood of the bodily life, and not, as is beyond question for Stier,[1] of the spiritual life; were Stier's view correct, the position of ζῶν and πιστεύων ('believeth') would have to be the reverse of what it is. The preceding ζήσεται ('shall live') is not intended to be taken up again, but the contrast to κἂν ἀποθάνῃ is to be named, and ζῶν and οὐ μὴ ἀποθάνῃ are then, in the change of their meanings, related to each other as previously were κἂν ἀποθάνῃ and ζήσεται. The necessity of this analogy refutes all the objections of Olshausen and Stier.

Jesus had testified to himself as the life of the future and as the life in the present, the former also according to the natural life, the latter at least according to the personal life. The raising of Lazarus was intended to prove this. For if Jesus has power to call back the soul which has already fallen into the realm of Hades, this is a proof that even there it is not lost to him, that even there it is still in communion with him the life. Therefore, whosoever by belief has entered into personal fellowship of life with him, has life even in death as to his person, and in that has at the same time a pledge of the new life for which his death-subjected nature may hope. If, moreover, the presence and power of life be in Jesus in such a comprehensive sense, it may at once be seen therefrom what is to be believed of and hoped for in him when he himself shall be given up unto death. This his disciples were to learn in general from this occurrence, for the speedily approaching time when they could use this knowledge.

Jesus thus made a demand on Martha's belief, namely,

[1] Stier, *Reden Jesu*, 3d ed., Leipzig 1873, vol. v. p. 28.

that she should cleave, not to the visible, but to the essential, which lies behind the visible, and from that point be assured of the future. Hence he turns to her with the urgent question : *Believest thou this ?* This direct turn can and is intended to be at the same time a help for her belief. And Martha answers the question affirmatively.

VERSE 27.

Martha had not indeed understood that conclusion in reference to Jesus himself, or the near-lying hope in reference to her brother ; yet she had understood the statement touching the life mediated by him even in death, and she acknowledged her belief in it : *Yea, Lord.* By this she affirms, in the first place, her belief on the word of Jesus which she had just heard. This ναὶ κύριε ('yea, Lord') refers to Jesus' question, and is not developed in what follows, so that what follows contains the answer (against Godet) ; but what follows confirms her yea. She believes that Jesus is the resurrection and the life ; for she believes that Jesus is the Messiah. Both, moreover, are so inwardly connected that she has recognised the former as a point lying in and given with the latter. Hence it is not at heart a new belief ; but this new point merely springs forth from her previous belief. It is not without reason that she says πεπίστευκα : *I* have—not now (thus Bengel), but when she united herself to Jesus in belief—won belief, and now *believe that thou art the Christ, the Son of God, which should come into the world.*

She designates him as the fulfilment of Israel, ὁ Χριστόσ ('the Christ'), as the completion of all divine revelation and communion (ὁ υἱὸσ τοῦ θεοῦ, 'the Son of God'), and as the salvation and expectation of the whole world (ὁ εἰσ τὸν κόσμον ἐρχόμενοσ, 'which should come into the world'). It is true that Martha does not mean 'Son of God' at first in the Johannean complete sense, but in the theocratical sense. Yet in that she at all finds it necessary to add this second definition to ὁ Χριστόσ, she shows that ὁ Χριστόσ is not enough for her, but that she desires to say a further thing of Christ : his personal relation to God. The third phrase, again, is an independent nearer definition of both the former ones. Ὁ ἐρχόμενοσ (' which should come ') is present, but used in the future meaning, which it has in this expression: הבא, the coming one, that is, he who will and shall come.—She does not intend to say by this 'that she expects the Messianic appearance as close at hand' (Meyer), but Jesus is to her indeed ὁ ἐρχόμενοσ, the one who is to come, and who now is there. It is the well-known ὁ ἐρχόμενοσ; compare Matt. xi. 3; Luke vii. 19, 20; in John vi. 14 it is, as here, put with εἰσ τὸν κόσμον.

With this she closes the confession. All that can be believed and known of Jesus is included in this threefold statement, which looks towards the three possible sides, to the history of salvation, to the fellowship of salvation, and to the need and hope of salvation. We might say: the first names the theme of Matthew's gospel, the third the theme of Luke's gospel, and the second the theme of John's gospel. And that which, in the higher combination of the scattered points, is the theme of the fourth gospel, is in direct generality and unity, the theme also of the second gospel.

She desired to confess her belief in Jesus in a complete, comprehensive manner, so as at the same time by this full joyful confession to show how certain it now also is to her that with Jesus is given life in death. By no means did she hastily try to end the conversation, which had taken a turn that went too high for her.[1]

Verse 28.

After these words she went away and called her sister. It is not said that Jesus sent her to bring her sister. But that follows naturally from φωνεῖ σε ('calleth for thee'); thus most commentators, against Brückner. Jesus had not replied to her confession. He had for the present led Martha far enough. Now, he wished to speak to her sister. Her calling her sister secretly is commonly said to be because of the hostile Jews (Lampe, Baumgarten-Crusius, Meyer, Gumlich). Perhaps it was in order to save her sister the troublesome witnesses of the first meeting, and

[1] See vol. i. p. 101 f.

of the new outburst of grief. *The teacher is there, and calls thee.* She does not say this ' quo celerius Mariam excitaret ' (' in order to urge Mary more swiftly '), Bengel. Mary did not need that. This announcement was indeed a matter of course. She calls Jesus ὁ διδάσκαλοσ (' the teacher ') : ' ita solebant inter se loqui de Jesu ' (' thus they were accustomed to speak of Jesus among themselves,' Bengel); for to them he had entered upon the place of the other masters of Israel ; compare xx. 16. As we see, the friendship between Jesus and them was based on the relation of teacher and scholar.

VERSE 29.

We have in the last words entered upon the second scene. Mary rose quickly to go to Jesus: *As soon as she heard that.*

VERSE 30.

For Jesus still (ἔτι, with ℵ B C) remained at the place where Martha had met him. This was certainly not in order to be in the neighbourhood of the grave (Olshausen, Hengstenberg), the situation of which he did not know; compare ver. 34. The reason for it is the same as the reason for the λάθρα (' secretly ') in ver. 28. He does not wish to have any disturbing witnesses of the first meeting with Mary (Meyer, Gumlich, Godet).

VERSE 31.

He does not indeed succeed in that. It is stated twice, ver. 29 and ver. 31, that she rose quickly and went forth. This is intended to hint at the violent movement of her feelings, which now also hastened her steps. The Jews ascribed it to a renewed violent emotion of grief (δόξαντεσ, ' thinking,' with ℵ B C L), and, according to the custom, hurried after her in order also at the grave to come to her aid with words of comfort. This alludes to the contrast with such comfort, offered in that which follows.

VERSE 32.

By the greater circumstantiality with which the emotion

is here described, the narrative permits us to see how much more violent the emotion of soul and the strength of the grief was in her case than in that of her sister. And this expresses itself likewise in the conduct of Mary. The very first words: *Then when Mary came where Jesus was, as she saw him*, are designedly thus chosen; and the following words: *she fell down at his feet* (αὐτοῦ πρὸσ τοὺσ πόδασ, according to the manuscripts), show the violence of her painful emotion of grief. The words with which she addressed Jesus are the same complaint as that in her sister's first words; only that, perhaps, it is not entirely a matter of indifference that in her address μοῦ ('my') precedes, whereas in ver. 21 it follows ἀδελφόσ ('brother'): *my* (emphatic) *brother had not died*. This occurs often in the New Testament, compare, for example, xiii. 6, and also elsewhere in Greek. By it the personal reference receives a stronger accent, corresponding to the individuality of Mary.

It is meant, as before, that in Jesus' presence death would have had no power over her brother, which makes her grieve at the very fact that Jesus could not have been present. But while Martha lifts herself from the grief, not merely to further conversation, but also to believing confidence and to the consolation of belief, Mary remains entirely in the realm of grief. She can bring no further word over her lips: her feelings can only find relief in tears. But by the very fact that he speaks no word of comfort to her, he calls her attention to his action. From the latter shall she then draw that knowledge of his essence which he gave to her sister at the very beginning, in order thereby to lead her to the understanding of his confirmatory action. Therefore Jesus is silent purposely, but not on account of the troublesome Jews (Meyer).

Verse 33.

Her woe, and the mourning tokens of the accompanying Jews, drew Jesus into a series of emotions, the order of and the single expressions for which have always been regarded as especially difficult to be understood.

We hold fast above all to the certain point that ἐμβριμᾶσθαι is always the expression only for indignation and angry emotion: 'infremo, vehementer irascor vel indignor;'[1] compare the detailed linguistic and literary proofs in Gumlich.[2] Βριμάομαι, from βρέμω, 'fremo,' expresses by way of imitation of the sound the low trembling tone of growling, of roaring, that proceeds from an object inwardly excited. Thence comes ἐμβριμάομαι, 'to breathe heavily,' exactly (Aeschylus[3]) and inexactly (Lucian[4]); hence Suidas: ἐμβριμᾶται, μετὰ αὐτηρότητοσ ἐπιτιμᾷ· ἐμβριμῆσαι, μετ' ὀργῆσ λαλῆσαι ('he reproves with severity:' 'to speak in anger'); thus also the Septuagint and the ancient versions. It has the same meaning in the five passages of the New Testament in which it is used, three times with, twice without τινί (object), four times of Jesus and once of the disciples as a strengthening of the usual ἐπιτιμᾶν; besides here and ver. 38, in Matt. ix. 30, Mark i. 43, xiv. 5. Thus it is here an expression for violent indignation and anger; Vulgate: 'infremuit spiritu;' Luther: he chafed in his spirit. Thus also all the Greek commentators explain it, as for example, Origen, Chrysostom, Theodore of Mopsuestia, Theodoret, and Theophylact; likewise the most of the earlier and later exegetes: Augustine, Nicolas de Lyra, Erasmus, Melanchthon, and the entire body of the exegetes of the Lutheran church; and, moreover, Lampe, Kuinoel, Strauss, Baur, Köstlin in his *Lehrbegriff*, Hilgenfeld, Stier, Ebrard, Besser, Meyer, Brückner, Godet. Exactly it is: he groaned with anger within himself. Hence it is neither here nor in ver. 38 to be understood of a strong emotion or of a violent convulsion of grief (thus Calvin, Olshausen, Maier, Lücke, Baumgarten-Crusius); nor is it to be considered as 'a grief that approaches indignation' (De Wette, Tholuck, Ewald).

This indignation, since ἐμβριμάομαι as a rule names one

[1] Grimm's edition of: *Wilkii Clavis N. T. philologica*, Leipzig 1862–1868.
[2] Gumlich, *Studien und Kritiken*, 1862, pp. 260–269.
[3] Aeschylus, 'Επτὰ ἐπὶ Θήβας, line 457, ed. Blomfield, Leipzig 1823, p. 45.
[4] Lucianus Samosatensis, *Menippus seu Necyomantia*, 20; *Opera*, ed. Jacobitz, Leipzig 1870, vol. i. p. 203 [484].

who expresses himself, is designated by τῷ πνεύματι ('in the spirit'), as one limited to the internality of the emotion of soul; compare ver. 38, ἐν ἑαυτῷ ('in himself'), and for this meaning of πνεῦμα ('spirit'), for example, xiii. 21. This latter passage also shows how the dative τῷ πνεύματι is to be understood. It is the same dative of reference as in the beatitudes, Matt. v. 3, 8, which gives the sphere in reference to which something occurs.[1] It is therefore not a designation of the object at which he was angry; so that it should designate the human emotion which seized upon him, and concerning which Jesus was angry according to his divine being, because the human feeling threatened to tear away the human person from its fellowship with the Logos, 'so that his divinity is angry at his moved humanity, and holds it together convulsively' (thus following the example of Origen, Chrysostom, Euthymius; among later scholars, especially Hilgenfeld repeatedly).[2] Such a view, however, is opposed not only by the parallel of ἐν ἑαυτῷ, ver. 38, but also by the notion of the πνεῦμα, which is not a passive object of determination, like ψυχή ('soul'), but the active, determining power of the internal life: vi. 63, τὸ πνεῦμά ἐστιν τὸ ζωοποιοῦν ('it is the spirit that quickeneth'); compare Hofmann[3] and Delitzsch.[4] As little does τὸ πνεῦμα designate the divine nature of Christ or the Logos (Zeller, Köstlin[5]), or the Holy Ghost (Cyril, Theophylact), so that he 'by means' of it (τῷ πνεύματι = τῇ δυνάμει τοῦ ἁγίου πνεύματοσ) was angry at his human sympathy.

The correct conception of τῷ πνεύματι finds its correspondent in ἐτάραξεν ἑαυτόν, *he troubled himself*, not merely: he troubled himself (Luther, Calov), and not: he let himself be troubled (De Wette), or in the sense of ἐταράχθη

---

[1] Compare Winer, *Grammatik des neutestamentlichen Sprachidioms*, § 31. 6 a, 7th ed., Leipzig 1867, p. 202.

[2] Hilgenfeld, *Die Evangelien*, Leipzig 1854, p. 296; *Historisch-kritische Einleitung in das Neue Testament*, Leipzig 1875, p. 709.

[3] Hofmann, *Der Schriftbeweis*, 2d ed., Nördlingen 1857, vol. i. p. 294.

[4] Delitzsch, *Biblische Psychologie*, 2d ed., Leipzig 1861, p. 96.

[5] Köstlin, *Der Lehrbegriff des Evangelium und der Briefe Johannis*, Berlin 1843, p. 141.

('he was troubled'), xiii. 21, but with intentional emphasis upon the personal activity on the part of Jesus. The reflexive does not intend merely to reproduce figuratively the view, so that the reader may at once see how Jesus shakes himself and shivers (Meyer); the expression would be too strong and too striking for that. In other cases it is always said of Jesus passively: τετάρακται, xii. 27, or ἐταράχθη, xiii. 21, and therefore the striking choice of the active must have been specially intended. It is true that ἑαυτόν ('himself') does not mean to limit the convulsion to the soul of Jesus (thus I earlier, and also Brückner), but comprehends the whole man inwardly and outwardly. Doubtless, however, the expression desires to designate the emotion as one that did not come upon Jesus, but which came forth from his innermost soul, so that the activity and the clear consciousness of Jesus remained intact (thus also Augustine, Brückner, Ebrard, Gumlich). Hence Bengel's words are correct: 'affectus Jesu non fuere passiones, sed voluntariæ commotiones, quas plane in sua potestate habebat: et hæc turbatio fuit plena ordinis et rationis summæ' ('the affections of Jesus were not passions, but voluntary commotions which he had entirely in his power; and this disturbance was full of order and of the highest reason').

What excited this violent convulsion of anger in Jesus? Before this (ὡσ εἶδεν, 'when he saw') the mournful words of Mary are named, and then her tears; and in contrast therewith, the weeping of the Jews. It must therefore stand in connection with these things. We have already seen that Jesus was not angry at his own emotion. Indeed, nothing is said about that before, and, moreover, he afterwards weeps.

Should it have been Mary's tears as a sign of unbelief (Lampe)? Or the therein revealed failure of his friends to know him, which want of knowledge combined itself with the wickedness of his enemies (Brückner)? That presupposes that Mary's address to Jesus was a reproach (Brückner). We have convinced ourselves, however, that this is not the case. Was the cause the unbelief of the

Jews? (Thus Kling.[1]) Or was it that of both? (Thus Theodore of Mopsuestia, Theodoret, Keim, and Strauss.[2]) But tears are not signs of unbelief; they are the involuntary utterance of the natural feeling of grief. Or was it the hypocritical tears of the Jews in contrast with the tears of Mary that moved him so much? (Thus Meyer.) For this, in my opinion, the violent convulsion of Jesus is too strong. Under such circumstances it would have been correct to speak of a being angry or the like, but not of such an internal convulsion. In that case we should have to assume a mingled feeling, and so save ourselves the more definite psychological explanation.

But as this, too, is not permissible if any other explanation still remains, the explanation will have to cleave to the course of the old method of understanding it, which found here an anger on the part of Jesus at death and its power. Thus say Theodore of Mopsuestia, Augustine, Lyra: 'iste enim fremitus Christi procedebat ex indignatione eius contra diabolum, per cuius suggestionem mors intravit in mundum, quem erat cito debellaturus,' 'for this groaning on the part of Christ proceeded from his indignation at the devil, by whose suggestion death entered into the world, and whom He was about to overcome,'[3] Erasmus, Calvin, Cornelius a Lapide; most Lutheran commentators, as Calov, Ebrard, Olshausen, Besser, Gumlich, and also Kahnis[4]—'there the unnatural character of death convulsed him the prince of life.' But it was not in a presentiment of his death, with which he should pay the penalty for the help he was here about to bring (Godet),—this seems to me artificial and unpsychological,—but it was that death, and he who has the power of death, should possess and exercise such power, and be able to cause such suffering. It is the most human sympathy, but in

---

[1] Kling, *Studien und Kritiken*, 1836, p. 674.

[2] Strauss, *Das Leben Jesu für das deutsche Volk bearbeitet*, Leipzig 1864, p. 474.

[3] Lyra (*Postilla in libros Novi Testamenti*, printed by Koberger at Nuremberg 1487) sheet q, fol. ii. A. a.

[4] Kahnis, *Die lutherische Dogmatik historisch-genetisch dargestellt*, Leipzig 1861, vol. i. p. 504.

the shape of anger against this power of opposition to life, this power which in all its convulsing strength here met him at the threshold of his own death.

It need not be said that he knew it before. For the effect of the veritable event before which we stand is quite different from that of the mere knowledge of it. But his internal anger is a threatening of this hostile power: he arms himself to war upon the enemy, who came to meet him in Lazarus' death. Cornelius a Lapide observes: 'se vicit et Lazarum suscitare voluit, qui fuit actus heroicæ fortitudinis, quem hoc fremitu patefecit. Sic milites instante prœlio fremunt et iras excitant acuuntque ad instantem pugnam arduam et periculosam; ira enim est cos virtutis et fortitudinis' ('he conquered himself, and he determined to raise Lazarus; an act of heroic fortitude, revealed in this groaning. Thus soldiers, when a battle is at hand, rage and excite their anger, and sharpen themselves for the arduous and dangerous conflict about to begin; for anger is the heart of virtue and fortitude ').[1]

Verse 34.

Jesus asks for the grave of Lazarus. This was not for effect, as for centuries the churchly exegetes have said, and is not to be explained upon the basis of the hypostatic union ('unio hypostatica'). The brevity of the question: *Where have ye laid him?* with the tone of decision, is at the same time occasioned by the sympathy which at this moment prevents his using many words. But the short answer: *Lord, come and see,* short because of grief, draws him, too, into the circle of the grief, and brings the feeling of grief to expression. Even in the previous indignation lay included the internal sympathy.

Verse 35.

Jesus wept. This is the third short phrase of the evangelist, the shortest verse, but just because of its brevity it is of the greatest, the most moving power. Hence also the

---

[1] Cornelius a Lapide, *Commentarius in Evangelium Johannis* [*Commentarius in Evangelia,* vol. ii.], Antwerp 1660, p. 420, A. a.

evangelist has made it stand clearly by itself, without placing it in connection with what precedes or with what follows, by particles. 'Lacrymatus est, non ploravit' ('he shed tears, he did not cry aloud'), Bengel. Jesus knew well that He would raise the dead man. But nevertheless that did not prevent his death from being a matter of grief. This is the human part of Jesus, that even his feelings were determined by the present, and stood under the influence of the instant. To this is to be added the fact that the fate of Lazarus had for Jesus a more general meaning, and was a reminder of the entire activity of the prince of death (compare Gumlich).

He weeps, not at the future judgment of Israel, as in Luke xix. 41 ff. at the sight of Jerusalem (against Strauss[1]), but at the judgment then present; that was, however, the suffering of death. As in Gethsemane and onwards from it he entered with his feelings into human death-suffering, so here he enters in human death-grief. Heb. ii. 17 f. recalls the fact also that he who was to help must have above all a feeling for the suffering out of which he was to afford help. Hence Hilgenfeld[2] is entirely right when, in the face of other representations of the Tübingen school (Zeller and Köstlin), he emphasizes the point that the passage before us not merely demands the assumption of a mere human corporality on the part of Christ, but also proves[3] the reality of a human person, which, as he expresses it, was united with the Logos. Keim,[4] however, without the least reason, finds the tears 'unnatural.' Jesus 'was not ashamed of tears' (Besser).

Verse 36.

His tears were not understood by all. Some, indeed, saw therein a sign of his love for Lazarus: πῶσ ἐφίλει ('how he loved'), in the imperfect, because referred to the time at which Lazarus still lived.

---

[1] Strauss, *Das Leben Jesu für das deutsche Volk bearbeitet*, Leipzig 1864.
[2] Hilgenfeld, *Das Evangelium und die Briefe Johannis nach ihrem Lehrbegriff dargestellt*, Halle 1849, p. 226 ff.
[3] Hilgenfeld, *ibid.* p. 260 f.
[4] Keim, *Geschichte Jesu von Nazara*, Zürich 1872, vol. iii. p. 71.

Verse 37.

When others of the Jews opposed to these: *Could not this man, who opened the eyes of the blind, have caused that even this man should not have died?* they thereby show evidently an internal position contrasted to that of the former speakers. Hence this cannot be an expression of good-will, which rested on a very strong belief in Jesus' miraculous power, as Gumlich[1] tries to prove, and as Lücke, Tholuck, De Wette, Brückner, and Hengstenberg more or less decidedly conceive it. It must be spoken from a contrasted internal posture, and therefore be meant in ill-will. Thus the most of the older commentators, as Chrysostom, Theophylact, Calvin, Bengel, also Meyer and Godet. But they do not deny his power (thus Meyer), for the words of these ill-willed people are a reply to ἐφίλει ('he loved'). Hence they deny Jesus' love. To them the tears are a sign of his impotence. Now it is too late. But he could have helped at an earlier period, if he had wished to. Why did he not come earlier? They appeal to the healing of the blind man. According to that explanation of Meyer's, they would deny this healing. We have no right to make such an assumption. They argue from the healing as a fact. How it may really have come to pass they leave undiscussed; for the people, the fact stood firm. Could he do that, he could also do this, namely, he could have kept Lazarus from death. Therefore he did not wish to. His tears thus seem to them hypocritical.

This, then, is the form of unbelief now, that denies not the power, but the love of Jesus. It could go no further. For if anything was proved through the whole life of Jesus, it was his love, ever ready to bear help. It is quite natural that the Jews should recall the healing of the blind and not the Galilean miracles (Strauss). The former had occurred but a short time before at Jerusalem, and had excited great attention. The Galilean miracles lay further from their circle of vision and from their knowledge, and might well also be problematical. This, therefore, in the mouth of

[1] Gumlich, *Studien und Kritiken*, 1862, pp. 297-307.

the Jerusalemites is directly a sign of historical truth (Brückner).

VERSE 38.

Jesus again groaned within himself. This new groaning is called forth by such failure to recognise his love: οὖν ('therefore') shows this. The explanation which conceives of the last speech of the Jews as a word of good-will and of belief (as Gumlich and the rest), must make the groaning of Jesus come in without any reason. But the groaning is evidently called forth by the ill-willed words of the Jews. It does not, however, exhaust itself upon them (thus commonly), but passes beyond them again to him who knew how to misuse the death of Lazarus for such a misinterpretation of Jesus' loving disposition. The indignation had led Jesus forth from the sphere of the overpowering feeling of grief, so that he now stood over the thing itself. In such a mood of anger against his opponents he goes to the grave with the sure step of certain victory. With this we are led to the third scene.

In the first place, the grave is briefly described, as far as was necessary to be able to understand the words of Jesus now to be cited. It was a rock-tomb (σπήλαιον, cave), such as the richer men had,[1] perhaps also with an entrance or an outer hall, and with different passages or rooms. It is hardly possible to decide whether it was hewn in the rock horizontally or perpendicularly. What follows does not speak necessarily for the former (against Lücke, De Wette). Yet it may at any rate not be improbable, and ἐπί ('upon'), as is well known, permits us to think of the stone as resting against the rock, and therefore as upright. As to the place now designated as Lazarus' grave, see above. Εἰσ τὸ μνημεῖον does not mean 'into,' but 'unto' the grave.

VERSE 39.

Ἄρατε τὸν λίθον, *Take ye away the stone;* Jesus commands,

---

[1] Compare Keil, *Handbuch der biblischen Archäologie,* 2d ed., Frankfort-on-the-Main 1875, p. 571; and Winer, *Biblisches Realwörterbuch,* 3d ed., Leipzig 1847, vol. i. p. 443 f., *sub voce* 'Gräber.'

with the tone of firm determination, as in the question, ver. 34. The words and the execution of them must put all in suspense and expectation—'suspensis omnium animis atque oculis' ('the minds and eyes of all being in suspense'), Titmann;—only Martha raises an objection: κύριε, ἤδη ὄζει ('Lord, by this time he stinketh'). It is commonly concluded from this that the usual embalming had not taken place. The Egyptian custom, Gen. l. 2 f., 26, laid the body, even if the brain and bowels were not removed, at least for seventy days in nitre.[1] In distinction from this, the Jewish custom consisted only in anointing the dead with costly oils, xii. 7, and wrapping them up with aromatic spices, xix. 39 ff.[2] It is not to be seen why this should here have been omitted. That they let it wait because they expected Jesus (thus I earlier), is an arbitrary assumption. It can in no wise be explained from the hope of the resurrection by Jesus (thus Hengstenberg), for the sisters did not have this hope; Martha only had it in a passing excitement of belief. But that whole argumentation is arbitrary. Martha could say this, even if her brother had been embalmed.

It is a delicate feature of the evangelist's, that he adds to Martha's name the words ἡ ἀδελφὴ τοῦ τετελευτηκότοσ ('the sister of him that was dead'). He did not need to describe her of whom so much had been said but a moment before. 'Causa horroris maioris notatur, ex natura et necessitudine' ('the reason for the greater horror is noted, from nature and necessity'), Bengel. She desires to save herself and Jesus the sight. Hengstenberg's opinion is a forced one, that she, 'in view of the corruption,' places 'before Jesus' eyes the greatness of the work which he is upon the point of executing.' 'She intends by this to make Jesus confirm his promise anew, and in that way strengthen her belief.' She does not expect the resurrection; she had understood Jesus' words of the essential life, and had contented herself with that. The words added: τεταρταῖοσ

---

[1] See Winer, *Biblisches Realwörterbuch*, 3d ed., Leipzig 1847, vol. i. p. 307 f., *sub voce* 'Einbalsamiren.'

[2] Keil, *Handbuch der biblischen Archäologie*, 2d ed., Frankfort-on-the-Main 1875, p. 571.

γάρ ἐστιν ('for he hath been dead four days'), evidently characterize the preceding ἤδη ὄζει ('by this time he stinketh') as a conclusion drawn by Martha (thus almost all modern commentators). Strauss,[1] indeed, conjectures that there was a 'smell of putrefaction;' and Keim[2] sees 'rationalism' in the assumption that there was not any smell observed. In this case the old painters would have struck the correct view, who make some of the figures in their pictures hold their noses and turn away! And yet this is opposed both by the express foundation for the words in the four days, and by the character of the rock-tomb.

It is another question whether Martha's conclusion was correct (thus also Gumlich, Stier, Hengstenberg) or not. Stier[3] appeals for the probability of her conjecture to the resurrection at the last day; but in this he fails to perceive the difference between that new-creative awakening and the revivifying of the old mortal body. The process of corruption might well have been checked from the very beginning by the working of divine power, for the sake of the revivifying. We cannot find in Martha's words an 'again approaching hopelessness' (De Wette), seeing that she is here no more hopeless than in ver. 27. The first interest, that of the bodily resurrection, has retired behind the belief which she has won, that her brother has not lost the true life in Christ. But this is combined with lack of belief that Christ can even now reveal himself as the life in the natural sphere of men.

Verse 40.

Jesus' words are intended to correct this fault of Martha's. He promises her the vision of the glory of God if she believes: that is the condition. The δόξα ('glory') is the ζωή ('life') in its realization and appearance in the sphere of natural life. When, now, Jesus here intends to reveal his divine life in the sphere of the natural life by the re-

---

[1] Strauss, *Das Leben Jesu für das deutsche Volk bearbeitet*, Leipzig 1864, p. 475.

[2] Keim, *Geschichte Jesu von Nazara*, Zürich 1872, vol. iii. p. 68, note 1.

[3] Stier, *Reden Jesu*, 3d ed., Leipzig 1873, vol. v. p. 40.

enlivening of his friend, he reveals this life as divine glory. As such, then, also the life is the object of vision. It is true that not vers. 25 and 26, but ver. 23 had spoken of this δόξα ('glory') as an appearance of the life. But the ὄψη ('shalt see') is contained in the present of the twenty-fifth verse, in ἐγώ εἰμι ἡ ἀνάστασισ ('I am the resurrection'). He had bidden her believe this too in his question : πιστεύεισ τοῦτο ('dost thou believe this?'). The fact that Martha remains silent shows that she resigns herself in will, and has entered upon a receptive state of expectation. Mary had so entirely sunk herself in Jesus, that in calm composure she lets herself be led, without excitement of her own thoughts and doubts.

Verse 41.

At Jesus' command they took away the stone that closed the grave. The received text adds (with E G H M, namely, the manuscripts of the so-called Byzantine recension): οὗ ἦν ὁ τεθνηκὼσ κείμενοσ ('where the dead was laid'). But the more important manuscripts omit this addition. A and K add merely οὗ ἦν ('where he was'), but that is evidently no less an addition. They believed they must at least add something for a nearer explanation ; but it was unnecessary. Lifting up his eyes,—' ἄνω amovit oculos ab objecto mortalitatis, in cælum' ('he cast his eyes upward, away from the object of mortality, unto heaven'), Bengel,—Jesus expresses his thanks, not a petition. He had already at an earlier period addressed himself in prayer to the Father.[1] This has been designated as inadmissible, because it is not expressly said.[2] But when Jesus begins with εὐχαριστῶ σοι ὅτι ἤκουσάσ μου ('I thank thee that thou hast heard me'), this is thanks for a hearing which has already taken place, and which has been inwardly experienced. To explain the words only from the anticipatory confidence (Hengstenberg), contradicts the sense of the words. Hence he only speaks the thanks for this aloud, to show what his relation to the Father is,

---

[1] Compare vol. i. p. 83.
[2] *Literarisches Centralblatt*, 1852, No. 46, col. 739. Thus also Hengstenberg.

that it is not only one of dependence, but also of the most intimate communion.

Verse 42.

Jesus proceeds: that he knew that the Father hears him always. This he says to prevent the impression that he in this gives especial thanks, because he has extraordinary reason for thanking; on the contrary, he always finds a hearing, and he knew that before he prepared himself to ask. He speaks his thanks aloud in this case only in order by that act to give testimony of his relation to the Father. At an earlier stage he would doubtless have made that which he here expresses in prayer the object of a self-witness in the form of a doctrinal statement. That time is past. Israel has now only the witness of his appearance in general. If it be unsuitable that Jesus should cause his intercourse of communion with the Father to come to view, it is just as unsuitable on the part of God when he answers aloud for the sake of the people, xii. 28, 30, a later prayer of Jesus, xii. 27, 28, and thus on his part causes the intercourse of communion between him and the Son to come to view as a testimony to the people. As the doctrinal intercourse with Israel is here followed by a testimony in prayer, so in a like manner the later instructions to the disciples are followed by the great comprehensive testimony in the high-priestly prayer.

Offence has often been taken at this prayer, and especially at the 'reflection' in ver. 42. In order to explain 'that which is not fitting in this turn,' they have attributed the words to the evangelist, who, 'led by the apologetic interest,' only 'lent them' to Jesus (De Wette, also Lücke: 'reflection of the evangelist'). On going further, they have spoken of a 'show-prayer' (Weisse), or seeming prayer (Baur), or finally, of an 'offensive grimace' of an 'actor,' and that too of an 'awkward one' (Strauss[1]). But as in the case of Jesus all must serve his vocation, so also must this appearance of his internal intercourse of fellowship with the Father.

[1] Strauss, *Das Leben Jesu für das deutsche Volk bearbeitet*, Leipzig 1864, p. 475 f.

From this point of view we are freed from the offence which Keim[1] takes at the circumstance that the 'thanking words of his address rather seek at the hands of men than of God, which is a breach of the religious reverence due to God,' and a 'sign of the overstrained dogmatics' of John. Keim,[2] indeed, thinks he knows besides 'that Jesus at the moment of the healings, with quite unimportant exceptions in poorly accredited accounts, did not pray, and that he likewise did not direct his disciples to heal with prayer.' If he contrasts with that the direct confidence, it is in truth no contrast at all. And if Jesus had the consciousness that all he did was given him of the Father and took its issue from him, as this plainly appears in John (for example, v. 19, 30, compare also Beyschlag[3]), then this dependent relation expresses itself even in the prayer, and the single utterances of it are only manifestations of a thing constantly repeating itself.

Verse 43.

With a loud voice Jesus called Lazarus out of the grave. Κραυγάζειν φωνῇ μεγάλῃ (' to cry out with a great voice ') is purposely heaped up to express the strength of the call. He had testified to himself as the one who was the resurrection. Thus the present preliminary resurrection served as a prefigurative pledge of the future and final one. Hence the pre-representation is also to make itself known in the form. In the loud voice the self-certain power and the utterance of might over death presents itself. Hence it is mentioned purposely. Whether or not a contrast be intended to the murmuring of the necromancers, Isa. viii. 19, xxix. 4 (Lampe, Bengel, Stier, Gumlich), is uncertain; but in any case the allusion is somewhat distant. *Lazarus, come hither*, come out, ' huc foras.' When the dead man at once comes forth at Jesus' call, the thing is not to be so conceived that Jesus' word should have served only the external mediating of the act of God; it is itself that which

---

[1] Keim, *Geschichte Jesu von Nazara*, Zürich 1872, vol. iii. p. 71, note 1.
[2] *Ibid.* 1871, vol. ii. p. 158.
[3] Beyschlag, *Christologie des Neuen Testaments*, Berlin 1866, p. 72.

works. Jesus owes to the Father only the utterance of the power which dwells within him. And, moreover, it is not to be thought that Lazarus had been previously raised by a secret influence, and then was only called forth (Lampe [1]). Jesus called the dead man from death when he calls him out of the tomb. But He calls him indeed by name, as if he were not dead, but as if he lived. For those who are his all live to him, ver. 25, as it is said of those who are God's, Luke xx. 38.

Verse 44.

The dead man comes forth wound around the hands and the feet with the bands ($\kappa\epsilon\iota\rho\iota\alpha\iota\sigma$),—the narrow strips of linen, elsewhere called ὀθόνια, xix. 40, xx. 5, 6, 7,—and with the face (ἡ ὄψισ, Rev. i. 16, like our 'visage') shrouded in the handkerchief (σουδάριον, xx. 7),[2] thus being in the complete dress of a corpse (Meyer). It is not necessary to assume for this a new miracle, a θαῦμα ἐν θαύματι ('miracle in a miracle;' Basil, Greek fathers, Lampe,[3] and Stier also, at least he is not against it[4]), whether according to the Egyptian custom the limbs were wrapped separately (Tholuck, Olshausen, De Wette, Baumgarten-Crusius, Maier), or, what is more probable, the wrapping was only loose, and was free enough to make it possible for him to move (for example, Meyer). It is at least not the evangelist's design to report a new miracle in these words; but he places before our eyes the contrast between the living person and his death-like appearance. He comes as a living man and yet appears as a dead man, so that they involuntarily feel: it is not 'he' who has torn himself from the sleep of death, but it is a foreign power which has only this moment come upon the dead man, and has snatched him from the realm of death. The bystanders feel this, and are astounded. Jesus had to remind them of what

---

[1] Lampe, *Commentarius . . . evangelii secundum Joannem*, Amsterdam 1726, vol. ii. p. 793.

[2] Concerning the treatment of the dead in general, see Winer, *Biblisches Realwörterbuch*, 3d ed., Leipzig 1848, vol. ii. p. 15 f., *sub voce* 'Leichen.'

[3] Lampe, *ut supra*, vol. ii. p. 795.

[4] Stier, *Reden Jesu*, 3d ed., Leipzig 1873, vol. v. p. 48.

they have to do: λύσατε αὐτόν κ.τ.λ., 'loose him, etc.' They are to make him entirely free from the shroud. Then first does he step back again into life, free and self-active.

Jesus has manifested himself as the prince of life, as the life of the resurrection, which has power over the realm of death. They are to be certain of this in regard to him.

Perhaps hardly any other gospel narrative has such a degree of plainness, directness, and internal truth. We are made sharers in the event, and in the internal emotions of every single moment. Upon this are wrecked the various explanations which have been attempted,—not only the insipid, now discarded, explanation of rationalism, that it was merely a seeming death (Paulus, Ammon),—but also the frivolous one of Renan, according to which Jesus lent himself to a comedy, which was to serve again to inflame the waning enthusiasm of his followers,—and as well the modern view, that we here have to do with a literary production which, by combination of the synoptic accounts of the two other alleged raisings of the dead, and of the account of the poor Lazarus, made up a miracle [1] that was intended to surpass all others. The complaints that it is unhistorical, unnatural, unpsychological (compare especially Keim [2]), have solved themselves for us in the opposite. The account is directly of the greatest psychological clearness of view and internal truth. The combining of it with those fragments of synoptic tradition is arbitrary, and the relation of a climax over against the other two raisings of the dead is conditioned by the historical situation: Jesus stood himself at the threshold of death.

If all miracles are σημεῖα ('signs') which are to show us the meaning of Christ and of his saving calling, the side upon which and the manner in which the σημεῖον ('sign') is to cause us to recognise Jesus, is determined in each case by the historical situation. It is thus determined here also. It was a sign for the disciples and for Israel; for us it has an importance only in connection with the certainty

---

[1] See above, p. 396 ff.
[2] Keim, *Geschichte Jesu von Nazara*, Zürich 1872, vol. iii.

of what Jesus is and did, a certainty which stands firm for
us even without this miracle. Spinoza is said to have
declared:[1] 'que s'il eût pu se persuader la résurrection de
Lazare, il auroit brisé en pieces tout son système, il auroit
embrassé sans répugnance la foi ordinaire des Chrétiens'
('that if he had been able to persuade himself of the resurrection of Lazarus, he would have broken his whole system
to pieces, he would have embraced without repugnance the
ordinary faith of Christians'). But the way to believe is
different from that. The evangelist, moreover, did not
report this story for that purpose. He wrote his gospel, not
for unbelievers, but for believers, so that they should recognise in Jesus the Son of God, who is the life, which shows
itself victorious over death. The miracle in itself alone does
not work this belief; the origin of belief is a moral process.
Where the corresponding internal moral posture is wanting,
all miracles are useless. This we see throughout in the
gospel; and it is true here.

(3.) VERSES 45-57.

The Effect.

VERSE 45.

The fact was somewhat overpowering for all. The common view is (Godet also, and I earlier) that two parts of
the Jews are spoken of: the one believed, the other informed on Jesus. But Meyer emphasizes correctly the
fact that it does not say τῶν ἐλθόντων ('of those who came'),
but οἱ ἐλθόντεσ ('those who came'). It is therefore true
of all the many who came, that they believed. But from
this fact we see what this belief was worth. It was
mediated by the vision of what Jesus did. The circumstance that θεᾶσθαι is chosen instead of ἰδόντεσ, does not
permit us to conclude that their beholding was directed at
the thing itself, which revealed itself in the act of Jesus

---

[1] Spinoza, according to Bayle, *Dictionnaire historique et critique*, 5th ed.,
Amsterdam 1740, vol. iv. p. 264, note (R) *sub fine.*

[Bayle notes that he was assured that Spinoza used this language to his
friends.—C. R. G.]

(thus I earlier). It is only intended to lay stress on the eyewitness, which extended to the series of separate events which they had experienced and seen. Mary is specially named as the one to whom they had come, because she is particularly prominent in this entire narrative as needing comfort.

VERSE 46.

Some, now, of these, not of the Jews in general, but of these who have become believers, tell the Pharisees what they had experienced. The Pharisees are designedly named, that is, not the possessors of power, but the representatives of orthodoxy. That offers the explanation of the design of the impartation. It was not an ill-intentioned design to denounce Jesus as a Goës, or as a dangerous man (thus mostly); in that case, the 'Jews' and not the Pharisees would have been spoken of. Nor was it with a good intention, namely, of determining the Pharisees also unto belief (thus especially Meyer); for by 'Pharisees' they are designated as an authority for the others. But in view of the want of independence of judgment in religious questions, which then reigned in lay circles, and of which we have repeatedly convinced ourselves, they desired to hear from the authorities how they ought to judge religiously of this miraculous event, the actuality of which is certain for them, that is, their πιστεύειν ('believing').

VERSE 47.

The next consequence is a meeting of the Sanhedrim. At the side of the 'high priests' the 'Pharisees' also are named; from the latter doubtless proceeded the suggestion, and from the former the call to the session (συνέδριον, thus here, and not the Sanhedrim itself, which must have had the article; this is the only time in John's gospel). At this session they arrive at that which in substance is the decisive decree. Hence John relates this session in greater detail. In doing it he has two points of view. On the one hand, he intends to show how in this the relation of Israel to Jesus came practically to an end; and, on the other hand, how even this action of the Jews must serve the saving will of God: it was all meant to occur in this way, ver. 51 f. The action of men, which as to substance is rooted in the disposition and in its internal self-determination, is in utterance taken into the service of higher purposes.

The former point of view first appears in ver. 47. The Pharisees called to their support the official power of the Sanhedrim and of the Sadducees, who were among the highest dignitaries, solely in order to rid themselves of this man. The assemblage is in embarrassment. But something must be done at once: τί ποιοῦμεν; *What do we?* They ask directly in the present, not τί ποιήσομεν; 'What shall we do?' Acts iv. 16. The indicative instead of the desiderative subjunctive: 'quid faciamus?' expresses the fact that there was not the least doubt that something must be done.[1] They really know very well what should be done, but they do not wish to speak out their thoughts and wishes plainly. It seems to me to be more suitable in such a question not to take τί ποιοῦμεν ὅτι together in the sense of 'in reference to the fact that' (De Wette, Lücke), or 'in the case that' (Baumgarten-Crusius), but to see in ὅτι κ.τ.λ. the reason for the question expressed in τί ποιοῦμεν (thus, for example, Lampe, Meyer): *for this man*—contemptuously—*doeth many signs.*

It is characteristic that they do not speak of a breach of the Sabbath or the like, and therefore make the claim of the law valid against him. By this they confess that all these reproaches were at heart to them only means to the end, though at any rate many separate Pharisees may have taken real offence at these things. The case was different for the majority. As they are alone, they do not need these excuses. The thing which now urges them to more decisive steps is the fact that Jesus does many signs. That becomes by degrees too offensive for them.[2] The last miracle of Jesus gives them but occasion to decree formally that which in consequence of the many previous miracles

---

[1] Winer, *Grammatik des neutestamentlichen Sprachidioms*, § 41. a. 3, 7th ed., Leipzig 1867, p. 267.

[2] Compare vol. i. p. 132 f.

they had already long ago determined in themselves. It is the whole action of Jesus that they wish to meet decidedly upon its course and put an end to. The contrast in the double ποιεῖν ('do,' 'doeth') was doubtless intended by the evangelist. They desire to overcome his action by their action, not knowing in the first place that they thereby must serve God's will, and in the second place that they are themselves to be overcome by the σημεῖον 'Ιωνᾶ τοῦ προφήτου ('sign of Jonah the prophet'). Bengel remarks on our passage: 'citius cedit mors virtuti Christi quam infidelitas' ('death yields more quickly to the power of Christ than infidelity does').

VERSE 48.

They sufficiently betray what urges them on by the words πάντεσ πιστεύσουσιν εἰσ αὐτόν ('all will believe on him'). It is the loss of the religious dominion over the people. But they must give themselves an appearance of another reason. By the hopes which he will excite as the supposed Messiah, Jesus will call forth insurrectionary movements; and that will offer the Romans an occasion for destroying the last relic of their independence. Ἀροῦσιν ἡμῶν καὶ τὸν τόπον καὶ τὸ ἔθνοσ ('They shall take away'), commonly it is said: 'land and people' (Luther, Bengel: 'territorium,' 'territory'); but τόποσ is too limited for that. To confine it to the temple (Lampe, De Wette, Baumgarten-Crusius, Lücke, Maier, Stier, Hengstenberg) is too narrow. The correct thing is doubtless to understand it of the capital, the proper (ἡμῶν, 'our') seat of the hierarchy. The fulfilment of the promise is connected with Jerusalem and its possession. As much more again of the land might be lost, if only the holy city with the temple remains unto them.

Hence, then, we must remain content with the first meaning of αἴρειν, 'to take away' (Meyer; Vulgate: 'tollent'); then afterwards Caiaphas makes an ἀπολέσαι ('to destroy') out of it (Lücke, De Wette, Baumgarten-Crusius, following Euthymius). Yet ἡμῶν does not depend on αἴρειν, and is not a genitive of separation (this is only poetic, in prose it is with a preposition), but it is made to precede emphatically: they fear for 'their' city and nation, that is, for their dominion over the same. Therefore they do not fear the destroying vengeance of the Romans for the temple and nation (Lücke), but only the loss of their dominion. This is characteristic of them, and therefore the evangelist cites it. Moreover, this fear is probably not at all meant in earnest, since they well knew the manner of Jesus' Messianic appearance. They only mirror it before themselves (against Meyer). But since they hypocritically played with such lies, it must needs come to pass that the lies in fact realized themselves, much more frightfully than they here lied to themselves. It was, it is true, in consequence of Messianic hopes and movements, which, however, only formed themselves, and hurled land and nation to destruction, because by this decree they had robbed themselves of the right Messiah and of the Messianic hope itself (compare Bengel). The evangelist wishes us to think of this fulfilment of the words of the Pharisees which had become prophetic.

Verse 49.

Caiaphas' heartless determination brings on the decision. He is purposely designated as the high priest of that year, ver. 49, 'anno illo memorabili quo moriturus erat Jesus' ('that memorable year in which Jesus was about to die,' Bengel), as is afterwards emphasized in ver. 51, and the intention is not merely to define the time. Least of all does this statement proceed from the singular conception that the office of the high priest changed every year (thus, after Baur, Strauss, and Scholten; against it, see Keim[1]). Not merely 'a Palestinian apostle must have known better than that,'[2] but as well every Gentile Christian who had but a moderate acquaintance with Jewish circumstances. The reference to the change, or at least the uncertainty of the high-priestly office at that time, by which Hengstenberg explains the expression, does not fit at all for Caiaphas,

---

[1] Keim, *Geschichte Jesu von Nazara*, Zürich 1867, vol. i. p. 133.
[2] Strauss, *Das Leben Jesu für das deutsche Volk bearbeitet*, Leipzig 1864, p. 78.

who was in office from about A.D. 18 to A.D. 36 (see Schürer[1]).

He places himself in a sharp contrast with the rest by the opening ὑμεῖσ ('ye'). Single voices may have indeed urged their opinion in a warning way, Luke xxiii. 51, but they were certainly altogether isolated, and gave no decided testimony for Jesus. As a whole, they wished to put an end to Jesus' activity, but they did not trust themselves to speak out the decisive word. Caiaphas in a sharp and bitter way reproaches them for this lack of courage and understanding, as he interprets it. Ὑμεῖσ, 'you people,' contemptuous, in the tone of pride which pervades this whole discourse. It is not passionate (Meyer), but cold intellectual pride;[2] and it is not to be explained as due to the general roughness of the Sadducees (thus Hengstenberg, appealing to Josephus,[3] and also Godet), but as individual. *Ye know nothing*, understand nothing, namely, in such questions of policy.

Verse 50.

And ye *consider not*, do not weigh the fact (λογίζεσθε, ℵ A B, not διαλογίζεσθε, see 2 Cor. x. 11), that policy and your advantage demand the sacrificing of one to save the whole. He says: συμφέρει ἡμῖν, or ὑμῖν ('it is expedient for us,' or 'for you;' the manuscripts are very uncertain as to the reading); therefore he has in view only their interest, the interest of the rulers (see Lampe[4]). He turns this: μὴ ὅλον τὸ ἔθνοσ ἀπόληται ('and that the whole nation perish not'), in such a way as if at heart the question was the welfare of the nation. The evangelist writes συμφέρει ἵνα, according to the later usage of ἵνα, instead of the infinitive in objective clauses, in which the original reference of aim is but dimly visible, if it has not entirely disappeared, in so far as such clauses always contain some-

---

[1] Schürer, *Lehrbuch der neutestamentlichen Zeitgeschichte*, Leipzig 1874, p. 419.

[2] See vol. i. p. 105.

[3] Josephus, *De Bello Judaico*, II. viii. 14; *Opera*, ed. Bekker, Leipzig 1856, vol. v. p. 153.

[4] Lampe, *Commentarius . . . evangelii secundum Joannem*, Amsterdam 1726, vol. ii. p. 807.

thing desirable and the like (compare Winer,[1] against Meyer). Εἶσ ('one') and λαόσ ('people') stand in contrast with each other. Hence at first λαόσ is chosen (the nation from the side of multitude, from ΛΑΩ, 'comprehendo, complector,' 'to comprehend, to embrace;' see Grimm[2]), and then after that ἔθνοσ (the people from the side of its unity, in character and customs). It is to be for the advantage of the many that the one is to be sacrificed. This and not substitution is what lies in ὑπέρ ('for'), as is always the case. But as to substance the relation is indeed of such a character, since the entire nation would have had to experience that which now merely the single one needs to experience: ἵνα μὴ ὅλον τὸ ἔθνοσ ἀπόληται ('that the whole nation perish not'). Bengel recalls 2 Cor. v. 15 (English version, 14): εἶσ ὑπὲρ πάντων ἀπέθανεν· ἄρα οἱ πάντεσ ἀπέθανον ('one died for all: then were all dead').

Verse 51.

This speech of Caiaphas', which at the same time is a fully characteristic expression for the meaning of the most fundamental Christian event, is for this reason the more worthy of remark for the evangelist, and thus it has become certain to him that Caiaphas did not clothe his thought in this prophetic expression without divine ordering. 'Caiphas cogitat de utilitate politica, sed spiritus prophetiæ ita eum gubernat, ut verbis utatur ad utilitatem spiritualem exprimendam idoneis. Caiphas et Pilatus Jesum condemnarunt: uterque tamen testimonium a suo ipsorum sensu alienum perhibuerunt. Caiphas hoc loco de sacerdotali morte Christi, Pilatus de regno, in titulo crucis' ('Caiaphas has political advantage in mind, but the spirit of prophecy so governs him that he uses words fit for expressing spiritual advantage. Caiaphas and Pilate condemned Jesus: yet each of them gave a testimony foreign to his own meaning: Caiaphas, in this place, concerning the priestly death of

---

[1] Winer, *Grammatik des neutestamentlichen Sprachidioms*, § 44. 8, 7th ed., Leipzig 1867, p. 314.

[2] Grimm's edition of *Wilkii Clavis N. T. philologica*, Leipzig 1862-1868, sub voce λαόσ.

Christ; Pilate, in the title on the cross, concerning the kingdom of Christ'), Bengel. The high priest was to speak just such a prophetic word. Most commentators (for example, Lücke, Olshausen, Baumgarten-Crusius, De Wette, Meyer, Maier, Godet) take the words of the evangelist (ἀρχιερεὺσ ὢν τοῦ ἐνιαυτοῦ ἐκείνου, 'being high priest that year') as if he ascribed to the high priest as such the gift of prophecy, as a remnant of the ancient questioning of Urim and Thummim, Ex. xxviii. 30; Num. xxvii. 21. But this had disappeared,[1] and the modern high-priesthood had lost its old splendour.

If, as is unquestionable, the word of Pilate is full of meaning for the evangelist, without the gift of prophecy being here bound to the office as such, but God having merely guided the words of just this official so significantly, the same thing must hold good of the then officiating high priest. Thence also, following Lampe's example, Brückner and Stier have justly protested against the above notion.[2] Nothing seems to justify that former view, and least of all the passage cited from Philo,[3] which 'idealizes the relation' (Meyer). What would then be intended by the addition of the words: τοῦ ἐνιαυτοῦ ἐκείνου ('of that year')? For this is not mechanical either here or at xviii. 13, where it is repeated, but is emphasized. Therefore he was to speak these prophetic words, not because he was high priest, but because he was high priest 'of that year.' Stier[4] rightly names it 'a deep irony of the most special providence for the centre of the world's history, that the perishing high-priesthood, against the knowledge and will of the bearer of the office, speaks at the very end concerning the true atoning offering.' The high priest was to do what belonged to his office, to present the sacrifice for the people.

He must designate Jesus as such an atoning sacrifice, for Jesus was to die as such. "Ὅτι before ἤμελλεν ('should')

---

[1] Josephus, *Antiquitates*, III. viii. 9; *Opera*, ed. Richter, Leipzig 1826, vol. i. p. 155 [164-166]; ed. Bekker, Leipzig 1855, vol. i. p. 163.

[2] See vol. i. p. 75 f.

[3] Philo, *De Creatione Principum*, § 8, Leipzig 1828, p. 101 f. [Mangey, vol. ii. p. 367].

[4] Stier, *Reden Jesu*, 3d ed., Leipzig 1873, vol. v. p. 52.

does not mean 'that' (De Wette), or 'in reference to the fact that' (Meyer). In that case, ver. 52 would not connect well, since it contains more than Caiaphas had expressed. Besides, God's decree of the death of Jesus is better named the reason than the contents of the high priest's unconscious anticipatory announcement. 'For Jesus, indeed, was to be the atoning sacrifice for the people, but an atoning sacrifice the value of which is universal:' thus the evangelist leads us to the comprehensive statement concerning the meaning of Jesus' death, in ver. 52. In this also the other point of view is sufficiently designated, for the sake of which the evangelist reports this decree, namely, to show that this action of the Jews must serve the saving will of God. This will, however, was an all-comprehensive one. Its realization began with Jesus' death.

Verse 52.

Jesus was not to die merely for Israel,—ὑπὲρ τοῦ ἔθνουσ, with reference to ver. 50, μὴ ὅλον τὸ ἔθνοσ, the people of Israel in its characteristic national peculiarities as contrasted with the Gentiles,—but ἵνα καὶ τὰ τέκνα τοῦ θεοῦ τὰ διεσκορπισμένα συναγάγῃ εἰσ ἕν ('that he should gather together in one the children of God that were scattered abroad'). Whereas the people of God in Israel form a closed unity, the children of God are scattered in the Gentile world. Compare 1 Pet. i. 1, διασπορά: in the world, which is foreign to their nature, they are scattered about as single persons. When they are called the children of God, the question arises, whether they are so named according to that which they were, or according to that which they became, upon the ground of which the evangelist views them in his mind. Hilgenfeld[1] follows the former conception in the sense of his Gnostic dualism, as if there were a natural divine sonship (so also Scholten;[2] but compare

---

[1] Hilgenfeld, *Das Evangelium und die Briefe Johannis, nach ihrem Lehrbegriff*, Halle 1849, p. 153; *Die Evangelien*, Leipzig 1854, p. 297; *Historisch-kritische Einleitung in das Neue Testament*, Leipzig 1875, p. 691 f.

[2] Scholten, *Das Evangelium nach Johannes*, Berlin 1867, third chapter, pp. 77–181.

against him, Beyschlag[1]). The same conception is followed by Reuss[2] with the rejection of a more particular explanation, and especially of the confirmation of it by election. Tholuck, Weiss,[3] Godet, and I earlier, took that conception on the basis of the preceding general moral state of preparation or of receptibility. But the foregoing stage is not the relation of sonship (compare Meyer). Nothing can be said of a being children of God, even in a preliminary manner, outside of the sphere of salvation, according to the Biblical and as well the Johannean view; compare my book on free-will:[4] 'the point of view is taken from the result, and from that looks out backwards.' Hence it is indeed said, 'respectu præcognitionis divinæ' ('in view of divine foreknowledge'), Bengel; compare also upon x. 16, concerning the 'sheep not of this fold.'[5] The evangelist looks forth from Israel over the whole world, and sees here the effect of the death of Christ in its all-comprehensive importance. Thus writes one who experienced the way in which the preaching of the cross was brought to the nations from Jerusalem, not merely delivering them, but even thereby at the same time gathering them together, and who, after that the church from the Gentiles had placed itself at the side of the church from Israel, then saw both unite into the one church of Jesus Christ in the world; compare Eph. ii. 11 ff. The fundamental thought of John is the κοινωνία ('communion'); compare chap. xvii. and 1 John i. 3. They were to be brought together, for they are scattered; quite different from the believers in Israel, who from the very outset were bound by the common history of salvation which completed itself on the ground of Israel. 'Præteritum denotat non eos qui sunt in dispersione, sed eos qui in dispersionem venerunt' ('the past denotes not those who are in the dispersion, but those who have come into the dispersion,' Gen. x. 32, xi. 8), observes Bengel.

[1] Beyschlag, *Studien und Kritiken*, 1875, p. 248 ff.
[2] Reuss, *Beiträge zu den theologischen Wissenschaften von den Mitgliedern der theologischen Gesellschaft zu Strassburg*, Erstes Heft, Jena 1847, p. 35.
[3] Weiss, *Der Johanneische Lehrbegriff*, Berlin 1862, p. 124.
[4] Luthardt, *Die Lehre vom freien Willen*, Leipzig 1863, p. 421.
[5] See above, p. 362 f.

History started from a unity; the 'one' humanity of God is its aim; the scattering abroad is the thing which has come in between. That which now binds the τέκνα θεοῦ ('children of God') together, is that new spirit of love which, as a previously unknown power, has gone forth into the world from Jesus' cross. This new spirit, however, is only the subjective existence of the πνεῦμα ἅγιον ('Holy Spirit'), which, having become free by Jesus' death and glorification, forms the unity of the humanity of God. For it is ἓν σῶμα ('one body') because it has ἓν πνεῦμα ('one spirit'), Eph. iv. 4; for ἐν ἑνὶ πνεύματι ἡμεῖσ πάντεσ εἰσ ἓν σῶμα ἐβαπτίσθημεν ('for by one spirit we are all baptized into one body'), 1 Cor. xii. 13, whence the apostle in the blessing names the κοινωνία τοῦ ἁγίου πνεύματοσ ('communion of the Holy Spirit'), 2 Cor. xiii. 13. This is the middle member which De Wette inquires for, and in the statement of which Paul agrees with John. The annulling of the law, which De Wette names for Paul, is based on this.

VERSE 53.

Caiaphas' speech had decided. Οὖν ('then') shows that it was approved. They no longer discuss the 'whether,' but their deliberations had the design already as their presupposition, and served only this aim: ἐβουλεύσαντο ἵνα ('they took counsel that'), ℵ B. Hence the point now was the ways and means. The evangelist has thus exhibited the decision of the Sanhedrim, which at base had long been ready, as the other effect of the raising of Lazarus; and at the same time he has also shown how the same, the decision, must serve the execution of God's saving will. By this means this third section of the chapter before us adds a third point to the preceding ones. The thought of death ruled the first section; that of life in and out from death, the second; in the third, the chief thought is, as we see, that of salvation, which is given to the world with the death here determined upon.

VERSES 54–57.

These verses follow as a conclusion for the whole account.

Verse 54.

When this verse relates that Jesus had withdrawn himself from the Jews because of such a determination on their part, it is easy to see that this is an anticipatory representation of the judgment which they have drawn upon themselves; compare vii. 34. First of all, it says: οὐκέτι παρρησίᾳ περιεπάτει ἐν τοῖσ Ἰουδαίοισ, ἀλλὰ ἀπῆλθεν κ.τ.λ. ('he walked no more openly among the Jews, but went thence, etc.'). The meaning of παρρησίᾳ περιεπάτει appears from vii. 4: it is the public self-testification in word and miracle. Because of their decree (οὖν, 'then,' ver. 54), Jesus withdrew this testimony from them. For he knew about it very well, even if it was not imparted to him by them (Lampe[1]). At the same time, Jesus shows by this that they will not carry out their will without his will, and that they will do it, not when they, but when he shall will it. When his time is come, he will come to them. This all serves as a testimony against them.

Ἀπῆλθεν ἐκεῖθεν ('went thence'), namely, from Bethany, that is, from the neighbourhood of Jerusalem, ver. 18: εἰσ τὴν χώραν ('unto the country') designates, therefore, the open country in distinction from the capital; compare ver. 55. He went towards the Jordan in a north-westerly direction, to the neighbourhood of the desert of Judea, εἰσ Ἐφραὶμ (without diacritical points, א: Ἐφρέμ) λεγομένην πόλιν ('unto a city called Ephraim'). The situation of this city is doubtful. According to Eusebius it lay eight, according to Jerome twenty miles (thus also Ritter[2]), north-east from Jerusalem; according to Josephus,[3] it was in the neighbourhood of Bethel. In 2 Chron. xiii. 19 occurs an Ephron (עֶפְרוֹן, for which the K'ri gives the dual form עֶפְרַיִן). Raumer identifies this both with the Ophra of Benjamin, the situation of which is conjectured to be at or in Tajibeh,

---

[1] Lampe, *Commentarius . . . evangelii secundum Joannem*, Amsterdam 1726, vol. ii. p. 815.

[2] Ritter, *Erdkunde*, Berlin 1852, vol. xvi. p. 531 ff.

[3] Josephus, *De Bello Judaico*, IV. ix. 9; *Opera*, Leipzig 1827, vol. vi. p. 405.

eastward (north-east) of Bethel, and with our Ephraim; compare Keil on 2 Chron. xiii. 19.[1] Thus also De Bruyn, on his great map of Palestine, 1874, identifies Ephraim and Ophra at Bethel; and Kiepert, on his new hand map of Palestine, places Ophra or Tajibeh at the same point. Ebrard[2] declares himself opposed to this situation, and demands a more easterly position from Jerusalem, because Jesus afterwards travelled to Jerusalem by way of Jericho. But he might very well have gone somewhat out of his way to pass through Jericho, in order to meet with the bands of pilgrims at that place.

How far he was active here, is not to be perceived. The contrast leads rather to the assumption that he devoted himself chiefly to his disciples, until the approach of the passover again occasioned his public appearance.

VERSE 55.

The Jews' Passover (compare ii. 13, vi. 4) led many ἐκ τῆσ χώρασ ('out of the country'),—that is, again, the open country, in contrast with the capital (Lücke, De Wette, Meyer, Godet), and not specially the neighbourhood in which Jesus had dwelt (Bengel, Olshausen); for it is a resumption of χώρα, ver. 54,—even before the feast, to Jerusalem, in order to subject themselves to Levitical purifications on behalf of the passover; compare Ex. xix. 10; Num. ix. 10; 2 Chron. xxx. 17 f.

VERSE 56.

They were accustomed to see Jesus in Jerusalem at this chief feast, and hence this verse follows with οὖν ('then'). Besides, they felt that the question for him must now be settled. They had thought they would find him already in Jerusalem: ἐζήτουν κ.τ.λ. ('they sought, etc.'). The seekers are presented to us standing in the temple, which reminded them of Jesus' previous self-testifications, and speaking with each other: this situation is intended to depict the

---

[1] Keil, *Ueber die nachexilischen Geschichtsbücher*, Leipzig 1870, p. 264.
[2] Ebrard, *Wissenschaftliche Kritik der evangelischen Geschichte*, 3d ed., Frankfort-on-the-Main 1868, p. 561.

tension in which they were. Although Israel had thrust its Messiah from it, yet Israel was not free to ignore him. They could not rid themselves of the expectation and the unrest which he excited in them. Their question is best taken as a double question (De Wette, Meyer, Godet, against Lücke). *What do ye think? That he will not come?* For in the other explanation his not coming would be assumed as already certain (Meyer). They do not say this either because they presuppose fear on the part of Jesus, or because they know of the plans of their rulers (Baumgarten-Crusius).

Verse 57.

There is no occasion for the former suggestion, and δέ ('now') (without καί, ℵ A B L, against D E G and Godet) contradicts the latter suggestion. Because Jesus now has made his attempt so often, and always in vain, they wonder whether he will not give it up. We see in this the correct feeling as to the situation, namely, that Jesus' public activity approaches its end. Only they understand it falsely. In so far, however, as in this restless expectation the sting betrayed itself, which Jesus' self-testification had left behind in them, these words find a sharp contrast in the command of the Sanhedrim, ver. 57 (against Meyer, who takes δέ as explanatory, as if γάρ, 'for,' stood there).

The closing words of this chapter introduce the further history. The gospel proceeds to the account of the arrest. Only, between the announcement here and the execution, come in those parts which the character of the gospel requires it to make especially prominent. First of all, however, the history led to this point required a conclusion, which at the same time should form the transition to what follows. The next section serves this purpose.

END OF VOL. II.

In two volumes, demy 8vo, price 21s.,

Growth of the Spirit of Christianity,
FROM THE FIRST CENTURY TO THE DAWN OF THE LUTHERAN ERA.

BY THE
REV. GEORGE MATHESON, M.A., B.D.,
AUTHOR OF 'AIDS TO THE STUDY OF GERMAN THEOLOGY.'

CONTENTS.

CHAPTER
- I. The Originality and Oldness of the Christian Religion.
- II. Preparation for the Cross.
- III. The Ingathering.
- IV. Birthplace of the Spirit of Christianity.
- V. Transition from Infancy into Childhood.
- VI. The Hopes of Childhood.
- VII. Breaking up of Home Associations.
- VIII. Extinction of Home Associations.
- IX. Independent Speculations of the Child-Life.
- X. Influence of Worldly Contact.
- XI. Moral Struggles of the Child-Life.
- XII. Fluctuations of the Struggle.
- XIII. Decline of the Ideal.
- XIV. The Child-Life under the World's Tuition.
- XV. Last Efforts of the Self-Will.
- XVI. The Reconciliation Completed.
- XVII. Close of the Child-Life.
- XVIII. Characteristics of the New Period.
- XIX. First Practical Influences of the Christian Spirit.
- XX. First Intellectual Stage of the School-Life.
- XXI. Protestant Influence of Mohammedanism.

CHAPTER
- XXII. First Revolt of the School-Life.
- XXIII. The Church under New Guardianship.
- XXIV. The Church become the World.
- XXV. Revival of Aspiration.
- XXVI. First Glimmerings of the Romantic Age.
- XXVII. Expanding of Christian Intelligence.
- XXVIII. Second Revolt of the School-Life.
- XXIX. Last Triumph of the Temporal Papacy.
- XXX. Search for a Rule of Conduct.
- XXXI. Discovery of a New Well-Spring.
- XXXII. Decline of the Temporal Papacy.
- XXXIII. Third Revolt of the School-Life.
- XXXIV. Close of the School-Life; the Negative Reformation Completed.
- XXXV. The Independence of Youth.
- XXXVI. The Moral Preparation of Youth.
- XXXVII. The Intellectual Preparation of Youth in its Relation to Art and the Reformation.
- XXXVIII. The Dawn of a New Day.

BY THE SAME AUTHOR.

In crown 8vo, Third Edition, price 4s. 6d.,

Aids to the Study of German Theology.

'The Author has done his work well, and has given us a real help to the understanding of German theology.'—*Princeton Review.*

'A work of much labour and learning, giving in a small compass an intelligent review of a very large subject.'—*Spectator.*

'An excellent and modest book, which may be heartily recommended.'—*Academy.*

'A helpful little volume; helpful to the student of German theology, and not less so to the careful observer of the tendencies of English religious thought.'—*Freeman.*

'The writer or compiler deserves high praise for the clear manner in which he has in a brief compass stated these opinions.'—*Christian Observer.*

Just published, in demy 8vo, price 12s.,

THE SCRIPTURAL DOCTRINE OF SACRIFICE.

By ALFRED CAVE, B.A.

BOOK I.—PREPARATORY.

PART I. THE PATRIARCHAL DOCTRINE OF SACRIFICE.
PART II. THE MOSAIC DOCTRINE OF SACRIFICE.
PART III. THE POST-MOSAIC DOCTRINE OF SACRIFICE.

BOOK II.—PLEROMATIC.

'We have nothing but praise for its clearness, its method, its thoroughness, and its tolerance. We most warmly commend Mr. Cave's book to the study of the clergy, who will find it full of suggestiveness and instruction.'—*English Churchman.*

'A thoroughly able and erudite book, from almost every page of which something may be learned. The author's method is exact and logical, the style perspicuous and forcible—sometimes, indeed, almost epigrammatic; and as a careful attempt to ascertain the teaching of the Scripture on an important subject, it cannot fail to be interesting even to those whom it does not convince.'—*Watchman.*

'We wish to draw particular attention to this new work on the deeply-important subject of sacrifice. . . . If we can induce our readers not only to glance through the book, but to read every line with thoughtful care, as we have done, we shall have earned their gratitude.'—*Church Bells.*

'It would be difficult to point to any modern theological work in English which reveals more abundant and patient scholarship, a more vigorous and comprehensive view of a great question. The subject is large and the literature enormous, the lines of investigation are numerous and intricate; but the author of the volume before us has displayed a fine mastery of voluminous material, and, after examining the scriptural phraseology in its historical development, positive declarations, and immediate inferences therefrom, he draws out his conclusions with great care, and contrasts them with views of a more speculative kind which have been advanced by distinguished scholars in Germany and England. The argument of the volume is sustained by logical compactness, lucidity of style, and considerable learning; it is a guide to the opinions of the principal writers on every part of the subject, and is pervaded by a fine spiritual tone.'—*Evangelical Review.*

'Mr. Cave has given us in this large volume a very thorough examination of the great doctrine of sacrifice. . . . And religious constructors will find in this work a perfect storehouse of information, and ample materials for expositions and defences. We cannot be mistaken in predicting for the book a cordial welcome.'—*Baptist Magazine.*

'It is of supreme and imperative importance that the inspired writings should be consulted upon a doctrine which so tests and determines our creed. To the "Volume of the Book" Mr. Cave appeals, resolved that, for the hour, its testimony respecting "sacrifice" shall alone be heard. Incidentally he betrays wide and patient reading on this theme; but all his reading is subordinated to his specific purpose of letting the Bible speak in clear and unmingled tones, and with great felicity and critical ability he enforces upon the attention everything the Scriptures have suggested and declared on this crucial doctrine of controversy and faith. An appendix of scholarly notes, and an index on Scripture passages referred to, and of subjects, etc. treated in this volume, complete a book on the doctrine of sacrifice which is almost without a rival for comprehensiveness and interest.'—*The Study and the Pulpit.*

Just published, Second Edition, demy 8vo, 10s. 6d.,

The Training of the Twelve;

OR,

EXPOSITION OF PASSAGES IN THE GOSPELS EXHIBITING THE TWELVE DISCIPLES OF JESUS UNDER DISCIPLINE FOR THE APOSTLESHIP.

BY

A. B. BRUCE, D.D.,

PROFESSOR OF DIVINITY, FREE CHURCH COLLEGE, GLASGOW.

'Here we have a really great book on an important, large, and attractive subject—a book full of loving, wholesome, profound thoughts about the fundamentals of Christian faith and practice.'—*British and Foreign Evangelical Review.*

'It is some five or six years since this work first made its appearance, and now that a second edition has been called for, the author has taken the opportunity to make some alterations which are likely to render it still more acceptable. Substantially, however, the book remains the same, and the hearty commendation with which we noted its first issue applies to it at least as much now.'—*Rock.*

'The value, the beauty of this volume is that it is a unique contribution to, because a loving and cultured study of, the life of Christ, in the relation of the Master of the Twelve.'—*Edinburgh Daily Review.*

'The volume is of permanent value, and we trust that its author may favour us with others of like character.'—*Freeman.*

'It is of no mean order as a profoundly devout piece of practical divinity.'—*Wesleyan Methodist Magazine.*

'It was by the first edition of this invaluable book that Dr. Bruce became known to English students as a theological writer. A more scholarly, more helpful book has not been published for many years past.'—*Baptist Magazine.*

BY THE SAME AUTHOR.

In one volume, 8vo, price 12s.,

THE HUMILIATION OF CHRIST

IN ITS PHYSICAL, ETHICAL, AND OFFICIAL ASPECTS.

(Sixth Series of Cunningham Lectures.)

'These lectures are able and deep-reaching to a degree not often found in the religious literature of the day; withal, they are fresh and suggestive. . . . The learning and the deep and sweet spirituality of this discussion will commend it to many faithful students of the truth as it is in Jesus.'—*Congregationalist.*

'We have not for a long time met with a work so fresh and suggestive as this of Professor Bruce. . . . We do not know where to look at our English Universities for a treatise so calm, logical, and scholarly.'—*English Independent.*

'The title of the book gives but a faint conception of the value and wealth of its contents. . . . Dr. Bruce's work is really one of exceptional value; and no one can read it without perceptible gain in theological knowledge.'—*English Churchman.*

'The writer gives evidence of extensive and accurate theological learning in the topics of which he treats, and he shows that he has theological grasp as well as learning.'—*Church Bells.*

In crown 8vo, price 5s.,

THE LEVITICAL PRIESTS.

A CONTRIBUTION TO THE CRITICISM OF THE PENTATEUCH.

By SAMUEL IVES CURTISS, Jr.,
DOCTOR OF PHILOSOPHY, LEIPZIG.

CHAPTER I. Introduction.
" II. The Ordination and Duties of Levi.
" III. The Inheritance of Levi.
" IV. The Blessing of Levi.
" V. The Modern Critic's Bridge.
" VI. Joshua—2 Kings.
" VII. The Credibility of the Chronicler.
" VIII. The Prophets and the Priests.
" IX. The Authorship of Deuteronomy and the Middle Books of the Pentateuch.

APPENDIX I. The Sources of the Chronicler.
" II. The Meaning of the word Thorah in Hos. iv. 6.
" III. The Authorship of Isaiah xl.–lxvi.
" IV. The text of הכהנים הלוים.

Extract from Preface by Dr. Delitzsch.

THE Author of the following work has made himself thoroughly acquainted with the writings of the chief representatives of this theory, and seeks by means of sober arguments to show (1) that the history of the people of Israel, as it lies before us in the historical books, presupposes a distinction in rank between the priests and the Levites, which reaches back to the time of Moses, and existed throughout all the periods of Israelitish history; (2) that the post-exilic books are in no way favourable to the opinion that the priestly hierarchy is a product of the time of Ezra; (3) that Deuteronomy, where it treats of religious privileges, does indeed assign them to the tribe of Levi, but yet so that these privileges—without contradicting the older legislation, which Deuteronomy recapitulates in an abridged form, and accommodates to changed circumstances—may be relatively distributed to the sons of Aaron and the Levites. He shows—and this deserves special attention—that the post-exilic Chronicles contain passages which in a Deuteronomic manner entirely obliterate the distinction between priests and Levites, while other passages emphasize it.

In crown 8vo, price 5s.,

FAITH IN GOD:
SERMONS
BY
THE LATE REV. JAMES HAMILTON, M.A.
EDITED BY
REV. WILLIAM SCRYMGEOUR.

Just published, in crown 8vo, price 5s.,

THE SYMBOLIC PARABLES

OF

THE CHURCH, THE WORLD, AND THE ANTICHRIST,

Being the Separate Predictions of the Apocalypse,

VIEWED IN THEIR RELATION TO THE GENERAL TRUTHS OF SCRIPTURE.

By Mrs. STEVENSON.

'An excellent treatise, containing much clear thought, and written as intelligibly as the subject would permit. To students of prophecy the book ought to be an attractive one; and to every one who desires to have a clearer understanding of his Bible, it will give much valuable assistance.'—*Glasgow Herald.*

'This is a sober, well-written, and instructive treatise on the Apocalypse. It is exceedingly suggestive, and the theory the author expounds holds well together. The key seems to fit every ward of the lock. This volume is worthy of the most serious consideration of all who take an interest in prophecy.'—*Daily Review.*

'It is quite refreshing to meet with a treatise on the Book of Revelation like this, marked by good sense and reverence. Brief as it is, it throws more light on a difficult subject than many laboured tomes.'—*Methodist Recorder.*

'It deserves careful study from all to whom the Book of Revelation has been regarded as a mystic utterance not meant for them, for it has the great advantage of being comprehensible by the most simple and unlearned.'—*John Bull.*

'Preachers will here find a mine of valuable hints on the spiritual bearing of the symbols which John's Apocalypse contains.'—*Dickinson's Quarterly.*

Just published, in crown 8vo, price 4s.,

OUTLINES OF BIBLICAL PSYCHOLOGY.

By J. T. BECK, D.D.,

PROF. ORD. THEOL., TÜBINGEN.

Translated from the Third Enlarged and Corrected German Edition, 1877.

'In this little volume Dr. Beck has given us a valuable contribution to the study of this science.'—*Homiletic Quarterly.*

'This handbook of Dr. Beck's is an admirable summary, and cannot fail to be fruitful in rich and valuable thought to those who will take the trouble to study it.'—*Christian Age.*

'The smallness of the work should not lead to its being undervalued; it well deserves a place side by side with Delitzsch and Heard. . . . We do warmly recommend this volume as one of the most fresh and valuable contributions to theological literature of recent date.'—*Wesleyan Methodist Magazine.*

'We quite endorse Bishop Ellicott's statement that, for many readers, Beck's will be found to be the most handy manual on the subject.'—*Church Bells.*

Dr. LUTHARDT'S WORKS.

In three handsome crown 8vo volumes, price 6s. each.

'We do not know any volumes so suitable in these times for young men entering on life, or, let us say, even for the library of a pastor called to deal with such, than the three volumes of this series. We commend the whole of them with the utmost cordial satisfaction. They are altogether quite a specialty in our literature.'—*Weekly Review.*

APOLOGETIC LECTURES
ON THE
FUNDAMENTAL TRUTHS OF CHRISTIANITY.
Fourth Edition.
BY C. E. LUTHARDT, D.D., LEIPZIG.

'From Dr. Luthardt's exposition even the most learned theologians may derive invaluable criticism, and the most acute disputants supply themselves with more trenchant and polished weapons than they have as yet been possessed of.'—*Bell's Weekly Messenger.*

APOLOGETIC LECTURES
ON THE
SAVING TRUTHS OF CHRISTIANITY.
Third Edition.

'Dr. Luthardt is a profound scholar, but a very simple teacher, and expresses himself on the gravest matters with the utmost simplicity, clearness, and force.'—*Literary World.*

APOLOGETIC LECTURES
ON THE
MORAL TRUTHS OF CHRISTIANITY.
Second Edition.

'The ground covered by this work is, of course, of considerable extent, and there is scarcely any topic of specifically moral interest now under debate in which the reader will not find some suggestive saying. The volume contains, like its predecessors, a truly wealthy apparatus of notes and illustrations.'—*English Churchman.*

Just published, in demy 8vo, price 9s.,

ST. JOHN THE AUTHOR OF THE FOURTH GOSPEL.
BY PROFESSOR C. E. LUTHARDT,
Author of 'Fundamental Truths of Christianity,' etc.
Translated and the Literature enlarged by C. R. GREGORY, Leipzig.

'A work of thoroughness and value. The translator has added a lengthy Appendix, containing a very complete account of the literature bearing on the controversy respecting this Gospel. The indices which close the volume are well ordered, and add greatly to its value.'—*Guardian.*

'There are few works in the later theological literature which contain such a wealth of sober theological knowledge and such an invulnerable phalanx of objective apologetical criticism.'—*Professor Guericke.*

Crown 8vo, 5s.,

LUTHARDT, KAHNIS, AND BRÜCKNER.
The Church: Its Origin, its History, and its Present Position.

'A comprehensive review of this sort, done by able hands, is both instructive and suggestive.'—*Record.*

Just published, in demy 8vo, price 9s.,

HIPPOLYTUS AND CALLISTUS;
OR,
THE CHURCH OF ROME IN THE FIRST HALF OF THE THIRD CENTURY.
By J. J. IGN. von DÖLLINGER.

Translated, with Introduction, Notes, and Appendices,

By ALFRED PLUMMER, M.A.,
MASTER OF UNIVERSITY COLLEGE, DURHAM.

'That this learned and laborious work is a valuable contribution to ecclesiastical history, is a fact of which we need hardly assure our readers. The name of the writer is a sufficient guarantee of this. It bears in all its pages the mark of that acuteness which, even more than the unwearied industry of its venerated author, is a distinguishing feature of whatever proceeds from the pen of Dr. Döllinger.'—*John Bull.*

'We are impressed with profound respect for the learning and ingenuity displayed in this work. The book deserves perusal by all students of ecclesiastical history. It clears up many points hitherto obscure, and reveals features in the Roman Church at the beginning of the third century which are highly instructive.'—*Athenæum.*

'Dr. Döllinger's masterly volume. . . . The translator has not only given us an excellent version, in good and idiomatic English, but he has added notes, which are terse, brief, and thoroughly to the point, and has discussed in some excellent appendices, criticisms on writers who, having for the most part written since Döllinger, are not referred to in the original work.'—*Church Quarterly Review.*

Just published, in two volumes, demy 8vo, price 12s. each,

A HISTORY OF THE COUNCILS OF THE CHURCH.
From the Original Documents.

TRANSLATED FROM THE GERMAN OF

C. J. HEFELE, D.D., BISHOP OF ROTTENBURG.

VOL. I. (*Second Edition*), TO A.D. 325.
By Rev. PREBENDARY CLARK.

VOL. II., A.D. 326 TO 429.
By H. N. OXENHAM, M.A.

'The second volume strikes us as scarcely if at all inferior in importance to the first. The translation reads as if it were an original work.'—*Church Quarterly Review.*

'Of the thoroughness of Bishop Hefele's learning and eminent fairness as a historian it is needless to speak. He is acknowledged to be unrivalled in his own country as a scholar and a profound theologian.'—*Pilot.*

'This careful translation of Hefele's Councils.'—Dr. PUSEY.

'A thorough and fair compendium, put in the most accessible and intelligent form.'—*Guardian.*

'A work of profound erudition, and written in a most candid spirit. The book will be a standard work on the subject.'—*Spectator.*

'The most learned historian of the Councils.'—*Père Gratry.*

'We cordially commend Hefele's Councils to the English student.'—*John Bull.*

In two vols., demy 8vo, price 21s.,

History of Protestant Theology,

PARTICULARLY IN GERMANY,

Viewed according to its Fundamental Movement, and in connection with the Religious, Moral, and Intellectual Life.

TRANSLATED FROM THE GERMAN OF

Dr. J. A. DORNER, Professor of Theology, Berlin.

With a Preface to the Translation by the Author.

'Dr. Dorner is distinguished by massive breadth of thought, . . . by scholarly research, genial appreciation of all forms of culture, and a well-balanced judgment, swayed by a spirit of fairness to those who differ from him. . . . The work is in every way deserving of careful examination now, as it is likely to be afterwards valued as one deserving the highest confidence as a book of reference, on account of its ample research amongst materials on which competent judgment must rest. . . . We regard with satisfaction the appearance of such a work. The highest interests are promoted by a treatise at once scholarly and eminently suggestive, which deals with theology at once scientifically and historically.'—*Contemporary Review.*

'This masterly work of Dr. Dorner, so successfully rendered into English by the present translators, will more than sustain the reputation he has already achieved by his exhaustive and, as it seems to us, conclusive *History of the Development of Doctrine respecting the Person of Christ.*'—*Spectator.*

In demy 8vo, 700 pages, price 12s.,

A CRITICAL AND EXEGETICAL COMMENTARY

ON THE

BOOK OF PSALMS.

WITH A NEW TRANSLATION.

By JAMES G. MURPHY, LL.D., T.C.D.,

AUTHOR OF COMMENTARIES ON THE BOOKS OF GENESIS, EXODUS, ETC.

'This work aims, and not unsuccessfully, at bringing out the sense and elucidating the principle of each psalm. The notes are plain and to the purpose. It has plenty of matter, and is not diffuse.'—*Guardian.*

'Dr. Murphy's contribution to the literature of the Psalms is a most welcome addition. . . . We have no hesitation in predicting for it a cordial reception from all who can appreciate a sound and scholarly exegesis, and who are anxious to discover the full and exact meaning of the inspired word.'—*Baptist Magazine.*

'A scholarly, careful production. It gives explanations of difficult Hebrew forms and phrases, traces with skill and insight the connection in each psalm, and brings out the sense in a version that is clear and idiomatic.'—*Freeman.*

Just published, price 7s. 6d.,

ON CHRISTIAN COMMONWEALTH.

TRANSLATED AND ADAPTED (WITH THE REVISION OF THE AUTHOR)

From the German of
Dr. HENRY J. W. THIERSCH.

'There is such an evident fairness in Thiersch's way of looking at the question—such an absence of dogmatism, or, which comes to the same thing, of contemptuous indifference for those who do not agree with him—that we have been attracted to it in spite of our antecedent objection to the positions which he sets out from.'—*English Independent.*

'It displays, in fact, an intimate knowledge, and, we think, correct appreciation of the varying conditions of the great problem of Church and State.'—*Church Quarterly Review.*

'The work is thoughtful, earnest, and moderate in tone.'—*Scotsman.*

'In a rather thin octavo are discussed seventeen subjects, each one enough for a volume, yet the essays are neither shallow nor evasive; the writer is in earnest and goes at once to the root of the matter. The style is singularly clear, and the language is concise, quite unlike what is often the German manner. A hundred quotations might be made, leaving a hundred bits equally good. This book deserves to reach a tenth edition.'—*Record.*

Just published, in demy 8vo, Third Edition, price 10s. 6d.,

MODERN DOUBT AND CHRISTIAN BELIEF.

A Series of Apologetic Lectures addressed to Earnest Seekers after Truth.

By THEODORE CHRISTLIEB, D.D.,
UNIVERSITY PREACHER AND PROFESSOR OF THEOLOGY AT BONN.

Translated, with the Author's sanction, chiefly by the Rev. H. U. WEITBRECHT, Ph.D., and Edited by the Rev. T. L. KINGSBURY, M.A., Vicar of Easton Royal, and Rural Dean.

CONTENTS.

FIRST LECTURE.—The Existing Breach between Modern Culture and Christianity.
SECOND LECTURE.—Reason and Revelation.
THIRD LECTURE.—Modern Non-Biblical Conceptions of God.
FOURTH LECTURE.—Theology of Scripture and of the Church.
FIFTH LECTURE.—The Modern Negation of Miracles.
SIXTH LECTURE.—Modern Anti-Miraculous Accounts of the Life of Christ.
SEVENTH LECTURE.—Modern Denials of the Resurrection.
EIGHTH LECTURE.—The Modern Critical Theory of Primitive Christianity.

'We recommend the volume as one of the most valuable and important among recent contributions to our apologetic literature. . . . We are heartily thankful both to the learned author and to his translators.'—*Guardian.*

'All the fundamental questions connected with revealed religion are handled more or less fully. The volume shows throughout intellectual force and earnestness.'—*Athenæum.*

'We express our unfeigned admiration of the ability displayed in this work, and of the spirit of deep piety which pervades it; and whilst we commend it to the careful perusal of our readers, we heartily rejoice that in those days of reproach and blasphemy, so able a champion has come forward to contend earnestly for the faith which was once delivered to the saints.'—*Christian Observer.*

'We do not hesitate to describe this as the clearest, strongest, and soundest volume of apologetics from a German pen we have read. The author takes hold of the great central and critical points and principles, and handles them with extraordinary vigour and wisdom.'—*Watchman.*

'It is one of the best works on Christian Evidences as a modern question to be found in any language.'—*Freeman.*

In three volumes 8vo, price 31s. 6d.,

A COMMENTARY
ON THE
GOSPEL OF ST. JOHN.
BY F. GODET, D.D.,
PROFESSOR OF THEOLOGY, NEUCHATEL.

'This work forms one of the battle-fields of modern inquiry, and is itself so rich in spiritual truth that it is impossible to examine it too closely; and we welcome this treatise from the pen of Dr. Godet. We have no more competent exegete, and this new volume shows all the learning and vivacity for which the author is distinguished.'—*Freeman.*

Just published, in two volumes 8vo, price 21s.,

A COMMENTARY
ON THE
GOSPEL OF ST. LUKE.
BY F. GODET,
DOCTOR AND PROFESSOR OF THEOLOGY, NEUCHATEL.

Translated from the Second French Edition.

'We are indebted to the Publishers for an English translation of the admirable work which stands at the head of this review. . . . It is a work of great ability, learning, and research.'—*Christian Observer.*

'Marked by clearness and good sense, it will be found to possess value and interest as one of the most recent and copious works specially designed to illustrate this Gospel.'—*Guardian.*

KEIL AND DELITZSCH'S COMMENTARIES ON THE OLD TESTAMENT.
10s. 6d. each volume.

PENTATEUCH, 3 Vols.	(*Keil.*)
JOSHUA, JUDGES, AND RUTH, 1 Vol.	(*Keil.*)
SAMUEL, 1 Vol.	(*Keil.*)
KINGS, 1 Vol., AND CHRONICLES, 1 Vol.	(*Keil.*)
EZRA, NEHEMIAH, AND ESTHER, 1 Vol.	(*Keil.*)
JOB, 2 Vols.	(*Delitzsch.*)
PSALMS, 3 Vols.	(*Delitzsch.*)
PROVERBS, 2 Vols.	(*Delitzsch.*)
ECCLESIASTES AND SONG OF SOLOMON, 1 Vol.	(*Delitzsch.*)
ISAIAH, 2 Vols.	(*Delitzsch.*)
JEREMIAH AND LAMENTATIONS, 2 Vols.	(*Keil.*)
EZEKIEL, 2 Vols.	(*Keil.*)
DANIEL, 1 Vol.	(*Keil.*)
MINOR PROPHETS, 2 Vols.	(*Keil.*)

'This series is one of great importance to the biblical scholar; and as regards its general execution, it leaves little or nothing to be desired.'—*Edinburgh Review.*

Just published, in crown 8vo, price 6s.,

SERMONS
FOR THE
CHRISTIAN YEAR.
ADVENT—TRINITY.
BY PROFESSOR ROTHE.
TRANSLATED BY WILLIAM R. CLARK, M.A. OXON.,
Prebendary of Wells and Vicar of Taunton.

'The volume is rich in noble thoughts and wholesome lessons.'—*Watchman.*

'The sermons before us are wonderfully simple in construction and expression, and at the same time remarkably fresh and suggestive. . . . It is a mind of real keenness, singularly pure and gentle, and of lofty spirituality, that expresses itself in these discourses.'—*Weekly Review.*

Just published, in two vols., large crown 8vo, price 7s. 6d. each,

THE YEAR OF SALVATION.
WORDS OF LIFE FOR EVERY DAY.
A BOOK OF HOUSEHOLD DEVOTION.
BY J. J. VAN OOSTERZEE, D.D.

'A work of great value and interest. To the clergy these readings will be found full of suggestive hints for sermons and lectures; while for family reading or for private meditation they are most excellent. The whole tone of the work is thoroughly practical, and never becomes controversial.'—*Church Bells.*

'The *very best* religious exposition for everyday use that has ever fallen in our way.'—*Bell's Weekly Messenger.*

'This charming and practical book of household devotion will be welcomed on account of its rare intrinsic value, as one of the most practical devotional books ever published.'—*Standard.*

'Massive of thought, persuasive, earnest, and eloquent.'—*Literary Churchman.*

'As might have been expected from so clear and vigorous a thinker, every passage is valuable either as an exposition or a suggestion.'—HENRY WARD BEECHER in *Christian Union.*

BY THE SAME AUTHOR.
Just published, in crown 8vo, price 6s.,

MOSES:
A BIBLICAL STUDY.

'Our author has seized, as with the instinct of a master, the great salient points in the life and work of Moses, and portrayed the various elements of his character with vividness and skill. . . . The work will at once take its place among our ablest and most valuable expository and practical discourses.'—*Baptist Magazine.*

'A volume full of valuable and suggestive thought, which well deserves and will amply repay careful perusal. We have read it with real pleasure.'—*Christian Observer.*

Just published, price 9s.,

SAINT AUGUSTINE.

A POEM IN EIGHT BOOKS.

By the late HENRY WARWICK COLE, Q.C.

With Prefatory Note by the Bishop-Suffragan of Nottingham.

'Written in sonorous and well-sustained verse. The testimony borne to the dignity and the value of the two Sacraments and to the authority of the Scriptures, as the revelation of God, is, we consider, of special value, as coming from a learned and cultivated layman, of considerable repute at the Bar, in an age of prevalent scepticism.'—*Church Bells.*

'This work is evidently the outcome of lifelong study. In eight books the spiritual history of Augustine is carefully and minutely traced through all its varied and thrilling phases.'—*Watchman.*

Recently published, in demy 8vo, price 7s. 6d.,

THE MIRACLES OF OUR LORD

IN RELATION TO MODERN CRITICISM.

TRANSLATED FROM THE GERMAN OF

F. L. STEINMEYER, D.D.,

Ordinary Professor of Theology in the University of Berlin.

'This work vindicates in a vigorous and scholarly style the sound view of miracles against the sceptical assaults of the time.'—*Princeton Review.*

'We commend the study of this work to thoughtful and intelligent readers, and especially to students of divinity whose position requires a competent knowledge of modern theological controversy.'—*Wesleyan Methodist Magazine.*

In demy 8vo, price 6s.,

THE SERVANT OF JEHOVAH.

A Commentary, Grammatical and Critical, upon Isaiah lii. 13–liii. 12.

WITH DISSERTATIONS UPON THE AUTHORSHIP OF ISAIAH XL.–LXVI., AND UPON THE MEANING OF EBED JEHOVAH.

By WILLIAM URWICK, M.A.,

Of Trinity College, Dublin; Tutor in Hebrew, New College, London.

'This is a very able and seasonable contribution to biblical literature.'—*Watchman.*

'The commentary evinces the great ability, accurate and extensive scholarship, and admirable judgment of the author.'—*Weekly Review.*

'We can sincerely congratulate the author on the learning and fidelity with which he has executed his task.'—*Record.*

Just published, price 5s.,

MESSIANIC PROPHECY:

Its Origin, Historical Character, and Relation to New Testament Fulfilment.

By Dr. EDWARD RIEHM,
PROFESSOR OF THEOLOGY, HALLE.

Translated from the German, with the Approbation of the Author,
By the Rev. JOHN JEFFERSON.

'Undoubtedly original and suggestive, and deserving careful consideration.'—*Literary Churchman.*

'Its intrinsic excellence makes it a valuable contribution to our biblical literature.'—*British and Foreign Evangelical Review.*

'The product of a well-balanced mind, which is able to weigh conflicting theories and to assign them their due proportion.'—*English Independent.*

'The subject is one confessedly of profound interest, and has been ably treated. . . . Even if his readers may not coincide with all his views, much valuable information will be gathered from the Author's lucubrations, which deserve careful consideration.'—*Christian Observer.*

In demy 8vo, price 7s. 6d.,

SERMONS TO THE NATURAL MAN.

By WILLIAM G. T. SHEDD, D.D.,
Author of 'A History of Christian Doctrine,' etc.

'These sermons are admirably suited to their purpose. Characterized by profound knowledge of divine truth, and presenting the truth in a chaste and attractive style, the sermons carry in their tone the accents of the solemn feeling of responsibility to which they owe their origin.'—*Weekly Review.*

In demy 8vo, price 12s.,

INTRODUCTION TO THE PAULINE EPISTLES.

By PATON J. GLOAG, D.D.,
Author of a 'Critical and Exegetical Commentary on the Acts of the Apostles.'

'Those acquainted with the Author's previous works will be prepared for something valuable in his present work; and it will not disappoint expectation, but rather exceed it. The most recent literature of his subject is before him, and he handles it with ease and skill. . . . It will be found a trustworthy guide, and raise its Author's reputation in this important branch of biblical study.'—*British and Foreign Evangelical Review.*

'A work of uncommon merit. He must be a singularly accomplished divine to whose library this book is not a welcome and valuable addition.'—*Watchman.*

'It will be found of considerable value as a handbook to St. Paul's Epistles. The dissertations display great thought as well as research. The Author is fair, learned, and calm, and his book is one of worth.'—*Church Bells.*

In crown 8vo, Second Edition, price 4s.,

PRINCIPLES OF NEW TESTAMENT QUOTATION

Established and applied to Biblical Science.

BY REV. JAMES SCOTT, M.A., B.D.

'This admirable treatise does not traverse in detail the forms and formulæ of New Testament quotation from the Old, nor enter with minuteness into the philological and theological discussion arising around many groups of these quotations—the author confines his attention to the *principles* involved in them. . . . An interesting discussion vindicating the method thus analyzed is followed by a very valuable summation of the argument in its bearing on the Canon, the originality of the Gospels, the internal unity of Scripture, and the permanence of Revelation.'—*British Quarterly Review.*

'In terse and well-ordered style the Author deals with a subject too little studied and less understood. He shows himself to be, in the best sense of the word, rational in his method and conclusions. . . . Strength, acuteness, sound judgment, and reason, chastened by reverence, pervade this book, which, with pleasure, we commend to all students of Holy Scripture.'—*Record.*

'The book is thoughtful, learned, conscientious, and painstaking, and performs a service which ought to be heartily recognised.'—*Baptist Magazine.*

Recently published, in demy 8vo, price 9s.,

A CHRONOLOGICAL AND GEOGRAPHICAL INTRODUCTION TO

THE LIFE OF CHRIST.

By C. E. CASPARI.

TRANSLATED FROM THE GERMAN, WITH ADDITIONAL NOTES, BY

M. J. EVANS, B.A.

Revised by the Author.

'The work is handy and well suited for the use of the student. It gives him, in very reasonable compass and in well-digested form, a great deal of information respecting the dates and outward circumstances of our Lord's life, and materials for forming a judgment upon the various disputed points arising out of them.'—*Guardian.*

'In this work the Author affords us the results of many-sided study on one of the most important objects of theological inquiry, and on a knot of problems which have been so often treated, and which are of so complex a nature. The Author is unquestionably right in supposing that the so-called outworks of the life of Jesus have their value, by no means to be lightly esteemed. Their examination must be returned to ever afresh, until the historic or unhistoric character of the substance of the Gospel narrative has been brought out as the result of scientific examination. . . . In conclusion, we believe we can with full conviction characterize the whole work as a real gain to the scientific literature of the question, and a great advance on previous investigations, not doubting that the most important positions maintained by the Author will in all essential points win the approbation of the student.'—*Jahrbücher für Deutsche Theologie.*

'An excellent and devout work. We can strongly recommend it.'—*Church Quarterly Review.*

WORKS BY THE LATE
PATRICK FAIRBAIRN, D.D.,

PRINCIPAL AND PROFESSOR OF THEOLOGY IN THE FREE CHURCH COLLEGE, GLASGOW.

In crown 8vo, price 6s.,

PASTORAL THEOLOGY: A Treatise on the Office and Duties of the Christian Pastor. With a Biographical Sketch of the Author.

'This treatise on the office and duties of a Christian pastor, by the late Professor Fairbairn, is well deserving thoughtful perusal. Throughout the volume, however, there is a tone of earnest piety and practical good sense, which finds expression in many profitable counsels, embodying the result of large experience and shrewd observation. . . . Much of the volume is devoted to the theory and practice of preaching, and this part we can most heartily commend; it is replete with valuable suggestions, which even those who have had some experience in the ministry will find calculated to make them more attractive and efficient preachers.'—*Christian Observer.*

In crown 8vo, price 7s. 6d.,

THE PASTORAL EPISTLES. The Greek Text and Translation. With Introduction, Expository Notes, and Dissertations.

'We cordially recommend this work to ministers and theological students.'—*Methodist Magazine.*
'We have read no book of his with a keener appreciation and enjoyment than that just published on the Pastoral Epistles.'—*Nonconformist.*

In two volumes, demy 8vo, price 21s., Sixth Edition,

THE TYPOLOGY OF SCRIPTURE, viewed in connection with the whole Series of the Divine Dispensations.

In demy 8vo, price 10s. 6d., Fourth Edition,

EZEKIEL, AND THE BOOK OF HIS PROPHECY: An Exposition. With a new Translation.

In demy 8vo, price 10s. 6d., Second Edition,

PROPHECY, viewed in its Distinctive Nature, its Special Functions, and Proper Interpretation.

In demy 8vo, price 10s. 6d.,

HERMENEUTICAL MANUAL; or, Introduction to the Exegetical Study of the Scriptures of the New Testament.

In demy 8vo, price 10s. 6d.,

THE REVELATION OF LAW IN SCRIPTURE, considered with respect both to its own Nature and to its Relative Place in Successive Dispensations. (The Third Series of the 'Cunningham Lectures.')

Just published, in demy 8vo, price 6s.,

A TREATISE ON THE

Inspiration of the Holy Scriptures.

BY

CHARLES ELLIOTT, D.D.,

PROFESSOR OF BIBLICAL LITERATURE AND EXEGESIS IN THE PRESBYTERIAN THEOLOGICAL SEMINARY OF THE NORTH-WEST, CHICAGO, ILLINOIS.

Just published, in one large 8vo volume, Eighth English Edition, price 15s..

A TREATISE ON THE
GRAMMAR OF NEW TESTAMENT GREEK,

Regarded as the Basis of New Testament Exegesis.

Translated from the German [of Dr. G. B. WINER].

With large additions and full Indices. Second Edition. Edited by Rev. W. F. MOULTON, D.D., one of the New Testament Translation Revisers.

The additions by the Editor are very large, and will tend to make this great work far more useful and available for *English* students than it has hitherto been. The Indices have been greatly enlarged, but with discrimination, so as to be easily used. Altogether, the Publishers do not doubt that this will be the Standard Grammar of New Testament Greek.

'We gladly welcome the appearance of Winer's great work in an English translation, and must strongly recommend it to all who wish to attain to a sound and accurate knowledge of the language of the New Testament. We need not say it is *the* Grammar of the New Testament. It is not only superior to all others, but *so* superior as to be by common consent the one work of reference on the subject. No other could be mentioned with it.'—*Literary Churchman.*

www.ingramcontent.com/pod-product-compliance
Lightning Source LLC
Chambersburg PA
CBHW051855300426
44117CB00006B/400